RACE, CLASS, AND POLITICS

RACE, CLASS, AND POLITICS

☆ ☆ ☆ ☆ ☆ ☆ ☆ ☆ ☆ ☆ ☆ ☆ ☆

Essays on American Colonial and Revolutionary Society

GARY B. NASH

With a Foreword by
Richard S. Dunn

UNIVERSITY OF ILLINOIS PRESS

Urbana and Chicago

This book is printed on acid-free paper.

Library of Congress Cataloging-in-Publication Data

Nash, Gary B.
  Race, class, and politics.

  Includes index.
   1. United States—History—Colonial period, ca. 1600–
1775—Addresses, essays, lectures. 2. United States—
Social conditions—To 1865—Addresses, essays, lectures.
3. United States—Politics and government—Colonial
period, ca. 1600–1775—Addresses, essays, lectures.
4. United States—History—Revolution, 1775–1783—Social
aspects—Addresses, essays, lectures. 5. United States—
Race relations—Addresses, essay, lectures. I. Title.
E188.5.N37 1986   973.2   85-24489
ISBN 0-252-01211-9 (cloth)
ISBN 0-252-01313-1 (paper)

To the Memory of
Wesley Frank Craven

CONTENTS

FOREWORD

The history of colonial and revolutionary America is peculiarly susceptible to mythic, chauvinistic, and patriotic interpretation: for the past
two hundred years we have become habituated to a ritualistic scenario
populated by Pilgrims escaping from Old World persecution, by pioneers forging into the trackless wilderness, and by revolutionary heroes
creating a new republic. Most historians of early America, including the
present writer, accept a good part of this pious vision of the past,
however hard we may struggle to escape it. We remain Whigs at heart,
and all things considered, we believe that our colonial and revolutionary ancestors should be chiefly remembered for their religious idealism,
economic enterprise, social mobility, and participatory politics.

Gary B. Nash is not a Whig, and he has been vigorously challenging the standard pieties for more than twenty years. What interests him
most about colonial and revolutionary America is the development of
racial polarization, economic stratification, class consciousness, and political conflict. He measures past experience by concrete action, not
abstract ideals, and since he believes that one's opinions are generally
shaped by social and economic forces, he looks for evidence of social
dislocation and class conflict within early America. Furthermore, instead of writing history from the top down and celebrating the achievements of the political and social elite, he writes history from the bottom
up, and explores the efforts of those persecuted Native Americans,
blacks, and poor whites who struggled purposefully in the seventeenth
and eighteenth centuries against their elite oppressors.

Nash presents his revisionist interpretation most fully in three important books. In *Quakers and Politics: Pennsylvania, 1681–1726*
(1968), he dismisses the notion that William Penn's holy experiment
should be remembered for its idealism and liberalism, and argues that
the early history of this colony is chiefly significant for a quite different
reason: in Pennsylvania economic and social conflicts quickly plunged
the Quaker colonists into especially bitter and anarchic factionalism. In
his next book, much broader in scope, *Red, White, and Black: The
Peoples of Early America* (1974, 1982), Nash dismisses the standard

textbook portrayal of European colonists settling an empty wilderness and replaces it with a strikingly different account of triracial interaction among Indians, Africans, and Europeans, in which the settlers' brutal exploitation of the Native Americans and blacks is strongly emphasized. In his most recent book, *The Urban Crucible: Social Change, Political Consciousness, and the Origins of the American Revolution* (1979), Nash modifies the common law view that Boston, New York, and Philadelphia were dynamic boomtowns in the eighteenth century. He argues that each of these communities experienced rising stratification, poverty, and social tension, with the result that by the 1760s in Boston and by the 1770s in Philadelphia and New York, the lower orders staged an internal revolt against the local elite while also participating in the external revolution against British rule.

In addition to these three books, Nash has produced four edited volumes designed for undergraduate classroom use—*Class and Society in Early America* (1970), *The Great Fear: Race in the Mind of America* (1970), *The Private Side of American History: Readings in Everyday Life* (1975, 1979, 1983), and *Struggle and Survival in Colonial America* (1981)—and he has also published nearly thirty essays in scholarly journals and anthologies. Some of these essays are pilot studies for his larger books, while others explore new territory. They include some of his best and most pointed writing. Scattered as they are in many different publications, these pieces are not easily available to the general reader. At the request of the publisher, therefore, Nash has selected eleven of his favorite published essays and one unpublished essay—all dealing with questions of race, class, and politics in colonial and revolutionary America—and has collected them in the present volume.

Gary Nash is a historian with a strongly held set of beliefs—which he spells out very fully and frankly in the preface. He is an argumentative writer, which makes his essays fun to read. He frequently pursues the same line of argument, which helps to shape this collection of essays into a cohesive whole. And he always builds his case upon exhaustive documentary research. Unlike Carl Becker, Charles Beard, and the other Progressive historians of the early twentieth century whom Nash admires, he never offers speculative propositions derived from the armchair rather than the archives. On the contrary, Nash's interpretation is always supported—like an iceberg floating powerfully at sea—by a hidden mass of documentation drawn from painstaking and creative research in the primary sources.

The twelve essays in this volume are arranged in roughly chronological order. "The Social Development of Colonial America" appropriately introduces the chief themes that concern the author. In this broad essay he compares and contrasts the recent findings of social historians who have studied New England, the mid-Atlantic, and the South, and then argues that all of this particularistic work should be related to broader issues of race, gender, and class—as seen in his own concern with urban life, and with triracial interchange involving Indians and blacks—if we are to achieve a coherent picture of colonial social development. The next essay, "The Image of the Indian in the Southern Colonial Mind," pursues the theme of racial conflict. Here Nash examines the colonist's split view of the native American from the 1580s to the 1700s, arguing that a hostile image of the Indian as wild beast prevailed during the seventeenth century when the English settlers were exterminating the coastal tribes, succeeded by a much more benign image in the eighteenth century when the red man no longer posed a serious cultural threat. "The Framing of Government in Pennsylvania: Ideas in Contact with Reality" presents one of the most interesting arguments from Nash's first book, *Quakers and Politics.* Here he examines the process by which William Penn drafted the constitution for his colony in 1681–83, and argues that Penn was persuaded by a circle of wealthy Quakers who bought land and obtained offices from him to construct a relatively illiberal government, with power concentrated in the hands of the elite.

The next three essays are by-products of Nash's most recent book, *Urban Crucible.* "Slaves and Slaveowners in Colonial Philadelphia" demonstrates that slaveholding was far more extensive in this Quaker city than previously recognized and traces the pattern of slave ownership and of slave occupation. "The Failure of Female Factory Labor in Colonial Boston" describes in rather parallel fashion how impoverished women were employed as textile workers in this town between 1748 and 1759 and how the women rebelled against this scheme. "The Transformation of Urban Politics, 1700–1764" discusses the rise of purposeful crowd action in Boston, New York, and Philadelphia, climaxing with massive popular participation in the Philadelphia election of 1764. Here Nash argues that this new activity by the lower orders radicalized urban politics before the revolutionary struggle with Britain had even begun.

The final six essays move into the era of the American Revolution. "Urban Wealth and Poverty in Prerevolutionary America" discusses the growing poverty problem in Boston, New York, and Philadelphia. Using tax lists, probate records, and poor-relief payments, Nash shows that over time the gap between the richest and poorest inhabitants was growing, that households of the lower classes were declining in real income and wealth, and that especially in Boston a large number of people were being forced into the almshouse, or warned out of town. "Social Change and the Growth of Prerevolutionary Urban Radicalism" builds upon the arguments advanced in the two previous essays to contend that the lower orders in Boston, New York, and Philadelphia developed their own "popular" ideology which differed from the Whig ideology espoused by the revolutionary leadership. According to Nash, popular resentment against the traditional elite escalated in the three towns as urban poverty became a major problem, and this protest movement reached a crescendo in Boston in 1765 when the Stamp Act rioters destroyed the mansions of Andrew Oliver and Thomas Hutchinson. In a parallel essay, "Artisans and Politics in Eighteenth-Century Philadelphia," Nash explores the growing political consciousness of the craft workers in this town, focusing in particular on the triumph of the artisans in 1774–75 when they ousted the merchants from political control.

The final three essays turn to the Afro-Americans. "Thomas Peters: Millwright, Soldier, and Deliverer" is the biographical sketch of a North Carolina slave who joined the British army in 1776, and later led a large group of refugee black loyalists from Nova Scotia to Sierra Leone in Africa. "Forging Freedom: The Emancipation Experience in the Northern Seaport Cities, 1775–1820" examines the formation of free black communities in Boston, New York, and Philadelphia during the half-century following the Revolution. The reader may wish to compare this essay with the author's earlier discussion of the experiences of poor whites in these same towns during the half-century preceding the Revolution. Here Nash imaginatively uses census returns to establish black patterns of occupation, residence, household composition, naming practices, and church affiliation. He argues that the blacks, despite vicious persecution, had managed to establish viable communities of their own in the northern cities by 1820. The concluding essay, " 'To Arise Out of the Dust': Absalom Jones and the African Church of Philadelphia, 1785–95" is the most recent piece of work in this collection, the only one not hitherto published, and certainly one of the most interesting essays Nash has written. Here he traces the efforts of Jones, a former slave from Delaware, to form a black religious organization, the Free African Society, in 1787, and then to build an independent black church, the African Church of Philadelphia, in 1794—and he stresses that the blacks achieved this goal despite much criticism and opposition from their white patrons.

As he mentions in the preface, Gary Nash and I go back together a long way, to the fall of 1954, when he was a senior at Princeton and I was a graduate student trying to lead the weekly discussion meetings, known as precepts, in History 306, which was Professor Craven's course in American Colonial History. Precepting was a new experience for me, and a daunting one, because the young gentlemen at Princeton learned to talk so glibly about the books assigned for discussion that I could never be sure whether they had actually read them. One of those gentlemen quickly won my gratitude, because he always did his home-work and kept the discussion on target, then as now. He was a sandy-haired, clean-cut youth in those days, who wore his snappy NROTC uniform to class and seemed from my jaundiced graduate school per-spective to be designed by God for a military career. I was surprised five years later to receive a letter from him telling me that he too had become a graduate student at Princeton. Gary Nash's record since then speaks eloquently for itself. It gives me special pleasure to introduce this fine volume of essays. I only regret that Frank Craven, the teacher from whom Gary and I learned so much, did not live to see the dedication to this book. Frank was proud of all his graduate student "boys," but he was especially proud of Gary Nash.

RICHARD S. DUNN

PREFACE

Thirty-one years ago, daydreaming in a class in colonial American history, my attention was captured by a remarkable statement issued from the lectern. "Boys," said Wesley Frank Craven in his measured way, "very nearly the most important problem the colonists had to face was the Indian problem." "Boys," he called us because at Princeton University in the 1950s there were no women other than the office secretaries and the kitchen workers at the Prospect Street eating clubs. And "boys" because Frank Craven was the gentlest of paternalists, a man to whom the vocabulary of family and community came naturally.

The declaration about the "Indian problem" made its impression, and it was in class discussions that semester, under the tutelage of Richard Dunn, a graduate-student preceptor, that I discovered the fascination of early American history. Mr. Dunn, as we undergraduates addressed him then, has been kind enough to write a brief foreword to this book. Looking back, he was even kinder for giving me one of the few A's I received in my four-year tenure as an undergraduate. There seemed little reason at that time to be unduly serious about undergraduate studies, since I had no intention of pursuing an academic career and in any event had committed my first three post-baccalaureate years to the United States Navy.

Eight years after my initial encounter with Professor Craven, I sat again in one of his classes, this time a graduate seminar. As a somewhat overage entering graduate student, now trying to determine whether my casual fascination with history could be kindled into a career, I once more heard his words about the "Indian problem." This time they resonated differently, for I was becoming active in the civil rights movement that was gathering momentum in the early 1960s, and I was beginning to see the connections between the distant colonial past and the turbulent present.

Frank Craven probably knew nothing of my involvement in civil rights when he assigned to me, for my first oral seminar report, Cotton Mather's *Magnalia Christi Americana* (1702). But it proved a fortuitous choice. While dispatching me deep into the heart of the seventeenth-century Puritan mind—a territory far beyond my ken at that point in my studies—he had also led me, inadvertently perhaps, to Mather's famous judgment about the Pequots in their war with the Puritans in 1637. After describing the grisly encounter on the Mystic River, where the English and their Narragansett allies massacred an entire Pequot village, Mather concluded: "in a little more than *one hour,* five or six hundred of these barbarians were dismissed from a world that was *burdened* with them" (p.482). It was, for Mather, a brilliantly unambiguous display of divine intervention, demonstrating that the Puritans were the historical agents of God's design for mankind's redemption.

Later that semester Frank Craven assigned "his boys" a book that had been handsomely reviewed in the history jounals—Douglas Leach's *Flintlock and Tomahawk: New England in King Philip's War* (1958). I took it as a possible sign that the critical intelligence needed for a career in history might not be out of reach when I bristled at a statement in the preface by one of the reigning masters of early American history, Professor Samuel Eliot Morison of Harvard. The defeat of the treacherous Wampanoags and their allied tribes at the hands of New England soldiers in 1675–76, Morison pronounced in his own attempt to indicate the usability of the past, was of great interest "in view of our recent experiences of warfare, and of the many instances today of backward peoples getting enlarged notions of nationalism and turning ferociously on Europeans who have attempted to civilize them" (p. ix). It was not until a few years later that I discovered that Professor Craven might not have shared that view—he had written, fourteen years before Morison's outburst, a seminal article on "Indian Policy in Early Virginia," which attempted to see native Americans as something more than "savages" standing in the way of visionary European colonizers. Thus did the dawn of my historical consciousness break by stages.

Frank Craven, to whom this book is dedicated, was a master teacher and a wonderfully warm-hearted, wry, and orderly human being. He encouraged his students to explore on their own and to develop intellectual autonomy. This explains, I believe, the great variety of dissertation work done under his auspices. I could not have asked for, indeed I cannot imagine, a more balanced and kindly critic under whom to serve an apprenticeship. From him I learned two cardinal rules that he believed governed sound scholarship (and in my experience nothing since has proven him wrong). First, having conceived of a project, read everything written on the subject. "Getting on top of the bibliography," he called it. Second, immerse yourself in the sources. The first rule ensures a firm grasp of how historical thinking has developed, sharpens one's critical sensibilities, and leads, often unexpectedly, to sources that might have been overlooked. The second rule is too obvious to require comment, though examples are hardly wanting these days of books written from the armchair, not the archives.

The essays that follow, written between 1963 and 1983, represent a sample of my attempts, since that first graduate seminar with Frank Craven, to deal with questions of race, class, and politics in the early development of American society. Each of these organizing categories deserves a few words of explanation.

Race has compelled my attention because I believe that, since the first collision of African, European, and native American peoples in North America in the late sixteenth century, it has shaped the American experience. Racial inequality, often splicing together with class and gender inequality, has proved extraordinarily resistant in the quest to achieve the democratic ideals that American society has long professed. It would have been difficult to ignore the centrality of race while studying American history in graduate school in the 1960s, and race relations was a topic with which Frank Craven, a Southerner by birth and upbringing if not entirely by temperament, was deeply concerned, though he rarely allowed his politics to show in public.

Class also has been a focus of my work. Long ago I became convinced that those who obliterated class and class consciousness as useful categories for studying what they see as a seamless American society were misreading the historical record and ignoring what has always been a critical force in American history. In spite of the *general* material abundance in this society, despite the *relatively* great degree of opportunity, and notwithstanding the lack of a feudal past, most of the significant changes in our history have come because social groups began to behave in class-specific ways in response to events impinging on their well-being and manifested points of view and cultural characteristics peculiar to their rank. No amount of movement between ranks or vertical linkages between them rid preindustrial society of its social tensions, which grew rapidly in the late colonial period. After the American Revolution, as the nation industrialized, such class-related conflict swelled enormously.

Politics, simply put, is the end point of so much historical action that it should never be far from the historian's mind. If every problem is not addressed or solved in the political realm, surely it is to the political arena that all protesting groups, whether organized by class, race, gender, or any other category, ultimately point. In this sense, the pronouncements of many social historians of recent years that they are attempting to get beyond the traditional formula that made history simply the story of "past politics" is a little misdirected. What has been wanting is a political history enriched by an understanding of the social processes and social consciousness that underlie all political discourse and action. But social history unconnected to the history of political power is incomplete, if not sterile.

Categories such as race, class, and politics can organize historical inquiry, but assumptions shape it. The essays that follow proceed from a number of assumptions, and it is only fair to share them with the reader, though I am not so naive as to believe they will be accepted by all who find their way to this book. All thinking about the past ought to be conditional, as the dizzying changes in American historical writing over the last century ought to convince us. Moreover, the work of reconstructing and reinterpreting the past, I believe, is profoundly personal; hence I state these asumptions not as truths or infallible guidelines but as a series of propositions that readers may find helpful to have in mind as they approach these essays.

Proposition 1: That the historical record, as it has come from the hands of professional academics, has generally reflected the composition of the profession and the intellectual climate in which its practitioners write. When women began to enter Clio's ranks in substantial numbers, the field of women's history blossomed. Black history, though it has attracted some attention for more than a century, became a major topic only when the civil rights movement of the post–World War II period made the country reverberate with rhetoric, demonstrations, violence, and armed government intervention at the local level. The strident protests over civil rights, soon overlapped by those against the Vietnam War, ignited great interest in the 1960s and 1970s in the history of radical protest. Although I am a white, middle-class male, my historical interests have been shaped by the times I lived in and by my personal responses to the critical events of the era.

Proposition 2: That since the guild of American historians until the last generation was narrowly recruited, it is not surprising that a highly nationalistic, ethnocentric, male-centered, and elitist orientation prevailed in the writing of history and in the teaching of history at all levels of the educational system. Ezra Pound put it too kindly when he wrote: "Even I can remember / A day when the historians left blanks in their writings, / I mean for things they didn't know" (*The Cantos of Ezra Pound* [New York, 1970], p. 60). It is not so much a matter of not knowing; rather, we are faced with a selective and purposeful amnesia about the past. J. H. Plumb gets to the heart of the matter in pointing out that "the personal ownership of the past has always been a vital strand in the ideology of all ruling classes."

Proposition 3: That the celebrated past, which in all societies is a hallmark of history written by a narrowly constituted tribe of scholars drawn from the upper rank, is no longer serviceable. We are past celebration—or ought to be—not because celebration is in itself unworthy but because it disavows a rendering of the past that reveals the tragic mistakes, misshapen prejudices, and human avarice of which we are the historical legatees. What is the good of a romanticized past that encourages people to try to recapture that which never existed? History is worth writing and studying primarily because of its power to shape our thinking about our present and future. Fifty-four years ago, Carl Becker ruffled the American Historical Association by proclaiming in his presidential address that "the history that lies inert in unread books does no work in the world." Becker was a Progressive historian, which meant that he identified with the Progressive movement that was attempting to fashion remedies to the social and political corrosions that had accompanied the rise of industrial capitalism. He intended the history he wrote to be part of the struggle for democratic reform in American society. The historian's role, he insisted, was to help society "understand what it is doing in the light of what it has done and what it hopes to do." To do otherwise, Becker warned, would ensure that the public "will leave us to our own devices, leave us it may be to cultivate a species of dry professional arrogance growing out of the thin soil of antiquarian research." Becker's wisdom is as fresh and relevant today as it was during the Great Depression when he made these statements. I am sometimes called a "neo-Progressive," a label that pleases me because I hope my work has some utility in the wrestling with the awesome problems of contemporary American life.

Proposition 4: That when historians attempt to write the history of the faceless, voiceless majority, they are rendering more than simple justice to the forgotten masses of people who have been omitted from the record. To rescue them from oblivion would hardly be worth the trouble if they were truly the "unthinking multitide," the "sheeplike masses," the "rabble" that the eighteenth-century gentry labeled them. We do not study ordinary people merely because they existed but because common men and women, individually and collectively, influenced and sometimes even dictated the course of historical development. Moreover, in all societies, regardless of size and organization, people of all positions and conditions form an indivisible whole where what appears at first glance to be personal and private behavior often assumes, upon closer inspection, a public and political dimension. I doubt that there are many critical events in the history of any society in which common people did not play an integral role.

Proposition 5: That there are two histories to write in recovering black history, women's history, native American history, laboring-class history, and the history of ethnic groups; the history of popular politics, popular religion, and popular culture; the history of childhood and the history of the family. One is the history of exploitation and oppression of subordinate groups, defined by race, class, gender, and religion. It befits a society founded on democratic principles to explore this history, learn from it, and apply that knowledge to a country still much in flux, still receiving waves of immigrants, still attempting to reconcile gaping chasms between the promise and the reality of American life. This history is often written as a history of victimization, and too often it treats the victims as ciphers—passive figures always acted upon but never themselves the agents of history. The other history, closely connected and ultimately of greater importance, is a history of struggle against such exploitation. It reconstructs how persistently and creatively the oppressed and restricted have coped with the barriers placed in their way. It demonstrates how frequently they survived their hardships rather than being overcome and immobilized by them, and explores how some of them even managed to thrive in the face of everything. To understand this hidden history is to be empowered by it, for it wipes away the sense of insurmountable odds, of inevitability, which are the great inhibitors of change.

Proposition 6: That try as we may to be "objective" about the past, the first critical task for every historian is the selection of a topic and the formulation of organizing questions around which to develop a study. This is a personal and inherently political—or at least epistomological—choice. Objectivity is a term that is more appropriately used to describe our search for evidence relating to a chosen subject and our treatment of that data once accumulated. I claim no objectivity in the topics I have chosen to investigate historically, nor do I believe others can do so. I strive, however, for objectivity in combing the surviving record for evidence and in evaluating what I have unearthed.

The essays in this book trace how social and racial groups related dynamically to each other in preindustrial America, how power and wealth were distributed, and how a polyglot people explored the meaning and uses of freedom. They are all part of my endeavor to recount and analyze how a triracial American society and a complex American culture developed over the first half of our four-hundred-year history. Taken as a whole, I hope they may be read as part of a history befitting the American democratic creed, contributing in a small way to what the incomparable Perry Miller called "the invigoration that comes from contending against society for the welfare of society" (quoted by Ann Douglass, "The Mind of Perry Miller," *New Republic* [Feb. 3, 1982], p. 30).

My intention in writing about early American history has been to reveal, on the one hand, the structures of wealth, status, and power within which all members of society lived their lives; and, on the other hand, to trace the behavior and recreate the inward experience of various social groups in the society—Afro-Americans, women, artisans, the poor, merchants, and clergymen. The structural transformations that took place in the colonizers' society for two centuries after Europeans began exploiting North America were very great. But these evolving structures limited rather than dictated life at various levels of society, always leaving room for choice and initiative by ordinary people.

In many of the essays that follow I found it necessary to draw upon sources that had scarcely been touched when I embarked on graduate studies, though since then they have been increasingly valuable to social historians. One of the most exciting "mysteries of the craft" of history is tracking down and learning to use previously unexploited sources. Sometimes one stumbles upon them unawares. Such was the case when I first looked at the 1767 assessors' lists for Philadelphia, which had found their way to the Van Pelt Library at the University of Pennsylvania. I imagined that these lists, when set alongside earlier tax lists, would allow me to analyze how the distribution of wealth had changed in Philadelphia from the early days of Penn's "greene country towne" to the eve of the American Revolution. This presumed a connection between the division of wealth in a community and the political contentedness of its members.

To my delight the tax assessors' reports showed not only the taxable wealth for each citizen but listed the various forms of assessable property—land, houses, silver plate, and, to my surprise, indentured servants and slaves. I had not turned many pages of this fascinating document when it became evident that the number of households with slaves (who were listed only if they were between the ages of fifteen and sixty) was very substantial. Almost nothing in my prior work on Philadelphia—and virtually nothing in the secondary literature—indicated that slave labor formed a vital part of the Quaker city's economy. Yet here was proof of slaves in the households of not just merchants and professionals but also artisans and mariners. My study of wealth distribution had to be pushed aside while I further pursued the matter of urban slavery in the North. Sometimes the documentary record takes command of the investigator and demands that one set forth in unexpected directions. It is a reason to eschew too much planning of a project before the research has begun.

The quest for sources that reveal life at the lower levels of society has by no means been exhausted, as I hope the reader will discover in the essays at the end of this book which deal with the black community in the northern seaports after the American Revolution. In ships' crew lists and maritime registration records, tax lists, city directories, manuscript censuses, almshouse dockets, church records, probated wills and inventories of estate, wage records, military pension files, vagrancy registers, court records, material culture, and oral history we have available the means for pushing forward with a more comprehensive and dynamic history of the American peoples.

I am unable to untangle the various influences on me as an undergraduate at Princeton University between 1951 and 1955; but in addition to Wesley Frank Craven, those who made history come alive for me were Gordon Craig, Charles Sellers, Ralph Powell, Eric Goldman, Jeter Isely, and "Jinx" Harbison. A little tardily, I acknowledge my debt to them. The indebtedness grew greatly during graduate studies at Princeton, where aside from Frank Craven's tutelage I learned most about the historian's craft from David Donald, Robert Lively, and Robert R. Palmer. (The latter also fueled my determination to make a place for myself in the historical profession by attempting to dissuade me from entering the graduate program at age twenty-nine on the grounds that I would be "a worn-out old hack" struggling to put my children through college by the time I reached my present age. As it stands, he proved at least halfway correct.)

All of the essays in this book are much the better for the careful and supportive criticism they have received at the hands of a number of generous colleagues and friends. My individual debts for these essays were acknowledged in their place of original publication, but collectively I express my gratitude again to Joyce Oldham Appleby, William Abbot, Ira Berlin, David B. Davis, Richard S. Dunn, James G. Henretta, Kenneth Lockridge, Jesse Lemisch, James T. Lemon, Donald G. Mathews, Michael McGiffert, John Murrin, Stephen Patterson, Cynthia J. Shelton, John Shy, Peter Wood, and Alfred F. Young.

For support in carrying out research I gratefully acknowledge the Princeton University Research Fund, the Research Committee of the Academic Senate at the University of California, Los Angeles, the Guggenheim Memorial Foundation, the American Council of Learned Societies, and the American Philosophical Society. Librarians and archivists at too many locations to name have been immensely helpful, and I thank them collectively for making research over the last two decades such a pleasure.

SHAPING A
TRIRACIAL SOCIETY

☆ ☆ ☆ ☆ ☆ ☆ ☆ ☆ ☆ ☆ ☆ ☆ ☆

1

THE SOCIAL DEVELOPMENT
OF COLONIAL AMERICA

THE HISTORY of social development in colonial America—portrayed in this paper primarily as the history of social relations between groups of people defined by race, gender, and class—is in glorious disarray. Disarray because all of the old paradigms have collapsed under the weight of the last generation of scholarship. Glorious because a spectacular burst of innovative scholarship, the product of those who have crossed disciplinary boundaries, transcended filiopietism, and been inspired in the best sense by the social currents of their own times, has left us with vastly more knowledge of the first century and a half of American history than we ever had before. But the more we have found out about the social development of early America, the less able we are to fit this knowledge into any of the existing frameworks that heretofore have guided us—the Whig framework, the Progressive framework, or the Consensus framework. Hundreds of fresh building blocks have been fashioned, each of them representing a challenge to the structures of earlier architects, but no new master builder has appeared to create an edifice out of these handsome new construction materials.

Colonial social historians of the last generation have done the most exciting, ingenious empirical research that can be found for any period of American history. By severely limiting spatial and chronological sweep, they have illuminated particular aspects of life as it unfolded in dozens of communities along the Atlantic seaboard from the early seventeenth to the late eighteenth century. Scholarly care has been lavished especially on the New England town. One may now read about twenty Puritan community studies published since the 1960s, and another dozen or more are seeking the light of print. The community-study

---

This essay first appeared under the title "Social Development," in Jack P. Greene and J. R. Pole, eds., *Colonial British America: Essays in the History of the Early Modern Era* (Baltimore: Johns Hopkins University Press, 1984), 233–61. Minor alterations have been made in the text and in the footnotes.

infection has spread southward to the mid-Atlantic region, where the records of town, church, and family have succumbed to the imaginative gaze and clever computations of another group of social historians. It has moved also to the tobacco colonies of the Chesapeake, where, substituting the county for the town, social historians have learned all the methodological lessons of their New England predecessors and done them several steps better. Only the rice coast has escaped the community-studies devotees, and surely it too will soon fall before their Gini coefficients, mortality calculations, family reconstitutions, and mobility measurements. But in all of these studies the sociological analysis, as opposed to the social, has been largely wanting. Sociological history—theoretically self-conscious history—"unfolds in a more grandiose fashion, peering down at large segments of the past from the lofty heights of imposing abstractions and generalization."[1] Its contribution is to analyze change broadly, to fathom the causes and nature of social development over extended periods of time.

So much creative work has been done during the last generation that it may seem that the time has arrived to build new models of social development. Yet this still may be premature because in spite of their many virtues, the innovative studies of the past two decades are so male-centered and oblivious to the black and native American peoples of colonial society that any new synthesis would necessarily be constructed with materials that present a skewed and incomplete picture of the social process in the prerevolutionary period.

If social development is defined as changing social relations between different groups in society, then the foundation of any such study must be rigorous analysis of the structural arrangements that did not strictly govern most human interaction but set the boundaries for it in the preindustrial period, as between masters and slaves, men and women, parents and children, employers and employees. Those relationships, moreover, must be examined within the context of a triracial society. This marks a fundamental difference between social development in England and America or in France and America. Of course other differences existed as well, but perhaps none was so great as that produced by the convergence of three broad cultural groups on the North American coastal plain in the seventeenth and eighteenth centuries. Some of the best work in colonial social history has been unmindful of this, drawing conceptually on European historical studies as if the colonies were pure offshoots of English society. While some inspiration can be drawn from the *Annales* school, the English Marxists, and other work accomplished at the macro- and micro-levels, we must regard the social development of colonial America as *sui generis* because of the triracial environment in which most colonists lived their lives. This racial intermingling had profound effects on the social formation of the colonies. Hence, in the years ahead colonial historians will be better advised to perfect their Spanish and Portuguese rather than their French and German. The work of the European historians will remain relevant to American historians, especially those studying the era of industrialization; but for the preindustrial era American historians will need to turn in a direction that has been consistently ignored for decades—the rapidly expanding social history of Spanish and Portuguese America.

Above structure is superstructure. Older arguments that the first determines the second or that base and superstructure are "separable concrete entities" are now passé.[2] Consciousness, cultural institutions, and ideology, it is widely agreed, are indissolubly a part of social development. While studies of social structure involving quantitative measurements stand out as one of the major achievements of the last generation of scholarship, a primary task for the next few decades is to reunite these contributions with studies of social change that deal with the transformations of value and consciousness, often expressed symbolically or ritually, that occurred in the colonial era. The advice of Raymond Williams, who calls for a "theory of social totality," is worth quoting at length. Williams pleads for revaluing " 'determination' toward the setting of limits and the exertion of pressure, and away from a predicted, prefigured, and controlled content. We have to revalue 'superstructure' toward a related range of cultural practices, and away from a reflected, reproduced or specifically dependent content. And, crucially, we have to revalue 'the base' away from the notion of a fixed economic or technological abstraction, and toward the specific activities of men [and women], in real social and economic relationships, containing fundamental contradictions and variations and therefore always in a state of dynamic process."[3]

Presuming that it is the interaction of social structure and social consciousness—worked out in the confrontation of three broad cultural groups—that is the bedrock upon which a theory of social development in colonial America must be built, we must be mindful of regional distinctions. It is not to be believed that the social development of a region where male and female colonizers were roughly equivalent in number and where African slaves and Indian inhabitants were relatively few could evolve the same social relationships as a society where male colonizers greatly outnumbered female colonizers for four generations and where the ratio of white to black and white to red was drastically different than in the prior case. The discussion that follows therefore moves regionally from North to South, although for the sake of emphasis I have separated the discussion of Afro-American and native American social development from that of the European colonizers.

As many historians have noted, the wave of community studies of pre-revolutionary New England make the several hundred thousand souls who lived in this region one of the most studied human populations in the annals of history. This is sometimes rationalized with the claim that the New England Puritan town was the prototypical American community. Yet, in terms of its social development, the New England town may be exceptional rather than typical of the early American experience. Especially in its transition to a market economy, a theme that will be resorted to on several occasions in this essay, it may have been the least dynamic region of the British mainland colonies. In its reliance upon free labor, mostly organized in family units, and in the depth of its attachment to communal values it was also atypical of the colonial experience. The point is not apparent in the work of a number of historians who have argued that the intrusion of individualistic, commercialized relations on a corporate, communalized ethos fermented the antinomian controversy in Boston in the 1630s, lay behind the witchcraft trials in Salem in the 1690s, gave meaning to the Great Awakening in many New England towns in the 1740s, partially inspired the American Revolution of the 1770s, and fueled the Second Great Awakening in the early 1800s. Taken together, these accounts make it appear that the transition to mercantile capitalism was occurring—and causing social trauma—at widely spread points in time within a region smaller than the state of North Dakota.[4] But much of the evidence in the New England community studies suggests that social change occurred very slowly. The inhabitants of the early Puritan towns were, in fact, much less peasant in outlook and behavior than Kenneth Lockridge would have us believe, experienced a longer and less divisive transition to a commercialized economy in the late seventeenth century than Paul Boyer and Stephen Nissenbaum portray, and by the end of the colonial era had witnessed less change in social relations than other regional populations in America.[5] In no part of North America, in fact, was rural England more faithfully recreated than in New England.[6]

This is not to argue that no alterations occurred but only that they were slower and more subtle than in other areas, leaving New England's communities unusually stable and relatively static in comparison with communities in other parts of colonial America. In the early years challenges to customary social relations may have been raised with what seemed frightening rapidity to the Puritan leaders by Mortonites, Gortonites, Hutchinsonians, Pequots, and Quakers, each with an alternate vision of how to structure society and mediate between different groups within it. But in each case the "outsiders" were bested and expelled without having affected the deeper-running social processes. Thus, a peculiar Puritan blend of participatory involvement within a hierarchically structured society of lineal families on small community-oriented farms perpetuated itself. The relatively fixed nature of this society owed something to the thin migratory flow into New England by other than English immigrants, the smallest flow in any area of English colonization. It owed much also to the visionary quality of Puritan ideology, the persistence of which was aided by the fact that New England remained a region populated by a culturally homogeneous people. Finally, the economic marginality of the region, which hindered commercial development and obviated the need for bound labor, ensured that New England's social development would change at an unimpressive pace compared with that in other areas.

No historian labors in the eye-straining, frustratingly incomplete, and sometimes nearly intractable sources of local records in order to prove the changelessness of the society he or she is studying. So nearly all of New England's community historians have emphasized change. Change there was, to be sure: demographic shifts at first in fertility, mortality, and marriage age, made possible in the founding generations by the general healthfulness of the climate and the wide availability of land that gave to the extended English family a durability greater than that of its English counterpart; changes in land prices, farm sizes, and patriarchal authority influenced by the new demographic contours; and changes from open-field to independent farming and from partible inheritance to primogeniture as the people-land ratio changed.[7]

In demonstrating these shifts the historians of early New England have made a major contribution, especially in the area of historical demography, where the old model of the extended English family evolving into the nuclear colonial family has been nearly stood on its head. Yet, while we now have a rich demographic history of New England, the economic history of the region is woefully underdeveloped. It is this gap in scholarship that has led to some exaggerated claims for social changes extending beyond the family to society at large. Very slowly, no doubt, the Puritan was becoming a Yankee, to invoke those two overused ideal types. Yet at the end of six generations of settlement social differentiation in the interior New England towns remained considerably less than in most other places in the Europeanized New World; the economy remained relatively underdeveloped; the threshold of expectations remained relatively fixed; and individualistic, opportunistic behavior was not nearly so pronounced as was continued attachment to family and community. New England was not so stable, so undifferentiated, so unlitigious, so religiously harmonious, or so consensual as Michael Zuckerman has argued; but the least favorable physical environment in eastern

North America combined with the cultural restraints imposed by Puritanism to retard the advent of behavioral characteristics associated with the spread of the market economy in a way that sets New England off somewhat from the rest of the British mainland colonies.

Because New England's economy was ill suited to the use of slave labor, except in a few areas such as the Narragansett region of Rhode Island, and because the native population was nearly eliminated by disease and war between 1615 and 1675, by the late seventeenth century the colonizers' society was left to develop relatively unaffected in formal ways by the cultures of non-Europeans.[8] Where New England's history did intersect with the history of "outside" forces was through its peoples' long involvement in a series of exhausting wars against the French in Canada and their Indian allies. These conflicts sapped the productive energies of New England's communities, inflicted casualty rates associated with modern wars, and dislocated the economy, especially in Massachusetts, in ways that produced social strain.[9] Still, so long as New Englanders could comprehend these wars as struggles of the people of light against the people of darkness, social development in the region was not significantly altered.

In summary, New Englanders had come from parts of England undergoing a transformation that involved widespread enclosure of land, unprecedented geographical mobility, widening social differentiation, and a quickening pace of commercial relations. In New England these developments were arrested for much of the seventeenth century as immigrants built a social system where family and community outweighed material acquisition, restless individualism was held in check, and the household mode of production remained the dominant form of economic existence. Over the fifteen decades separating the arrival of the Pilgrims from the beginnings of the American Revolution the morselization of land increased geographical mobility, widened social disparities, and eroded patriarchal authority. But in no place in colonial America did the earliest forms of social development—land use, social differentiation, labor force, mode of production, religious ideology, political institutions, legal codes, and moral discipline—remain so close to the founding patterns as in the *relatively* cohesive, *relatively* insular, and *relatively* homogeneous communities of New England.[10]

THE MID-ATLANTIC

If New England stands as the most homogeneous area in British America in the colonial period, the mid-Atlantic represented the most heterogeneous. This diversity has been noticed most frequently in terms of the ethnic and religious mosaics of New York and Pennsylvania, where religious sects flourished, ethnic enclaves proliferated, and a great commingling of different variants of transplanted European culture occurred. In New York this was so initially because of the cosmopolitan Dutch presence in the area, which was followed by English intrusion, Puritan migration, Huguenot and Jewish arrivals, and German and Scotch-Irish immigration. In Pennsylvania the founding English and Welsh Quakers ensured that they would be engulfed by other religions and ethnic stocks shortly after they grafted themselves onto the scattered Swedish, Finnish, and Dutch settlements by adopting an open-door policy to all newcomers, in vivid contrast to the New Englanders, who used rhetoric, law, and even the hangman's noose to keep outsiders from their doors.

This ethnic and religious heterogeneity in the mid-Atlantic was important to the pluralistic development of the region. But more vital were the forms of social organization imposed upon this temperate grain and cattle area by the founding colonizers of the region and by its basic ecology. If the New England way was to stress individual economic activity within communally oriented towns, the mid-Atlantic contained a variety of economic modes and social formations. In parts of New York and New Jersey some men aggrandized baronial estates and practiced a form of exploitative agrarian capitalism based on leasing land to hundreds of tenant farmers.[11] Though often called manor lords, most of them were more interested in land speculation and maximizing rental income than in exercising the privileges and responsibilities traditionally associated with feudal tenure. While landlordism may not have been as exploitative of tenant farmers as has sometimes been claimed, and while some farmers may have regarded tenantry as a necessary step on the road to a freehold farm, capitalistic manorialism nonetheless stunted the economic development of areas where it prevailed and introduced class disparities that were the most exaggerated for any rural area north of the Chesapeake.[12]

Within the same ecological zone, in other parts of New York and New Jersey and in Pennsylvania and northern Delaware, the social organization evolved very differently: toward a society of freeholders; a competitive market economy; a system of land use and transfer that stressed the commodity value of land; the considerable use of slave, indentured, and wage labor by individual owners of medium-sized farms; and a social ethos notable for the most fully articulated defense of self-interest in colonial America.[13] The prevailing ideal in this region was familial without being communal, so that most farmers were competitively involved in a market economy and many more than in New England utilized credit and purchased the bound labor of indentured servants and slaves.

These commercial farmers of the region watered by the Delaware and Susquehanna rivers engaged in no dramatic antinomian controversies or witchcraft trials, and even the Great Awakening there was mild by comparison with that in New England. Hence, we find little of the social conflict that is said to have been causally joined to the transition to a market economy in New England. Disputes with proprietors and their agents abounded, and Quaker Pennsylvania was wracked by the Keithian controversy in the early years of settlement. But chronic social division was not characteristic of the mid-Atlantic region. What stands out is the rapid settlement of the land by individual farmers, who rarely settled in towns and exhibited several of the key characteristics of a system of commercial agriculture—production of foodstuffs for an export market; purchase rather than home manufacture of cloth; high volume of turnover in land for speculative purposes; and investment in nonfamily labor, whether bound or free. The contrast in growth and development of these two northern regions is notable. Seven decades after it was founded, New England had a population of 93,000, which drew but little on an external labor supply and imported goods from England at a rate of about one pound per capita annually. Seven decades after its founding, the region embracing Pennsylvania, New Jersey, and Delaware contained about 220,000 people who were heavily involved in the slave and indentured servant trade and imported from England nearly twice as much per capita as their New England counterparts.[14]

We will need many more community studies of the mid-Atlantic before parity with the state of knowledge for New England is reached; but it is already apparent that real differences existed between the social development of most of New England (excluding parts of the Connecticut River Valley and the Narragansett region) and that of most of the mid-Atlantic region. These differences help reconcile the ongoing argument between James Lemon and James Henretta, two of the principal contributors to recent discussions of social evolution in early America. The argument is largely a false one because Henretta is mainly painting the New England scene, while Lemon is portraying the mid-Atlantic landscape. To be sure, the two regions were not altogether different. The lineal family was important in Pennsylvania, as in New England. Agricultural production for market was not unknown in Massachusetts or Connecticut; "traditional" values were not changeless in one area or entirely swept away in the other. But distinct patterns of social development occurred because the forms of economic existence varied, as did the ideological outlook, partly brought from the homelands of the respective settlers and partly remolded by conditions in the new land. Henretta believes that Lemon assumes "a false homogeneity in colonial

society" but himself portrays "the historically distinct social and economic system that developed in America," as if all colonists traveled the
same road toward a commercialized economy and at the same pace.[15]

At the heart of the problem, then, lies the dialectic between inherited
cultural norms and economic systems brought to the New World and the
transforming effects of the colonizers' new environment. In the mid-Atlantic, as in New England, traditional values set limitations on how fast
and in what ways social relationships changed. But the tempo and character of change depended in turn on the possibilities afforded by particular environments. Following Percy Bidwell, Henretta admits "a direct
relationship between the material environment, on the one hand, and the
consciousness and activity of the population on the other" and concludes that in America "acquisitive hopes had yielded to geographic
realities," thus preserving the precommercial *mentalité*.[16] But geographic
realities varied greatly between stony, thin-soiled New England and the
rich alluvial soils of Pennsylvania which proved so wonderfully suited to
grain production. It was not the "differential access to an urban and
international market" that marked the mid-Atlantic off from New England but the productivity of the soils and the greater availability of
cleared land in the early period of settlement. The latter fact, not yet fully
studied, is likely explained by the pre-Columbian history of the region.
Far more agricultural than their Algonquian counterparts of the more
northerly latitudes, the native inhabitants of the mid-Atlantic had left far
greater amounts of tillable soil to the European immigrants.

Nor did the cultural constraints circumscribing "the extent of involvement in the market economy" apply with equal force in New
England and the mid-Atlantic. Puritan communalism kept its grip on
New Englanders far longer than did the weaker Quaker communalism
of Pennsylvania and New Jersey, partly because the environment itself
in New England was less conducive to the breaking out of a bourgeois
ethos and partly because New England attracted, or permitted, far
fewer non-Puritan immigrants than Pennsylvania attracted, or recruited,
non-Quaker newcomers. Even the communally oriented Germans of
Pennsylvania make a frail reed upon which to base an argument for
resistance to a commercialized, commoditized culture, because the Mo-
ravian and Mennonite sectarians represented only a small fraction of
the entire pool of newcomers after 1715, which was heavily composed
of Scotch-Irish and nonsectarian Germans.

Thus, while Henretta's argument for the persistence of a precommercial ethos has substantial relevance for New England (the maritime
towns, the Connecticut River Valley, and the Narragansett country excepted), Lemon's model is more appropriate for the mid-Atlantic. It is
likely that additional local studies will show that there the rate of land

transfer was higher, social differentiation proceeded faster, per capita accumulation of goods was substantially higher, farmers produced more extensively for external markets, and the bourgeois mentality, less re- strained by the community ideal, was developed more fully by the time of the Revolution.

With deeper research the different patterns of social development in New England and the mid-Atlantic may also make better sense of the contrasting resonances of the Great Awakening in the two regions, which in itself offers clues to the course of deeper-running social changes. The much greater intensity of the Awakening in New England can be partly accounted for by the stronger grip that millennialism always had in the region of colonial America that maintained its cul- tural insularity longest and thus kept alive the sense of providential mission. But the searing force of the Awakening in New England is also attributable to the incipient strain produced by economic marginality (rather than by the transition to capitalism), a disordered monetary system, growing poverty in the port towns, and a series of debilitating wars between 1675 and 1763. The flame-throwing itinerant evangelist James Davenport never preached in Lancaster, Pennsylvania, or Albany, New York; but it seems unlikely that he could have touched off the emotional explosions that occurred when he scorched the townspeople of New London, Connecticut, and Boston, Massachusetts. The Great Awakening in the middle colonies emerged from doctrinal differences within the Presbyterian and Dutch Congregational churches and served primarily to reach a large number of people who were poorly minis- tered to, if served at all, by the established clergy. In New England thousands who had been on the fringes of organized religious activity "flew to Christ"; but a far greater number were swept into the evangeli- cal net because of the precariousness of their position—an insecurity that now could be expressed through the vehicle of religion, which, amid an ethos of community and cultural homogeneity, was more ap- propriate than the vehicle of politics. Militant and evangelical Protes- tantism was best suited to the people in British America who had best maintained their religious and ethnic unity, who were geographically contiguous to the French papist enemy, and who inhabited the least hospitable physical environment along the North American coastal plain.

THE SOUTH

In the Chesapeake and along the rice coast of South Carolina and Georgia local societies developed so differently than in either the mid- Atlantic or New England that they may be designated hinterlands of exploitation rather than of settlement.[17] Three interlocking factors governed the unique development of these areas: first, the peculiarly dismal demographic history of the seventeenth-century South; second, the rapid growth of export-propelled economies; and third, the heavy reliance on bound labor. A spectacular burst of empirical research, almost all of it appearing since 1965, has reshaped our understanding of the colonial South's unique social development and the extent to which it differed from northern social evolution in ways that go far beyond the contrasts implied in the hallowed dichotomy of Cavalier and Yankee.

Scholarship in the 1970s has nearly reversed the old characterization of the South as precapitalist and neofeudal because it lacked economic diversification and developed a partriarchal planter class whose members supposedly buried capital in the creation of an ostentatious plantation life instead of ploughing it back into productive use. Chesapeake historians, by delving into the economic history of the Chesapeake tobacco coast—in contrast to the New England community historians, who have only scratched the surface of this subject—have pieced together a comprehensive picture of the interaction between cultural traditions and physical environment. These studies portray Chesapeake settlers building a highly exploitative and capitalist economy far more rapidly than did settlers in New England, if we can judge this transition by the rapidity of land exchange, the rise of land speculation, the commoditization of labor, the movement from subsistence to commercial agriculture, and the use of deficit spending to increase production.[18]

The new history of the Chesapeake stresses the development of a staple crop, in wide demand in the metropolitan area, as an engine of growth. Tobacco filled this function for Virginia, Maryland, and southern Delaware in the seventeenth century. Initially, high prices for the leaf spurred investments in the development of the region, which led to large importations of white bound labor and the rapid expansion of output. Over the course of the seventeenth century tobacco prices declined sharply, but for producers this was offset by lower costs in producing, transporting, and marketing the crop. As tobacco prices dropped, the nicotine addiction fell within reach of a broader range of consumers; and even though the limits of the English market had been reached by about 1680, creating a period of stagnation for about three decades, the eighteenth century brought a dizzying new expansion of the market, as France became a major consumer of Chesapeake-produced sotweed.

Subject to booms and depressions far more intense than fluctuations in the northern agricultural sector, Chesapeake tobacco growers became mainland America's foremost users of credit instruments and were the most deeply involved in the international marketplace. With roughly the same population as New England, the Chesapeake colonies exported to and imported from England commodities with aggregate values from six to ten times greater than those imported and exported by their northern counterparts.[19] Even if New England's trade volume is doubled to reflect its extensive participation in the West Indies economy (remembering that the Chesapeake-West Indies commerce, although very considerable, has hardly been studied), the difference in the degree of commercialization in the two regions is marked.

The far more dynamic character of the Chesapeake economy has sometimes been shrouded because so much emphasis has been given to the southern reliance on bound as against free labor, a factor that for some historians disqualifies the region's economy as capitalistic. In fact, it was the ability of southern planters to procure and control a large and unfree labor force—reversing the historical rise of free labor in early modern Europe—that led to a rate of growth, market orientation, and accumulation of wealth that outstripped the performance of New England.[20] The factors that led to changing this labor force from primarily white indentured servants in the seventeenth century to primarily African slaves in the eighteenth has now been pieced together in a skillful examination of both the supply and the demand sides of the phenomenon.[21]

One of the major accomplishments of the Chesapeake social historians has been to show how the rapid development of an economy that increased tobacco exports from 15 million pounds in 1670 to 100 million pounds in 1770 occurred amidst ghastly demographic conditions that contrast severely with those in other parts of English America. Mortality rates in the seventeenth-century Chesapeake colonies were probably twice as high as New England's in this period. The region also suffered a badly skewed ratio of males to females that left more than half the males womanless for most of the century. These two factors, fearful mortality and a wildly unbalanced sex ratio, produced a dismally low fertility rate, probably not one-fourth of New England's. Yet the population of the Chesapeake grew as rapidly as New England's because of an immigration rate that dwarfed that of the Puritan colonies.[22] New Englanders in the second half of the seventeenth century were mostly the children and grandchildren of healthy, fertile founding immigrants; in the same period Marylanders and Virginians were mostly newly arrived immigrants replacing the sickly and infertile settlers of earlier years.

Social development within a society so demographically sterile and socially mobile but so economically dynamic could not help but differ drastically from northern patterns. First, the labor force was predominantly young, predominantly male, and predominantly unmarried for most of the seventeenth century. Second, by the end of the seventeenth century southern society was relying increasingly on black slave labor. Between 1690 and 1770 the Afro-American population of the South grew from about 13,000 to 410,000. Hence, the advent of a less transitory and more family-centered white society in the South, marked by decreased white immigration, lower mortality rates, more balanced sex ratios, and family formation, occurred simultaneously with the adoption of a labor force that required massive coercion and intimate interracial contacts.[23] Third, because the plantation system was based on dispersed holdings of land, where capital and labor were concentrated as nowhere else on the mainland, the rules governing the supervision of the labor force tended to be set individually by employer-owners rather than by local instruments of government as in New England and the mid-Atlantic. Fourth, the rapidly expanding staple economy produced a much more stratified social system than in the North, with a small number of extremely wealthy planters, who owed their fortunes to land speculation as well as tobacco production; a comparatively shriveled middle class, kept small because of the difficulties for small producers to compete with large planters, the domination of artisan work by black slaves, and the general absence of towns; a sizable white tenant class, which in both absolute and relative terms was growing in the eighteenth century; and a massive number of slaves, who constituted from 40 to 60 percent of the total population in various regions of the South on the eve of the Revolution.

Relying increasingly on chattel slavery in the eighteenth century, this staple-producing society was marked by greater volatility and violence than historians have usually recognized. The substitution of black slave labor for white indentured labor at first seemed to promise differently. The tobacco coast in the 1660s and 1670s seethed with discontent, as servants, who had obligingly died off before serving their term of service during the era when English adventurers launched the tobacco economy, began to live longer and form a class of landless, impoverished, socially blocked, and armed freemen—the stuff of which frontier Indian wars and civil rebellions are made. By relocating their reservoir of servile labor from the impoverished rural villages of England and Ireland to the villages of West Africa, while at the same time turning internal class tensions into external violence against native occupiers of fertile land, late-seventeenth-century southern colonizers were able to forge a consensus among upper- and lower-class whites. With new land available through dispossession of Indians, and the pipeline carrying new indentured servants shut down, lower-class southern whites became aspiring landowners, desirous of owning their own black bondsmen and bondswomen, and thus emerged as a stabilizing force in the eighteenth-century plantation society rather than a source of disequilibrium as in the seventeenth. Race became the primary badge of status in a world that heretofore had relied primarily on religious and economic distinctions in creating lines of social stratification.[24]

Despite its promise of allowing for social development free of class tension, racial slavery could only temporarily mend rifts in white society. In fact, the new availability of land following the Chesapeake Anglo-Indian war of 1675–76 and the greater degree of family formation as sex ratios became more balanced in the late seventeenth century were powerful dissolvents of the social acids that ate at the fabric of society in Bacon's and Culpepper's rebellions in the 1670s. Far from narrowing rifts in white society, however, slavery greatly enhanced the class power of the large planters, leading to a concentration of wealth and political leverage and, as it evolved into its patriarchal form in the eighteenth century, allowing the planter to extend his dominance over family, including secondary wives and illicit offspring, poor kin, and neighboring smallholders.[25] But power derived from extensive landholdings and fields full of gang laborers had its limits. Even the creation of a white solidarity myth, which "asserted the unity of the free population, the oneness of those who owned slaves and those who did not" and "assured those whose importance had been reduced, whose labor had been cheapened, that they shared with the slaveholder a fundamental superiority," could not prevent the rise of tensions within white society.[26] By the mid-eighteenth century these tensions were manifesting themselves, and they would continue to rive southern society during the Revolution, when a much larger part of the lower class in the South than in the North turned out under the colors of the loyalists rather than fight alongside a patriot planter class. More delving into this topic is needed, especially for North Carolina and South Carolina, where social historians have only begun to make inroads, but there are signs in recent research that the pressures for racial solidarity among whites were breaking down in the eighteenth century.[27] Comparatively hidden from sight because they frequently took the form of social banditry or localized disruptions rather than being played out on the public stage of provincial politics, the incipient divisions riddling the southern colonies were much greater than in New England or the middle colonies. Social cohesion, attachment to community, the mediating role and moderating effects of local institutions, and a vision of a larger purpose were all attenuated in the staple economies of the South. To no small extent this was related to the peculiar demographic history of the region, where the unbalanced sex ratio, redressed only after four generations, produced a male-centered rather than a family-centered society and an extremely high population turnover, which made attachment to community and social stability elusive. Zuckerman may sometimes have confused the ideal with the real in his study of New England's eighteenth-century communities, but surely the agricultural villages he studied *were* "peaceable kingdoms" compared with either the tidewater or the piedmont counties of Virginia, Maryland, or the Carolinas, all of which lacked most of the centripetal forces operating in the North.

Social volatility and endemic violence in the South also owed much to Indian-white relations. It is customary to think of the South as a much more biracial society than the North, but it was also more triracial. The interaction with small coastal tribes in the early period of settlement was not very different in the two regions. In both cases European diseases did their deadly work, and the remaining strokes were delivered in a series of wars that culminated in New England and the Chesapeake in 1675. The Euro-Indian confrontation in the Carolinas produced similar results in a different way: the pitting of one local tribe against another for the purposes of primitive accumulation and a disencumbering of the land through an Indian slave trade.[28]

A major North-South difference evolved, however, in relations between the colonizers and the powerful, populous interior tribes. Northern colonists competed little for the land of the Iroquois, since they were valued as trading partners and since it was widely understood that to push them into the arms of the French was suicidal. In the South the Creeks and Cherokees stood in a different relationship to the coastal settlers. Their trade was valued, as was their political neutrality, given Spanish pretensions in this part of the world; but by the eighteenth century the rapid growth of the settler population and the expanding export market for staples such as rice, indigo, and tobacco caused covetous eyes to turn toward native lands. Moreover, holding in bondage a slave population that after 1690 was tripling every twenty-five years in Virginia and Maryland and quadrupling in South Carolina, white colonizers warily regarded the Creeks and Cherokees as providers of refuge for escaping slaves and even as potential coconspirators with blacks against the white population. One solution was to pit the Creeks and Cherokees against each other in a game of double elimination. Another was to render them both dependent on the English through the trade connection. Whatever the strategy, the colonizers of the South were more continuously, intimately, and violently involved in exploiting the Indian societies of their region than were their counterparts in New England or the mid-Atlantic. The mixing of gene pools and cultural traits was also more extensive in the South than elsewhere, affecting social development in ways that historians have only begun to explore.

In sum, environment triumphed over imported cultural traditions more completely than in any other region. The result was a highly developed system of extracting an economic surplus through the coercion of an internal black labor force and the fitfully successful manipulation of an external labor force of indigenous people. This process proceeded all the faster because the southern colonies lacked widely shared assumptions about a controlling social ideal, such as characterized New England's communities. Nonetheless, the social development of the South did in time produce ideological constructs peculiar to the region. New expectations and new labor processes emerged amid ecological conditions far different than in the North and eventually gave birth to an ideology that legitimized and gave a veneer of respectability to the highly exploitative economic system based on the racial division of labor.

In New England, it may be said, institutions such as religious ideology, participatory local government, and a town form of settlement greatly restrained economic ambition, which in any case was dampened by the geographical realities of the region. Amid different geographical realities, southern colonizers cast away restraining ideologies and institutions, developed a labor process unknown in England, and gradually articulated an ideology of racial paternalism.

THE CITIES

Even though only about 5 percent of the eighteenth-century colonizers lived in cities (and none of these cities exceeded sixteen thousand in 1750 or thirty thousand in 1776), the commercial capitals of British North America were the cutting edge of social change. Almost all the alterations that have been discussed so far first occurred in the seaports and then radiated outward to the villages, farms, and plantations of the hinterland.

In the half-century between 1690 and 1740 Boston, New York, and Philadelphia blossomed into commercial centers that rivaled such British provincial ports as Hull, Bristol, and Glasgow. This urban growth reflected the development of the hinterlands to which they were symbiotically linked. Gradually these seaports—along with others such as Newport, Providence, Baltimore, Annapolis, Norfolk, and Charleston—were drawn into the international marketplace, which included not only England, Scotland, and Ireland but also Newfoundland, the West Indies, Africa, and the Iberian peninsula. Increasingly a part of an Atlantic world, urban merchants, politicians, and even artisans made economic decisions in consonance with an emerging commercial ethic that was eroding traditional restraints on entrepreneurial activity.[29]

That the cities stood at one end of a continuum of social development can be seen in the rate of geographical mobility, the distribution of wealth, the rapidity of property transfer, the extent of poverty, the level of investment in bound and wage labor, and the reliance on modern credit instruments. All of these phenomena have been examined in some detail in recent years, although the lesser port towns and the inland marketing centers still largely await study.[30] Persistence rates, for example, which according to Lockridge were as high as 99 percent in seventeenth-century Dedham, were much lower in the cities, where as much as 10 percent of the population annually were in- or out-migrants. The wealth profile in the maritime centers was much more asymmetrical than in rural areas, with the top 10 percent of the urban wealthholders typically holding about 70 percent of the wealth, whereas in northern farming communities at mid-eighteenth century they usually controlled about 40 percent. Those without property typically constituted about 30 percent of the adult males in farming areas of the North by the time of the Seven Years' War but nearly double that percentage in the urban centers. Bound labor—black slaves and white indentured servants—filled roughly half of the laboring roles of the commercial ports at the end of the colonial period but less than one-quarter of them in the northern countryside.[31]

Another mark of urban social devlopment was occupational specialization and the rise of the professions. In every farming village of the North and on most large southern plantations a variety of artisans practiced their crafts. But in the seaboard commercial centers the occupational range increased enormously, not only because shipbuilding and metalworking flourished but because crafts such as shoemaking and furniture making were divided into subspecialties in the eighteenth century. While artisans in twenty-seven different trades resided in Germantown, Pennsylvania, on the eve of the American Revolution, for example, more than eighty skills were denoted on the tax lists of nearby Philadelphia. Likewise, the urban centers became professional seedbeds because they contained the major institutions of culture and higher learning, which rapidly increased in number during the prerevolutionary generation; a majority of the colonial lawyers, whose profession grew in tandem with urban commercial development; most of the government officials, whose ranks swelled with the increase in imperial authority in the eighteenth century; and more than their share of clergymen.[32] The growing density of social institutions, which was occurring everywhere in the eighteenth-century colonies but happened most extensively in urban areas, signaled the maturation of colonial society and played a vital role in the ability of the colonists to concert themselves politically and militarily when the imperial crisis erupted following the end of the Seven Years' War.

The spread of the entrepreneurial ethic in the eighteenth century, which was most noticeable in the commercial centers, where upper

artisans as well as merchants and shopkeepers threw off traditional
notions of political economy, was accelerated by the European wars
into which the colonies were drawn. The effect of these international
conflicts on colonial social development has gone largely unnoticed and
represents one of the important areas of research ahead. But it is evident, taking King George's War as an example, that New England was
drained of manpower and resources as its inhabitants engaged in costly
attempts to overcome the French enemy to the north. However, the war
also offered opportunities for merchants and others to conduct business
on a scale hitherto unknown and to amass profits through lucrative war
contracts and privateering. Becoming more stratified by wealth and
differentiated by occupation, urban people came to think of themselves
as belonging to economic groups that did not always share common
goals, began to behave in class-specific ways in response to events that
impinged upon their well-being, and manifested ideological points of
view and cultural differences peculiar to their rank. This is not to say
that all carpenters or all merchants occupied the same position along
the spectrum of wealth, or that all ship captains or all ship caulkers
thought alike, or that upper-class city dwellers consistently opposed
lower-class city dwellers because they occupied different social niches.
Evidence is abundant that vertical consciousness was always present in
a society where movement up and down the social ladder never stopped
and where the natural tendency of economic networks was to create a
common interest, as among merchant, shipbuilder, and mariner. Nonetheless, movement between ranks and vertical linkages that were a part
of a system of economic clientage could not prevent horizontal bonds
from growing stronger. People who had previously thought of themselves as belonging to the lower, middling, or upper ranks but had seen
no reason why this should imply incipient social conflict gradually came
to associate these rough identifiers of social standing with antagonistic
interests and made these differences the basis for political contention.[33]

Much more work needs to be done on the cities before these tendencies can be fully comprehended. Little is yet known about the productive and reproductive lives of urban women. Urban economic networks and economic clientage need further study, as do the phenomena
of cultural hegemony wielded from above and deference yielded from
below—modes of behavior that may have pertained to the rural populations of the eighteenth century more than the urban.

One aspect of urban development that troubled many contempo-
raries was the impoverishment of a substantial part of the population of
the northern seaports. In part the growth of poverty was a side effect of
the mid-century wars that extended over eighteen of the twenty-four
years between 1739 and 1763. Casualty rates in these conflicts ex-

ceeded those of twentieth-century wars and left in their wake large numbers of disabled men, as well as larger numbers of widows with dependent children, who became the labor force of the first textile factories in America, conceived not out of entrepreneurial inspiration but out of despair at the climbing poor rates and bulging almshouses. Since colonial armies were recruited mainly from the lower classes, and since the cities contained a disproportionate number of propertyless and marginal persons, the urban centers became scenes of considerable suffering at the end of these wars.[34]

The discovery of urban poverty has altered the thinking of some historians about social development in the eighteenth century. For many years it was assumed that progress was almost automatic in the thriving commercial centers of America. We now know differently. In the cities poverty challenged the governing modes of thought, shook confidence in the internal economic system, led to sharp questioning of the imperial relationship, and intensified class feeling. "He that gets all he can honestly, and saves all he gets (necessary Expenses excepted)," Poor Richard counseled, "will certainly become RICH." Such advice, for a growing number of urban dwellers, was only salt on wounds that were not self-inflicted. No amount of exhortation could convince the laboring poor of the relevancy of maxims written in an era of full employment and higher real wages than existed in the period following the end of the Seven Years' War. Out of the grievances of the urban laboring classes came much of the social force that saw in Revolution the possibility of creating a new social order.

Most of the tendencies associated with the development of a bourgeois society are most noticeable in the colonial commercial centers: the transition from an oral to a literate culture, from an organic to an associational patterning of human relationships, from a moral to a market economy, from ethnically and religiously homogeneous to heterogeneous communities, from roles assigned by ascription to roles gained by achievement, and from a communal to an individualistic orientation. In the work that lies ahead, however, it is important that these word pairings not entrap us in the much-used model of decline, which, as Thomas Bender points out, traces the movement from gemeinschaft to gesellschaft in terms of decay, declension, dissolution, and disintegration of "community." Enough has been discovered about the dynamics of social development in diverse seventeenth- and eighteenth-century locales to keep historians mindful that communities change at different rates of speed, sometimes in different directions, not always in unilinear fashion, and rarely with all members of the community cleaving to the same values and responding identically to the stimuli. Bender aptly asks: "Why cannot gemeinschaft and gesellschaft simultaneously shape social life," for both are "forms of human interaction that can act reciprocally on each other"?[35] We may ask also whether homogeneity is the *sine qua non* of community and whether the concept of *pro bono publico* is the only glue of social relations. Even in the seaport towns, where social development carried colonial people closest to the world we call modern, where stratification was most pronounced, population mobility greatest, the market orientation strongest, the concept of self-interest most widely accepted, and the populace the most heterogeneous in terms of ethnicity, occupation, and religion, communities existed and thrived. This is not to say that there was no social conflict. But conflict is not the same as decline or decay. In future work historians may better construct new paradigms of social change by concentrating on social process—the story of people struggling to create, oppose, defend, and legitimize new circumstances and new structural realities—rather than by nostalgically documenting the eclipse of community.

NATIVE AMERICANS

Ideally, a discussion of the role of native American societies in the social development of eastern North America should be regionally organized because there was no unified "Indian" experience and the various tribal histories that ethnohistorians have reconstructed are closely related to the histories of European colonizers in particular areas.[36] But space limitations permit only some general remarks about the underdeveloped field of native American history and its connection to the history of the colonizers. It is important to differentiate between coastal and interior tribes: even though disease and warfare thoroughly ravaged the numerous seaboard tribes by the third generation of settlement in every colony, these small societies profoundly affected the shaping of settler communities.

The process of decimation, dispossession, and decline among the Indian societies of the coastal areas occurred in different ways during the first century of European colonization. Everywhere that Europeans settled, a massive depopulation occurred as the invaders' diseases swept through biologically defenseless native societies. Yet this rarely broke the resistance of the native peoples. In New England that occurred only after the stronger coastal tribes, such as the Wampanoags and Narragansetts, finally succccumbed in a long war of attrition to an enemy who sought no genuine accommodation. In Virginia and Maryland the tidewater tribes genuinely strove for accommodation following their unsuccessful resistance movements of 1622 and 1644. But, as in New England, their inability to function in any way that served European society finally led to conflict initiated by whites. Even as friendly colonized people they were obstacles in the path of an acquisitive and expanding plantation society. In South Carolina it was not dead Indians but Indians alive and in chains that benefited the white settlers. The build-up of the colonizer population was slow enough, and the desire among the Indians for trade goods intense enough, that the white Carolinians, most of them transplanted from Barbados, where they had learned to trade in human flesh, could lure the coastal tribes into obliterating each other in the wars for slaves.[17]

The result was roughly the same in all the colonies along the seaboard. By the 1680s in the older colonies and by the 1720s in the new ones the coastal tribes were shattered. Devastated by disease and warfare, the survivors either incorporated themselves as subjects of stronger inland groups or entered the white man's world as detribalized servile dependents. Their desire for European trade goods, which kept them in close contact with European colonizers, and the persistence of ancient intertribal hostilities, which thwarted pan-tribal resistance, sealed their fate once the growth of the settler population made it apparent that their value as trading partners was incidental in comparison with the value of the land that their destruction would convert to European possession.

Although they were defeated, the coastal cultures served a crucial function for tribes farther inland. Their prolonged resistance gave interior societies time to adapt to the European presence and to devise strategies of survival as the white societies grew in size and strength. "People like the Iroquois," T. J. C. Brasser has pointed out, "owed a great deal to the resistance of the coastal Algonkians, and both peoples were well aware of this."[38] The coastal tribes provided a buffer between the interior Indians and the Europeans, and when the coastal tribes lost their political autonomy, their remnants were often incorporated into the larger inland tribes. This was important in the much stronger opposition that the Iroquois, Cherokees, and Creeks offered to European encroachment—a resistance so effective that for the first century and a half of European settlement the white newcomers were restricted to the coastal plain, unable to penetrate the Appalachians, where the interior tribes, often allied with the French, held sway.

During the first half of the eighteenth century the interior Indian societies demonstrated their capacity for adapting to the presence of Europeans and for turning economic and political interaction with them to their own advantage. Drawing selectively from European culture, they adopted through the medium of the fur, skin, and slave trade European articles of clothing, weapons, metal implements, and a variety of ornamental objects. To some extent this incorporation of material objects robbed the Indians of their native skills. But agriculture, fishing, and hunting, the mainstays of Indian subsistence before the Europeans came, remained so thereafter. European implements such as the hoe only made Indian agriculture more efficient. The knife and fishhook enabled the natives to fish and trap with greater intensity in order to obtain the commodities needed in the barter system. However, pottery making declined, and the hunter became more dependent upon the gun.

Yet, interaction with European societies over many generations sowed seeds of destruction within tribal villages. It is not necessary to turn Indians into acquisitive capitalists to explain their desire for trade goods. They did not seek guns, cloth, kettles, and fishhooks out of a desire to become part of bourgeois culture, accumulating material wealth from the fur trade, but because they recognized the advantages, within the matrix of their own culture, of goods fashioned by societies with a more complex technology. The utility of the Europeans' trade goods, not the opportunities for profit provided by the fur trade, drew native Americans into it, and from the Indian point of view, trade was carried on within the context of political and social alliance.[39]

Nonetheless, the fur trade required native Americans to reallocate their human resources and reorder their internal economies. Subsistence hunting turned into commercial hunting, and consequently males spent more time away from the villages trapping and hunting. Women were also drawn into the new economic organization of villages, for the beaver, marten, or fox had to be skinned and the skins scraped, dressed, trimmed, and sewn into robes. Among some tribes the trapping, preparation, and transporting of skins became so time-consuming that food resources had to be procured in trade from other tribes. Ironically, the reorientation of tribal economies toward the fur trade dispersed villages and weakened the localized basis of clans and lineages. Breaking up in order to be nearer the widely dispersed trapping grounds, Indian villagers moved closer to the nomadic woodland existence that Europeans had charged them with at the beginning of contact.

Involvement in the fur trade also altered the relationship of native Americans to their ecosystem. The tremendous destruction of animal life triggered by the advent of European trade undermined the spiritual framework within which hunting had traditionally been carried out and repudiated the ancient emphasis on living in balance with the natural environment. Trade also broadened vastly the scale of intertribal conflict. With Europeans competing for client tribes who would supply furs to be marketed throughout Europe, Indian societies were sucked into the rivalry of their patrons. As furs became depleted in the hunting grounds of one tribe, they could maintain the European trade connection only by conquering more remote tribes whose hunting grounds had not yet been exhausted or by forcibly intercepting the furs of other tribes as they were transported to trading posts. Thus, the Iroquois decimated the Hurons of the Great Lakes region in the mid-seventeenth century as part of their drive for beaver hegemony.[40]

While the interior tribes were greatly affected by contact with the colonizers, they nonetheless rejected much of what the newcomers presented to them as a superior way of life. Tribes such as the Iroquois, Creeks, and Cherokees were singularly unimpressed with most of the institutions of European life and saw no reason to replace what they valued in their own culture with what they disdained in the culture of others. This applied to the newcomers' political institutions and practices, system of law and justice, religion, education, family organization, and childrearing practices. Many aspects of Indian life were marked by cultural persistency in the long period of interaction with Europeans. Indian societies incorporated what served them well and rejected what made no sense within the framework of their own values and modes of existence.

Despite their maintenance of their traditional culture in many areas of life, the native Americans' involvement in the European trade network hastened the spread of epidemic diseases, raised the level of warfare, depleted ecozones of animal life, and drew Indians into a market economy that over a long period of time constricted their economic freedom. The interior tribes reorganized productive relations within their own communities to serve a trading partner who, through the side effects of trade, became a trading master.

Social development within the British mainland colonies proceeded in some unexpected ways because of the Indian presence. Unable to coordinate themselves militarily and politically in the first 150 years of settlement, English colonizers were unable to conquer or dislodge from their tribal homelands—as did their Spanish counterparts to the south— the powerful interior native American societies. Hence, the settlers' societies, restricted to the coastal plain, developed differently than if they had been free to indulge their appetite for land and their westward yearning. Higher mortality rates associated with the spread of epidemic diseases in more densely settled areas, the rise of tenantry in rural areas, underemployment in the cities at the end of the colonial period, the decline of indentured servitude because of the growing pool of landless free laborers, and the rise of class tensions in older seaboard communities are some of the social phenomena that may be attributed in part to the limitations placed upon westward movement by the controlling hand of the major eastern tribes in the trans-Allegheny and even the Piedmont region. The native American was also of primary importance in forging an "American" identity among English, Scotch-Irish, German, and other European immigrants in North America. In their relations with the native people of the land the colonizers in British North

American served a long apprenticeship in military affairs. Far more populous than the settlers of New France and therefore much more covetous of Indian land, they engaged in hundreds of military confrontations ranging from localized skirmishes to large-scale regional wars. The allegiance of the diverse immigrants to the land, the annealing of an American as distinct from an English identity, had much to do with the myriad ways in which the colonists interacted with a people who were culturally defined as "the others" but were inextricably a part of the human landscape of North America.[41]

AFRO-AMERICANS

Unless we wish to continue picturing some one million Africans brought to or born in America before the Revolution as mindless and cultureless drones, it will be necessary to push forward recent work on the social development of black society and then to incorporate this new corpus of scholarship into an overall analysis of colonial social development. It bears noting that a large majority of the persons who crossed the Atlantic to take up life in the New World in the three hundred years before the American Revolution were Africans. Their history is still largely untold because so much attention has been paid to the kind of slave systems Europeans fashioned in the New World—the black codes they legislated, their treatment of slaves, the economic development they directed—that the slaves themselves, as active participants in a social process, are often forgotten.

In attempting to remedy this gap, historians have borrowed heavily from the work of anthropologists. The encounter model of Sidney Mintz and Richard Price, developed with reference to the Caribbean world, is especially useful because it explores how Africans who found themselves in the possession of white masters five thousand miles from their homeland created institutions and ways of life that allowed them to live as satisfactorily as possible under the slave regimen imposed upon them by the master class. In their New World encounter with European colonizers the problem was not one of merging a West African culture with a European culture, because the human cargoes aboard slave ships were not a single collective African people but rather a culturally heterogeneous people from many tribes and regions. Hence, arriving slaves did not form "communities" of people at the outset but could only become communities through forging a new life out of the fragments of many old cultures combined with elements of the dominant European culture that now bounded their existence. "What the slaves undeniably shared at the outset," according to Mintz and Price, "was their enslavement; all—or nearly all—else had to be created by them."[42]

Major strides have been taken in tracing this process of social adaptation in the Chesapeake region and along the rice coast of South Carolina and Georgia, though much remains to be done.[43] Already, it is apparent that in this process of adaptation there was a premium on cultural innovation and creativity, both because slaves had to adjust rapidly to the power of the master class and because of the initial cultural heterogeneity of the Africans. Unlike the European colonizers, Africans were immediately obliged "to shift their primary cultural and social commitment from the Old World to the New." This required rapid adaptation, learning new ways of doing things that would ensure survival. It is not surprising, therefore, that Africans developed local slave cultures rather than a unified Afro-American culture. In adapting to North American slavery, they adopted "a general openness to ideas and usages from other cultural traditions, a special tolerance (within the West African context) of cultural differences."[44] Of all the people converging in seventeenth- and eighteenth-century North America, the Africans, by the very conditions of their arrival, developed the greatest capacity for cultural change.

The complexity of black culture in America cannot be understood without considering the evolution of distinct, regional black societies as they developed over the long course of slavery.[45] One of the accomplishments of the new social historians of the colonial South is to have broken much new ground on the life cycle, family formation, and cultural characteristics of the black population, which was increasingly creole, or American-born, as the eighteenth century progressed. This work makes it possible already to go beyond earlier studies of slave life in the colonies, which were based largely on studies of nineteenth-century sources, when discussing the development of Afro-American society in the eighteenth-century colonies.

How much of African culture survived under eighteenth-century slavery is an oft-debated question. There can be little doubt that slave masters were intent on obliterating every Africanism that reduced the effectiveness of slaves as laborers and that they had some success in this. It is also true that slavery eliminated many of the cultural differences among slaves, who came from a wide variety of African cultural groups—Fulanis, Ibos, Yorubas, Malagasies, Ashantis, Mandingos, and others. At the same time, it must be remembered that throughout the eighteenth century, unlike in the nineteenth, large numbers of new Africans arrived each year. Slave importations grew rapidly in the eighteenth century, so that probably never more than half the adult slaves were American-born. This continuous infusion of African culture kept alive many of the elements that would later be transmuted almost beyond recognition. Through fashioning their own distinct culture within the limits established by the rigors of the slave system, blacks were able to forge their own religious forms, their own music and dance, their own family life, and their own beliefs and values. All of these proved indispensable to survival in a system of forced labor. All were part of the social development of black society. And all affected the social development of white society as well.

WOMEN

One final aspect of social development, occasionally alluded to in this essay but indispensable to the work that lies ahead, concerns social relations defined by gender. In the last ten years, and especially in the last four or five, a wave of new work has appeared, some of it defined as women's history and some as demographic or family history.[46] This work shows how rich the possibilities are for those who wish to study the lives of women and female-male relationships. It is crucial to the construction of new paradigms of social development that these studies of women's productive and reproductive lives, which need to be studied with class, racial, and regional differences in mind, be pushed forward at an accelerated pace and then integrated with the studies of the much better understood male half of the population. It is out of the convergence of the already completed demographic and community studies and the studies of women, blacks, and native Americans still remaining to be done that a new understanding of the social development of colonial American will emerge.

NOTES

1. Bryan D. Palmer, *A Culture in Conflict: Skilled Workers and Industrial Capitalism in Hamilton, Ontario, 1860–1914* (Toronto, 1979), xiv.

2. Raymond Williams, *Marxism and Literature* (Oxford, 1977), 81.

3. Raymond Williams, "Base and Superstructure in Marxist Cutural Theory," *New Left Review,* no. 82 (1973): 5–6.

4. Michael Zuckerman, "The Fabrication of Identity in Early America," *William and Mary Quarterly,* 3d ser., 34 (1977): 183–84; Thomas Bender, *Community and Social Change in America* (New Bruswick, N.J., 1978), 47–49.

5. Kenneth A. Lockridge, *A New England Town: The First Hundred Years, Dedham, Massachusetts, 1636–1736* (New York, 1970); Paul Boyer and Stephen Nissenbaum, *Salem Possessed: The Social Origins of Witchcraft* (Cambridge, Mass., 1974).

6. Sumner C. Powell, *Puritan Village: The Formation of a New England Town* (Middletown, Conn., 1963); David Grayson Allen, *In English Ways: The Movement of Societies and the Transferal of English Local Law and Custom to Massachusetts Bay in the Seventeenth Century* (Chapel Hill, 1981).

7. Among the major community studies that wrestle with these changes, utilizing various methodologies, are: Powell, *Puritan Village;* Charles S. Grant, *Democracy in the Connecticut Frontier Town of Kent* (New York, 1961); John Demos, *A Little Commonwealth: Family Life in Plymouth Colony* (New York, 1970); Philip J. Greven, *Four Generations: Population, Land, and Family in Colonial Andover, Massachusetts* (Ithaca, 1970); Lockridge, *New England Town;* Darrett B. Rutman, *Winthrop's Boston: Portrait of a Puritan Town, 1630–1649* (Chapel Hill, 1965); Richard L. Bushman, *From Puritan to Yankee: Character and the Social Order in Connecticut, 1690–1765* (Cambridge, Mass., 1967); Robert G. Pope, *The Half-Way Covenant: Church Membership in Puritan New England* (Princeton, 1969); Michael Zuckerman, *Peaceable Kingdoms: New England Towns in the Eighteenth Century* (New York, 1970); Darrett B. Rutman, *The Husbandmen of Plymouth: Farms and Villages in the Old Colony, 1620–1692* (Boston, 1967); Boyer and Nissenbaum, *Salem Possessed;* Paul R. Lucas, *Valley of Discord: Church and Society along the Connecticut River, 1636–1725* (Hanover, N.H., 1976); Richard P. Gildrie, *Salem, 1626–1683: A Covenant Community* (Charlottesville, 1975); Robert A. Gross, *The Minutemen and Their World* (New York, 1976); and Patricia J. Tracy, *Jonathan Edwards, Pastor: Religion and Society in Eighteenth-Century Northampton* (New York, 1979).

8. The Puritan-Algonquian interaction in the first generations of settlement is treated from radically differing perspectives in Alden T. Vaughan, *New England Frontier: Puritans and Indians, 1620–1675* (Boston, 1965); Francis Jennings, *The Invasion of America: Indians, Colonialism, and the Cant of Conquest* (Chapel Hill, 1975); and Neal E. Salisbury, *Manitou and Providence: Indians, Europeans, and the Making of New England, 1500–1643* (New York, 1982).

9. Gary B. Nash, *The Urban Crucible: Social Change, Political Consciousness, and the Origins of the American Revolution* (Cambridge, Mass., 1979), chaps. 3–10.

10. This characterization is most explicitly argued in T. H. Breen and Stephen Foster, "The Puritans' Greatest Achievement: A Study of Social Cohesion in Seventeenth-Century Massachusetts," *Journal of American History* 60 (1973): 5–22; John J. Waters, Jr., "The Traditional World of the New England Peasants: A View from Seventeenth-Century Barnstable," *New England Historical and Genealogical Register* 130 (1976): 3–21; idem, "Patrimony, Succession, and Social Stability: Guilford, Connecticut in the Eighteenth Century," *Perspectives in American History* 10 (1976): 131–60; idem, "Family, Inheritance, and Migration in Colonial New England: The Evidence from Guilford, Connecticut," *William and Mary Quarterly,* 3d ser., 39 (1982): 64–86; and Christopher M. Jedrey, *The World of John Cleaveland: Family and Community in Eighteenth-Century New England* (New York, 1979).

11. Rowland Berthoff and John M. Murrin, "Feudalism, Communalism, and the Yeoman Freeholder: The American Revolution Considered as a Social Accident," in *Essays on the American Revolution,* ed. Stephen G. Kurtz and James H. Hutson (Chapel Hill, 1973), 263–76.

12. Cf. Sung Bok Kim, *Landlord and Tenant in Colonial New York: Manorial Society, 1664–1775* (Chapel Hill, 1978); and Edward Countryman, *A People in Revolution: The American Revolution and Political Society in New York, 1760–1790* (Baltimore, 1981), chaps. 1–3.

13. James T. Lemon, *The Best Poor Man's Country: A Geographical Study of Early Southeastern Pennsylvania* (Baltimore, 1972); Stephanie Grauman Wolf, *Urban Village: Population, Community, and Family Structure in Germantown, Pennsylvania, 1683–1800* (Princeton, 1976); Patricia U. Bonomi, "The Middle Colonies: Embryo of the New Political Order," in *Perspectives on Early American History: Essays in Honor of Richard B. Morris,* ed. Alden T. Vaughan and George Athan Billias (New York, 1973), 63–92; Jerome H. Wood, Jr., *Conestoga Crossroads: Lancaster, Pennsylvania, 1730–1790* (Harrisburg, Pa., 1979).

14. U.S. Bureau of the Census, *Historical Statistics of the United States: Colonial Times to 1970,* 2 vols. (Washington, D.C., 1975), 2:1168, 1176–77. The mid-Atlantic data are for Pennsylvania.

15. "Mr. Henretta Replies" *William and Mary Quarterly,* 3d ser., 37 (1980): 696–97.

16. James A. Henretta, "Families and Farms: *Mentalité* in Pre-Industrial America," *William and Mary Quarterly,* 3d ser., 35 (1978): 14; see also James T. Lemon, "Early Americans and Their Social Environment," *Journal of Historical Geography* 6 (1980).

17. The terms are taken from Lloyd Best, "Outlines of a Model of Pure Plantation Economy," *Social and Economic Studies* 17 (1968): 285–87.

18. Jacob M. Price, *France and the Chesapeake: A History of the French Tobacco Monopoly, 1674–1791, and of Its Relationship to the British and American Tobacco Trades,* 2 vols. (Ann Arbor, 1973); Carville V. Earle, *The Evolution of a Tidewater Settlement System: All Hallow's Parish, Maryland, 1650–1783* (Chicago, 1975); Russell R. Menard, "Secular Trends in the Chesapeake Tobacco Industry, 1617–1710," *Working Papers from the Regional Economic History Research Center* 1 (1978); Paul G. E. Clemens, *The Atlantic Economy and Colonial Maryland's Eastern Shore: From Tobacco to Grain* (Ithaca, 1980).

19. Bureau of the Census, *Historical Statistics of the United States, Colonial Times to 1970,* 1168, 1176–77.

20. Aubrey C. Land, "Economic Base and Social Structure: The Northern Chesapeake in the Eighteenth Century," *Journal of Economic History* 25 (1965): 639–54; idem, "Economic Behavior in a Planting Society: The Eighteenth-Century Chesapeake," *Journal of Southern History* 33 (1967): 469–85.

21. T. H. Breen, "A Changing Labor Force and Race Relations in Virginia, 1660–1710," *Journal of Social History* 6 (1973): 3–25; Edmund S. Morgan, *American Slavery—American Freedom: The Ordeal of Colonial Virginia* (New York, 1975); Russell R. Menard, "From Servants to Slaves: The Transformation of the Chesapeake Labor System," *Southern Studies* 16 (1977): 355–90; Lois Green Carr and Russell R. Menard, "Immigration and Opportu-

nity: The Freedman in Early Colonial Maryland," in *The Chesapeake in the Seventeenth Century-Essays on Anglo-American Society,* ed. Thad W. Tate and David L. Ammerman (Chapel Hill, 1979), 206–42.

22. Herbert Moller, "Sex Composition and Correlated Cultural Patterns," *William and Mary Quarterly,* 3d ser., 11 (1945): 415–42; Lorena S. Walsh and Russell R. Menard, "Death in the Chesapeake: Two Life Tables for Men in Early Colonial Maryland," *Maryland Historical Magazine* 69 (1974): 211–27; Morgan, *American Slavery–American Freedom;* Darrett B. Rutman and Anita H. Rutman, "Of Agues and Fevers: Malaria in the Early Chesapeake," *William and Mary Quarterly,* 3d ser., 33 (1976): 31–60; Carville V. Earle, "Environment, Disease, and Mortality in Early Virginia," in Tate and Ammerman, *The Chesapeake in the Seventeenth Century,* 96–125.

23. Daniel Blake Smith, "Mortality and Family in the Colonial Chesapeake," *Journal of Interdisciplinary History* 8 (1977–78): 403–27; Lorena S. Walsh, " 'Til Death Us Do Part': Marriage and Family in Seventeenth-Century Maryland," in Tate and Ammerman, *The Chesapeake in the Seventeenth Century,* 126–52.

24. William McKee Evans, "Race, Class and Myth in Slaveholding Societies" (Paper presented at a meeting of the Southern Historical Association, Louisville, 1981).

25. For the rise of patriarchalism see Daniel Blake Smith, *Inside the Great House: Planter Family Life in Eighteenth-Century Chesapeake Society* (Ithaca, 1980); Gerald W. Mullin, *Flight and Rebellion: Slave Resistance in Eighteenth-Century Virginia* (New York, 1972), chap. 1; T. H. Breen, "Horses and Gentlemen: The Cultural Significance of Gambling among the Gentry of Virginia," *William and Mary Quarterly,* 3d ser., 34 (1977): 239–57; Jack P. Greene, *Landon Carter: An Inquiry into the Personal Values and Social Imperatives of the Eighteenth-Century Virginia Gentry* (Charlottesville, 1965); and Rhys Isaac, *The Transformation of Virginia, 1740–1790: Community, Religion, and Authority* (Chapel Hill, 1982).

26. Evans, "Race, Class, and Myth."

27. Ronald Hoffman, *A Spirit of Dissension: Economics, Politics, and the Revolution in Maryland* (Baltimore, 1973); David Curtis Skaggs, *Roots of Maryland Democracy, 1753–1776* (Westport, Conn., 1973); Rhys Isaac, "Evangelical Revolt: The Nature of the Baptists' Challenge to the Traditional Order in Virginia, 1765 to 1775," *William and Mary Quarterly,* 3d ser., 31 (1974): 345–68; Gregory A. Stiverson, *Poverty in a Land of Plenty: Tenancy in Eighteenth-Century Maryland* (Baltimore, 1977); Marvin L. Michael Kay, "The North Carolina Regulation, 1766–1776: A Class Conflict," in *The American Revolution: Explorations in the History of American Radicalism,* ed. Alfred F. Young (De Kalb, Ill., 1976), 71–123; Rhys Isaac, "Preachers and Patriots: Popular Culture and the Revolution in Virginia," in ibid., 125–56; Ronald Hoffman, "The 'Disaffected' in the Revolutionary South," in ibid., 273–316; Richard R. Beeman and Rhys Isaac, "Cultural Conflict and Social Change in the Revolutionary South: Lunenburg County, Virginia," *Journal of Southern His-*

tory 46 (1980): 525–50; Richard R. Beeman, "Social Change and Cultural Conflict in Virginia: Lunenburg County, 1746 to 1774," *William and Mary Quarterly,* 3d ser., 35 (1978): 455–76.

28. Verner W. Crane, *The Southern Frontier, 1670–1732* (Durham, 1929).

29. Carl Bridenbaugh, *Cities in the Wilderness: The First Century of Urban Life in America, 1625–1742* (New York, 1938); idem, *Cities in Revolt: Urban Life in America, 1743–1776* (New York, 1955); Jacob M. Price, "Economic Function and the Growth of American Port Towns in the Eighteenth Century," *Perspectives in American History* 8 (1974): 123–86; Carville V. Earle and Ronald Hoffman, "Staple Crops and Urban Development in the Eighteenth-Century South," ibid. 10 (1976): 7–78; Carville Earle, "The First English Towns of North America," *Geographical Review* 67 (1977); 34–50; Nash, *Urban Crucible.*

30. See, however, Wolf, *Urban Village;* and Wood, *Conestoga Crossroads.*

31. The many studies on wealth distribution in the colonial period are recapitulated in Alice Hanson Jones, *The Wealth of a Nation to Be: The American Colonies on the Eve of the Revolution* (New York, 1980); and Peter H. Lindert and Jeffrey Williamson, *American Inequality: A Macro-economic History* (New York, 1980), chap. 1. For migration see Douglas L. Jones, *Village and Seaport: Migration and Society in Eighteenth-Century Massachusetts* (Hanover, N.H., 1981). For bound labor in the cities see Gary B. Nash, "Slaves and Slaveowners in Colonial Philadelphia," *William and Mary Quarterly,* 3d ser., 30 (1973): 223–56; and Sharon V. Salinger, "Colonial Labor in Transition: The Decline of Indentured Servitude in Late Eighteenth-Century Philadelphia," *Labor History* 22 (1981): 165–91.

32. On lawyers see John M. Murrin, "The Legal Transformation: The Bench and Bar of Eighteenth-Century Massachusetts," in *Colonial America: Essays in Politics and Social Development,* ed. Stanley N. Katz (Boston, 1971), 415–19; and William E. Nelson, *Americanization of the Common Law: The Impact of Legal Change on Massachusetts Society, 1760–1830* (Cambridge, Mass., 1975). On education see Lawrence A. Cremin, *American Education: The Colonial Experience, 1607–1783* (New York, 1970).

33. Nash, *Urban Crucible,* chaps. 7–13.

34. Douglas L. Jones, "The Strolling Poor: Transiency in Eighteenth-Century Massachusetts," *Journal of Social History* 8 (Spring 1975): 28–54; Billy G. Smith, "The Material Lives of Laboring Philadelphians, 1750 to 1800," *William and Mary Quarterly,* 3d ser., 38 (1981): 163–202; Gary B. Nash, "Poverty and Poor Relief in Pre-Revolutionary Philadelphia," ibid. 33 (1976): 3–30; Raymond A. Mohl, "Poverty in Early America: A Reappraisal: The Case of Eighteenth-Century New York City," *New York History* 50 (1969): 5–27.

35. Bender, *Community and Social Change,* 31, 33.

36. For a review of recent work see James Axtell, "The Ethnohistory of Early America: A Review Essay," *William and Mary Quarterly,* 3d ser., 35 (1978): 110–44.

37. An overview and synthesis of recent work in this area is given in Gary B. Nash, *Red, White, and Black: The Peoples of Early America,* 2d ed. (Englewood Cliffs, N.J., 1982), chaps. 3–6.

38. T. J. C. Brasser, "The Coastal Algonkians: People of the First Frontiers," in *North American Indians in Historical Perspective,* ed. Eleanor Burke Leacock and Nancy O. Lurie (New York, 1971), 73.

39. Calvin Martin, *Keepers of the Game: Indian-Animal Relationships and the Fur Trade* (Berkeley, 1978).

40. Bruce G. Trigger, *The Children of Aataentsic: A History of the Huron People to 1660,* 2 vols. (Montreal, 1976).

41. James Axtell, "The Indian Impact on English Colonial Culture," in *The European and the Indian: Essays in the Ethnohistory of Colonial North America* (New York, 1981), 272–315.

42. Sidney W. Mintz and Richard Price, *An Anthropological Approach to the Afro-American Past: A Caribbean Perspective,* ISHI Occasional Papers on Social Change, no. 2 (Philadelphia, 1976), 4–11; the quote is from p. 10.

43. The most important work includes Mullin, *Flight and Rebellion;* Peter H. Wood, *Black Majority: Negroes in Colonial South Carolina from 1670 through the Stono Rebellion* (New York, 1974); Russell R. Menard, "The Maryland Slave Population, 1658–1730: A Demographic Profile of Blacks in Four Counties," *William and Mary Quarterly,* 3d ser., 32 (1975): 29–54; Allan Kulikoff, "A 'Prolifick People': Black Population Growth in the Chesapeake Colonies, 1700–1790," *Southern Studies* 16 (1977): 391–428; idem, "The Origins of Afro-American Society in Tidewater Maryland and Virginia, 1700 to 1790," *William and Mary Quarterly,* 3d ser., 35 (1978): 226–59; idem, "The Beginnings of the Afro-American Family in Maryland," in *Law, Society, and Politics in Early Maryland,* ed. Aubrey C. Land, Lois Green Carr, and Edward C. Papenfuse (Baltimore, 1977); Daniel C. Littlefield, *Rice and Slaves: Ethnicity and the Slave Trade in Colonial South Carolina* (Baton Rouge, 1981); and Philip D. Morgan, "Black Society in the Lowcountry, 1760–1810," in *Slavery in the Era of the American Revolution,* ed. Ira Berlin and Ronald Hoffman (Charlottesville, 1982). For a comprehensive view of recent work see Peter H. Wood " 'I Did the Best I Could for My Day': The Study of Early Black History during the Second Reconstruction, 1960 to 1976," *William and Mary Quarterly,* 3d ser., 35 (1978): 185–225.

44. Mintz and Price, *An Anthropological Approach,* 26.

45. Ira Berlin, "Time, Space, and the Evolution of Afro-American Society in British Mainland North America," *American Historical Review* 85 (1980): 44–78.

46. For a review of the demographic literature see Daniel Blake Smith, "The Study of the Family in Early America: Trends, Problems, and Prospects," *William and Mary Quarterly,* 3d ser., 39 (1982): 3–28. Among the recent work in women's history see esp. Ben Barker-Benfield, "Anne Hutchinson and the Puritan Attitude toward Women," *Feminist Studies* 1 (1972): 65–96; Alexander Keyssar, "Widowhood in Eighteenth-Century Massachusetts: A Problem in the History of the Family," *Perspectives in American History* 8 (1974): 83–

119; D. Kelly Weisberg, " 'Under Greet Temptations Heer': Women and Divorce in Puritan Massachusetts," *Feminist Studies* 2 (1975): 183–94; Katherine A. Jacob, "The Woman's Lot in Baltimore Town, 1729–1797," *Maryland Historical Magazine* 71 (1976); Nancy F. Cott, "Divorce and Changing Status of Women in Eighteenth-Century Massachusetts," *William and Mary Quarterly,* 3d ser., 33 (1976): 586–614; John Faragher, "Old Women and Old Men in Seventeenth-Century Wethersfield, Connecticut," *Women's Studies* 4 (1976): 110–31; Lois Green Carr and Lorena S. Walsh, "The Planter's Wife: The Experience of White Women in Seventeenth-Century Maryland," *William and Mary Quarterly,* 3d ser., 34 (1977): 542–71; Jean P. Jordan, "Women Merchants in Colonial New York," *New York History* 58 (1977): 416–36; Mary Dunn, "Saints and Sisters: Congregational and Quaker Women in the Early Colonial Period," *American Quarterly* 30 (1978): 582–601; Gary B. Nash, "The Failure of Female Factory Labor in Colonial Boston," *Labor History* 20 (1979): 165–88; Marylynn Salmon, "Equality or Submersion? Feme Covert Status in Early Pennsylvania," in *Women of America: A History,* ed. Carol Ruth Berkin and Mary Beth Norton (Boston, 1979), 92–111; Linda K. Kerber, *Women of the Republic: Intellect and Ideology in Revolutionary America* (Chapel Hill, 1980); Mary Beth Norton, *Liberty's Daughters: The Revolutionary Experience of American Women, 1750–1800* (Boston, 1980); Lyle Koehler, *A Search for Power: The 'Weaker Sex' in Seventeenth-Century New England* (Urbana, 1980); Alan D. Watson, "Women in Colonial North Carolina: Overlooked and Underestimated," *North Carolina Historical Review* 58 (1981): 1–22; Laurel Thatcher Ulrich, *Good Wives: Image and Reality in the Lives of Women in Northern New England, 1650–1750* (New York, 1982); Joan R. Gundersen and Gwen Victor Gampel, "Married Women's Legal Status in Eighteenth-Century New York and Virginia," *William and Mary Quarterly,* 3d ser., 39 (1982): 114–34; Marylynn Salmon, "Women and Property in South Carolina: The Evidence from Marriage Settlements, 1730 to 1830," *William and Mary Quarterly,* 3d ser., 39 (1982): 655–85.

2

THE IMAGE OF THE INDIAN IN
THE SOUTHERN COLONIAL MIND

T HE CHANGING IMAGE of the native inhabitants of North America provides a penetrating glimpse into the fears, desires, and intentions of
Englishmen in colonial America. From the guileless primitive of certain
sixteenth-century writers, to the savage beast of colonial frontiersmen, to
the "noble savage" of eighteenth-century social critics, the Indian has furnished the social, intellectual, and cultural historian with an important
analytical tool. Just as Europeans saw in Africa and Africans not what actually existed but what their prior experience and present needs dictated,
so in America the image of the Indian was molded by the nature of colonization and the inner requirements of adventuring Englishmen.[1]

Understanding the English image of the Indian not only reveals the
conscious and unconscious workings of the Anglo-American mind, but
also gives meaning to English relations with the Indian and to English
policies directed at controlling, "civilizing," and exterminating him. Images of the Indian were indicators of attitudes toward him. Attitudes, in
turn, were closely linked to intentions and desires. These intentions and
desires, acted out systematically over a period of time and often provok-
ing responses from the natives which tended to confirm and reinforce
first impressions, became the basis of an "Indian policy." Thus, images
of the Indians in colonial America are of both explanatory and causa-
tive importance. They help us penetrate the innermost thoughts and
psychic needs of Englishmen confronting a distant, unknown, and terri-
fying land, and they provide a basis for understanding English interaction with the native inhabitants over a period of close but abrasive
contact which lasted for more than one hundred fifty years.[2]

The early 1580s mark a convenient point to begin a study of the
images of the Indian refracted through the prism of the English mind. It
was then that Elizabethan England, already a century behind Spain and
Portugal in exploiting the potentialities of the New World, took the first
significant steps toward extending her power across the Atlantic. Two

This essay first appeared in *William and Mary Quarterly,* 29 (1972): 197–230. Alterations have been made in the footnotes.

attempts at settlement in North America in 1583 and 1584, one by Sir Humphrey Gilbert, among the most active promoters of English colonization, and the other by his half brother, Walter Raleigh, the best known and most romantic of the early adventurers, were undertaken. Gilbert sailed the northern route, and made a landfall in Newfoundland with five ships and 260 men. He then turned west and disappeared at sea, leaving the other ships to return to England. Raleigh, plying the familiar southern route, touched land on the upper Carolina coast, left a small contingent on what was to be called Roanoke Island, located at the mouth of Albemarle Sound, and returned to England with two natives of the region. Thus began an era of English participation in the great race for colonial possessions that was to occupy—at times preoccupy—Europe for the next two centuries.[3]

What images of the Indians were lodged in the minds of men like Gilbert and Raleigh as they approached the forbidding coast of North America? One can be sure that they experienced the uncertainty and apprehension that regardless of time or place fill the minds of men who are attempting to penetrate the unknown. But in all likelihood they also had well-formed ideas about the indigenous people of the New World. Legends concerning other worlds beyond the sunset had reverberated in the European mind for centuries.[4] And, beginning with Columbus's report on the New World, published in several European capitals in 1493 and 1494, a mass of reports and stories had been circulating among sailors, merchants, and geographers who were participating in voyages of discovery, trade, and settlement.[5]

From this considerable literature, men like Gilbert and Raleigh were likely to derive a split image of the natives of North America. On the one hand they had reason to believe that the Indians were savage, hostile, beastlike men, whose proximity in appearance and behavior was closer to the animal kingdom than the kingdom of men, as western Europeans employed that term to describe themselves. As early as the first decade of the sixteenth century Sebastian Cabot had paraded in England three Eskimos taken captive on his voyage to the Arctic in 1502.[6] A contemporary described the natives as flesh eating, primitive specimens who "spake such speech that no man coulde understand them, and in their demeanour like to bruite beasts."[7] In 1556, curious Englishmen could read an account of Giovanni da Verrazano's voyage of 1524 to North America, including descriptions of the natives which could have been little cause for optimism concerning the reception Europeans would receive in the New World.[8] Other accounts were filtering back to England from fishermen operating off the Newfoundland Banks or from explorers such as Martin Frobisher, whose three attempts to find the Northwest Passage in the 1570s led to the publication of a number of descriptions of the northern reaches of the lands across the Atlantic.[9] The accounts from the Frobisher voyages were filled with descriptions of crafty, brutal, loathsome half-men whose cannibalistic instincts were revealed, as Dionyse Settle wrote in 1578, by the fact that "there is no flesh or fishe, which they finde dead, (smell it never so filthily) but they will eate it, as they finde it, without any other dressing."[10]

Other unsettling accounts also became available through the translation of Spanish and Portuguese writers. Sebastian Munster's *A Treatyse of the newe India . . .* was published in English in 1553; Peter Martyr's *The Decades of the newe worlds or west India* two years later; Jean Ribault's *The whole and true discoverye of Terra Florida . . .* in 1563; Nicolas Le Challeux's *A true and perfect description, of the last voyage or Navigation attempted by Capitaine John Rybaut . . . into Terra Florida . . .* in 1566; and André Thevet's *The New found worlde, or Antarcticke, . . .* in 1568.[11] In all of these works Englishmen of the day could read accounts which suggested that the people of the New World were not only primitive—simply by not being English one was that—but bestial, cannibalistic, sexually abandoned, and, in general, moved entirely by passion rather than reason.

But another vision of the native was simultaneously entering the English consciousness. Columbus had written of the "great amity towards us" which he encountered in San Salvador in 1492 and described a generous, pastoral people living in childlike innocence.[12] Thenceforth, the accounts which Englishmen read were tinged with a romantic image of the New World, as if, Howard Mumford Jones has written, to fill some psychic need of a dreary, tired Europe.[13] Just a few years before the Gilbert and Raleigh voyages, Englishmen could read in translation Nicholas Monardes's *Joyfull Newes out of the Newe Founde Worlde, . . .* which limned America as a horn of plenty, an earthly paradise where nature's bounty allowed men to live for centuries in sensual leisure.[14] To some extent this positive side of the image of the New World was based on the friendly reception which Europeans had apparently received in Newfoundland, parts of Florida, and elsewhere on the continent. Gilbert, for example, was familiar with the testimony of David Ingram, one of about a hundred sailors set ashore on the northern coast of the Gulf of Mexico by John Hawkins in 1568. Upon his return to England, Ingram wrote of the tractable and generous nature of the natives who provided food and were "Naturally very courteous, if you do not abuse them."[15] Other accounts confirmed the notion that the natives as well as the climate in some parts of the New World would be hospitable.[16]

Three books published in the early 1580s, as the Roanoke voyages were being launched, provide a clearer insight into this split vision of English writers as they pondered the nature of the people inhabiting the lands of the New World. Two were written by the Richard Hakluyts, uncle and nephew—the greatest colonial publicizers and promoters of their age.[17] With pen rather than sword the Hakluyts inspired Elizabethan courtiers, adventurous sons of the lesser nobility, and merchants with venture capital to enter the colonial sweepstakes before Spain and Portugal, already firmly established in South America and the West Indies, laid claim to the whole of the New World. The third was penned by Sir George Peckham, who had acompanied Sir Humphrey Gilbert on the Newfoundland voyage of 1583 and left his impressions, *A True Reporte, of the late discoveries, . . . of the Newfound Landes . . . ,* as the latest guide for Englishmen eager to unravel the mysteries of North America.[18]

In all of these tracts the ambivalence and confusion in the English mind is readily apparent. Hakluyt the elder could write of the New World as "a Country no less fruitful and pleasant in al respects than is England, Fraunce or Germany, the people, though simple and rude in manners, and destitute of the knowledge of God or any good lawes, yet of nature gentle and tractable, and most apt to receive the Christian Religion, and to subject themselves to some good government."[19] In the same vein, the younger Hakluyt wrote in 1584 of a "goodd clymate, healthfull, and of goodd temperature, marvelous pleasaunte, the people goodd and of a gentle and amyable nature, which willingly will obey, yea be contented to serve those that shall with gentlenes and humanitie goo aboute to allure them."[20] These were useful promotional statements. And yet the Hakluyts could not banish the thought that planting English civilization in the New World would not be all gentleness and amiability. Festering in their minds was knowledge of the Spanish experience in America. They had read carefully every account of the Spanish conquest of Mexico, especially Bartholome de las Casas's *The Spanish Colonie, or Briefe Chronicle of the acts and gestes of the Spaniardes in the West Indies,* translated in 1583.[21] Las Casas deplored the reign of death and terror which the Spanish had brought to aboriginal culture in the name of Christianity. In his own propaganda for colonization Hakluyt felt moved to quote several Spanish authors who labeled their countrymen "helhoundes and wolves"—men who claimed they had conquered and pacified the Indians, but who in reality had engaged in a policy bordering on genocide. The Indians, according to Hakluyt's source, "not havinge studied Logicke concluded very pertinently and categorically that the Spaniardes which spoiled their Contrie, were more dangerous than wilde beastes, more furious then Lyons, more fearefull and terrible then fire and water."[22]

Did the same experience await the English? Few doubted that they enjoyed the same technological superiority as the Spanish. If they desired, they could thus lay waste to the country they were entering. Moreover, the English experience with the Irish, in whose country military officers like Gilbert and Raleigh had been gaining experience in the subjugation of "lesser breeds" for several decades, suggested that the English were fully capable of every cruelty contrived by the Spanish. Thus, as the elder Hakluyt pointed out, if the English were not well received, they might be obliged to employ force to show the Indians the advantages of participating in the benefits of English civilization. "If we finde the countrey populous," he wrote in 1584, "and desirous to expel us, and injuriously to offend us, that seeke but just and lawfull trafficke, then by reason that we are lords of navigation, and they not so, we are the better able to defend our selves by reason of those great rivers, and to annoy them in many places." Hakluyt concluded that the English might find it necessary to "proceed with extremetie, conquer, fortifie, and plant in soiles most sweet, most pleasant, most strong, and most fertile, and in the end bring them all in subjection and to civilitie."[23] So the bitter would be mixed with the sweet.

George Peckham, writing contemporaneously with the Hakluyts, gave an even clearer expression of the emerging formula for colonization: exterior expressions of goodwill and explanations of mutual benefits to be derived from the contact of two cultures, but lurking beneath the surface the anticipation of violence. In his promotional pamphlet, *A True Reporte, . . . of the Newfound Landes,* Peckham began with elaborate defenses of the rights of maritime nations to "trade and traficke" with "savage" nations and assured Englishmen that such enterprises would be "profitable to the adventurers in perticuler, beneficial to the Savages, and a matter to be attained without any great daunger or difficultie." Some of the natives, Peckham allowed, would be "fearefull by nature" and disquieted by the "straunge apparrell, Armour, and weapon" of the English, but "courtesie and myldnes" along with a generous bounty of "prittie merchaundizes and trifles: As looking Glasses, Bells, Beades, Braceletts, Chaines, or Collers of Bewgle, Christall, Amber, Jett, or Glasse" would soon win them over and "induce theyr Barbarous natures to a likeing and a mutuall society with us."[24]

Having explained how he hoped the English *might* act, and how the natives *might* respond, Peckham went on to reveal what he must have considered the more likely course of events:

> But if after these good and fayre meanes used, the Savages nevertheles will not be heerewithal satisfied, but barbarously wyll goe about to practise violence either in repelling the Christians from theyr Portes and safe Landinges or in withstanding them afterwards to enjoye the rights for which both painfully

and lawfully they have adventured themselves thether; Then in
such a case I holde it no breache of equitye for the Christians
to defende themselves, to pursue revenge with force, and to
doo whatsoever is necessary for attayning of theyr safety: For
it is allowable by all Lawes in such distresses, to resist violence
with violence.[25]

With earlier statements of the gentle and receptive qualties of the
Indians almost beyond recall, Peckham reminded his countrymen of
their responsibility to employ all necessary means to bring the natives
from "falsehood to truth, from darknes to lyght, from the hieway of
death, to the path of life, from superstitious idolatry, to sincere christianity, from the devil to Christ, from hell to Heaven." Even more revealing of his essentially negative image of the Indian, he wrote that the
English, in planting their civilization, would aid the Indians by causing
them to change "from unseemly customes, to honest maners, from dis-
ordred riotous rowtes and companies, to a wel governed common
wealth."[26]

Thus, two conflicting images of the Indian were wrestling for as-
cendance in the English mind as the first attempts to colonize in the
New World began. At times the English tended to see the native as a
backward but receptive man with whom amicable and profitable relations might be established. This image originated not only in the uto-
pian anticipation of the New World but in the desire to trade with the
Indians. The early voyages were not primarily intended for the purpose
of large-scale settlement and agricultural production. A careful reading
of the promotional literature of this period will show that the English
were primarily interested in a mercantile relationship. Trade with the
Indians, the search for gold and silver, and discovery of the Northwest
Passage were the keys to overseas development. Trade was expected to
be a major source of profit. Not only would the natives provide a new
outlet for English woolens, but all of the rich and varied commodities of
the New World would flow back to England in ample measure. Since
trade was the key to success in these bold new adventures, a special
incentive existed for seeing the Indian as something more than an intractable savage. For the Spanish and Portuguese colonizers in the New
World (and for the English in Ireland) land had been the key. But land
conquest did not figure importantly in Elizabethan planning. In fact, it
would undermine attempts to establish a mercantile relationship. Instead well-fortified trading posts would be established at the heads of
rivers where the natives would come to trade. In this mercantile approach to overseas adventuring the English promoters were strongly
influenced by English participation in the Levantine and Muscovy trade
where English merchants had operated profitably for half a century, not

invading the land of foreign peoples and driving them from it, but "trafficking" among them without challenging their possession of the land. In Hakluyt's *Notes on Colonization,* written five years prior to the Roanoke voyages, the recommendations for approaching the natives are almost identical to those given for adventurers seeking the Northeast passage in 1580.[27]

Thus, one side of the image of the native had its source not only in the idyllic visions of the New World, but in the intentions of the Elizabethan adventurers. It was only a friendly Indian who *could* be a trading Indian. If trade was the key to overseas development, then it is not surprising that English promoters suggested that the Indian might be receptive and generous—a man who could be wooed and won to the advantages of trade.

But the creation of a tractable Indian, amenable to trade, could never blot from the English mind the image of the hostile savage who awaited Christian adventurers. Most of the Elizabethan adventurers had been involved in the English invasions of Ireland and the Netherlands where they had learned that indigenous peoples do not ordinarily accept graciously those who come to dominate them. They had special reasons for anticipating the darker side of the Indian's nature because they were familiar with the literature on the "savages" of the New World and were well acquainted with the Spanish and Portuguese overseas experience. With hostility on their minds, it was impossible to picture the Indian as a purely benign creature. Regardless of the natural temperament of the New World man, his contact with Europeans thus far had rarely been pacific. To imagine the Indian as a savage beast was a way of predicting the future and preparing for it and of justifying what one would do, even before one caused it to happen.

The experience at Roanoke Island between 1584 and 1587 illustrates how preconceptions affected the initial Anglo-Indian contacts. For Englishmen it was their first settlement in the New World. Initially, several hundred men attempted to maintain themselves on the island while making exploratory trips into the mainland wilderness. For three years the settlement struggled for existence, kept alive by fresh infusions of men and supplies from England. But left to its own resources, when the Spanish Armada prevented provisioning ships from leaving England in 1588, the tiny colony perished.[28]

Three accounts of the Roanoke experience survive.[29] Because they were written at least partially as promotional pamphlets, intended to inspire further attempts at settlement, they must be used cautiously as a source of information. Though differing in detail, all of the accounts agree that the Indians of the Carolina region were receptive to the English. Arthur Barlowe, a member of the first expedition, wrote that "we were entertained with all love, and kindnes, and with as much boutie, after their manner, as they could possibly devise. Wee found the people most gentle, loving, and faithfull, void of all guile, and treason," and noted that the Indians were "much grieved" when their hospitality was shunned by the suspicious English.[30] Other accounts, though less roseate, also suggest that the natives were eager to learn about the artifacts of Europeans, and, though wary, extended their hospitality.[31] Since the English came in small numbers, the Indians probably did not regard them as much of a threat. They were no doubt as curious about the English as the English were about them.[32] So far as one can tell from the surviving evidence, no conflict occurred until the English, upon discovering a silver cup missing, dispatched a punitive expedition to a nearby Indian village. When the Indians denied taking the cup, the English, determined to make a show of force, burned the village to the ground and destroyed the Indians' supply of corn. After that, relations deteriorated.[33] Aware of their numerical disadvantage and the precariousness of their position, the English used force in large doses to convince the natives of their invulnerability. As one member of the voyage admitted, "Some of our companie towardes the ende of the yeare, shewed themselves too fierce, in slaying some of the people, in some towns, upon causes that on our part, might easily enough have bene borne withall."[34]

In spite of these difficulties, the principal members of the Roanoke colony who returned to England entertained considerable respect for Indian culture. Thomas Hariot wrote that "although they have no such tooles, nor any such craftes, sciences and artes as wee; yet in those things they doe, they shewe excellencie of wit."[35] John White, a painter of some skill, who had accompanied the Roanoke expedition, brought back more explicit testimony of the Indians' culture—in the form of scores of sketches and watercolors which show the Indians at various aspects of work and play. White's drawings reveal a genuine appreciation of the Indians' ability to control their environment through their methods of hunting and agriculture, their family and communal life, and other aspects of their culture.[36]

For two decades after the failure at Roanoke, Englishmen launched no new colonial adventures. Although a few English ship captains, who represented merchants dabbling in the West Indies trade, looked in on the coast of North America in hopes of bartering with the natives, and reported that their relations with them were generally friendly,[37] the next attempt at colonization did not come until the Virginia Company of London completed its plans in December 1606. The arrival of the first Virginia expedition in April 1607, with more than one hundred men in three ships, marked the beginning of permanent English pres-

ence in North America. Henceforward, Indians and Englishmen would
be in continuous contact.

The crucial difference between the Roanoke colony of the 1580s
and the settlement at Jamestown in 1607 was that the latter, after the
first few years, was planned as a permanent community. From this
point onward, Englishmen came to America not merely to trade with
the natives or to extract the riches of the land but to build an enduring
society—an extension of England overseas. It was this shift in intention
that reshaped the nature of the contacts between English and Indians
and consequently altered the English image of the native as well as the
Indian perception of the Englishman. Permanent settlement required
acquisition by whites of land—land which was in the possession of the
Indian. That single fact was the beginning of a chain of events which
governed the entire sociology of red-white relations.

For Englishmen, the Indians' occupation of the land presented a
problem both of law and morality. Even in the 1580s, George Peckham,
an early promoter of colonization, had admitted that many Englishmen
doubted their right to take possession of the land of others.[38] In 1609
the thought was amplified by Robert Gray, who asked rhetorically, "By
what right or warrant we can enter into the land of these Savages, take
away their rightfull inheritance from them, and plant ourselves in their
places, being unwronged or unprovoked by them."[39] It was a logical
question to ask, for Englishmen, like other Europeans, had organized
their society around the concept of private ownership of land and regarded this as an important characteristic of their superior culture. They
were not blind to the fact that they were entering the land of another
people, who by prior possession could lay sole claim to all the territory
of mainland America. To some extent the problem was resolved by
arguing that the English did not intend to take the Indians' land but
wanted only to share with them the resources of the New World where
there was land enough for all. In return, they would extend to the
Indians the advantages of a richer culture, a more advanced civilization,
and, most importantly, the Christian religion. Thus, in 1610 the governing council in Virginia advertised to those at home that the English "by
way of marchandizing and trade, doe buy of them [the Indians] the
pearles of earth, and sell to them the pearles of heaven."[40] A few decades later, Samuel Purchas, who took up the Hakluyts' work of promoting colonization in the seventeenth century, gave classic expression
to this explanation: "God in wisedome having enriched the Savage
Countries, that those riches might be attractive for Christian suters,
which there may sowe spirituals and reape temporals."[41] Spirituals to be
sown, of course, meant Christian doctrines; temporals to be reaped
meant land.

A second and far more portentous way of resolving the problem of land possession was to deny the humanity of the Indians. Thus, Robert Gray, who had asked if Englishmen were entitled to "plant ourselves in their places," answered by arguing that the Indians' inhumanity disqualified them from the right to possess land. "Although the Lord hath given the earth to children of men, . . . the greater part of it [is] possessed and wrongfully usurped by wild beasts, and unreasonable creatures, or by brutish savages, which by reason of their godles ignorance, and blasphemous idolatrie, are worse then those beasts which are of most wilde and savage nature."[42] This was an argument fraught with danger for the Indian, for whereas other Englishmen, such as William Strachey, secretary of the resident council in Virginia at this time, were arguing that "every foote of Land which we shall take unto our use, we will bargayne and buy of them,"[43] Gray was suggesting that present and future acts of godlessness or savagery, as defined by the English, would entitle the colonists unilaterally to seize or occupy land. This notion that by their nature the "savages" had forfeited their right to the land was only occasionally mentioned in the early years. But in the 1620s, after a major war had been fought, the idea would gain greater acceptance.

Little evidence exists on which to base unequivocal assertions about English attitudes toward the Indians in 1607, at the moment of initial contact. But it seems likely that given their belief that the Roanoke colony had been reduced to a pile of bones by the Indians a generation earlier, the English were not very optimistic about the receptiveness of the indigenous people. This pessimistic view must have been greatly intensified when the Jamestown expedition was attacked near Cape Henry, following their first debarkation in the New World. Hereafter, the English would proceed with extreme caution, as well they might, given the size of their expedition. Violence was anticipated, and when Indians approached the English in outwardly friendly ways, the worst was suspected. Thus, when Christopher Newport led the first exploratory trip up the newly named James River, just weeks after a tiny settlement had been planted at Jamestown, he was confused by what he encountered. The Indians, a member of his group wrote, "are naturally given to trechery, howbeit we could not finde it in our travell up the river, but rather a most kind and loving people."[44] This account reveals that the English were wined and dined by the Indians who explained that they were "at oddes" with other tribes, including the Chesapeake tribe that had attacked the English at Cape Henry, and were willing to ally with the English against their enemies.[45] It is clear from ethnological research that the Indians of the Chesapeake region, composing some thirty different tribes, were not monolithic in cultural characteristics and were undergoing internal reorganization. The most powerful tribe, the Pamunkey, of which Powhatan was chief, had been attempting for some time before the arrival of the English to consolidate its hold on lesser tribes in the area, while at the same time warding off the threats of westerly tribes of the Piedmont. From the available ethnographic evidence, it appears that Powhatan saw an alliance with the English as a means of extending his power in the tidewater area while neutralizing the power of his western enemies.[46]

But the English, who were quick to comprehend the intertribal tensions as well as the linguistic differences among the Indians of the region, could apparently not convince themselves that some tribal leaders regarded the English as threatening while others found their arrival potentially to their advantage. Perhaps because they viewed their position as so precarious (the Jamestown settlement was in a state of internal crisis almost from the moment of landfall), they could only afford to regard all Indians as threatening. Thus, hostile and friendly Indians seemed different only in their outward behavior. Inwardly they were identical. The hostile Indian revealed his true nature while the friendly Indian feigned friendship while waiting for an opportunity to attack, thus proving even more than his openly warlike brother the treacherous nature he possessed.

Over the first few years of contact, during which time the Jamestown settlement was reprovisioned from England with men and supplies, the confusion in the English mind was revealed again and again. In the summer of 1607, when food supplies were running perilously low and all but a handful of the Jamestown settlers had fallen too ill to work, the colony was saved by the Indians who brought sufficient food to keep the struggling settlement alive until the sick recovered. This, too, was seen by many as an example of Powhatan's covert hostility rather than an attempt to serve his own interests through an alliance with the English. "It pleased God (in our extremity)," wrote Smith, "to move the Indians to bring us Corne, ere it was halfe ripe, to refresh us, when we rather expected . . . they would destroy us."[47] As a man of military experience among "barbarian" people in all parts of the world, Smith was not willing to believe that the Indians, in aiding the colony, might have found the survival of the English in their own interest. Hostility was on his mind, sporadic hostility had already been experienced, and thus all acts, friendly or foul, were perceived as further evidence of the natives' irreversible hostility and innate savagery. The records left by the English would be couched hereafter in these terms. Outright conflict was taken as the norm because it represented the logical result of contact with a people who were hostile and treacherous by nature. Friendly overtures by Powhatan and other tribal leaders, who hoped to use the English to consolidate their own position, were seen as further examples of the dissembling nature of the Indians. One reads of "these cunning tricks of their Emperour of *Powhatan*," or of "their slippery designes," or of "perfidious Savages," or that "I know their faining love is towards me not without a deadly hatred."[48] Increasingly, of course, this was true, as Powhatan, finding his efforts to build a mutually profitable relationship fading, withheld trading privileges and assumed an uncooperative stance.

It was John Smith who, more than any other figure, wrought the most significant change in English attitudes and policy toward Powhatan. As the Jamestown settlement struggled for existence in 1607 and 1608, plagued by hunger, disease, dissension, and a remarkable refusal of most of its participants to work for their own survival, Smith emerged as the "strong man." Experienced in military exploits, skilled in cartography, seemingly indestructible, Smith initiated an aggressive Indian policy, based on the burning of Indian canoes, fields, and villages, in order to extort food supplies and to cow Powhatan and other tribal leaders. "The patient Councel, that nothing would move to warre with the Salvages," was replaced by a policy of terrorization, which "brought them [the Indians] in such feare and obedience, as his very name would sufficiently affright them."[49] It is not easy to fathom Smith's perception of the situation, especially since so much of the information for this period must be gleaned from his own accounts. But certainly important in Smith's assessment of the Indians' intentions was the petty theft of English implements by Indians who circulated in the English settlements in the first year, the confession of two Indians in May 1608 (under duress if not torture) that Powhatan was the recipient of the stolen objects and was secretly plotting to wipe out the colony,[50] and Smith's worldwide military experience, which convinced him that with "heathen" people the best defense was a good offense. On the last point Smith wrote that "the Warres in *Europe, Asia,* and *Affrica,* taught me how to subdue the wilde Salvages in *Virginia* and *New-England,* in *America.*"[51]

In the short run most of the colonists thought that Smith's policy of intimidation paid off. As it was later written, "Where before, wee had sometime peace and warre twice in a day, and very seldome a weeke but we had some trecherous villany or other," now the Indians, both the openly hostile and the professedly friendly, were tamed.[52] But Smith's ruthless and indiscriminate approach disturbed some Virginia leaders who thought that on several occasions he mercilessly killed and attacked Indians who had done the English no harm and thus destroyed chances of profitable trade with the Indians while sowing the seeds for future discord. But Smith convinced most in the colony, as well as the managers of the London-based Virginia Company, of the efficacy of his strategy. The new attitude toward the Indians is apparent in the orders for Sir Thomas Gates, who sailed from England in 1609 to take command of the colony. In 1606 the Company had instructed: "In all your passages you must have great care not to offend the naturals, if you can eschew it."[53] Now Gates was ordered to effect a military occupation of the Chesapeake region, to make all tribes tributary to him rather than Powhatan, to extract corn, furs, dye, and labor from each tribe in proportion to its number, and, if possible, to mold the natives into an agricultural labor force as the Spanish had attempted in their colonies.[54] As the English settlement gained in strength following the arrival of six hundred additional colonists in 1610, Gates continued Smith's policy of intimidation, as did his successor, Sir Thomas Dale. In 1610 and 1611, following sporadic violence by both sides, three attacks by the English took the lives of a significant part of the population of three tribes and destroyed the tribal centers of Appomattucks and Kecoughtan.[55] In 1613, the English kidnapped Powhatan's favorite daughter, Pocahontas, who had acted as intervening savior in 1608 when Powhatan conducted a mock execution of the captured John Smith. Pocahontas immediately won the love of John Rolfe, a leader in the colony, and Powhatan was reluctantly persuaded of the political advantages of allowing the first, and perhaps the only, Anglo-Indian marriage in Virginia's early history. A period of peace followed, and this, one suspects, further confirmed many in their view that the English policy, as it had evolved, was the best that could be devised.[56]

In spite of his tendency to read hostility and savagery into the Indians' character, the early leaders of the Virginia colony manifested a strong curiosity about native culture and in their writings did not suppress their respect for it. John Smith, as has been indicated, was the foremost proponent in the early years of cowing the Indians through repeated demonstrations of the English martial spirit and superiority in weapons. But in his descriptions of Indian culture Smith revealed a genuine respect for the native way of life. He marveled at the Indians' strength and agility, their talent for hunting and fishing, their music and entertainment. He noted that civil government was practiced by them, that they adhered to religious traditions, and that many of their customs and institutions were not unlike those of the Europeans. Smith's statement that "although the countrie people be very barbarous; yet have they amongst them such government, as that their Magistrats for good commanding, and their people for du subjection, and obeying, excell in many places that would be counted very civill" illustrates the tendency to define the native as a hostile savage but still to retain an avid interest in his way of life.[57] William Strachey, who served as secretary to the colony from 1610 to 1611, and Henry Spelman, who lived among the Indians for four years, also wrote appreciatively about Indian life. Borrowing liberally from Smith and other authors, Strachey wondered how the Indians could have effected "so generall and grosse a defection from the true knowledg of God." But with this off his chest, he went on to portray the natives as "ingenious enough in their owne workes" and in possession of much of the apparatus of "civilized" society.[58] Alexander Whitaker, an Anglican minister who proselytized among the Indians, wrote that some men "are farre mistaken in the nature of these men, for besides the promise of God, which is without respect of persons, made as well to unwise men after the flesh, as to the wise, etc. let us not thinke that these men are so simple as some have supposed them: for they are of body lustie, strong, and very nimble: they are a very under-standing generation, quicke of apprehension, suddaine in their dis-patches, subtile in their dealings, exquisite in their inventions, and in-dustrious in their labour."[59] Whitaker's comments indicate the division of opinion that may have been growing in Virginia, with some men beginning to blot from their minds some of the positive characteristics of Indian society they had earlier observed.

Notwithstanding misconceptions on both sides, the English and the Indians lived in close contact during the first years. Neither mutual distrust nor intermittent conflict nor casualties on both sides kept the English from trading with the Indians when they could, from sporadi-cally conducting experiments in proselytizing and educating the Indians, and even from fleeing to Indian villages where some of the settlers found life more agreeable than at Jamestown where a military regimen prevailed after 1608. After the colony's ability to survive and overmatch the Indians was established, Indians were frequently admitted to the white settlements as day laborers. Though perhaps accepting hostility as the norm after the first few years, both sides were tacitly agreeing to exploit the dangerous presence of the other as best they could.[60]

Although the documentary record becomes much thinner after 1612, it appears that it was in the decade following this date that a major change in Indian relations occurred in Virginia. The Virginia Company of London gave up its plans for reaping vast profits through Indian trade or the discovery of minerals and instead instituted a liberal land policy designed to build the population of the colony rapidly and ultimately to make it an agricultural province of such productivity that land sales would enrich its investors. When the cultivation of tobacco was perfected, giving Virginia a money crop of great potential, and further promotional efforts were rewarded with a new influx of settlers after 1619, the availability of land became a critical question for the first time in the colony's existence. As more and more men began push-ing up the James River and its tributaries in the second decade of settlement to carve tobacco plantations out of the wilderness, the Indians of the region perceived that what had heretofore been an abrasive and often violent relationship might now become a disastrous one. It was the tension of a rapidly growing—and spreading—population that provided the highly combustible atmosphere that in 1622 was ignited by the murder of a greatly respected Indian of the Powhatan confederacy. The result was a well-coordinated, all-out attack on the white settlements in that year.

In studying the colonial image of the Indian, the details of the "massacre" of 1622 are less important than the effect it had on English perceptions of the natives. It was, of course, a genuine disaster for the Virginia Company of London, which was shortly to go bankrupt, and for the weary Virginia settlement, which lost about one-third of its inhabitants. But more important, it confirmed beyond doubt what most Englishmen had suspected from the beginning: that all Indians were inherently treacherous, cunning, and infinitely hostile. No longer would it be necessary to acknowledge an obligation to civilize and Christianize the native. Even though several leaders in the colony confided that the real cause of the Indian attack was "our owne perfidiouse dealing with them,"[61] it was generally agreed that henceforward the English would be free to hunt down the native wherever he could be found. A no-holds-barred approach to "the Indian problem" was now adopted. Whereas before the colonists claimed (at least officially) that they followed the principle of retributive justice, only engaging in attacks against the natives when they had been assaulted, now they were entitled to put aside all restraint and take the offensive. As one leader wrote revealingly after the Indian attack:

> Our hands which before were tied with gentlenesse and faire usage, are now set at liberty by the treacherous violence of the Sauvages. . . . So that we, who hitherto have had possession of no more ground then their waste and our purchase at a valuable consideration to theire owne contentment, gained; may now by right of Warre, and law of Nations, invade the Country, and destroy them who sought to destroy us: whereby wee shall enjoy their cultivated places, turning the laborious Mattocke into the victorious Sword (wherein there is more both ease, benefit, and glory) and possessing the fruits of others labours. Now their cleared grounds in all their villages (which are situate in the fruitfullest places of the land) shall be inhabited by us, whereas heretofore the grubbing of woods was the greatest labour.[62]

A note of grim satisfaction that the Indians had succeeded in wiping out one-third of the English settlement can be detected. Now the colonizers were entitled to devastate Indian villages and to take rather than buy the best land of the area. John Smith, writing two years after the attack, noted that some men held that the massacre "will be good for the Plantation, because now we have just cause to destroy them by all meanes possible."[63]

Another writer gave clear expression to his genocidal intent when he reasoned that the Indians had done the colonists a favor by sweeping away the previous English reluctance to annihilate the Indians. Now the colony would prosper. The author relished in enumerating the ways that the "savages" could be exterminated. "Victorie," he wrote, "may bee gained many waies: by force, by surprize, by famine in burning their Corne, by destroying and burning their Boats, Canoes, and Houses, by breaking their fishing Weares, by assailing them in their huntings, whereby they get the greatest part of their sustenance in Winter, by pursuing and chasing them with our horses, and blood-Hounds to draw after them, and Mastives to teare them."[64]

Once the thirst for revenge was slaked, the only debatable question was whether the extermination of the Indians would work to the benefit or disadvantage of the colony. John Martin, a prominent planter, offered several "Reasons why it is not fitting utterlye to make an exterpation of the Savages yett," and then assured his readers that it was not genocide he was against but the destruction of a people who, if properly subjected, could enrich all of the Virginians through their labor.[65] Martin's advice was ignored and during each summer in the decade following the attack of 1622, the provincial government dispatched raiding parties to destroy Indians and their crops wherever they could be found. In 1629 a peace treaty was negotiated but then rejected because it was decided by the Virginia Council that a policy of "perpetual enmity" would serve the colony better.[66] Rather than interpret the massacre of 1622 as the culmination of conflicting interests and acts of violence on both sides, the Virginians sought its origins in the nature of the native man. Because of the attack he had launched, the Indian had defined himself in a way that justified any course of action that the English might devise.

In the aftermath of the massacre of 1622 an unambiguously negative image of the Indian appeared. It would be strengthened and confirmed by later Indian attacks in 1644 and 1675. Words such as "perfidious," "cunning," "barbarous," and "improvident" had been used heretofore in describing the native, but his culture still commanded considerable respect in English eyes. After 1622, the Indians' culture was seldom deemed worthy of consideration. More and more abusive words crept into English descriptions of the Indian. Negative qualities were projected onto him with increasing frequency. Words like "beastly," "brutish," and "deformed" can be found in descriptions of the Indians after 1622. Whereas John Smith and others had described them as "ingenious," "industrious," and "quick of apprehension," Edward Waterhouse, writing after the massacre, informed his readers that the Indians "are by nature sloathfull and idle, vitious, melancholy, slovenly, of bad conditions, lyers, of small memory, of no constancy or trust . . . by nature of all people the most lying and most inconstant in the world, sottish and sodaine: never looking what dangers may happen afterwards, lesse capable then children of sixe or seaven yeares old, and lesse apt and ingenious."[67] This vocabulary of abuse reflects not only the rage of the decimated colony but an inner need to provide a justification for colonial policy for generations to come. Hereafter, the elimintion of the Indians could be rationalized far more easily, for they were seen as vicious, cultureless, unreconstructable savages rather than merely as hostile and primitive men, though men with an integral culture and a way of life worthy of notice.[68]

The psychological calculus by which intentions governed white attitudes can be seen more clearly by studying the views of Englishmen who genuinely desired amicable relations with the Indians. The Quakers of Pennsylvania and West New Jersey, who were the most important early practitioners of pacifism in the New World, threatened no violence to the Indians when they arrived in the Delaware River Valley in the last quarter of the seventeenth century. It was pacifism, not violence, that was on the minds of the Quakers. Eager to avoid the conflict which had beset other colonies and committed ideologically to banishing violence and war, the Quakers viewed the Indian in a different light. Though regarding him as backward and "under a dark Night in things relating to Religion," they also saw him as physically attractive, generous, mild tempered, and possessed of many admirable traits. William Penn, the proprietor of the colony, gave new expression to old speculations that the Indians were the "Jews of America," the descendants of the Lost Tribes of Israel. He found their language "lofty" and full of words "of more sweetness or greatness" than most European tongues.[69] Though Quaker relations with the Indians were not so benign as some historians have suggested, it is significant that not a single incident of organized violence between Indians and Quakers occurred during the colonial period. The deterioration of Indian relations in Pennsylvania can be traced primarily to the rapid influx after 1713 of German and Scotch-Irish settlers whose land hunger and indifference toward the Indians, combined with the Anglo-French wars of the mid-eighteenth century, set the frontier in flames for a quarter century.

In the southern colonies the image of the Indian also began to change once the resistance of the natives to the territorial encroachment of white settlers faded. In almost all the colonies, concerted attacks by the Indians lasted only into the third generation. Thereafter the Indians who had survived contact with European culture either moved beyond the reach of the colonizers, at least temporarily, or lived within white communities in a subservient status. Thus, in Virginia the last significant Indian attack came in 1675. In South Carolina, settled six decades later, the last major Indian offensives were mounted in the Tuscarora and Yamasee wars of the early eighteenth century. Later in the eighteenth century Indian tribes fought English settlers on numerous occasions, but always as adjuncts of their French or Spanish allies who armed, directed, and controlled them, rather than as independent nations.[70]

When the precariousness of the English position was eliminated as a significant factor in Anglo-Indian relations, and when large-scale attacks on white communities had subsided, the image of the Indian began to change, at least among the literate or reflective element of society. Because the social context of Indian-white relations was changing, the white community was far better disposed emotionally to see the Indian as another cultural group rather than simply as the enemy. In the first half of the eighteenth century a number of colonial observers began to develop a new image of the Indian. Unlike later writers, who from seaboard cities or European centers of culture sentimentalized the native into a "noble savage," these men knew of Indian life from firsthand experience as missionaries, provincial officials, and fur traders. Close to Indian culture, but not pitted against the native in a fight for land or survival, they developed clearer perspectives on aboriginal life. Not yet seized by the certainty that they were fulfilling a divine mission in North America, they were able to take a more anthropological approach to Indian society rather than assaying it only in terms of its proximity to English culture.[71]

All of the components in the revised image of the Indian emerging in the eighteenth century were linked together by the basic assumption that the Indians' culture was worth examining on its own terms. This in itself was a significant change, since during the period of Indian attacks most colonists had regarded the Indians as cultureless. Samuel Purchas's charge of 1625 that the Indians were "bad people, having little of humanitie but shape, ignorant of Civilitie, or Arts, or Religion: more brutish then the beasts they hunt, more wild and unmanly then that unmanned wild Countrey, which they range rather then inhabite" was a classic statement of the earlier view of the worthlessness or absence of Indian culture.[72] But now Englishmen began to discover all of the missing elements in the Indians' cultural makeup—government, social structure, religion, family organization, codes of justice and morality, crafts and arts.

So far as can be ascertained from the surviving sources, an unpublished anonymous account of 1689, perhaps by the Anglican minister John Clayton, was the first attempt since John Smith's description of 1612 to take Indian culture seriously. "The Indians in Virginia. . ." assumed a reportorial tone and described Indian customs, though not the Indians' character, in a neutral way.[73] Far more significant was Robert Beverley's *The History and Present State of Virginia . . .* , published in 1705, almost a century after the planting of the Jamestown settlement and at a time when the Indian population of the settled regions of the colony had declined from an estimated eighteen thousand in 1607 to about two thousand. Even in the chapter headings he used—"Religion and Worship," "Laws and Authority," "Learning and Language," "Marriage and Children," and "Crafts"—Beverley revealed a new attitude toward the native. Much of what he saw in Indian culture reminded him of classical Spartan life. Beverley used words like "strange" or "remarkable" to describe Indian customs, but completely absent from his account were those earlier adjectival indicators such as "beastly," "savage," "primitive," "monstrous," and "idolatrous."[74] In Beverley's description can be seen the beginning of a new genre of literature on the Indian—a genre which included a foretaste of the "noble savage" tradition, but which was more fundamentally rooted in a desire to describe the Indians' culture than to use it as a foil for demonstrating the decadence of western civilization.

Four years later, John Lawson, a proprietary officeholder who traveled extensively among the tribes of South Carolina and Georgia, published a lengthier description of Indian culture. In *A New Voyage to Carolina,* Lawson attempted to describe the material culture of the southern tribes and to examine their social, political, and religious institutions. Lawson's account was not free of judgmental statements about the "imbecilities" of certain native customs or their "lazy, idle" habits. But like Beverley he seems to have made a conscious attempt to step back from his own cultural standards when observing the music, dancing, games, marriage and family customs, medicine, religion, and government of the southeastern tribes among which he traveled for eight years.[75]

Some eighteenth-century writers were, however, still employing words like "savage," "monstrous," and "idolatrous" to describe the Indians. William Stith's *The History of the First Discovery and Settlement of Virginia . . .* , published in 1747, pictured the Indian as inherently treacherous and barbarous. Relying heavily on the early accounts of Virginia by John Smith and Thomas Hariot, Stith insisted that the English had always treated the Indians "with the utmost Humanity and Kindness, out of the Hope and Desire, of thereby alluring and bringing them over, to the Knowledge of God and his true Religion." At Jamestown, the Indians had been "fed at their Tables, and even lodged in their Bedchambers; so that they seemed, entirely to have coalesced, and to live together, as one People." The Indians had repaid this generous treatment, Stith claimed, with perfidious attacks on the English settlement.[76] The Anglican minister Hugh Jones, writing in 1724, was equally prepared to assign blame for Anglo-Indian hostility to the natives and to describe them as savage and idolatrous. But Jones also found the Indians serious in debate and possessed of "tolerable good notions of natural justice, equity, honor, and honesty." Although he could not persuade himself that the Indians would ever rise to the level of Christianity, Jones was far more appreciative of native culture than his seventeenth-century predecessors.[77]

The most complete statement of the integrity of Indian culture came from James Adair in his *History of the American Indians . . . ,* published in 1775 and based on forty years of experience as an Indian trader on the frontiers of South Carolina and Georgia. In an argument extending to more than two hundred pages, Adair labored to prove the descent of the American Indians from the ancient Jews. In matters as widely separated as adherence to theocratic government, genius for language and rhetoric, and manner of embalming the dead, Adair found links between Semitic and Indian culture. Like a number of others who were describing the Indians, Adair was impressed with the "plain and honest law of nature" which governed native society and by the strong sense of religion that gave meaning and coherence to native life.[78]

Just as a new view of native culture was appearing in the eighteenth century, ideas about the Indians' character traits—or what would come to be called personality—were undergoing a marked change. Widespread agreement cannot be found among colonial writers, of course, for each was influenced by his own background and by his special purposes in writing about the Indians. Moreover, the personality of the Indian was in the process of change as he struggled to adapt to the presence of more and more Europeans and African slaves in his ancestral lands. But despite significant differences, eighteenth-century colonial observers of Indian character were far more favorable than those of an earlier period, when the ultimate outcome of Anglo-Indian confrontation had still been in doubt.

On one point agreement was nearly unanimous: the Indians were extraordinarily brave. Both men and women were fired with the most unswerving loyalty to their tribe and endowed with incredible stoicism under torture and duress.[79] At the same time, most observers thought the Indians were revengeful, never forgetting an ill deed or an injustice. Agreement was general that this was a weakness in the Indian, though to identify this as a defect was ironic inasmuch as colonial Indian policy was unambiguous on the need to administer swift and severe retribution for every Indian offense.[80]

Predictably, observers took a variety of positions on the honesty of the natives. The old image of the cunning, deceitful, treacherous Indian retained its currency.[81] But other observers insisted that the Indians were more straightforward and honorable in matters of trade and land exchange than the English. For example, Edmond Atkin, who was appointed southern superintendent of the Indians in 1756, was convinced that "in their publick Treaties no People on earth are more open, explicit and Direct. Nor are they excelled by any in the observance of them."[82]

In the more favorable image of the Indian that was emerging, an element of considerable importance, because it related to the origins of Anglo-Indian hostility, concerned the attitude of Indians toward strangers. After the first concerted Indian attacks of the seventeenth century, writers had characterized the native as brutish, vicious, and hostile by nature. But in the eighteenth century, men who traveled among or negotiated with the Indians discovered that hospitality and generosity were important in the Indians' structure of values.[83] Robert Beverley made the point explicitly by noting that the Indians had been "at first very fair and friendly" and provided the provisions that kept the struggling Jamestown colony alive during the first hard winter.[84] Edmond Atkin charged that the English had received "a very hospitable Reception" at Roanoke Island but were rewarded for their pains by the leader of the colony, Richard Grenville, who punished the Indians for the action of a native "who did not know the difference of Value between [the silver cup] and a horn Spoon."[85] Missionaries of the Society for the Propagation of the Gospel, the evangelical arm of the Anglican church, also reported on the equable temperament and generosity of the natives. In 1706, for example, Francis Le Jau's first impressions of the Yamasee Indians in South Carolina were of a "very quiet, sweet humor'd and patient [people], content with little."[86]

Physical attractiveness also commanded the attention of eighteenth-century commentators. In the previous century the Indian had not been regarded as physically repulsive, as was the African in some cases, but neither had the Indian women been generally regarded as suitable for marriage. Now, early in the eighteenth century, it was proposed that the Indians had an uncommonly handsome physique which commended them for racial intermixture. William Byrd, one of Virginia's largest plantation owners and a man who kept the pleasures of the flesh and the mind in exquisite balance, described the Indians as strong, handsome, and at least as attractive as the first English settlers. Byrd was sufficiently impressed by the Indians' outward features to suggest that intermarriage should offend the tastes of nobody. If practiced earlier, he argued, a century of bloodshed might have been avoided. Their fine bodies, wrote Byrd in a revealing comment, "may make full Amends for the Darkness of their Complexions." If the English had not been "so Squeamish" and imbued with a "false Delicacy," they might have made a "prudent alliance" with the Indians of the Chesapeake region to everyone's benefit. Byrd believed the Indians had been offended by this rejection and could never "perswade themselves that the English were heartily their Friends, so long as they disdained to intermarry with them." He advised that a lost opportunity might still be reclaimed by intermarriage—the "Modern Policy" in French Canada and Louisiana.[87] Robert Beverley took a similar view. He described Indian males as "straight and well proportion'd, having the cleanest and most exact limbs in the World." As for the native woman, she was "generally Beautiful, possessing uncommon delicacy of Shape and Features, and wanting no Charm, but that of a fair Complexion." Like Byrd, Beverley regretted that intermarriage had not occurred.[88] Lawson was another who remarked on the admirable stature of the Indian men, commenting on their "full and manly" eyes, their "sedate and majestick" gait, and their strength and agility. Indian women were no less appealing. They were described as "fine shap'd Creatures . . . as any in the Universe" and their smiles "afford the finest Composure a Face can possess."[89]

Closely tied to physical attractiveness in the minds of white writers was the notion of cleanliness—both of body and mind. Earlier colonists, perhaps projecting their own feelings of embarrassment and guilt, had frequently remarked on the nakedness and open sexual relations of the Indians, concluding that the natives were dirty and lewd. Beverley, however, wrote that Indian marriage was "most sacred and inviolable" and that the women were relaxed, good humored, and full of dignity. Though white men charged unmarried Indian women with promiscuity, he was convinced that this was only a projection of "the guilt of their own consciences," and added that white men, who kept their women in tight rein, were "not very nice in distinguishing betwixt guilt, and harmless freedom" when they saw the familiarity and openness of young Indian girls.[90] Adair was in agreement. He found the native women "of a mild amiable soft disposition: exceedingly soft in their behaviour," and compared Indian marriage and divorce traditions with those of the ancient Hebrews. The tribes of southeastern America had high moral standards, inhabited "clean, neat dwelling houses," and were critical, with much cause, of the laxity of white morals.[91] The Anglican missionary Le Jau, after observing both white and red settlements in South Carolina for a year, concluded that the Indians "make us ashamed by their life, Conversation and Sense of Religion." Whereas English settlers talked about religion and morality, the Indians lived it.[92] Lawson, however, was offended by the Indian practice of fornication before marriage and the readiness of Indian women to prostitute themselves to fur traders. But in personal habits he found the natives clean and "sweet."[93]

The ability to take a more dispassionate view of the Indian allowed discussion of the effects of white society on the Indians' way of life. Earlier, when the Indian had been seen simply as a savage, it was logical to assume that the confrontation of cultures could only benefit the indigenous man. If Europeans were civilized and Indians were heathen, cultural interaction would necessarily improve the inferior group. But eighteenth-century observers, more wont to take Indian culture on its own terms, frequently concluded that colonizing Europeans had perverted rather than converted the Indian. The English had introduced drunkenness and covetousness, Beverley complained, and robbed the natives of much of their "Felicity, as well as their innocence."[94] Almost every prerevolutionary eighteenth-century writer agreed that the Indians had been debauched by rum, and educated in thievery, avariciousness, and immorality. The lowest elements of white society, in most frequent contact with the natives, gave the Indians cause to suspect the superiority of white Christian culture to which they were incessantly urged to aspire.[95] Fur traders were no better, constituting a "Wretched sort of Men," as one Anglican missionary put it.[96] Agreement was general among the Society for the Propagation of the Gospel that it was impossible to convert the natives until the "white barbarians" of the frontier areas, as Benjamin Franklin called them, had been brought within the pale of civilization.[97]

Ironically, the new image of the Indian was emerging at a time when the native qualities most likely to gain the admiration or respect of white society were disappearing. Ravaged by alcohol and European diseases, decimated by wars in which they fought at a technological disadvantage, the tribes of the coastal area were losing many of the age-old skills and cultural attributes which commended them to eighteenth-century observers. Even while the new view of him formed, the indigenous American was in some areas slipping into a state of dependency which eroded white respect enormously. As the gun and knife replaced the bow and arrow, as the kettle and fishhook replaced hand-fashioned implements, and as rum became the great painkiller for those whose culture was undergoing rapid change, the grudging respect of white culture turned to contempt. While the colonial intelligentsia was discovering the integrity of native culture in the eighteenth century, the ordinary farmer and frontiersman found less and less to admire in Indian life. For the Indian the limited respect of European colonizers had come too late to halt the process of cultural change which would leave his image impaired and his power to resist further cultural and territorial aggrandizement fatally weakened. For the colonist, the image of the native, so useful in the past, would continue to reflect the needs and intentions of a restless, ambitious people.

NOTES

1. For the Elizabethan image of the African, see Winthrop D. Jordan, *White Over Black: American Attitudes Toward the Negro, 1550–1812* (Chapel Hill, N.C., 1968). His pervading theme, that white attitudes toward the African reflected attempts of Englishmen to resolve their own problems of identity, parallels Roy Harvey Pearce's organizing thesis in *The Savages of America: A Study of the Indian and the Idea of Civilization* (Baltimore, 1953).

2. I have focused this study on the southern colonies, especially Virginia, excluding from consideration Puritan New England and, for the most part, the Middle Atlantic colonies. A whole range of factors—including geography, the Indians' cultural characteristics and prior contacts with Europeans, Puritan theology, and the psychic life of the seventeenth-century Puritan community—affected attitudes and relations in these areas.

3. For the exploits of Gilbert and Raleigh, see David Beers Quinn, ed., *The Voyages and Colonizing Enterprises of Sir Humphrey Gilbert,* Hakluyt Society Publications, 2d Ser., 83–84 (London, 1940), hereafter cited as *Voyages of Gilbert;* Quinn, ed., *The Roanoke Voyages, 1584–1590,* ibid., (London, 1955), hereafter cited as *Roanoke Voyages;* and Quinn, *Raleigh and the British Empire* (London, 1947).

4. Loren Baritz, "The Idea of the West," *American Historical Review,* 71 (1960–61): 618–40. See also William H. Babcock, *Legendary Islands of the Atlantic: A Study in Medieval Geography* (New York, 1922).

5. A general treatment of this literature, as literature, is given in Howard Mumford Jones, *O Strange New World; American Culture: The Formative Years* (New York, 1964), 1–70.

6. For a consideration of English reactions to the Indian at home, see Sidney Lee, "The American Indian in Elizabethan England," in *Elizabethan and Other Essays,* ed. Frederick S. Boas (Oxford, 1929), 263–301; and Carolyn Foreman, *Indians Abroad, 1493–1938* (Norman, Okla., 1943).

7. Richard Hakluyt, *Divers voyages touching the discoverie of America, and the Ilands adjacent unto the Same* (1582), Hakluyt Soc. Pub., 1st Ser., 7 (London, 1850), 23, hereafter cited as *Divers voyages.*

8. "The Relation of John Verrazanus,..." ibid., 55–71. By this time three accounts of the New World were available in English. They are reprinted in Edward Arber, ed., *The first Three English books on America. [?1511]–1555 A.D. Being chiefly Translations, Compilations, etc., by Richard Eden, ...* (Birmingham, 1885).

9. The most important were George Best, *A True Discourse of the late voyages of discoverie, for the finding of a passage to Cathaya, ...* (1578);

Dionyse Settle, *A true reporte of the laste voyage into the West and Northwest regions,* . . . (1577); and Thomas Ellis, *A true report of the third and last voyage into Meta Incognita:* . . . (1578). All are reported in Vilhjalmur Stefansson, ed., *The Three Voyages of Martin Frobisher* . . . (London, 1938).

10. Stefansson, ed., *Voyages of Frobisher,* 2:23.

11. For a compilation of books in English describing the overseas world before 1600, see George B. Parks, *Richard Hakluyt and the English Voyages* (New York, 1928), 270–76; and John Parker, *Books to Build an Empire: A Bibliographical History of English Overseas Interests to 1620* (Amsterdam, 1965).

12. Cecil Jane, ed., *The Journal of Christopher Columbus* (New York, 1960), 23–24.

13. Jones, *O Strange New World,* 10–13.

14. Trans. John Frampton (London, 1577).

15. Quinn, ed., *Voyages of Gilbert,* 105:285.

16. Jones, *O Strange New World,* 1–34.

17. *Divers voyages,* and *Discourse of Western Planting* (1584). The latter is reprinted in E. G. R. Taylor, ed., *The Original Writings & Correspondence of the Two Richard Hakluyts,* Hakluyt Soc. Pub., 2d Ser., 76–77 (London, 1934), 77:211–326. Herafter cited as *Writings & Correspondence.*

18. (London, 1583).

19. Taylor, ed., *Writings & Correspondence,* 76:164–65.

20. Ibid., 77:223. Hakluyt was quoting from Ribault's *Whole and true discoverye.*

21. (London, 1583).

22. Hakluyt, *Discourse of Western Planting,* in Taylor, ed., *Writings & Correspondence,* 77:309–10, 257–65. The quotations are from pp. 309–10. Spanish cruelty toward the natives was a stock theme in the literature of English expansionists. See, for example, ibid., 212, 223, 241; and Quinn, ed., *Roanoke Voyages,* 104:490–91. The influence of Spanish colonization on English expectations of the New World, including the key notion that the Indians could be employed as an agricultural labor force, is discussed by Edmund S. Morgan, "The Labor Problem at Jamestown, 1607–18," *Amer. Hist. Rev.* 76 (1971): 597–600.

23. *Inducements to the Liking of the Voyage intended towards Virginia* . . . (1585), in Taylor, ed., *Writings & Correspondence,* 77:329–30.

24. Quinn, ed., *Voyages of Gilbert,* 84:450–52.

25. Ibid., 453.

26. Ibid., 467–68.

27. Cf. *Notes on Colonisation* . . . (1578), written for Gilbert's voyage; *Instructions for the North-East Passage* . . . (1580); and *Voyage intended towards Virginia,* all reprinted in Taylor, ed., *Writings & Correspondence,* 76:116–22, 147–58; 77:327–38.

28. The best accounts of the Roanoke colony, from an English point of view, are Wesley Frank Craven, *The Southern Colonies in the Seventeenth Century, 1607–1689* (Baton Rouge, La., 1949), 27–59; and David Beers Quinn's introduction to *The Roanoke Voyages.*

29. Thomas Hariot, *A briefe and true report of the new found land of Virginia* . . . (1588); Arthur Barlowe, *Discourse of the First Voyage* . . . (1585); and Ralph Lane, *Discourse on the first colony* . . . [1586?]. All were first published in 1589 in Richard Hakluyt, *The Principall Navigations, Voyages, Traffiques & Discoveries of the English Nation* . . . , 12 vols. (Glasgow, 1903–5 [orig. publ. London, 1589]), and are reprinted in Quinn, ed., *Roanoke Voyages*, 104:317–87, 91–116, 255–94.

30. Quinn, ed., *Roanoke Voyages*, 104:108. Although at first glance one might dismiss such comments as colonizing propaganda, it must be understood that all of the accounts had to come to terms with the fact that conflict did break out and ultimately led to the extinction of the English settlement. Given the unhappy ending of the story, it is less likely that the authors would falsify the Indians' initial reactions to the arrival of the English.

31. Ibid., 368–72, 376.

32. Of the attempts by anthropologists to analyze the reaction of the tribes in the Chesapeake region to the arrival of the English, the best is Nancy Oestreich Lurie, "Indian Cultural Adjustment to European Civilization," in James Morton Smith, ed., *Seventeenth-Century America: Essays in Colonial History* (Chapel Hill, N.C., 1959), 33–60. Lurie draws upon and extends the work of an earlier generation of anthropologists including Maurice Mook, James Mooney, John R. Swanton, and Frank G. Speck.

33. Quinn, ed., *Roanoke Voyages*, 104:191–92, 246, 259, 265, 271, 286–88.

34. Ibid., 381–82.

35. Ibid, 371.

36. Paul Hulton and David Beers Quinn, *The American Drawings of John White, 1577–1590* (Chapel Hill, N.C., 1964).

37. Edward Arber and A. G. Bradley, eds., *Travels and Works of Captain John Smith* . . . (Edinburgh, 1910), 1:335–39.

38. *A True Reporte* . . . *of the Newfound Landes*, in Quinn, ed., *Voyages of Gilbert*, 84:449–50.

39. *A Good Speed to Virginia* (1609), quoted in Wesley Frank Craven, "Indian Policy in Early Virginia," *William and Mary Quarterly*, 3d Ser., 1 (1944): 65. A useful essay on the subject is Wilcomb E. Washburn, "The Moral and Legal Justifications for Dispossessing the Indians," in Smith, ed., *Seventeenth-Century America*, 15–32. For another early seventeenth-century rationale, see William Strachey, *The Historie of Travell into Virginia Britania (1612)*, eds. Louis B. Wright and Virginia Freund, Hakluyt Soc. Pub., 2d Ser., 103 (London, 1953), 7–29. Hereafter cited as *Historie of Travell into Virginia*.

40. *A True Declaration of the Estate of the Colonie in Virginia*, . . . (1610), in Peter Force, comp., *Tracts and Other Papers, Relating Principally to the Origin, Settlement, and Progress of the Colonies in North America, from the Discovery to the Year 1776* (Washington, D.C., 1844), 3, Nos. 1, 6.

41. Samuel Purchas, *Hakluytus Posthumus or Purchas His Pilgrimes* . . . (Glasgow, 1906 [orig. publ. London, 1625]), 19:232.

42. *A Good Speed to Virginia* (London, 1609), ed. Wesley Frank Craven (New York, 1937), n.p.

43. Strachey, *Historie of Travell into Virginia,* eds. Wright and Freund, 26.

44. [Gabriel Archer?], "A Breif discription of the People," in Philip L. Barbour, ed., *The Jamestown Voyages Under the First Charter, 1606–1609,* Hakluyt Soc. Pub., 2d Ser., 86–87 (London, 1969), 86:103–4. Hereafter cited as *Jamestown Voyages.*

45. Ibid., 82–86. Powhatan swiftly attacked the Chesapeake tribe, killing several of its leaders and replacing them with "trusted kinsmen." Lurie, "Indian Cultural Adjustment," in Smith, ed., *Seventeenth-Century America,* 41.

46. Lurie, "Indian Cultural Adjustment," in Smith, ed., *Seventeenth-Century America,* 38–47. Wesley Frank Craven, the most careful student of the English Indian policy in the first half of the seventeenth century, takes the view that Powhatan, like his Indian enemies, never regarded an alliance with the English as advantageous and plotted their destruction from their first arrival. "Indian Policy in Early Virginia," *Wm. and Mary Qtly.,* 3d Ser., 1 (1944): 68–70. Though there is evidence to dispute this interpretation of Indian motives, it is preferable to the older, naive, and sentimental view of the Indians as hapless and helpless victims whose disinterested goodwill and hospitality toward the English was met with hostility and violence. To imagine that the Indians were unable to comprehend what was in their self-interest and incapable of perceiving English intentions is to give them less than their due and consign them to an essentially passive role in what surely must have been a dynamic process.

47. "A True relation," in Arber and Bradley, eds., *Travels and Works of Smith,* 1:8–9. George Percy wrote of the same event: "If it had not pleased God to have put a terrour in the Savages hearts, we had all perished by those wild and cruell Pagans, being in that weake estate as we were." *Observations gathered out of a Discourse . . . ,* in Barbour, ed., *Jamestown Voyages,* 86:144–45.

48. Arber and Bradley, eds., *Travels and Works of Smith,* 1:38; Susan M. Kingsbury, ed., *The Records of the Virginia Company of London* (Washington, D.C., 1906–35), 3:175, 93; Arber and Bradley, eds., *Travels and Works of Smith,* 1:35.

49. Arber and Bradley, eds., *Travels and Works of Smith,* 1:107.

50. Ibid., xiv, 24–27, 32–33, 35–38, 106–7.

51. *Advertisements For the unexperienced Planters of New-England, . . .* (1631), ibid., 2:925.

52. Ibid., 411.

53. Ibid., 1:xxxv, 122–23.

54. Kingsbury, ed., *Virginia Company Records,* 3:14–21. A few years later Gov. Thomas Dale saw divine approval of this course of action. "Now may you judge Sir," he wrote, "if the God of battailes have not a helping hand in this, that having our swords drawn, killing their men, burning their houses, and taking their corne: yet they tendred us peace, and strive with all allacrity to

keep us in good oppinion of them; by which many benefits arise unto us."
Ralph Hamor, *A True Discourse of the Present State of Virginia* (1615), ed. A.
L. Rowse (Richmond, 1957), 54–55.

55. Ben C. McCary, *Indians in Seventeenth Century Virginia* (Williamsburg, Va., 1957), 78.

56. The Rolfe-Pocahontas union, and its political implications, are best
told in the primary source material by Hamor, *True Discourse,* ed. Rowse; and
in the secondary literature by Bradford Smith, *Captain John Smith, His Life and
Legend* (Philadelphia, 1953); and Philip L. Barbour, *Pocahontas and Her
World . . .* (Boston, 1970). The view of the Anglican minister, Alexander Whitaker, that the dual policy of ruthless militarism and political intermarriage was
the best policy is expressed in a letter written in 1614 and reprinted in Hamor,
A True Discourse, ed. Rowse, 59–61.

57. *A Map of Virginia . . . ,* in Arber and Bradley, eds., *Travels and Works
of Smith,* 1:43–84. Smith's statement on the civility of Indian society was
copied almost verbatim by Strachey. See *Historie of Travell into Virginia,* eds.
Wright and Freund, 77.

58. Strachey, *Historie of Travell into Virginia,* eds. Wright and Freund,
53, 74–116. Spelman's account is in Arber and Bradley, eds., *Travels and
Works of Smith,* 1:cv–cxiv.

59. Whitaker, *Good Newes from Virginia* (1613), quoted in Pearce, *Savages of America,* 13.

60. Lurie, "Indian Cultural Adjustment," in Smith, ed., *Seventeenth-Century America,* 48–50.

61. Kingsbury, ed., *Virginia Company Records,* 4:117–18, 89.

62. Edward Waterhouse, *A Declaration of the State of the Colony and
Affaires in Virginia, With a Relation of the Barbarous Massacre . . .* (1662),
ibid., 3:556–57.

63. Arber and Bradley, eds., *Travels and Works of Smith,* 2:578–79.

64. Waterhouse, *State of the Colony,* in Kingsbury, ed., *Virginia Company
Records,* 3:557.

65. "The Manner Howe to Bringe the Indians into Subjection," ibid.,
705–7.

66. McCary, *Indians in Virginia,* 80; Craven, "Indian Policy," *Wm. and
Mary Qtly.,* 3d Ser., 1 (1944): 73. See also William S. Powell, "Aftermath of the
Massacre: The First Indian War, 1622–1632," *Virginia Magazine of History
and Biography,* 66 (1958): 44–75.

67. Barbour, ed., *Jamestown Voyages,* 136: 104; 137:354; Waterhouse,
State of the Colony, in Kingsbury, ed., *Virginia Company Records,* 3:562–63.

68. Promotional literature would continue to minimize Anglo-Indian hostility and reiterate the old notions of converting the natives to Christianity. This
literature is included in P. Lee Phillips, "List of Books Relating to America in
the Register of the London Company of Stationers, from 1562 to 1638,"
American Historical Association, *Annual Report* (Washington, D.C., 1897),
1251–61.

69. William Penn, *A Letter from William Penn, . . . to the Committee of*

the Free Society of Traders . . . (1683), in Albert Cook Myers, ed., *Narratives of Early Pennsylvania, West New Jersey and Delaware, 1630–1707* (New York, 1912), 230, 234. A descriptive study of Indian origins, as viewed by colonizing Europeans, is Lee Eldridge Huddleston, *Origins of the American Indians: European Concepts, 1492–1729* (Austin, Tex., 1967).

70. A general treatment of eighteenth-century Indian wars is provided in Howard H. Peckham, *The Colonial Wars, 1689–1762* (Chicago, 1964).

71. It is doubtful that a new view of the Indian ever made much progress below the upper stratum of society. Among frontiersmen, who still competed for land with the native and whose contacts with him remained abrasive, the old stereotypes remained basically unchanged throughout the eighteenth century. The same was true in the middle and lower classes of the seaboard cities and towns. Only when geographical and social distance separated the two groups could a new popular image emerge. For treatment of the frontier image of the Indian see Lewis O. Saum, *The Fur Trader and the Indian* (Seattle, Wash., 1965).

72. Purchas, *Purchas His Pilgrimes,* 19:231.

73. Stanley Pargellis, ed., "An Account of the Indian in Virginia," *Wm. and Mary Qtly.,* 3d Ser., 16 (1959):228–43.

74. Ed. Louis B. Wright (Chapel Hill, N.C., 1947), 159–23, *passim.*

75. John Lawson, *A New Voyage to Carolina, . . .* ed. Hugh T. Lefler (Chapel Hill, N. C., 1967), 19, 38.

76. (Williamsburg, Va., 1747), 210.

77. Hugh Jones, *The Present State of Virginia . . .* (1724), ed. Richard L. Morton (Chapel Hill, N.C., 1956), 54–58.

78. James Adair, *The History of the American Indians . . .* (London, 1775).

79. Ibid., 413; Wilbur R. Jacobs, ed., *Indians of the Southern Colonial Frontier: The Edmond Atkin Report and Plan of 1755* (Columbia, S.C., 1954), 62, 68; William K. Boyd, ed., *William Byrd's Histories of the Dividing Line betwixt Virginia and North Carolina* (Raleigh, N.C., 1929), 3, 222; Jones, *Present State of Virginia,* ed. Morton, 56; Lawson, *Voyage to Carolina,* ed. Lefler, 207, 243.

80. Adair, *History of the Indians,* 4; Jones, *Present State of Virginia,* ed. Morton, 56–57.

81. For example, Jones, *Present State of Virginia,* ed. Morton, 57; Adair, *History of the Indians,* 4–5.

82. Jacobs, ed., *Report and Plan of 1755,* 38. This affirmation of the Indians' sense of honor had been noted by some of the original members of the Jamestown expedition. George Percy wrote: "It is a generall rule of these people; when they swere by their God which is the Sunne, no Christian will keep their Oath better upon this promise." *Observations gathered,* in Barbour, ed., *Jamestown Voyages,* 136:143. Atkin, however, found the Choctaw Indians "subtle, Deceitful, Insolent." Jacobs, ed., *Report and Plan of 1755,* 7.

83. Adair, *History of the Indians,* 422–24; Jacobs, ed., *Report and Plan of 1755,* 38; Beverley, *History and Present State of Virginia,* ed. Wright, 188–89; Lawson, *New Voyage to Carolina,* ed. Lefler, 23, 35, 243.

84. Beverley, *History and Present State of Virginia*, ed. Wright, 29.

85. Jacobs, ed., *Report and Plan of 1755*, 39.

86. Frank J. Klingberg, ed., *The Carolina Chronicle of Dr. Francis Le Jau, 1706–1717*, University of California Publications in History, 53 (Berkeley and Los Angeles, 1956), 19.

87. Boyd, ed., *William Byrd's Histories of the Dividing Line*, 3–4.

88. Beverley, *History and Present State of Virginia*, ed. Wright, 159, 38–39. The degree of miscegenation between white males and Indian women—the reverse was almost certainly rare—has been often disputed but rarely supported with convincing evidence. Wilbur R. Jacobs believes that mixed marriages were a rarity. "British-Colonial Attitudes and Policies Toward the Indian in the American Colonies," in Howard Peckham and Charles Gibson, eds., *Attitudes of Colonial Powers Toward the American Indian* (Salt Lake City, 1969), 90–92. Herbert Moller has argued that demographic ratios, both male to female and white to nonwhite, have been the controlling factor in the incidence of interracial sexual relations. "Sex Composition and Correlated Culture Patterns of Colonial America," *Wm. and Mary Qtly.*, 3d Ser., 2 (1945): 113–53. Both Beverley and Byrd noted the contrast between English and French or Spanish attitudes toward intermarriage with the Indians. Gov. Alexander Spottswood claimed in 1717 that he had never heard of an Anglo-Indian marriage during his seven years in Virginia. R. A. Brock, ed., *The Official Letters of Alexander Spottswood* . . . (Virginia Historical Society, Collections, N.S., 2 [Richmond, 1885]), 227. This statement should be taken with caution, since only a few years earlier, Lawson noted interracial mating. *Voyage to Carolina*, ed. Lefler, 195–96. The English government encouraged racial intermarriage in Nova Scotia between 1719 and 1766. See J. B. Brebner, "Subsidized Intermarriage with the Indians: An Incident in British Colonial Policy," *Canadian Historical Review*, 6 (1925): 33–36. The entire subject of interracial contact, both Anglo-Indian and Afro-Indian, needs further investigation.

89. Lawson, *Voyage to Carolina*, ed. Lefler, 176–77, 189.

90. Beverley, *History and Present State of Virginia*, ed. Wright, 170–71, 4–5.

91. Adair, *History of the Indians*, 413–16.

92. Klingberg, ed., *Chronicle of Le Jau*, 24.

93. Lawson, *Voyage to Carolina*, ed. Lefler, 40–41, 189–90, 180.

94. Beverley, *History and Present State of Virginia*, ed. Wright, 233.

95. Adair, *History of the Indians*, 4–5; Jacobs, ed., *Report and Plan of 1755*, 23–26; Boyd, ed., *William Byrd's Histories of the Dividing Line*, 116–20; Lawson, *Voyage to Carolina*, ed. Lefler, 18, 211, 239–46; Klingberg, ed., *Chronicle of Le Jau*, 54.

96. Klingberg, ed., *Papers of Johnston*, 53.

97. Klingberg, *Anglican Humanitarianism in Colonial New York* (Philadelphia, 1940), 54; Klingberg, *An Appraisal of the Negro in Colonial South Carolina: A Study in Americanization* (Washington, D.C., 1941), 54, 68.

3

THE FRAMING OF
GOVERNMENT IN PENNSYLVANIA:
Ideas in Contact with Reality

LITTLE IS KNOWN of the pressures and influences which bore upon William Penn as he pieced together the instruments of government for his "Holy Experiment" between March 4, 1681, when he received his charter from Charles II, and April 25, 1682, when his Frame of Government was published in London. Most historians, upon reading the widely heralded Frame of 1682, have been content to believe that Penn was given the rare opportunity of forging a government of his own and that the result was a pure distillation of his political philosophy, drawn from studies of classical Republican writers, his practical experience since 1675 in the affairs of West New Jersey, and the counsel of a few intimate advisers such as Algernon Sidney, the radical parliamentarian, and Benjamin Furly, the Rotterdam Quaker merchant.

This uncomplicated view assumes a confidence in the Quaker founder on the part of his principal supporters that probably never existed. Penn, in all likelihood, was far from a free agent in the work of constituting a government. William Markham, his cousin and a trusted adjutant in the colony for many years, indicated as much when he later wrote: "I know very well it [the Frame of Government] was forced from him by friends who unless they received all that they demanded would not have settled the country."[1] But beyond this intriguing comment little direct evidence of such pressures survives to illuminate the government-making process in 1681 and 1682; nor is it likely that any interplay between Penn and his supporters was recorded at the time.

But what is evident from an examination of Penn's remaining correspondence and from a close analysis of the various drafts of government fashioned in 1681 and 1682 is that the ideal state which Penn had constructed theoretically in the 1670s in a series of essays and pam-

---

This essay first appeared in *William and Mary Quarterly*, 23 (1966): 183–209. Minor alterations have been made in the footnotes.

phlets was transmuted to a considerable degree as a consequence both of a metamorphosis in his own thinking, once proprietarial authority was thrust upon him, and of the concessions he necessarily made to those whose support was indispensable in the founding of his New Jerusalem on the Delaware. The Frame of 1682, and the Frame of 1683, which was ultimately adopted in its place, represent, in effect, a failure of ideas in contact with realities.

At the root of Penn's problems in formulating a system of government was the need to capitalize his colonial enterprise. Fragmentary evidence, including the language of Penn's petition to the Crown for a patent in America, suggests that Penn himself was in financial straits in the early 1680s, perhaps because of his failing estates in Ireland and England.[2] That he had not subscribed even a partial share in the West Jersey enterprise, of which he was a principal mover, may be further evidence of his strained resources. And even if his finances were not in decay at the time, it would have been difficult, if not impossible, for Penn to underwrite singlehandedly such an undertaking. Penn later wrote that the expenses of petitioning for his patent and launching his visionary scheme had cost him £10,000 in the first two or three years.[3]

As a colonial promoter of no little experience, Penn must have recognized that the success of his colony hinged as much on his ability to attract wide financial support as to recruit settlers. The lessons of nearly a hundred years of English colonization were clear: success was unthinkable without the steady infusion of capital during the early years of settlement. Again and again colonial ventures had foundered on the rocks of inadequate financial backing, especially proprietary experiments such as those of Sir Ferdinando Gorges and the Carolina proprietors. Fortunately, by the 1680s English Quakerism, though identified chiefly with yeomen and shopkeeper-artisans, had attracted a considerable number of merchants and well-to-do gentry. Within a decade or so the "Richest Trading Men in London" were Quakers, according to one contemporary observer.[4] Upon these men Penn would count for a large part of his financial support.

Penn was singularly well connected in Quaker society to make his appeal. Not only in his endeavors for West New Jersey but as one of the intellectual leaders of the Quaker movement, he had circulated for years among the most affluent Friends, establishing cordial relations with merchants of note in all the urban centers of Quakerism—Dublin, Cork, Bristol, and London—and with the Quaker gentry in the countryside. Throughout the Quaker world his name drew admiration for his courageous efforts in the law courts and at Whitehall on behalf of the faith. No less intimate was his association with the religious leaders of the movement—George Fox, William Meade, Alexander Parker, George

Keith, Robert Barclay, Benjamin Furly, and others. Penn was often a companion on their proselytizing trips through England, Scotland, and Ireland, and even into the Rhineland and Holland.[5] When the Pennsylvania charter was granted in 1681, these friendships paid dividends. Every "Publick Friend," as the religious leaders were known, was a potential spokesman for Penn's undertaking. There were few who did not respond. Over the Society's well-developed lines of communication word went out: Penn's charter had passed the seals; plans were being readied; land grants could be obtained through Penn's agents in most of the major towns.

But even the exciting word of Penn's grant was probably not enough to attract the broad support of affluent Quakers. By 1682 a Friend intent on immigration to America or with capital to invest had a choice of three colonies dominated by Quakers: Pennsylvania, West Jersey, and East Jersey—the latter purchased by twelve Quaker proprietors, including Penn, even as plans for Pennsylvania went forward. Penn, like colonial promoters before him, had to pitch his appeal for backing on the argument that his colony was not only a haven for the oppressed but also a sound and perhaps astute investment. He had said himself in 1681 that "though I desire to extend religious freedom [in Pennsylvania], yet I want some recompense for my trouble."[6] Similarly, Penn recognized that he could best mobilize the support of well-to-do Friends by presenting Pennsylvania not only as a religious refuge—a place for the English Quakers to build their own "city on a hill"—but also as a field ripe for economic exploitation. The same motives which induced Quaker men of means to purchase shares in East and West Jersey, and to trade them speculatively throughout the 1680s, were at play in the purchase of large blocks of land in Pennsylvania.[7] Penn, in effect, was competing for investors with the other Quaker provinces. Thus, Robert Barclay, his promotional agent in Scotland, wrote in 1681 that the cheap price of East Jersey land "makes thine seem dear." "Thou has land enough," cautioned Barclay, "so need not be a churle if thou intend to advance thy plantation."[8]

The success of Penn's appeal to wealthy Quakers is evident in an analysis of the men who bought property directly from Penn in the first year of settlement. One surviving list of such First Purchasers, as those entitled to city lots were styled, shows land sales as of May 22, 1682, and reveals that of about 469 buyers, 41 subscribed to 241,000 acres, nearly half the total sales.[9] Another, which probably records purchases through late 1684, counts 751 purchasers, 69 of whom absorbed 380,000 of the 860,000 acres sold.[10] In both lists large purchasers, the "lords" or "barons" as Penn styled them, took up 5,000 acres or more each. What is notable is that while about two-thirds of the early purchasers immigrated to Pennsylvania, only about one-third of the baronial buyers—men with 5,000 acres or more—did so. Of 56 large purchasers in the first list, only 13 moved to Pennsylvania. On the last list only 20 of 69 pulled up roots in the Old World.

This upper stratum upon which Penn depended so heavily was studded with Quaker merchants, particularly from London, and to a lesser degree from Bristol and Dublin. Regardless of which list of purchasers is used, mercantile wealth is identifiable in more than half of the names. Richard Marsh, Robert Turner, Thomas Callowhill, Samuel Carpenter, Samuel Claridge, James Claypoole, Joseph Fisher, John Fuller, James Lyell, and many more—practically a roll call of eminent Quaker merchants in England and Ireland, with a scattering from elsewhere—make up the list. The other great investors were a potpourri of professional men, well-circumstanced landowners, and Penn's relatives and personal associates.[11] The purchases of some of these investors represented venture capital, mostly advanced for speculative purposes by men who had no intention of going to Pennsylvania. Of those who planned to take up life in the province, most, including the merchants, purchased land on the assumption that it would appreciate rapidly as new settlers sought property in Philadelphia and the surrounding countryside. A few of the gentry or prosperous yeomen, men like John Simcock, Thomas Brassey, Joseph Growden, and the landed leaders of the Welsh migration, sought a new life in the colony as country gentlemen. In short, Pennsylvania was founded primarily by yeomen and artisans who left England for both religious and economic reasons. But Penn, while seeking such sturdy settlers, relied on a far smaller number of wealthy men for the purchase of nearly half of the land and, what is more, for political leadership on the Delaware.

It is not surprising that in attempting to attract the support of the upper stratum of English Quakers Penn offered handsome rewards to those who would join him in the work of nation-building in the wilderness. It is not too much to say, in fact, that Penn, in forging plans for his colony, placed himself and his principal associates at the vital center of economic and political affairs. The distribution of land, the conferral of profitable offices, and the organization of government were all a part of this pattern.

From the earliest stages of planning, Penn conceived of a colony centering on a river capital, the seat of government and the hub of commercial activity. Property in the city was not offered for direct sale but reserved entirely for dividends meted out to the purchasers of the first 500,000 acres in proportion to country land "taken up upon rent," that is, purchased in fee simple from the proprietor and subject to an annual quit rent of one shilling per hundred acres.[12] Buyers of these "country lots" received 2 percent of their purchase in the form of "city lots," obviously to be the most valuable real estate in the province. The larger the purchase, the greater was the dividend in the capital city.[13]

Such an arrangement worked to the mutual benefit of Penn and the major investors. The tantalizing offer of a dominant position in city realty stimulated large purchases of land; the buyers, in turn, only one-third of whom would immigrate, could anticipate a handsome return on their investment as incoming settlers bid for property in the commercial center of the province. Whether Penn at this time privately offered the largest investors first consideration in the allocation of waterfront property is not known. Such a promise is not unlikely though, for when Penn actually assigned the city lots, after his arrival in October 1682, he did just this, situating his relations and those "that he had the Greatest regard for" on the most advantageous sites.[14]

As an additional means of welding to his interest a circle of wealthy adherents who would follow him to Pennsylvania, Penn utilized an enormous power of patronage. The proprietor, as will later be discussed, reserved for himself the right to appoint initially all proprietary, provincial, and county officers; each would serve, barring misbehavior, for life. Penn put this broad appointive power to good use. As Table 1 indicates, positions of profit and power went almost uniformly to men whose tangible commitment to the Holy Experiment was substantial.[15] Also noteworthy is that in striking contrast to both East and West New Jersey, the other Quaker colonies in the New World, dual officeholding was not forbidden in Pennsylvania and in fact was common practice.

Nicholas More, a purchaser of 10,000 acres, was appointed provincial secretary and clerk of the council, both positions of high influence. More was also president of the Free Society of Traders, a joint-stock company founded by a group of London Quakers, who, capitalizing on special privileges granted the company by Penn, planned to occupy a central position in the economic life of the young colony. Once in Pennsylvania, Penn added to More's titles by commissioning him chief justice of the provincial court. To Robert Turner, Penn's former agent in Dublin and a purchaser of 6,000 acres, went a seat on the powerful Board of Property created to administer the allocation of land in Penn's absence. Turner also sat on the provincial bench and in the Philadelphia county court and later became provincial treasurer. William Markham, Penn's kinsman and purchaser of 5,000 acres, functioned before Penn's arrival as deputy governor and thereafter as proprietary secretary and member of the Board of Property. Thomas Holme, another large landholder, was appointed Markham's assistant before Penn's arrival and then as receiver general for the Lower Counties (later the province of Delaware), surveyor general for the colony, and justice of the Philadel-

Table 1. Initial Appointments to Provincial and Proprietary
Offices in Pennsylvania

Office	Name	Land Purchased (Acres)	Religion	Occupation in England
Deputy Governor	William Markham	5,000	Anglican	Gentleman
Assistant Deputy Governor	Silas Crispin[a]	5,000	Quaker	Gentleman
	Thomas Holme	5,000	Quaker	Gentleman
Commissioners for	Silas Crispin[a]	5,000	Quaker	Gentleman
Settling the	William Haige	500	Quaker	Merchant
Colony	Nathaniel Allen	2,000	Quaker	Cooper
	John Bezar	1,000	Quaker	Maltster
Keeper of the Seal	Thomas Rudyard[b]	5,000	Quaker	Lawyer
	Thomas Lloyd	5,000	Quaker	Gentleman
Master of the Rolls	Thomas Rudyard[b]	5,000	Quaker	Lawyer
	Thomas Lloyd	5,000	Quaker	Gentleman
Receiver-General	Christopher Taylor	5,000	Quaker	School-teacher
Receiver-General for the Lower Counties	Thomas Holme	5,000	Quaker	Gentleman
Register-General	Christopher Taylor	5,000	Quaker	School-teacher
Provincial Sec'y and Clerk of Provincial Council	Richard Ingelo	500	Quaker	?
	Nicholas More	10,000	Anglican	Gentleman
Provincial Treas.	Robert Turner	6,000	Quaker	Merchant
Chief Justice of Provincial Court	Silas Crispin	5,000	Quaker	Gentleman
	Nicholas More	10,000	Anglican	Gentleman
Provincial Judges	William Welch		Quaker	Merchant
	William Wood	2,500	Quaker	Merchant
	Robert Turner	6,000	Quaker	Merchant
	John Eckley	1,250	Quaker	Yeoman
Attorney-General	John White	?	Quaker	?
Commissioners of	James Claypoole	10,000	Quaker	Merchant
Property	Robert Turner	6,000	Quaker	Merchant
	Thomas Lloyd	5,000	Quaker	Gentleman
	Samuel Carpenter	5,000	Quaker	Merchant
Proprietary Secretary	Philip Lehnman	1,000	Quaker	Gentleman
Proprietary Steward	James Harrison	5,000	Quaker	Shopkeeper

[a] Died en route to Pennsylvania
[b] Relinquished appointment to assume lieutenant-governorship of East New Jersey
[c] Served only five months

phia county court. Thomas Rudyard, Penn's trusted solicitor and legal draftsman in London, was rewarded for his 5,000-acre purchase with the important offices of Master of the Rolls and Keeper of the Seal. Hardly a position of influence or profit in the early years was allowed a man without at least a 5,000-acre investment in the province. Most appointees were also stockholders in the Free Society of Traders.

Of the First Purchasers of 5,000 acres or more who came to Pennsylvania before 1684, in fact, only four—John Simcock, Joseph Growdon, Thomas Brassey, and Griffith Jones—were not installed in high places. The first three chose to eschew city life in Philadelphia and established estates in the country where they were appointed to the county courts and assumed leading roles in county affairs. Jones was a special case. Well known to Penn as a Quaker merchant of London, he alone was left out of office, perhaps because of a querulous nature which was to involve him in litigation and acrimonious dispute during the next two decades. Looking at the question in another way, it can be said that of all the important officeholders, only three—William Clarke, William Welch, and William Haige—were not large buyers of Penn's real estate. Each of these men, however, was proprietor and vast landowner in West Jersey, and earlier an intimate of Penn in England. All were merchants, all were Quakers; Haige and Clarke, who preceded Penn to the Delaware, were already experienced in matters in settlement. Haige and Welch died within a few years but Clarke lived on to become Penn's most trusted officeholder in the Lower Counties and the most important figure on the lower Delaware Bay.

That Penn should establish an administrative and economic system which delivered power and advantage to those who invested most heavily in his plan is hardly surprising. Like any prudent manager of a large enterprise he sought support in the wealthiest and most experienced sector of his constituency. Conversely, these men, in return for financial backing and for their willingness to start life anew in a distant wilderness, expected compensation. Notwithstanding what has been written about Quaker egalitarianism, one searches in vain for evidence that Pennsylvania was ever conceived as an economic or political democracy in nineteenth- or twentieth-century terms. Nothing could have been more natural than the transplanting of an ordered society where position and power resided in those whose stake in the venture was the largest.

Beyond the terms of land distribution and the pattern of patronage, one must turn to the most central aspect of the governmental apparatus which was constructed in London in 1681 and 1682—the Frame of 1682, a constitutional scheme under which Pennsylvania was to be governed. The absence of conclusive evidence leaves any hypothesis open to question, but there are strong indications that Penn's circle of backers caused him to deviate markedly from his own ideas on government in favor of a system more to their liking and advantage. At the same time, in accommodating their demands, Penn seems to have taken a second hard look at the experiment he was promoting and to have sought powers as proprietor and governor that earlier he might have considered extreme.

It needs to be understood, in discussing Penn's political ideas, that consistency was never a characteristic feature of the proprietor's thinking, and that even at the time when plans for Pennsylvania were going forward Penn was capable of philosophical vacillation.[16] On the one hand, he had long been in the vanguard of those Restoration critics who contended that English rights and liberties were being endangered by creeping licentiousness and authoritarianism. His efforts on behalf of religious toleration and civil liberties in the 1670s were unmatched by any Englishman of his time. In memorials to Parliament, the sheriffs of London, and to justices and Lords; in speeches before parliamentary committees and Charles II; and in treatises such as *The Great Case of Liberty of Conscience* (1670), *England's Present Interest* (1675), *An Address to Protestants of all Persuasions* (1679), *England's Great Interest in the Choice of This New Parliament* (1679), and *One Project for The Good of England* (1679), Penn had enunciated a call for moderation and sympathy in affairs of church and state and for a recognition of the populace as the ultimate source of political sovereignty. Here was a man entirely at home with "commonwealth-men" of his era, who sought to follow Milton's injunction that Englishmen must teach the nations how to live. But at the same time, Penn revealed himself an essentially conservative thinker, committed to a political order based on property, in favor of a social system which upheld "all reasonable distinction and those civil degrees that are amongst people," and filled with a downright aversion to the "mob" and the "rabble."[17] That freedom was endangered "by the ambitions of the populace which shakes the constitution,"[18] was not an atypical statement for Penn to make in the 1670s. At moments, indeed, Penn seemed to project a nostalgic longing for the feudal past with its well-ordered society and its "old time Nobility and Gentry."[19] Even in America he likened his provincial councilors to the English "Knights of Shires."[20]

Despite these sometimes antagonistic tendencies in his thought, Penn did commit himself wholeheartedly to one constitutional document of the 1670s—the West New Jersey Concessions and Agreements of 1677, published as fundamental law for the western half of the Jerseys, which Edward Byllynge purchased in 1675. Although Penn's authorship of the Concessions and Agreements has been questioned, there is little doubt that many of his ideas found expression in the document and that as a trustee of the colony he gave it his full consent.[21] In this sense it is indicative of his thinking on matters of civil polity during this period. By its provisions the Concessions delivered all legislative power to an assembly chosen by the "inhabitants, freeholders and proprietors" of the colony. The legislature was also to constitute courts and define the jurisdiction of each, appoint the principal public officers, choose its own speaker, meet and adjourn as it saw fit, and appoint a ten-man commission to act in an executive capacity. Justices of the peace and local officeholders were to be elected. Complete freedom of religion and explicit guarantees of trial by jury were included.[22] As Penn and five other trustees wrote even before the document was published, "we lay a foundation for after ages to understand their liberty as men and christians, that they may not be brought in bondage, but by their own consent; for we put the power in the people. . . ."[23]

The West Jersey Concessions perhaps went further than even Penn might have been expected to go. "Only rarely in the progress of limited government have men been able to achieve out of conflict and suffering such enlightened views of human society," it has recently been written of those who formulated the document.[24] By personal preference, Penn might have hewed closer to the enlightened constitutional theory of the time, which prescribed a balance of strong and independent governmental powers as the safeguard against tyranny.[25] Just such a system was believed to be embodied, at least theoretically, in the English government—an equilibrium of monarchy, aristocracy, and democracy as represented by King, Lords, and Commons. Most of the colonies, distributing power among governor, council, and assembly, after the English example, reflected this emphasis on equipoise. Also, Penn might logically have made other modifications of the concept of limited government simply because his charter to Pennsylvania was proprietarial in form.

Beyond such conjectures one can move to firmer ground, guided by a series of seventeen constitutional drafts in which the evolution of the Frame of 1682 can be traced.[26] That the end product varied so significantly from Penn's expressed views of earlier years and even from his initial attempts to formulate a constitution is clear evidence that either his political philosophy underwent a complete reorientation, or, as is more likely, that he yielded to the demands of persons he was in no position to ignore.

The first draft of the Frame of 1682 projected a system far less liberal than governments in other colonies, themselves not so committed to government by consent as the West Jersey plan. The governor was to be assisted by a parliament consisting of two houses. The upper chamber, analogous to the House of Lords, would include the first fifty purchasers of 5,000 acres or more; they would comprise a self-perpetuating aristocracy, their seats devolving to their heirs. Styled "lords," the members were to sit and adjourn at their own pleasure, nominate all officers in church and state, and delegate committees drawn from both houses to supervise financial and military affairs. Their consent was necessary to the passage of laws. The lower house contained "renters"—the smaller landowners—or their delegates. Theirs was the function of initiating laws.[27]

Although it has been suggested that Penn was not the author of such a "government by a landed aristocracy," the two-house parliament, stripped of the hereditary feature in the upper chamber, was the essence of the next five drafts, many of them interlineated in Penn's hand.[28] The only major innovation was the addition of a council, chosen by the proprietor from a double list of names nominated by the parliament, to assist in the executive functions of government. Untouched was the power of the lower house to initiate legislation and the right of the large landowners to sit as an upper house with power to nominate most provincial and county officers and to pass on bills presented by the lower chamber. Though somewhat unwieldy, it was a scheme of government which attempted a rough division of power among the governor, the two houses of parliament, and the executive council.

But abruptly, after the first six drafts, an entirely new direction was taken. Departing from the previous formula, the new draft greatly magnified the power of both proprietor and large landowners while reducing that of the lower house. Behind the shift, apparently, was a lengthy critique of the earlier drafts by Thomas Rudyard, Penn's lawyer and one of his closest advisers.[29] Although there is no direct evidence that Rudyard's criticisms reflected the ideas of the men around Penn, a number of factors point to this conclusion. As a prominent London Quaker and a man of affairs, Rudyard was in close touch with almost all of Penn's substantial supporters. He had first been connected with Penn in 1670 at the renowned Penn-Meade trial, and by 1681 was deeply involved in Quaker affairs in East and West New Jersey. It was to Rudyard's home in George Yard, Lombard Street, that prospective emigrants came in that year to obtain details of West Jersey or to purchase land. Similarly, throughout the period when Penn was piecing together a model of government, Rudyard, himself a purchaser of 5,000 acres, was busily drawing up land deeds and other documents for Pennsylvania.[30] That he was appointed deputy governor of East New Jersey only six months later was a measure of the confidence which moneyed Quakers placed in him. It is difficult to believe that his appraisal of the drafts of government, as they had evolved by late 1681, were not related to the objections of other important Pennsylvania investors.

The interest of such men in the pattern of government was doubtless great—and hardly unexpected. This was an era alive with the controversial questions of a possible Catholic succession, foreign domination, parliamentary privileges, and the legitimate boundaries of the King's power. Leading their lives in the urban centers of English life, the Quaker elite was keenly aware of, if not actually involved in, these significant political issues. Ten of the major purchasers, as proprietors of West New Jersey, knew well of the dispute that raged between Edward Byllynge and the inhabitants of the colony even as the plans for Pennsylvania went forward. The issue involved the right to elect a deputy governor. Byllynge, chief proprietor of the colony, claimed the privilege for himself since the Duke of York, in confirming his title to West Jersey in 1680, had conferred upon him the right of government. The popularly elected assembly, on the other hand, viewed this as an invasion of a right belonging solely to it under the Concessions of 1677.[31] The controversy was an object lesson in the potential dangers of a proprietary government, especially should the proprietor attempt to exercise his authority from England. It was natural that Penn's supporters, as prudent businessmen, should act to protect their investment in Pennsylvania by safeguarding against such possibilities. Who knew when Penn, the "true and absolute Proprietor," might die, to be succeeded by a son or heir whose interests were antagonistic to their own? Or who could guarantee that Penn, like Byllynge, might not become a distant source of power, an absentee proprietor exercising prerogative power from England?

Rudyard, in his appraisal of Penn's drafts of government, argued that the proprietor must alter his initial conception of a landed aristocracy sitting as an upper house with powers analogous to the Lords in England. Such a system was based on an early plan, copied from West Jersey, to sell one hundred "proprieties" of 5,000 acres or more, allowing men of more slender means to buy land in turn from these proprietors.[32] This system had already been discarded in favor of a more flexible program whereby Penn offered small tracts to husbandmen and yeomen while advertising baronial estates to a limited number of wealthy men who would enjoy semi-autonomous privileges, renting out lands to tenants, holding seignorial courts, and exercising administrative authority within their domains.[33] Viewing the sluggish market for manorial tracts, Rudyard questioned whether there would be enough proprietors for the upper house of the bicameral parliament. Even if there were, he argued, such an aristocratic system would "reflect on us as a people who affect Grandure beyond our pretensons, and sett up that in state pollity which in our religious Capacity we have struck against beyond any people whatsoever." Needed instead was a less formal system, based not on some abstract idea of a provincial nobility, but on a working aristocracy vested with a central and functional role in the government. Legislative power, suggested Rudyard, should be concentrated in a single house, controlled by the wealthiest members of the community—not by prescription but simply out of the natural acquiescence which lesser settlers would yield to such men. In England persons of modest income, but entitled to vote, were twenty to forty times more numerous than those of great estate. But rarely, if ever, was a man of less than £500 to £1,000 yearly income elected. So it would be in Pennsylvania. To concentrate the 5,000-acre proprietors in an upper house as planned would be doubly disadvantageous. Not only would they lack the legislative initiative, but the lesser freemen, seeing their betters congregated in an upper house, would be encouraged to elect men of their own station to the lower house—a situation which "may in all probability breed differences and Emulations between the upper and lower houses, and hinder dispatch of busyness."[34]

It may have been at this point, though the absence of dates on many of the drafts makes sequential ordering indeterminable, that Penn wrote his most liberal draft of government, "The Fundamentall Constitutions of Pennsylvania."[35] The document, which is among the most carefully wrought of Penn's constitutional drafts, is prefaced by the proprietor's reflections on theories of government—an essay which in content and phraseology closely parallels the preamble to the Frame of 1682. Central to the Fundamental Constitutions was the idea that the preponderant governmental power should rest with the freeholders. The legislative assembly would consist of two houses. The lower house, comprising 384 members, elected annually, and enjoying all the privileges known to the English House of Commons, would alone propose and pass laws. By an extraordinary clause, each member was required to bring instructions from his electors to the first session of the assembly where a copy would be made and registered. No money bill could be voted upon until referred to the freemen in each of the electoral districts. The second branch of government, the council, would include 48 members chosen by the lower house from among its own members for three-year terms. In legislative matters the council was purely a consultative body, sitting with the governor to make recommendations upon bills initiated in assembly, but possessing no negative power. Council's most important function was to exercise executive supervision in the colony through its committees of justice, trade, treasury, and "manners and education." Further articles in the Fundamental Constitutions provided for the annual election in cities and towns of justices of the peace, bailiffs, sheriffs, and constables. In the counties the governor or his deputy would choose sheriffs and justices from a double list presented by the electorate. Individual liberties were protected by guarantees of freedom of religion, due process, jury trial in the vicinage, habeas corpus, monthly sessions of county courts, and the prohibition of imprisonment for debt. That the Fundamental Constitutions contrasted so sharply with earlier drafts of government and that the document was given close consideration is indicative of Penn's fluid state of mind as blueprints for his government were on the drawing board in London.

Penn's close associate in Rotterdam, Benjamin Furly, was among those consulted in the drafting of the Fundamental Constitutions. Indeed, Furly believed that Penn had committed himself to these articles of government, which he deemed excellent.[36] But at some point in the early months of 1682 Penn reverted to a far less liberal scheme of government. New constitutional drafts were made, providing for an upper house of the seventy-two men in the colony "most eminent for vertue Wisdom and Substance," to be elected by the freemen. The right of initiating legislation, except in bills related to "Publick moneys," was transferred from the lower to the upper house. Several drafts later the lower chamber was stripped of any role whatsoever in the initiation of legislation, leaving it with only a right of consent. The ultimate step came in the fourteenth draft. The functions of the governor's council and the upper house of the legislature were combined, fusing in one body control of legislative, executive, and judicial matters according to a pattern not unfamiliar in other colonies.[37]

What remained was an emasculated lower house, restricted to a nine-day annual session, and allowed only to approve or negate laws proposed by council, to impeach criminals, and, after Penn died, to nominate county sheriffs, coroners, and justices of the peace. It could not initiate legislation as could Parliament at home or the lower houses in neighboring colonies. Nor could it elect its own speaker, as had been allowed in earlier drafts, or sit on its own adjournment, another right commonly enjoyed in adjacent provinces. In fact, as Penn subsequently pointed out, the lower house had no real existence of its own, but represented simply those delegates chosen annually to sit in a "General Assembly" with the councilors and to pass on laws structured by the governor and council. It did not possess the power even to debate a proposed law or to ask for the amendment of a clause within it. "The Assembly, as they call themselves," wrote Penn later in attacking the ambitions of the self-styled lower house,

> is not so, without Governor and P[rovincial] councel, and that no Speaker clarke [clerk] or book [minutes] belong to them that the people have their representatives in the Pro. Councell

to prepare, and the Assembly as it is called, has only the power of I or no, yea or nay. If they turn debators, or Judges, or complainers, you overthrow the Charter quite in the very root of the constitution of it, for that is to usurp the P[rovincial] councels part in the Charter and to forfit the Charter itself: here would be two assemblys and two representatives, whereas they are but one, to two works, one prepares and proposes, the other assents or denys—the negative voyce is by that in them, and that is not a debateing, mending, altering, but an accepting power.[38]

The council, on the other hand, was endowed with sweeping legislative, executive, and judicial powers. Included was the all-important right of initiative and also authority (with the governor) to erect courts, preserve the peace and safety of the province, situate cities, ports, and market towns, regulate all matters relating to public buildings, roads, and marketplaces, judge impeached criminals, execute the laws, and supervise the treasury. The proprietor, as governor, also possessed extensive powers. He sat as the presiding officer in council where he held a triple vote. More important he held sole power of appointment to all proprietary, provincial, and county officers—judges, treasurers, masters of the rolls, sheriffs, justices of the peace, and coroners. Only after the initial round of appointments—the appointees would serve for life barring misbehavior—would the power to nominate a double list of officers for the governor's choice devolve on council, for provincial officers, and the electorate in each country, for county officers.[39]

In comparison with either the West New Jersey Concessions and Agreements of 1677 or the New York Charter of Libertyes of 1683, Penn's Frame of 1682 represents a rather restrictive system of government. In both neighboring colonies the lower house existed as a discrete legislative body, possessing power of initiative and the right to meet on its own adjournment without time limitations. West New Jersey adopted a far more liberal voting requirement—in effect, all free male inhabitants were qualified—and provided, in contrast to Pennsylvania, the appointment of administrative and judicial officers through either public election or assembly choice.[40] Even in East New Jersey the impossibly complex Fundamental Constitution of 1683 conferred greater power on the elected assembly than was allowed in Pennsylvania, and provided for the election of justices of the peace, sheriffs, and petty officers by the freemen of the boroughs and hundreds.[41]

Penn, in short, had finally determined on a constitutional system where political power was concentrated in the governor and his council. Belatedly he had realized, or been made to understand, that neither his initial plans for a parliamentary system nor his later more liberal schemes were feasible or acceptable. Men of substance, upon whom he relied for leadership and financial backing, would not exchange carefully cultivated estates in England for the uncertainties of a proprietary wilderness unless they were conceded extensive power.

What has obscured the vision of many historians in pondering the division of power in the final frame of government is the provision that the seventy-two councilors (the council was reduced to eighteen in the first year of settlement) be elected by the freemen. Historians have sometimes read twentieth-century democracy back into seventeenth-century documents. But men of influence at the time, as Thomas Rudyard stated, knew what sort of man should and would reach office. The "Laws Agreed Upon in England," a series of forty statutes to be ratified in Pennsylvania, indicated plainly that any Christian of twenty-one years who possessed one hundred acres of land (fifty acres if he had been released from indenture within the preceding year) or who paid scot and lot, a property owners' municipal tax, was eligible to vote.[42] This probably enfranchised about one-half the adult males or one-eighth of the total population.[43] But who attained the high office of councilor was another question. Men of this era understood—and early elections in Pennsylvania would confirm their belief—that only those of considerable estate, demonstrably successful in their private affairs and proven leaders at the local level, could expect to reach the council. Early Pennsylvania was to be a deferential society, hierarchically structured and paternalistic, for Quakers had no more difficulty than did other Englishmen in reconciling spiritual egalitarianism with a traditional view of the natural ordering of social classes. An elective council little threatened the pivotal position which Penn's moneyed supporters expected to occupy.

Two of Penn's advisors, neither of whom intended to immigrate to Pennsylvania, well knew that Penn had forsaken earlier ideals of balanced government and openly expressed their dismay at the concentration of political power in the hands of a proprietary-oriented elite. Algernon Sidney, Penn heard, attacked the Frame of Government as "the basest laws in the world, and not to be endured or lived under. . . ." Even "the Turk was not more absolute" than the proprietor, claimed Sidney according to reports reaching Penn's ears.[44]

Benjamin Furly, Penn's learned friend in Rotterdam, was no less vehement in opposition. He had seen earlier drafts of government, especially the Fundamental Constitutions, before the lower house had been stripped of the initiative. "I wonder who should put thee upon altering them [the earlier drafts] for these, And as much how thou couldst ever yield to such a thing. . . . Who has turned you aside from these good beginnings to establish things unsavory and unjust," demanded Furly.

Specifically the Rotterdam merchant lamented the curtailment of the assembly's initiative and power to sit on its own adjournment. This "divesting of the peoples representatives (in time to come) of the greatest right they have . . . will lay morally a certain foundation for dissention amongst our successors." The "patronizers of this new frame," he warned prophetically, would be repugnant to future assemblies. Englishmen, Furly warned, "can never, by any prescription of time be dispossessed of that naturall right of propounding laws to be made by their representatives." To have a "great nation" ruled by only such laws as forty-eight men [a quorum of council] should think fit, and they susceptible to be "corrupted" by a governor with a triple voice in council, "is not consistent with the publick safety which is and always will remain, the supreme law." Finally, Furly expressed his dismay that the assembly had lost its vote in the appointment of public officials and that nowhere in the frame was the legislative veto power of the governor explicitly denied.[45]

Among other critics of Penn's frame of government were George Hutcheson and Jasper Batt, two of the best-known Quakers in the west of England in the late 1670s. Hutcheson, a proprietor of West New Jersey and one of its most important officeholders and politicians after immigrating to the Delaware in 1681, reported that Penn was "reflected upon" in West Jersey for his government and laws.[46] Batt, who preached at George Fox's funeral and was denoted the "greatest seducer in all the West" by the Bishop of Bath and Wells,[47] was more specific. When he first viewed the Frame of 1682 in the company of Penn's London associates, Batt confided, he was ready to accept its worth. But returning to the west country he encountered trenchant criticisms of a governmental scheme, which, upon closer examination, revealed the virtually unshakeable control which the governor and those close to him could potentially exert. The Frame, Batt pointed out, did not specifically allow the governor a negative voice in the passage of laws. But four distinct clauses of the Frame stated that all laws must be prepared by the governor and the provincial council. "What need the Governor a negative voyce in passing of lawes," chided Batt, "when he have it before, and none must be prepared or offered but what he first assents unto. . . . Indeed if no bills were to be past into law in England by the Commons but what the king first with his Council prepared for them, there were no need of the kings passing them at last. To me here is all the difference, the Governor there must first passe it, and here the king after passe it." Penn, concluded Batt, exercised more power in government than the king in England, not to speak of his expansive tenurial rights as proprietor.[48]

No conspiratorial overtones need be attached to this apparently conscious attempt of Penn and the principal colonizers to vest themselves with effective political control. These were men whose own sufferings as members of a persecuted sect had bred in them a keen sense of history and a watchful attitude toward their fellow men. Too, they were transferring their estates to a colony granted under semifeudal conditions. It is not surprising that those who risked their fortunes and uprooted their lives would seek every possible security for life in the Delaware wilderness. Likewise they might well have expected special concessions in the allocation of land and first consideration in the distribution of profit-bearing offices. But no advantage outweighed that of political control—of a governmental system insulated to the greatest possible degree from pressures exerted from above and below.

Penn did not find the arguments for a weak assembly and a strong council unconvincing. He was highly aristocratic himself and in political theory no dogmatist. "I do not find a model in the world," he wrote in the preface to the Frame of 1682, "that time, place, and some singular emergences have not necessarily altered; nor is it easy to frame a civil government, that shall serve all places alike." To this statement he added another defense of his pragmatic approach—and one which suggests some need to justify his departure from original plans:

> There is hardly one frame of government in the world so ill designed by its first founders, that, in good hands, would not do well enough. . . . Governments, like clocks, go from the motion men give them, and as governments are made and moved by men, so by them they are ruined too. Wherefore governments rather depend upon men, than men upon governments.[49]

It was this emphasis on the personnel rather than on the structure of government, quite the reverse of conventional Whiggish dogma, that permitted Penn to be swayed from initial plans for a government modeled on more advanced thinking. Moreover, his outlook on man at this time, while he was in the full euphoria of establishing a Quaker utopia, was Lockean rather than Hobbesian.[50] Almost all of the great early purchasers were fellow Quakers, many of them close associates and intimate friends. Penn had every reason to believe that his Holy Experiment would be safe in their hands, especially since he planned personally to assume the role of governor in Pennsylvania. "Let men be good," he pronounced, "and the government cannot be bad."[51]

Furthermore, Penn had compromised only one element in his plans for government. Inviolably secure was the cornerstone of religious toleration, the object of a whole decade of labors in England. Also firmly rooted were an enlightened judicial system and penal code, positive safeguards for property and individual liberty, and such Harringtonian devices as the use of the secret ballot, controls against political chicanery, and the rotation of offices.[52] Here was a constitution which, despite its departures from his earlier concepts of government, could translate his noble vision into reality.

As complex and protracted as the organization of the machinery of government had been, a final crisis could not be averted when the Frame of 1682 was submitted for ratification in Pennsylvania. Shortly after his arrival in Pennsylvania in October 1682, Penn called for the election of seven delegates from each of the six counties erected. On December 4, 1682, the forty-two representatives gathered at Chester to confirm or revise the Frame of 1682, the "Laws Agreed upon in England" (a combined civil and criminal code, including certain fundamental laws concerned with the protection of individual rights), and a series of additional laws drafted by the proprietor after his arrival.[53] It was no surprise that most of Penn's supporters and officeholders secured election—Holme, Taylor, More, Clarke, Simcock, Jones, Withers, Brassey, and others.[54] But from the three Lower Counties came representatives of the older Swedish, Dutch, and English settlers, most of them apprehensive about the sudden takeover of territory and government by the proprietor and his small circle. For nearly a decade English tobacco planters had been drifting into the lower Delaware area from adjacent counties in Maryland, taking up land patents under the Duke of York's deputies and gradually replacing the Swedes. When Penn received his charter more than one thousand people populated the Lower Counties—Sussex, Kent, and New Castle—arranged in a tier from the mouth of the Delaware Bay northward to the town of New Castle.[55] Now their representatives seemed little ready to accede to the proprietor's requests. The speakership nearly fell to a non-Quaker, "Friends carrying it but by one voyce, and that through the absence of 2 of the other side that were not Friends," Penn wrote in dismay.[56]

The confrontation of old and new, Quaker and non-Quaker, Penn's associates and independent adventurers, had grave consequences for the entire machinery of proprietary management. In a series of moves the convention struck at Penn's system. Proposals were made, as Benjamin Furly had predicted, to overthrow the council's monopoly in initiating legislation by allowing "any Member [of the lower house to] offer any Bill, publick or private, tending to the publick Good, except in Case of levying Taxes." Nineteen of the ninety laws proposed by Penn were rejected outright. Most significant, both the Frame of 1682 and the law confirming the charter of the Free Society of Traders were voted down.[57] Obviously a majority of representatives had arrayed themselves against central aspects of Penn's governmental system. Fissures in the community had been opened that would not quickly heal.

A new attempt to ratify the constitutional instruments was made three months later in March 1683. Recognizing that the 72 councilors and 200 representatives to the General Assembly allowed by the Frame of 1682 was far too cumbersome and unrealistic a number for the sparsely populated frontier society, Penn consented to the election of 3 councilors and 9 assemblymen from each county.[58] When the election returns were in, it was clear that council would be dominated by Penn's associates. Half of the councilors chosen were principal officeholders and purchasers of land, while several others, Quakers who had settled on the Delaware before Penn's grant, were now equally bound to the proprietor. In the lower house of the General Assembly sat an uneasy company of Quaker and non-Quaker, new settler and old, English and non-English. One characteristic alone bound them together: almost none was tied to the proprietor by appointive office or involvement in the Free Society of Traders. Those from the upper counties were Quaker with few exceptions; from the Lower Counties came mostly non-Quaker settlers of the pre-Penn era.[59]

The principal task of the General Assembly was to model a new frame of government in place of the rejected Frame of 1682. Debate focused on the proper distribution of power among proprietor, council, and assembly—the same thorny problem mooted so laboriously in England.[60] But now, assent was needed from the very body which had been relegated to virtual impotency—the lower house. By rights, the matter should not have come before that body at all, for by Penn's reckoning the Frame of 1682 would be endorsed by the ratifying convention dominated by his associates. And even if the Frame should fail, Penn might logically have reasoned, the lower house would defer to the "wisdom, virtue, and ability" of the provincial councilors in the work of devising a new Frame. Now, the assembly was becoming instead the agency of antiproprietary sentiment. Half the seats were occupied by non-Quakers from the Lower Counties, and others by those eager to enlarge the assembly's role. Only an unsubstantial minority, composed of Quakers from the Upper Counties, remained firm in their support of Penn, demonstrating an allegiance more characteristic of the councilors.[61] Council, though supporting Penn on the whole, sought subtle reductions of his power.

Upon one issue, the unmanageable size of both legislative houses, there was general accord. Accordingly, the council and assembly were reduced from 72 and 200 respectively to 18 and 36 in the new Frame of Government under preparation. Agreement was reached on little else. Of foremost concern was the question of the governor's voice in legislative matters. In England, Penn, eager to promote his colony, had at first reserved for himself only a single voice in council and no negative power at all. In its final form, however, the Frame of 1682 allowed him a triple voice in council, a virtual negative in the preparing of bills, as Jasper Batt had indicated, and power to withhold approval of any constitutional alterations. Once in Pennsylvania Penn apparently took a harder look at his charter from the king. Two provisions were clear: firstly, laws were to be made by the proprietor "with the advice, assent, and approbation of the freemen." As was later pointed out, this seemed to mean that Penn was obliged by the specifications of his charter to reserve a negative power for himself.[62] Secondly, Penn was obliged to "stand security" to the Crown for any damages resulting from colonial violations of the acts of trade, as ascertained in any English court. In effect, Penn was assuming financial liability for the behavior of his entire colony. It was a provision unknown to earlier colonial charters and reflective of attempts in England to obtain adherence to the navigation acts, frequently evaded and ignored in the colonies during the previous decade.

Meeting with council, Penn announced his intention to obtain either a negative voice in legislation or the colonists' countersecurity for observance of the navigation acts. After lengthy debate the council agreed to allow the governor a negative voice rather than cast a lien on their own estates.[63] At the same time the councilors' appetite for power was satisfied by curbing the governor's right to act in matters of justice, trade, finance, or defense without their "advice and consent."[64] Since virtually every public matter came under one of these heads, council obtained a large degree of control over the proprietor's executive authority.

The Assembly only reluctantly accepted the innovation of the governor's negative power in the new Frame of 1683, for a majority in that body continued to chafe at the insignificant role allowed them. Repeating a request made at the December 1682 convention, they proposed that the lower house be allowed the power of initiative. Although council and proprietor spurned this proposal, they were "condescential" to the less important request that the Assembly be allowed the privilege of conferring with the upper house. It was a concession only large enough to whet the appetite of a majority in the assembly who outspokenly cast "Reflections and Aspersions . . . upon the Governor," according to the complaint of Penn's supporters.[65] Endorsement of the Free Society of Trader's charter could not be obtained.

On April 2, 1683, after more than three weeks of deliberations, the new constitution, called the Frame of 1683 or the Charter of Liberties, was endorsed by the General Assembly and engrossed on parchment. That evening, before the members of the General Assembly and other inhabitants of Philadelphia who attended the session, Penn signed the constitutional document under which Pennsylvania was governed until Penn's rights of government were suspended a decade later.[66]

At best the constitution represented a bundle of compromises which failed to satisfy any of the parties involved. Nicholas More, the colony's largest landowner and one of its leaders, adamantly opposed the changes and maintained in heat that those who were party to it might be "impeacht for Treason for what you do."[67] The allegiance of other members of the proprietary circle was no more enduring. The lower house, as the representatives to the General Assembly collectively thought of themselves, never gave up their struggle for greater power and recognition. So inflamed did subsequent relations become between the council and assembly and between factions within each body, that Penn, within two years, was imploring the colonial leaders "for the love of God, me and the poor country [to] be not so governmentish, so noisy and open in your dissatisfactions."[68] A year later he wrote in despair at the political confusion in his colony, "It almost temps me to deliver up the colony to the K[ing]—and lett a mercenary government have the tameing of them."[69] Already the Holy Experiment was in disarray, plagued by factionalism, disorderly pursuit of office, and acrimonious dispute over the proper form of government. From such political instability Pennsylvania would not recover for several decades.

NOTES

1. Markham to Gov. Benjamin Fletcher, May 26, 1696, *Calendar of State Papers, Colonial Series, America and West Indies, 1696–97* (London, 1904), 17.

2. Penn's petition is in Samuel Hazard, ed., *Annals of Pennsylvania From the Discovery of the Delaware, 1609–1682* (Philadelphia, 1850), 474. See also Charles M. Andrews, *The Colonial Period of American History* (New Haven, 1934–38), 3:278.

3. Penn to James Logan, Sept. 14, 1705, in Edward Armstrong, ed., *The Correspondence of William Penn and James Logan . . .* (Philadelphia, 1879–80), 2:71; Penn to Robert Harley, Feb. 9, 1704, in Historical Manuscripts Commission, *Reports, Duke of Portland Manuscripts*, 4 (London, 1897), 80.

4. Charles Leslie, *The Snake in the Grass* (London, 1698), 362, quoted in Frederick B. Tolles, *Meeting House and Counting House: The Quaker Merchants of Colonial Philadelphia, 1682–1763* (Chapel Hill, 1948), 48.

5. The intimacy of Penn with the leading figures of the Society of Friends can be traced in William C. Braithwaite, *The Second Period of Quakerism* (London, 1921), and in John L. Nickalls, ed., *The Journal of George Fox* (Cambridge, Eng., 1952).

6. Penn to ———, July, 1681, quoted in William R. Shepherd, *History of Proprietary Government in Pennsylvania* (New York, 1896), 175.

7. For trading of East N.J. shares, see, for example, James Claypoole to Thomas Cooke, Nov. 11, 1682, Claypoole Letter Book, Historical Society of

Pennsylvania, Philadelphia. All manuscript sources quoted hereafter are at Hist. Soc. of Pa. unless otherwise noted.

8. Barclay to Penn, Nov. 29, 1681, Francis F. Hart Collection. The competition for settlers led to serious friction between Pennsylvania and West New Jersey in the early years of settlement. See *New Jersey Archives,* 1st Ser., 1 (Newark, 1880), 415–21.

9. The list is printed in Hazard, ed., *Annals,* 637–42.

10. Pennsylvania Cash Accounts, Penn Papers. Cf. John E. Pomfret, "The First Purchasers of Pennsylvania, 1681–1700," *Pennsylvania Magazine of History and Biography,* 80 (1956): 148–50.

11. Biographical data on the first generation of colonists must be sought in widely scattered sources. The most important are the eighty-nine volumes of the *Pa. Mag. of Hist. and Biog.* for which the *Index* to volumes 1–75 is an invaluable aid; editorial notes in Norman Penney, ed., *The Journal of George Fox* (Cambridge, Eng., 1911), and Norman Penney, ed., *The Short Journal and Itinerary Journals of George Fox* (Cambridge, Eng., 1925); John W. Jordan, ed., *Colonial Families of Philadelphia* (New York, 1911); Wilfred Jordan, ed., *Colonial and Revolutionary Families of Philadelphia* (New York, 1933–60); Joseph Besse, *A Collection of the Sufferings of the People Called Quakers . . .* (London, 1753); William W. Hinshaw, ed., *Encyclopedia of American Quaker Genealogy* (Ann Arbor, 1936–50); and the extensive collections, both manuscript and published, at the Genealogical Society of Pennsylvania, the Historical Society of Pennsylvania, and Friends House, London.

12. A statement of terms on which land could be purchased and held, the Conditions and Concessions, was issued in July 1681. Hazard, ed., *Annals,* 516–20.

13. Lawrence Lewis, Jr., *An Essay on Original Land Titles in Philadelphia* (Philadelphia, 1880), 65–68.

14. Minutes of the Board of Property, Oct. 20, 1712, in *Pennsylvania Archives,* 2d Ser. (Harrisburg, 1874–90), 19:532.

15. Most of the early appointments are listed in John Hill Martin, *Martin's Bench and Bar of Philadelphia . . .* (Philadelphia, 1883) and in *Pa. Archives,* 2d Ser., 9:607–766. Neither compilation, however, is wholly accurate and has been here corrected and supplemented by the multitude of commissions found in the Penn Papers, Pemberton Papers, Etting Collection and Society Miscellaneous Collection, Historical Society of Pennsylvania; the Penn Manuscripts and Ancient Documents, American Philosophical Society; and Deed Books C-1, C-2, E-1/5 and E-2/5, Recorder of Deeds, City Hall, Philadelphia.

16. Penn's inconstancy in political philosophy is best discussed in Edward C. O. Beatty, *William Penn as a Social Philosopher* (New York, 1939), 20–41. For other views of his political theory see Mary Maples, "A Cause to Plead: The Political Thought and Career of William Penn from 1660 to 1701" (unpubl. Ph.D. diss., Bryn Mawr College, 1959); and Richard J. Oman, "William Penn: A Study in the Quaker Doctrine of Political Authority" (unpubl. Ph.D. diss., University of Edinburgh, 1958).

17. Joseph Dorfman, *The Economic Mind in American Civilization,*

1606–1933 (New York, 1946–59), 1:80, quoting Penn, *An Address to Protestants.*

18. Quoted in Beatty, *William Penn,* 38.

19. William Penn, *Some Account of the Province of Pennsilvania* (London, 1681), in Albert C. Myers, ed., *Narratives of Early Pennsylvania, West New Jersey and Delaware* (New York, 1912), 205. For this vein in Penn's thinking see also Anthony N. B. Garvan, "Proprietary Philadelphia as Artifact," in Oscar Handlin and John Burchard, eds., *The Historian and the City* (Cambridge, Mass., 1963), 177–201.

20. Penn to William Clarke, ca. Feb. 1683, *Pa. Archives,* 2d Ser., 7:6.

21. See John L. Nickalls, "The Problem of Edward Byllynge. Part 2. His Writings and Their Evidence of his Influence on the First Constitution of West Jersey," in Howard H. Brinton, ed., *Children of Light* (New York, 1938), 111–31; and John E. Pomfret, "The Problem of the West Jersey *Concessions* of 1676/77, *William and Mary Quarterly,* 3d Ser., 5 (1948): 95–105. Despite such arguments, the authorship of Byllynge is not wholly proven. In all likelihood Byllynge participated in the preparation of the Concessions but played a secondary role to the more active Quaker trustees of West New Jersey—Nicholas Lucas, Gawen Lawrie, and Penn.

22. Aaron Leaming and Jacob Spicer, *The Grants, Concessions, and Original Constitutions of the Province of New Jersey . . .* (2d ed. Philadelphia, 1881), 382–411.

23. Lawrie, Penn, Lucas, Byllynge, John Eldridge, and Edmond Warner to Richard Hartshorne, Aug. 26, 1676, *N.J. Archives,* 1st Ser., 1:228.

24. Julian P. Boyd, *The Fundamental Laws and Constitutions of New Jersey* (Princeton, 1964), 3.

25. Maples, "A Cause to Plead," 77–78.

26. The drafts are in Charters and Frames of Government, Penn Papers, foll. 49–149.

27. Ibid., foll. 49–51.

28. Sydney G. Fisher, *The True William Penn* (Philadelphia, 1906), 222. Drafts 2–6 are in Charters and Frames of Government, foll. 53–61, 71–77. The following discussion of the efforts to fabricate a constitution is based on an analysis of the various drafts in this collection. These drafts are now published in *The Papers of William Penn, II:1680–1684,* Richard S. Dunn and Mary Maples Dunn, eds. (Philadelphia, 1982).

29. Charters and Frames of Government, fol. 63.

30. John E. Pomfret, "The Proprietors of the Province of West New Jersey, 1674–1702," *Pa. Mag. of Hist. and Biog.,* 75 (1951): 136–37; *The Present State of the Colony of West-Jersey, 1681* (London, 1681), in Myers, ed., *Narratives,* 195; William Penn, *Some Account of the Province of Pennsilvannia* (London, 1681), ibid., 215. For Rudyard, also see Alfred W. Braithwaite, *Thomas Rudyard,* Supplement no. 27 to the *Journal of the Friends Historical Society* (London, 1956).

31. John E. Pomfret, *The Province of West New Jersey, 1609–1702* (Princeton, 1956), 111–12.

32. Penn, *Some Account of Pennsilvania*, 208–9.

33. Charters and Frames of Government, fol. 63; also see Pomfret, "First Purchasers of Pennsylvania," 146.

34. Charters and Frames of Government, fol. 63.

35. Ibid., foll. 73, 119–25, and reprinted in *Pa. Mag. of Hist. and Biog.*, 20 (1896): 283–301.

36. "B[enjamin] F[urly] Abridgment out of Holland and Germany . . . ," in Julius F. Sachse, "Benjamin Furly," *Pa. Mag. of Hist. and Biog.*, 19 (1895): 303–4.

37. Charters and Frames of Government, foll. 79–117, 127–41.

38. Penn to Robert Turner, one of the Commissioners of State, July 18, 1688, reprinted in Samuel Hazard, ed., *The Register of Pennsylvania*, 4 (Philadelphia, 1829), 105.

39. The final version of the Frame of 1682 is printed in Francis N. Thorpe, ed., *The Federal and State Constitutions, Colonial Charters, and Other Organic Laws* . . . (Washington, 1909), 5:3052–9.

40. Pomfret, *Province of West New Jersey*, 95-99. For a recent appraisal of the New York Charter of Libertyes, see David S. Lovejoy, "Equality and Empire: The New York Charter of Libertyes, 1683," *Wm. and Mary Qtly.*, 3d Ser., 21 (1964): 493–515.

41. John E. Pomfret, *The Province of East New Jersey, 1609–1702, the Rebellious Proprietary* (Princeton, 1962), 140–43.

42. Thorpe, ed., *Federal and State Constitutions*, 5:3060.

43. Two samples of early immigrants yield information on the ratio of indentured servants to free men. "A Partial List of the Families Who Arrived at Philadelphia between 1682 and 1687," *Pa. Mag. of Hist. and Biog.*, 8 (1884): 328–40, records 89 heads of families and 192 indentured servants. A Bucks County census taken in 1684 tabulated 61 heads of family and 80 servants. For the latter see ibid., 9 (1885), 223–33.

44. Quoted in William I. Hull, *William Penn; A Topical Biography* (London, 1937), 229.

45. Furly's lengthy criticism of the Frame of 1682 is reprinted in *Pa. Mag. of Hist. and Biog.*, 19 (1895): 297–306. John Locke, who lived in exile at Furly's house in Rotterdam in 1687 and 1688, studied a copy of Penn's Frame in 1686. Locke found the constitution imprecise, fragmentary, and occasionally arbitrary in the large powers conferred upon council, although he made no comments on the circumscribed role allowed the lower house. See Maurice Cranston, *John Locke* (London, 1957), 261–62.

46. Hutcheson to Penn, Mar. 18, 1683, Penn Papers, Friends House, London.

47. John Whiting, *Persecution Exposed* . . . (London, 1715), 108.

48. Jasper [Batt], Ans[wer] to W[illiam] P[enn]'s Letter, ca. 1684, Swarthmore Manuscripts, 6, Friends House, London.

49. Thorpe, ed., *Federal and State Constitutions*, 5:3052–54.

50. Beatty, *William Penn*, 17.

51. Frame of 1682 in Thorpe, ed., *Federal and State Constitutions*, 5:3054.

52. Penn's emphasis upon these requisites of good government is considered in Beatty, *William Penn*, 24–32; and Mary Maples, "William Penn, Classical Republican," *Pa. Mag. of Hist. and Biog.*, 81 (1957): 152–55.

53. Edwin B. Bronner, *William Penn's "Holy Experiment"* (New York, 1962), 33–35.

54. Not all of the delegates are known, but seventeen are mentioned in the minutes of the session which appear in *Votes and Proceedings of the House of Representatives of the Province of Pennsylvania*, in *Pa. Archives*, 8th Ser. (Harrisburg, 1931–35), 1: 1-13. Hereafter cited as *Votes*.

55. For the early settlement of the Lower Counties see J. Thomas Scharf, *History of Delaware, 1609–1888* (Philadelphia, 1888), 23–68.

56. Penn to Jasper [Batt], Feb. 5, 1682/83, in *Pa. Mag. of Hist. and Biog.*, 6 (1882): 467–72; the addressee is there mistakenly identified as Jasper Yeates.

57. *Votes*, 1:1–13.

58. Penn to William Markham, Feb. 5, 1682/83, in *Pa. Mag. of Hist. and Biog.*, 6 (1882): 466–67.

59. For the membership of assembly and council see *Votes*, 1:13; and *Minutes of the Provincial Council of Pennsylvania, From the Organization to the Termination of Proprietary Government*, 1 (Philadelphia, 1852), 57–69. Hereafter cited as *Minutes*.

60. Proceedings of the General Assembly, Jan. 12, 1682–83, are in *Votes* 1:13–43.

61. Penn's adherents comprised about one-sixth of the assembly. Included were John Songhurst, Thomas Wynne, William Yardley, Nicholas Waln, Thomas Fitzwater, John Blunston, Thomas Brassey, and John Bezar.

62. James Logan to Penn, Dec. 20, 1706, *Penn-Logan Correspondence*, 184.

63. The debate over Penn's veto power was later recalled by Penn and Logan. See ibid.; and Penn to Logan, May 10, 1705, ibid., 2:17. For mention of the question in council, see *Minutes*, 1:60–61.

64. *Votes*, 1:18–19.

65. Ibid., 14–15, 18.

66. Bronner, *Penn's "Holy Experiment,"* 40.

67. *Minutes*, 1:59.

68. Penn to Council, Aug. 19, 1685, Gratz Collection. For the decay of government in the early years see Gary B. Nash, "The Free Society of Traders and the Early Politics of Pennsylvania," *Pa. Mag. of Hist. and Biog.* 89 (1965): 147–73.

69. Penn to Thomas Lloyd, Nov. 17, 1686, Parrish Collection, Proud Papers, 2:5.

4

SLAVES AND SLAVEOWNERS IN COLONIAL PHILADELPHIA

ALTHOUGH HISTORIANS have recognized the importance of slavery in the social and economic life of colonial America, they have associated the institution primarily with the plantation economy of the southern colonies. Textbooks in colonial history and black history rarely mention urban slavery in the northern colonies or take only passing notice of the institution and conclude that the small number of slaves in northern cities served as domestic servants, presumably in the households of the upper class. The history of slavery in the colonial period is particularly obscure for Philadelphia, the largest city in British North America on the eve of the Revolution. In the extensive literature on William Penn's colony the inquiring student finds only the most impressionistic information regarding the number of slaves in the city, the pattern of slave ownership, the use of slaves, and the interplay of demand for black and white bound labor. None of the historical accounts of Philadelphia published in the last century deals directly with slavery, thus leaving the impression that the institution was incidental to the development of Philadelphia as an urban center.[1]

To some extent this gap in our knowledge can be explained by the traditional dependence of historians upon literary evidence. In the case of Philadelphia they have been unusually handicapped by the fact that not a single official census was taken in the city during the colonial period. Although census data revealing the racial composition of the population are intermittently available for New York from 1698 to 1771 and for Boston from 1742 to 1770, historians of colonial Philadelphia have had to rely on the widely varying comments of residents and travelers to estimate the slave population.[2] Thus, the opinion of Gov. William Keith, who reported in 1722 that Pennsylvania had few slaves "except a few Household Servants in the City of Philadelphia,"

This essay first appeared in *William and Mary Quarterly*, 30 (1973): 223–56. Alterations have been made in the text, several tables, and the footnotes.

and the view of Andrew Burnaby, who recorded nearly forty years later that "there are very few Negroes or slaves" in Philadelphia, and the comment of Benjamin Franklin, who wrote in 1770 that in the northern cities slaves were used primarily as domestic servants and that in North America as a whole "perhaps, one family in a Hundred . . . has a slave in it," have taken on unusual weight in the historical record.[3] To be sure, visitors to Philadelphia occasionally conveyed a different impression. For example, after visiting the city in 1750, Peter Kalm, the Swedish botanist, noted that in earlier decades slaves had been bought "by almost everyone who could afford it, the Quakers alone being an exception." Kalm added that more recently Quakers had overcome their scruples "and now . . . have as many negroes as other people."[4] But Kalm's view seems to have been regarded as a minority report and is seldom cited by historians.

Despite the absence of census data, other kinds of evidence are available to indicate that slaveholding in Philadelphia was far more extensive than has generally been believed. It is known, for example, that in December 1684, just three years after the coming of the Quaker founders of the colony, a shipload of 150 African slaves arrived in Philadelphia. Transported by a Bristol mercantile firm, the slaves were eagerly purchased by Quaker settlers who were engaged in the difficult work of clearing trees and brush and erecting crude houses in the budding provincial capital. So great was the demand for the slaves, according to one prominent settler, that most of the specie brought to Philadelphia by incoming settlers was exhausted in purchasing the Africans.[5] Thus at a time when the population of Philadelphia was probably about two thousand, 150 slaves became incorporated into the town's social structure. Although little evidence is available to indicate the extent of slave importation in the next few decades, a survey of inventories of estates from 1682 to 1705 reveals that about one in fifteen Philadelphia families owned slaves in this period.[6]

It is unlikely that slaves entered the city at more than a trickle in the next few decades, at least in part because of the high import duties imposed after 1712. But the reduction of the import duty to £2 per head in 1729 and the lapse of any duty after 1731 seem to have triggered a significant increase in slave importations. Although most Quaker merchants withdrew from the trade in the 1730s after a period of controversy within the Society of Friends regarding the morality of importing and trading slaves, merchants of other religious persuasions gladly accommodated the growing demand for slave labor.[7] Some indication of this new importance of slavery can be inferred from the burial statistics which were recorded in Philadelphia in 1722, 1729, 1731–32, and 1738–44, and published annually beginning in 1747.[8] Whereas only 26 Negroes died in Philadelphia in 1722, 97 were buried there in 1729, 102 in 1731, and 83 in the following year. These figures tend to confirm the observation of Ralph Sandiford, an early Quaker abolitionist, who wrote in 1730 that "we have *negroes* flocking in upon us since the duty on them is reduced to 40 s *per* head for their importation."[9] Indeed, the proportion of black deaths in the annual death toll during the early 1730s was the highest in the city's history (Tables 1 and 2).

Following a period of relatively heavy imports in the early 1730s, the traffic in slaves seems to have slackened considerably. Correspondingly, the number of black deaths declined in the late 1730s and did not again reach the level of the period from 1729 to 1732 until after 1756. This leveling off of the slave trade at a time when the city was growing rapidly cannot be satisfactorily explained in economic terms since the high import duties of the earlier period had not been reinstated. Instead, it must be attributed to a preference for German and Scotch-Irish redemptioners and indentured servants who flooded into Philadelphia between 1732 and 1754. Although these immigrants had been attracted to Pennsylvania in substantial numbers since 1716, their numbers increased dramatically beginning in 1732.[10] The relative decline in black deaths between 1732 and 1755 suggests that city dwellers with sufficient resources to command the labor of another person usually preferred German or Scotch-Irish indentured servants to black slaves when the former were readily available, even though indentured labor was probably somewhat more expensive.[11]

The beginning of the Seven Years' War in 1756 marked the onset of a decade in which slavery and slavetrading reached their height in colonial Philadelphia. This can be explained largely by the sudden drying up of the supply of indentured German and Scotch-Irish laborers who had disembarked at Philadelphia in record numbers between 1749

Table 1. Burials in Philadelphia, 1722–55

	Average Burials Per Year		
Year	White	Black	Percent Black
1722	162	26	13.8
1729–32	396	94	19.2
1738–42	418	51	10.9
1743–48[a]	500	64	11.3
1750–55	655	55	7.7

[a]Based on deaths registered in 1743–44 and 1747–48. The bills of mortality for 1745–46 are not extant.

and 1754.[12] Historians have never made clear the reasons for this stoppage, although most have implied that the wartime disruption of transatlantic traffic put an end to the Palatine and Scotch-Irish emigration.[13] The answer, however, originates on land, not at sea. Beginning in the fall of 1755, the English commanders in the colonies began recruiting indentured servants in order to bolster the strength of the British units, which were reeling under the attacks of the French and their Indian allies on the western frontier.[14] About two thousand Pennsylvania servants had been recruited by the end of 1755 according to one estimate, and the problem was serious enough by early 1756 to warrant a strong message from the Assembly to the governor warning that "if the Possession of a bought Servant . . . is . . . rendered precarious . . . the Purchase, and Of Course the Importation, of Servants will be discouraged, and the People driven to the Necessity of providing themselves with Negro Slaves, as the Property in them and their Service seems at present more secure."[15]

Rather than reversing the policy of luring servants into the British army while offering partial financial recompense to their owners, Parliament legitimized and extended the practice in a law which was carried to the colonies in July 1756 by Lord Loudoun, the new British commander-in-chief. By this time Benjamin Franklin was issuing firm warnings to the English government and predicting what had already happened: the continuing enlistment of servants, he wrote, "will . . . intirely destroy the Trade of bringing over Servants to the Colonies, either from the British Islands or Germany."[16] As Franklin explained, "no Master for the future can afford to give such a Price for Servants as is sufficient to encourage the Merchant to import them" when the risk of losing a newly purchased servant to the British army remained so great.[17] With little hope for a reversal of English policy, Pennsylvanians seeking bound labor turned to black slaves. According to one of Philadelphia's largest merchants, writing in September 1756, "all importations of white Servants is ruined by enlisting them, and we must make more general use of Slaves."[18] If those with capital to invest in human labor had heretofore preferred white indentured labor to black slave labor, even at some economic disadvantage, by late 1756 their options had been narrowed and they turned eagerly, in the face of the rising cost and unpredictability of white labor, to African slaves.

The shift to black slave labor is reflected both in the shipping records and in the annual bills of mortality in Philadelphia. Importation of slaves, which according to a recent study had averaged only about twenty a year in the 1740s and about thirty a year in the early 1750s, began to rise sharply. Although precise figures are not available, it appears that at least one hundred slaves entered Philadelphia in 1759.

By 1762, probably the peak year of slave importations in the colony's history, as many as five hundred slaves may have arrived, many of them directly from Africa. In each of the following years between one and two hundred disembarked.[19]

Corroborating evidence of this rapid expansion of slavery is provided by the burial statistics of blacks during these years. Whereas burials had averaged 51 a year from 1738 to 1742, 64 a year from 1743 to 1748, and 55 a year from 1750 to 1755, they rose sharply to an average of 91 annually from 1756 to 1760, when unprecedented numbers of slaves were sold in the city, and remained at an average of 87 a year in the next three five-year periods (Tables 1 and 2).

What makes this rapid growth of slavery in Philadelphia especially noteworthy is that it occurred at precisely the time the prerevolutionary abolitionist movement, centered in Philadelphia and led by John Woolman and Anthony Benezet, was reaching its climax.[20] Attempting to end the slave trade through appeals to conscience at a time when white indentured labor was becoming unreliable and expensive, these ideologues found their pleas falling on ears rendered deaf by sudden changes in the economics of the labor market.

The rapid wartime growth of the slave trade ended as fast as it had begun. By the beginning of the 1760s, with the war subsiding and British recruiting sergeants no longer at work, the influx of Germans and Scotch-Irish redemptioners and servants recommenced.[21] As indicated in Table 3, the Scotch-Irish immigration, which throughout the colonial period flowed predominantly through Philadelphia, had begun an upward swing in 1760; within three years ships crowded with Palatine immigrants were also disgorging their passengers on the Philadelphia docks. Concurrently the slave trade tapered off. The import duties, reported annually to the Assembly by the customs officer at Philadelphia, indicate that from September 1764 to September 1768, when German and Scotch-Irish immigration had almost reached prewar levels, slave imports dropped to an annual average of sixty-six. Between 1768 and 1770 they declined to less than thirty per year,[22] and by the

Table 2. Burials in Philadelphia, 1756–75

| Year | Average Burials per Year | | |
	White	Black	Percent Black
1756–60	917	91	9.2
1761–65	990	87	8.1
1766–70	856	87	9.2
1771–75	1,087	87	7.4

end of the latter year the Pennsylvania slave trade had all but ceased.[23] Given the choice once more between black slaves and white indentured servants, Philadelphians and other Pennsylvanians chose the latter to satisfy their requirements for bound labor.

For the years from 1767 to 1775 the size and composition of the black population in Philadelphia can be charted with unusual precision because abundant records with which the social historian can work have survived: transcripts of the tax assessors' reports for 1767, 1769, 1772, and 1774, an enumeration of taxable slaves in the city in 1773, and constables' returns for 1775.[24] Unlike earlier tax lists, which indicate only the total rateable estates of the city's inhabitants, the assessors' reports for these years record each category of assessable wealth, including land, buildings, ground rents, slaves, servants, and livestock. In addition, the constables' returns of 1775 list all heads of household and include for each house the number—and in most cases the ages—of all tenants, hired and bound servants, slaves, and children. As specified by law, the tax assessors listed only slaves between twelve and fifty and servants between fifteen and fifty years of age as assessable property,[25] so the totals obtained from these lists must be adjusted to account for slaves and servants outside of these age limits.

The tax assessors' reports of 1767 indicate a total of 814 slaves between the ages of twelve and fifty in the city of Philadelphia. If we include as a part of urban Philadelphia the district of Southwark, which lay along the Delaware River immediately south of the city and contained many of the shipyards, ropewalks, tanneries, sail lofts, and ship

Table 3. Number of Immigrant Ships Arriving in Philadelphia

Year	German	Irish	Total	Year	German	Irish	Total
1750	15	6	21	1763	4	15	19
1751	16	0	16	1764	14	8	22
1752	19	3	22	1765	5	10	15
1753	19	5	24	1766	5	20	25
1754	19	5	24	1767	5	13	18
1755	2	2	4	1768	4	7	11
1756	1	1	2	1769	4	11	15
1757	0	6	6	1770	7	12	19
1758	0	3	3	1771	9	19	28
1759	0	2	2	1772	8	15	23
1760	0	7	7	1773	15	17	32
1761	1	8	9	1774	6	15	21
1762	0	10	10	1775	2	13	15

chandlers' offices associated with the maritime commerce of the city, the number of slaves is swelled to 905.[26]

To this number we must add slaves who were under twelve or over fifty years of age. Unfortunately almost no data for determining the age structure of the slave population in Philadelphia are available for the years before 1775. It is virtually certain, moreover, that by 1775 the age distribution had changed markedly after a decade of declining importations. It is reasonable, however, to infer the age distribution of Philadelphia slaves from coeval census data for New York City slaves. In the enumerations of 1731 and 1737, 23.5 percent and 25.3 percent, respectively, of the slaves in New York City were under ten years of age. In the census reports of 1746, 1749, 1756, and 1771, the black population was divided into those sixteen and over and those under sixteen. The under-sixteen segment was, respectively, 48.7, 43.7, 41.2, and 36.2 percent of the whole slave population. These figures indicate that the proportion of children was declining and that Negroes of twelve years or younger made up about 25 to 30 percent of the slave population of New York City in the decade before the Revolution. Census data for eight counties of New Jersey between 1726 and 1772 and for the entire province of New York between 1703 and 1771 show a fairly low range of variation in the age distribution of slaves and thus reinforce one's confidence in estimating that about 30 percent of the slaves in Philadelphia were too young to be included in the tax assessors' reports in 1767.[27]

Slaves over fifty years of age are estimated to have composed 5 percent of the Philadelphia slave population in 1767. The Philadelphia constables' reports of 1775, which give the ages of most of the city's slaves, reveal that 7.6 percent of the slaves were over fifty. Because the age structure of the slave population probably advanced from 1767 to 1775 as a result of a low birth rate and a marked decrease in slave importations, this figure was probably nearer 5 percent for the former year. Comparable data from New York City show that 6.7 percent of male slaves were over sixty in 1746, 3.7 percent in 1749, 6.0 percent in 1756, and 2.8 percent in 1771.[28]

After adjusting the total of 905 taxable slaves to account for those of nontaxable ages, we can estimate that in 1767, at a point only a few years after what was probably the apogee of slaveholding in the colonial period, almost 1,400 slaves served their masters in Philadelphia. In a total population of about 18,600, slaves represented 7.5 percent of the city's inhabitants.[29]

As importations of black slaves subsided following the reopening of the white indentured servant trade, the slave population in Philadelphia entered a period of substantial decline. Between 1767 and 1773 the

number of slaves between twelve and fifty years old in Philadelphia
decreased from 905 to 669 and the approximate total number of slaves
from 1,392 to 945. The number of slaves dropped again, although
slightly, in 1774 and then decreased sharply in the following year
(Table 4).[30]

How is one to explain this precipitous decline of the slave population, which between 1767 and 1775 reduced the number of slaves in the
city by more than half? Given the intensity of the abolitionist campaign
during these years, one might suspect that the manumission of slaves
was the major factor. Benjamin Rush's assertion in May 1773 that
three-quarters of his fellow Philadelphians "cry out against slavery"
seems to confirm such a view.[31] But even among Quakers, the only
vigorous opponents of slavery in Philadelphia, manumissions were rare
until late in 1775, a year after the Yearly Meeting of the Society of
Friends took a strong stand against slaveholding and began systematic
visitations to Quaker slaveholders in order to encourage private manumissions. In fact, as the carefully kept Quaker records reveal, only
eighteen slaves were manumitted in Philadelphia between 1766 and
1775, and of these fourteen belonged to "persons not in Membership
with Friends."[32]

The real explanation of the rapidly declining number of slaves was
the inability of the slave population to reproduce itself in a period when
slave importations had virtually ceased. This is made manifest by corre-
lating the data from the annual mortality bills and the constables' reports of 1775. The mortality bills reveal that between 1767 and 1775,
679 blacks, almost all of them slaves, were buried in the "Strangers
Burialground"—an average of about seventy-five per year. In an era
when slave importations were inappreciable, one side effect of this
heavy death toll was to alter the age structure of the slave population.
Many female slaves passed beyond the age of fertility and were not
replaced by younger slave women. This further depressed a fertility rate
which even in periods of substantial importation was far below the

Table 4. Slave Population in Philadelphia, 1767–75

Year	Slaves between 12 and 50	Estimated Slave Population	Approximate Total Population	Percent Slave
1767	905	1,392	16,000	8.8
1769	856	1,270	16,850	7.9
1772	774	1,069	18,225	5.9
1773	669	945	18,700	5.1
1774	658	869	19,175	4.5
1775	450	672	19,650	3.4

white birth rate for two major reasons. First, male slaves outnumbered female slaves in almost all places and times during the colonial period, and Philadelphia, so far as can be ascertained from the limited data, was no exception. Second, in a city where more than half of the slaveholders owned only a single adult slave, sexually mature male and female slaves infrequently lived together under the same roof, thus further reducing the incidence of conception.[33]

The low fertility rate of slave women in the northern regions in general was noted by several eighteenth-century amateur demographers. Franklin, for example, remarked in 1751 that only by constant importation was the African population maintained.[34] Edward Wigglesworth, professor of divinity at Harvard, ventured the same opinion in 1775, writing that "a large annual importation from Africa [was required] to keep the stock good."[35] That these impressions of knowledgeable observers applied with special force to Philadelphia after slave importations dropped off in the late 1760s is evident from the age structure of slaves listed on the constables' reports of 1775. These lists give the ages of 89 percent of the city's slaves of whom only 10.7 percent were under ten years of age. Data for other areas indicate approximately the same age structure.[36] From 1767 to 1775, when the slave population averaged about one thousand, 679 blacks had been buried in Philadelphia and fewer than 100 black children had been born and survived infancy. This excess of deaths over births can only be explained by an extremely low birth rate, a drastically high infant mortality rate, or a combination of the two.[37]

While the slave labor force was contracting rapidly, the number of free blacks in Philadelphia grew slowly. Free blacks had lived in the city at least as early as 1717 when the Anglican church recorded the baptism of a free black woman.[38] Although it is extremely difficult to trace the growth of the free black community during the next half century, some scattered evidence is available to throw a glimmer of light on these Philadelphians. Between 1748 and 1752 fourteen blacks, some adults and some children, were baptized in the Anglican church.[39] And in 1751, the *Pennsylvania Gazette* printed the complaint of one Philadelphian who upbraided a number of free blacks, who "have taken Houses, Rooms, or Cellars, for their Habitations," for creating disorders with "Servants, Slaves, and other idle and vagrant Persons."[40] By 1768 eight free black children were attending an Anglican school established ten years before for the eduction of blacks, and in 1770 a Quaker school for blacks had enrolled thirty-six children of free blacks.[41] Twenty-seven free blacks are mentioned in the Anglican baptism records between 1756 and 1765 and in the following decade forty-one additional free blacks were cited.[42] From this scattered and incomplete evidence it seems likely that the free black population was at least 150 in 1770. Occasional manumissions in the early 1770s may have swelled the number of free blacks to about 250 on the eve of the Revolution.[43]

These population estimates can be combined with the statistics compiled from the bills of mortality to approximate a crude death rate for 1767, when slavery was near its peak in Philadelphia. By calculating the slave population at 1,392 (Table 4) and adding 100 free blacks, an estimated black population of 1,492 is obtained. With black burials averaging 102 annually in Philadelphia in the five-year period 1765 to 1769, this indicates a crude death rate of 68.4. Although this figure seems startlingly high, it is not out of range with the death rate of Negroes in prerevolutionary Boston where between 1725 and 1775 the crude decadal mortality rate varied between 56 and 86.[44]

By examining the tax assessors' reports of 1767 it is also possible to draw a collective profile of slaveowning Philadelphians for that year. The assessors' reports disclose that of the 3,319 taxpayers in the city 521 (15.7 percent) owned slaves. Because taxpayers who owned only slaves under twelve or over fifty years of age do not appear on the assessors' returns as slaveowners, this total must be increased somewhat. The constables' reports of 1775 show that almost 14 percent of the slaveowners in that year owned only slaves whose ages fell outside the taxable limits. If this pattern applied in 1767, more than seventy slaveowners would not be revealed by the assessors' returns and the total number of slaveowners should be increased to about 590.[45] A still more accurate measurement of how extensively slavery permeated the social structure can be made by keeping in mind that the number of taxpayers and the number of householders were by no means the same. Of the 3,319 taxpayers in 1767, 337 were assessed a poll tax, indicating that they were single freemen, usually living at the home of their parents or renting lodging in the house of another. Others—perhaps as many as 10 percent—were tenants.[46] It is clear from the tax assessors' reports that very few tenants or persons assessed a poll tax owned slaves. By conservative estimate, then, the number of householders could not have numbered more than about 80 percent of the number of taxpayers. Calculating the number of households in Philadelphia at about 2,655 (80 percent of the total number of taxpayers) and the number of slaveowners at about 590, we can estimate that slaves resided in the homes of more than one in every five families in Philadelphia in 1767.

To understand how many Philadelphians participated in the institution of slavery, one must also take into account the shifting composition of the slaveowning group in the city. Although only fragmentary evidence remains by which to trace the sale or transfer after death of slaves, some indication of the turnover in slaveownership can be inferred by comparing the tax assessors' reports of 1767 and 1769. On the 1769 list 125 persons appear as slaveowners who had not been assessed for slave property in 1767. Including these "new" owners, over 700 Philadelphia families, representing about one-quarter of the households in the city, were involved in slavekeeping in the closing years of the 1760s. However moderate the treatment of slaves and whatever the quasi-familial status of some bondsmen and women, the master-slave relationship and the ownership of other human beings as chattel property were extensively woven into the fabric of city life. If John Woolman was correct in believing that slaveholding, even by the kindliest of masters, did "yet deprave the mind in like manner and with as great certainty as prevailing cold congeals water," and that the absolute authority exercised by the master over his slave established "ideas of things and modes of conduct" that inexorably molded the attitudes of children, neighbors, and friends of slaveholders, then Philadelphia, at least for a brief period, was indeed deeply involved in the "peculiar institution."[47]

In sharp contrast to the towns of the colonial South, most slaveowners in Philadelphia held only one or two adult slaves. Of the 521 slaveowners appearing on the 1767 tax list, 57 percent owned only a single slave between twelve and fifty years of age and another 26 percent owned but two (Table 5). If slaves under twelve and over fifty years of age were included, these figures would be somewhat, but probably not significantly, changed. In all likelihood, this pattern of ownership reflects the limited possibilities for employing slaves in gang labor in a city where most of the productive labor, outside of ship building and a few enterprises such as bakeries, brickyards and ropewalks, was still carried out in the small shop of the individual artisan.

That slaveowning in Pennsylvania was predominantly an urban phenomenon is made apparent by comparing the number of slaves in the city with figures for outlying rural areas. In Chester and Lancaster

Table 5. Pattern of Slave and Servant Ownership
in Philadelphia in 1767

Number of Taxable Slaves or Servants	Number of Slaveowners	Percent of Slave-owners	Number of Servant-owners	Percent of Servant-owners
1	297	57	169	72
2	136	26	55	24
3	56	11	6	3
4 or more	32	6	3	1
	521	100	233	100

counties, the most densely populated and agriculturally productive areas in the colony, slaves numbered only 289 and 106 respectively on the assessors' lists of 1759. Only 4.2 percent of the taxpayers in Chester County and 1.2 percent in Lancaster County owned slaves in that year.[48] Although it might be expected that the large importations of the early 1760s would have increased the incidence of slaveholding somewhat in these areas, this did not in fact happen. By 1773–74 the number of slaves reported by the tax assessors in Chester and Lancaster counties had dropped to 237 and 52 respectively, while the number of taxable white inhabitants was increasing sharply between 1760 and 1770—from 4,761 to 5,484 in Chester County and from 5,635 to 6,606 in Lancaster County.[49]

Even in Philadelphia County, immediately to the north and west of the city, slaveowning never approached the level obtained in the city. In 1767 only 206 of 5,235 taxpayers (3.9 percent) owned a total of 331 taxable slaves.[50] Thus the incidence of slaveholding in the city was about four times that of the surrounding countryside. No tax lists for Philadelphia County are extant before 1767, making it impossible to determine whether slaveholding was increasing or decreasing at this time. But it appears that slaveholding was near its peak in 1767; by 1772 the number of slaves had dropped from approximately 502 to 457 and two years later had declined to 410 (Table 6).[51]

The tax assessors' lists also reveal that slaves composed more than three-quarters of the unfree labor in the city in 1767 and that slaveholders outnumbered servantholders more than two to one (Tables 5 and 6). The five-year period between 1755 and 1760, when almost no indentured servants entered the colony and most of those already there completed their terms of servitude, serves to explain this emphasis on black labor. That 104 ships arrived in Philadelphia with Scotch-Irish and German immigrants in the six intervening years before the tax list

Table 6. Composition of the Unfree Labor Force
in Philadelphia, 1767–75

Year	Philadelphia City				Philadelphia County			
	Slaves	Servants	Total	Percent Slaves	Slaves	Servants	Total	Percent Slaves
1767	1,392	395	1,787	77.9	502	422	924	54.3
1769	1,270	482	1,752	72.5	536	443	979	54.7
1772	1,069	558	1,627	65.7	457	389	846	54.0
1773	945	673	1,618	58.4	440	426	866	50.8
1774	869	762	1,631	53.3	410	467	877	46.7
1775	673	869	1,542	43.6	—	—	—	—

of 1767 was drawn[52] suggests that for at least a brief period in the early 1760s slaves may have represented as much as 85 to 90 percent of the city's bound laborers. After 1767, however, with slave importations reduced to a trickle and white indentured servants crowding into the city, the composition of the unfree labor force underwent equally sudden changes, reverting to what was probably the pre-1755 pattern. By 1775 white servants, who less than a decade before had composed less than one-quarter of the unfree labor force, constituted 56 percent of Philadelphia's bound workers (Table 6).[53]

A different pattern prevailed in the rural areas outside Philadelphia as indicated in Table 6 by the figures for Philadelphia County. Whereas white indentured servants made up only 22 percent of the unfree labor force in 1767 in the city, they constituted almost half of the bound laborers in the surrounding county. Seven years later this pattern had changed only slightly in Philadelphia County, where the incidence of both servantholding and slaveholding was always much lower than in the city.

What also claims our attention is the fact that at a time when the population of the city was growing rapidly the demand for bound labor, either black or white, was shrinking. Between 1767 and 1775, when urban Philadelphia grew from approximately 18,000 to 25,000, the number of servants and slaves declined from 1,787 to 1,542. Whether this was a long-range trend reflecting changes in the organization of work and the growing profitability of wage versus bound labor is impossible to determine without examining a series of postwar assessors' reports.[54] But it is possible that on the eve of the Revolution a plentiful supply of free wage laborers, created by rural overpopulation in the hinterland, decreased the demand for bound labor in Philadelphia. Or the sources of indentured labor in Germany and Ireland may have been drying up. Whatever the reasons, those with money to invest in human labor were turning more and more in the last third of the eighteenth century from the bound to the wage laborer.

By analyzing the 1767 tax list it is also possible to establish the correlation between economic status, as measured by assessable wealth, and slave ownership. As might be expected, slaveowners were concentrated in the upper wealth bracket. Only 5 percent of Philadelphia's 521 slaveowners in 1767 came from the bottom half of the white wealth scale, and these 26 individuals owned only 28 of the 905 taxable slaves in the city. Almost two-thirds of the slaveowners had sufficient wealth to place them in the top quarter of the property owners and one-third of them, holding 44 percent of the city's slaves, came from the wealthiest tenth of the population. This unsurprising correlation between wealth and slave ownership parallels the Boston pattern of 1771 (Table 7).[55]

Table 7. Economic Status of Philadelphia and Boston Slaveholders

	Number and Percent of Slaveholders	
Position Among All Taxables	Philadelphia (1767)	Boston (1771)
Bottom 50%	26 (5.0%)	17 (5.4%)
Upper-middle 25%	151 (28.9%)	70 (22.0%)
Top 25%	344 (66.1%)	231 (72.6%)
	521	318

Slaveowners in the city were distributed through the top half of the social scale to a far greater degree than in the rural areas. Whereas the top 10 percent of the taxpayers in Philadelphia owned 44 percent of the city's slaves, the upper tenth in Philadelphia County owned 77 percent of the slaves, in Chester County 58 percent, and in Lancaster County 60 percent.[56] This tendency for slaveholding to be heavily concentrated in the upper reaches of rural society but to be diffused through the middle strata of urban society is probably best explained by the greater prosperity enjoyed by those at the middling levels of city life. In Philadelphia County, for example, the top tenth of the wealth holders included all those with estates of £24 or more. In the city, by contrast, a taxpayer needed at least £60 of taxable property to count himself or herself in the wealthiest tenth of the community. Put differently, more people in the city than in the country had amassed sufficient wealth to afford a slave, and it seems likely that this contributed to the much higher incidence of slaveholding and servantholding in Philadelphia than in outlying areas.

The correlation between wealth and slave ownership can be misleading, however. At first glance it seems to indicate that slaveholding was restricted to the elite in Philadelphia and thus, like the building of stately townhouses and the flourishing of the arts in the third quarter of the eighteenth century, was a part of cultivating the genteel life. This view is reinforced by scanning the list of slaveholders, which is studded with names of prominent pre-Revolutionary Philadelphians—merchants, professionals, proprietary officeholders, and political magnates such as John Baynton, Thomas Bond, Thomas Cadwalader, Benjamin Chew, John Dickinson, Benjamin Franklin, Joseph Galloway, Thomas Lawrence, Samuel McCall, Samuel Mifflin, Robert Morris, Edward Pennington, Edmund Physick, Edward Shippen, Joseph Shippen, Robert Waln, Thomas Wharton, and Thomas Willing. But an analysis of the occupations of slaveowners reveals that slaves were owned by a wide range of artisans and even by men such as mariners and carters who commanded little leverage in the social and political life of the city and could hardly be considered proto-aristocrats.

As Table 8 indicates, about one-third of the taxable slaves in the city were owned by merchants and shopkeepers. Many of these slaves were doubtless household servants, while others were being held for sale by merchants engaged in the slave trade or were contracted out for day labor. Ninety-five slaves (10.5 percent) were held by thirty-nine "professional" men—sixteen doctors, ten lawyers, nine officeholders, two conveyancers, a clergyman, and a teacher. Innkeepers or tavern-holders owned thirty-four slaves, and widows and "gentlemen" accounted for thirty-one more.

Nearly half of the city's slaves are included in these categories. But the other half were owned by artisans, men associated with maritime enterprise, or, in a few cases, by laborers. Almost every occupational category in the city included at least one slaveholder and some, such as bakers, metalworkers, woodworkers, and ropemakers, were heavily represented.

That slave labor was used extensively by artisans and craftsmen is also revealed by the small number of Philadelphians who held 4 or more slaves of assessable age—men, in other words, who were employing labor on a fairly large scale by prerevolutionary standards. Only 32 of 521 slaveholders in Philadelphia were included in this group. Of these, 8 were merchants, including such prominent figures of Philadelphia society as William Allen, perhaps the wealthiest man in Philadelphia, Isaac Coxe, Samuel Howell, John Hughes, later appointed stamp distributor, Archibald McCall, Samuel McCall, Samuel Mifflin, and Thomas Willing. Six lawyers, including John Dickinson (whose 11 slaves made him the second largest slaveholder in the city), John Ross, and John Lawrence were also among this group, as were 2 proprietary officials, James Tilghman and Benjamin Chew. But among the other large slaveholders were 5 bakers, 3 ropemakers, a sailmaker, a goldsmith, and a ferry-man whose slaves apparently operated the ferries that plied the Delaware River between Philadelphia and Burlington, New Jersey. The largest slaveowner in Philadelphia was John Phillips, whose 13 slaves manned the city's largest ropewalk in Southwark.[57]

Perhaps most surprising is the large number of ship captains and mariners who owned slaves. Almost 10 percent of the slaveowners were men whose work took them to sea. It is possible that these Philadelphians purchased female slaves to assist their wives with household tasks while they were away. But given the racial attitudes of colonial Americans and the general apprehension of slaves that existed in all urban centers, it is more likely that most of these seagoing Philadelphians purchased slaves to work on board ship. The substantial number of mariners and ship captains who owned slaves suggests that the American merchant marine may have been far more heavily manned by black

Table 8. Occupations of Philadelphia Slaveholders in 1767

Occupational Group	Number and Percent of Slaveowners		Number and Percent of Taxable Slaves Owned	
Merchants and retailers	161	31.2%	291	32.2%
Professionals (including doctors, lawyers, officeholders)	39	7.5%	95	10.5%
Service trades (including tavernkeepers, barbers, printers)	30	5.6%	48	5.2%
Wood-, metal-, and stone-workers	66	12.6%	104	11.5%
Cloth- and leatherworkers	56	10.7%	97	10.7%
Food processors (including butchers, bakers, brewers millers)	31	6.0%	70	7.7%
Maritime trades (including captains, mariners, shipwrights, and sail-, rope-, and blockmakers)	75	14.2%	122	13.5%
Miscellaneous (including widows)	31	6.1%	44	4.9%
Unknown	32	6.1%	34	3.8%
	521		905	

labor than has been previously recognized.[58] It is especially likely that slaves owned by mariners were black sailors. The constables' reports reveal that all but two of the thirty-two mariners owning slaves were married, but twenty-three of them owned no house, renting their quarters from others. Nine of them had no taxable assets other than their slaves, suggesting that these mariners, who were generally located in the lower reaches of society, had used the small amount of capital they possessed to purchase a slave and thus increase their share of the profits from Atlantic voyages.

Mariners were not alone in preferring slave labor to real estate as a field for investment. Of the 521 slaveowners, only 190 (36.4 percent) owned a house or property in Philadelphia. The other 331 rented their dwellings, preferring to put excess capital into the acquisition of a slave or two rather than purchasing or building a house. Of course both the incidence of slave ownership and home ownership increased with the level of wealth in Philadelphia, so that many men in the top echelon owned both real and human property. But for a significant number of middle-class Philadelphians with limited capital to invest, acquisition of slaves took precedence over the purchase of a house. Indeed, for one-eighth of the slaveholders their human property represented their only taxable assets. Typical of these Philadelphians were men and women like Charles Jenkins, a mariner living in Southwark; John Dowers, a sail-maker in Mulberry Ward; William Benning, a staymaker in Walnut Ward; and Widow Sinclear, who kept a tavern in Walnut Ward. Thus a great many of Philadelphia's slaveowners appear to have been small entrepreneurs who lacked the assets to purchase or maintain a slave merely for the social prestige it would confer. Instead, most of these city dwellers seem to have purchased slaves, particularly after the white in-dentured labor supply became uncertain, as a means of carrying on their crafts and small-scale industries and thereby improving their fortunes.

Correlations between slave ownership and religious affiliation are difficult to establish because church membership records are incomplete for the pre-Revolutionary period. But the Society of Friends was assidu-ous in record keeping, and therefore it is possible to identify almost all of the Quaker slaveholders and determine whether the incidence of slaveholding among Friends differed from that of non-Friends. This is of special significance because for Quakers buying, selling, or even own-ing a slave involved a direct conflict of economic interest and ideology. Whereas an Anglican, Presbyterian, German Lutheran, Methodist, or member of any other religious group in Philadelphia could participate in the institution of slavery secure in the knowledge that it was justified both by his church and by the prevailing philosophies of the Western world, Quakers could not. Since the 1690s individual Quakers had been developing piecemeal the argument that slaveowning was sinful and only by dissociating themselves from it could they cleanse themselves of impurities.[59] Individual arguments of this kind were followed by official action. Periodically after 1730 the Philadelphia Yearly Meeting advised its members not to buy or sell slaves. More importantly, prodded by the tireless work of John Woolman, the Yearly Meeting agreed in 1758 to exclude Friends who bought or sold slaves from meetings for business and to refuse their contributions as tainted money. Although it would not institute a policy of disownment, as Woolman urged, the Yearly Meeting appointed a committee which, with the assistance of Friends

appointed by the various Quarterly Meetings, was to visit all slaveholders and convey the message that slave ownership, although not yet
cause for disownment, was no longer consistent with the Quaker view
of just relations among the brotherhood of man. Woolman himself took
up the task of making independent visits to dozens of Philadelphia
slaveowners, asking them to look into their hearts to ascertain whether
their ownership of slaves did not reveal an immoral lust for gain.[60]
These visitations, together with the official pronouncements of the
Yearly and Quarterly Meetings, involved every Quaker slaveholder by
the late 1750s in a situation where economic interest and ideology were
in direct conflict. Increasing the tension was the fact that the uncertainties and rising price of white bound labor, owing to the recruitment of
indentured servants by the British army beginning in late 1755, created
new inducements for the purchase of black labor at the very time that
the Quaker leaders were taking fresh steps to end the involvement of
Friends in the institution of slavery.

The best method of estimating the size of the Quaker segment of the
entire Philadelphia population, in order to lay a basis for comparing the
ratio of Quakers to non-Quakers on the list of slaveowners in 1767, is to
establish the number of Quaker and non-Quaker deaths during this era.
On the annual bills of mortality Quaker burials represented between
12.4 and 13.9 percent of the total number of white burials in the city for
every five-year period from 1755 to 1774; for the period as a whole
Quaker burials represented 12.8 percent of the same total. In the list of
slaveowners in 1767, it is possible to identify 88 members of the Society
of Friends, or 16.9 percent of the total of 521.[61] Although the burial
statistics indicate only the approximate size of the Quaker community, it
seems safe to conclude that Friends were somewhat overrepresented
among Philadelphia slaveholders in proportion to their numbers. Confirmation of this extensive involvement by Friends in slavekeeping can be
found in Quaker documents themselves. To be sure, a prominent Philadelphia Quaker, James Pemberton, wrote in 1762 that the "In[i]quetous
[slave] traffic hevy of late [has] lamentably Increas'd here, tho' the members of the Society Appear entirely clear of being Concernd in the Importation and there are few Instances of any purchase of them."[62] But only
three months earlier the Philadephia Yearly Meeting had regretfully
noted an "increase of Slaves among the members of our religious Society" in its report to the London Yearly Meeting.[63] And among the slaveowners identified in the 1769 assessors' reports are the names of at least
seven Quakers who had not owned slaves two years before. The evidence
is substantial, then, that when faced with a direct choice between forgo-
ing the human labor they needed or ignoring the principles enunciated by
their leaders and officially sanctioned by the Society through its Quar-

terly and Yearly Meetings, the rank and file of Philadelphia Friends chose the latter course. More than twenty years of abolitionist campaigning by men such as Woolman and Benezet, and the increasing commitment of the Society of Friends to ending slavery, culminating in the decisions of 1758, failed to stem the influx of slave labor into Philadelphia, to bring about more than a handful of manumissions, or even to prevent an increase in slaveownership among Quakers. Not until about 1764, by which time white bound labor had become as available as before the war, did Quakers stop buying slaves; and not until the eve of the American Revolution was the ideological commitment of the Quaker leadership able to prevail over the membership at large in the matter of manumission.

The religious affiliations of non-Quakers cannot be readily identified, given the fragmentary state of church records for several groups such as the Baptists, Roman Catholics, and Swedish Lutherans. But an analysis of surnames in the list of 521 slaveholders indicates that at least one group eschewed slaveholding to a remarkable degree. This was the German element in Philadelphia, composed of German Lutherans and German Calvinists. German Lutherans ranked just behind the Anglicans as the largest religious group in the city and, combined with German Calvinists, accounted for 23 percent of the burials in Philadelphia between 1765 and 1769, a five-year period bracketing the tax assessment of 1767. Although they contributed virtually nothing to the antislavery literature of the period, they seem to have had a strong aversion to slaveholding. Only 17 of the 521 (3.3 percent) slaveowners can be identified as Germans—an incidence of slaveholding that clearly distinguishes them from all other ethnic and religious groups in the city. This abstinence from slaveholding can only partly be explained in economic terms, for while it is true that the Philadelphia Germans were concentrated in the lower half of the wealth structure, thus putting the ownership of a slave beyond the means of many, a sizeable number of Germans enjoyed a modest affluence. Perhaps of equal importance was the aversion to slaveholding which the immigrants from the Palatinate expressed beginning with the Germantown petition of 1688 against slavery and continuing through Christopher Sauer, the German printer in Philadelphia who almost always refused to accept advertisements for runaway slaves or slave sales in his German-language newspaper at a time when Benjamin Franklin had no compunction about printing them in the *Pennsylvania Gazette*.[64] The Philadelphia Germans had no reservations about purchasing indentured servants, most of whom were their countrymen, but they drew the line there and only rarely ventured to purchase African slaves.[65]

On the eve of the American Revolution, the slave population was dwindling as a result of private acts of manumission and, more importantly, because of the virtual cessation of the slave trade and natural decrease. As the Second Continental Congress convened in Philadelphia, slavery was moving slowly into its twilight period in the largest city in British North America.[66] But the long history of slavery in the city and the wholesale substitution of black for white bound labor in the late 1750s and early 1760s demonstrate that even in the center of colonial Quakerism the appeals of antislavery ideologues went largely unheeded whenever they interfered with the demand for bound labor.

NOTES

1. See, for example, Ellis Paxson Oberholtzer, *Philadelphia, A History of the City and its People: A Record of 225 Years* (Philadelphia, 1912); J. Thomas Scharf and Thompson Westcott, *History of Philadelphia, 1609–1884*, 1 (Philadelphia, 1884); John F. Watson, *Annals of Philadelphia, and Pennsylvania . . .*, 3 (Philadelphia, 1857); Carl and Jessica Bridenbaugh, *Rebels and Gentlemen: Philadelphia in the Age of Franklin* (New York, 1942); Carl Bridenbaugh, *Cities in Revolt: Urban Life in America, 1743–1776* (New York, 1955); Horace Mather Lippincott, *Early Philadelphia: Its People, Life and Progress* (Philadelphia, 1917); Struthers Burt, *Philadelphia, Holy Experiment* (New York, 1945).

2. Edward R. Turner, the most thorough student of slavery in Pennsylvania, concluded that "it is almost impossible to obtain satisfactory information as to the number of negroes in colonial Pennsylvania" and made no attempt to calculate the slave population of Philadelphia at any point in the colonial period except by inference, such as in stating that "when fairs were held in Philadelphia as many as a thousand negroes sometimes gathered together for carousal and barbaric rejoicing." "Slavery in Colonial Pennsylvania," *Pennsylvania Magazine of History and Biography*, 35 (1911): 143, 149. On the eve of the Revolution two independent estimates placed the slave population of Pennsylvania as high as 100,000 and as low as 2,000. Evarts B. Greene and Virginia D. Harrington, *American Population Before the Federal Census of 1790* (New York, 1932), 114. The latest population estimates make no mention of Philadelphia but set the number of slaves in the colony at 6,000 in 1770. U.S. Department of Commerce, Bureau of the Census, *Historical Statistics of the United States, Colonial Times to 1957* (Washington, D.C., 1960), 756.

3. Keith to Board of Trade, Dec. 18, 1722, Board of Trade Papers, Proprieties, 2, R. 42, Historical Society of Pennsylvania, Philadelphia, and cited in Edward Raymond Turner, *The Negro in Pennsylvania; Slavery—Servitude—Freedom, 1639–1861* (Washington, D.C., 1911), 11, n.40; Burnaby, *Travels Through the Middle Settlements in North America in the Years 1759 and 1760 . . .*, 2d ed. (Ithaca, N.Y., 1960), 57 [Benjamin Franklin], "A Conversation between an ENGLISHMAN, a SCOTCHMAN and an AMERICAN on the Subject

of SLAVERY" (1770), in Verner W. Crane, "Benjamin Franklin on Slavery and American Liberties," *PMHB,* 62 (1936): 5.

4. Adolph B. Benson, ed., *Peter Kalm's Travels in North America: The English Version of 1770,* rev. ed., 2 (New York, 1964), 206.

5. Nicholas More to William Penn, Dec. 1, 1684, Albert C. Myers Collection, Box 2, #6, Chester County Historical Society, Chester, Pa.

6. Gary B. Nash, *Quakers and Politics: Pennsylvania, 1681–1726* (Princeton, N.J., 1968), 278, n.69. The inventories are in Philadelphia Wills and Inventories, Book A (1682–99) and Book B (1699–1705), photostatic copies at Hist. Soc. of Pa.

7. Turner, *Negro in Pa.,* 4–6; W.E. Burghardt Du Bois, *The Philadelphia Negro: A Social Study* (Philadelphia, 1899), 411–18, where the legislation concerning import duties is listed; Darold D. Wax, "Negro Imports into Pennsylvania, 1720–1766," *Pennsylvania History,* 32 (1965): 256, n.9; and Wax, "Quaker Merchants and the Slave Trade in Colonial Pennsylvania," *PMHB,* 86 (1962): 145. For early Quaker controversy concerning the slave trade see Thomas E. Drake, *Quakers and Slavery in America* (New Haven, Conn., 1950), 34–47.

8. The figures for 1722, 1729, and 1731–32 were printed in the *American Weekly Mercury* and are summarized, except for 1729, in Samuel Hazard *et al.,* eds., *Pennsylvania Archives,* 8th Ser. (Harrisburg, Pa., 1931), 4: 3517. The figures for 1738 to 1744 are reproduced in Leonard W. Labaree et al., eds., *The Papers of Benjamin Franklin* (New Haven, Conn., 1959–), 3, 439. Bills of mortality, which distinguished race and religious affiliation, were published annually between 1747 and 1775 by the Anglican church in Philadelphia and are available, except for 1749 and 1750, on microcard as listed in Charles Evans, *American Bibliography: A Chronological Dictionary of all Books, Pamphlets, and Periodical Publications Printed in the United States . . . 1639 . . . 1820* (Chicago, and Worcester, Mass., 1903–59).

9. *The Mystery of Iniquity; In a Brief Examination of the Times . . . with Additions,* 2d ed. (Philadelphia, 1730), 5.

10. Seventeen ships carrying German immigrants had entered Philadelphia between 1727, when records are first available, and 1731. In the next two years 18 ships arrived and after a three-year period in which arrivals dropped to 2 or 3 a year, the greatest influx in the colony's history began. For the next 17 years, from 1737 to 1754, an average of 11 ships a year, carrying about 40,000 German immigrants, disembarked their passengers at Philadelphia. The number of ships arriving each year and calculations of the average number of immigrants per ship are given in Ralph Beaver Strassburger and William John Hinke, *Pennsylvania German Pioneers: A Publication of the Original Lists of Arrivals In the Port of Philadelphia from 1727 to 1808* (Pennsylvania-German Society, *Publications,* 42–44 [Norristown, Pa., 1934], 1:xxix, xxxi. Abbot Emerson Smith presents evidence indicating that Strassburger and Hinke underestimated the Palatine immigration by about 15%. *Colonists in Bondage: White Servitude and Convict Labor in America, 1607 to 1776* (Chapel Hill, N.C., 1947), 320–23. While most of these Palatines made their way to rural areas north and west

of Philadelphia, that a substantial number remained in the city is evident from the sharp increase of deaths listed in the annual mortality bills for "Dutch Calvinists," "Dutch Reformed," and "Strangers." The number of arriving Irish and Scotch-Irish indentured servants is much less certain. A recent study puts the figure below 30,000. See R.J. Dickson, *Ulster Emigration to Colonial America, 1718–1775* (London, 1966), 59.

11. Darold D. Wax's examination of sale prices leads him to conclude that servants, presumably with full terms to serve, were sold at about half the price of the average slave. "The Demand for Slave Labor in Colonial Pennsylvania," *Pa. Hist.*, 34 (1967): 344. Turner estimates that slaves cost about three times as much as white servants. *Negro in Pa.*, 10–11. The relative profitability of slave as opposed to indentured labor in a colonial urban environment has never been calculated to my knowledge, but I tentatively conclude that indentured labor was somewhat more expensive than slave labor.

12. At least 22 ships crowded with German and Scotch-Irish immigrants had reached Philadelphia in each year between 1752 and 1754. But from 1755 to 1760 an average of only 4 ships a year carrying German and Scotch-Irish immigrants arrived in Philadelphia (Table 3). Strassburger and Hinke, *German American Pioneers*, 1:xxx, and Dickson, *Ulster Emigration*, Appendix E. That the general transatlantic traffic continued to flow is evident from the statistics on the import and export of goods at Philadelphia and from the fact that the city's merchants had no difficulty importing slaves. Imports from England declined 40% in 1755 from the previous two-year level but from 1757 to 1760 were at all-time highs. Exports declined about one-third from 1756 to 1760 partially as a result of the war in some of the wheat-producing areas of central Pennsylvania, but still remained high enough to indicate that the Atlantic traffic was far from halted. The shipping data are from *Hist. Stat. of the U.S.*, 757.

13. Geiser, *Redemptioners and Indentured Servants*, 39, and C. Henry Smith, *The Mennonite Immigration to Pennsylvania in the Eighteenth Century* (Pa.-Ger. Soc., *Pubs.*, 35 [Norristown, Pa., 1929]), 204, 217.

14. Stanley McCrory Pargellis, *Lord Loudoun in North America* (New Haven, Conn., 1933), 105–8, 116–19.

15. The estimate was by William Peters in a letter to Thomas Penn, proprietor of Pennsylvania. Cited in Labaree et al., eds., *Franklin Papers*, 6:397, n.2 For the plea of the Assembly, see ibid., 397–98.

16. Pargellis, *Lord Loudoun*, 116–23, and Franklin to Sir Everard Fawkener, July 27, 1756, Labaree et al., eds., *Franklin Papers*, 6:472–76.

17. Franklin to Fawkener, July 17, 1756, Labaree et al., eds., *Franklin Papers*, 6:472–76. In addition to the inadequate compensation made by the British army for enlisted servants, the Pennsylvanians complained that they were unable to replace their servants at such critical points in the agricultural cycle as harvest or seedtime when they were lured away by the British recruiting sergeants. Thus it was the undependability as well as the cost of indentured servants that led to the transition to slave labor.

18. Thomas Willing to Coddrington Carrington, Sept. 3, 1756, Willing

and Morris Letter Book, 221, Hist. Soc. of Pa., quoted in Darold Duane Wax, "The Negro Slave Trade in Colonial Pennsylvania" (Ph.D. diss., University of Washington, 1962), 32.

19. Wax, "Negro Slave Trade in Pa.," 47–48. In 1761, 24 Philadelphia merchants, petitioning the governor to withhold his approval of a £10 per head duty passed by the Assembly, referred to the continuing scarcity of labor owing to "near a total Stop to the importation of German and other white Servants." The petition is published in William Renwick Riddell, "Pre-Revolutionary Pennsylvania and the Slave Trade," *PMHB,* 52 (1928): 16–17. That heavy importations continued from 1762 to 1766 in spite of the imposition of what the Assembly meant to be a prohibitory £10 duty testifies to the insistent demand for labor, white and black, at this time.

20. For extensive treatments of the abolitionist campaign, none of which attempts to measure the success of the abolitionists in bringing about private manumissions of slaves, see Drake, *Quakers and Slavery,* chaps. 3 and 4; Zilversmit, *First Emancipation,* chap. 3; and David B. Davis, *The Problem of Slavery in Western Culture* (Ithaca, N.Y., 1966), chap. 10.

21. The number of German ship arrivals listed in Table 3 is given in Strassburger and Hinke, *German American Pioneers,* 1:xxx, and can be regarded as nearly accurate since Pennsylvania law required the registration of all alien arrivals. The Scotch-Irish arrivals, based primarily on shipping advertisements in the *Belfast News Letter,* are tabulated in Dickson, *Ulster Emigration,* Appendix E. The newspaper files are incomplete from about 1750 to 1755, so the figures for these years may be too low.

22. Slave importations from 1761 to 1771, as calculated from the customs accounts, are tabulated in Wax, "The Negro Slave Trade in Pa.," 48. Thomas Riche, a Philadelphia merchant, was a few years premature in asserting in 1764 that "the time is over for the sale of Negroes here." Riche Letter Book, 1764–71, Hist. Soc. of Pa., quoted in Wax, "Negro Imports into Pa.," *PMHB,* 32 (1965): 255.

23. According to Benezet, more slaves were exported than imported in Philadelphia by 1773. Benezet to Granville Sharp, Feb. 18, 1773, Sharp Letter Book, Library Company of Philadelphia, cited in Wax, "Negro Imports into Pa.," *Pa. Hist.,* 32 (1965): 255.

24. Transcripts of the 1767 assessors' reports are at the Van Pelt Library, Univ. of Pa., Philadelphia. I have used microfilm copies of the 1769 and 1774 tax lists, at Hist. Soc. of Pa., where a transcript of the 1772 assessors' reports is also deposited. The constables' returns of 1775 are in the Philadelphia City Archives, City Hall, hereafter cited as constables' returns of 1775. A facsimile of the 1773 report, from Joseph Galloway to the earl of Dartmouth, is in B. F. Stevens, *Facsimiles of Manuscripts in European Archives relating to America, 1773–1783* . . . (London, 1889–1895), 24:2086.

25. The basic tax law governing the assessment for servants and slaves was passed in 1764 and continued in force throughout the prerevolutionary period. White servants of fifteen to twenty years of age were valued at 30s.;

slaves of twelve to fifty years of age were valued at £4. James T. Mitchell and Henry Flanders, comps., *The Statutes at Large of Pennsylvania from 1682 to 1801,* Vol. 6: *1759 to 1765* (Harrisburg, Pa., 1899), 358.

26. Southwark's urban character and rapid growth enabled it to become a municipality with powers equivalent to those of the counties by an act of the Assembly in May 1762. Scharf and Wescott, *Philadelphia,* 256–57. See also Margaret B. Tinkcom, "Southwark, A River Community: Its Shape and Substance," American Philosophical Society, *Proceedings,* 114 (1970), 327–42.

27. The New York census data are in Greene and Harrington, *American Population,* 97–102. The New Jersey data are summarized by J. Potter, "The Growth of Population in America, 1700–1860," in D. V. Glass and D. E. C. Eversley, ed., *Population in History: Essays in Historical Demography* (London, 1965), 656–57. Data for Newport, R.I., in 1755 show that 39.5% of slaves were under age sixteen, if one interprets the designation "boys" and "girls" as referring to persons under sixteen and the designations "men" and "women" as referring to persons over sixteen. Greene and Harrington, *American Population,* 67. In New Haven and New London, Conn., in 1774, 48.0% of the slave population were under the age of twenty. Charles J. Hoadly, *Public Records of the Colony of Connecticut, from October, 1772, to April, 1775, Inclusive,* 14 (Hartford, Conn., 1887), 483–92.

28. Constables' returns of 1775. The New York City figures are derived from Greene and Harrington, *American Population,* 99–102.

29. Although no census was taken in the city during these years, a series of enumerations of houses and taxable inhabitants allows for calculations of crude population levels of 7,800 in 1740 and 10,700 in 1755. Actual counts of houses that were made in 1749 and 1769 are given in Watson, *Annals of Philadelphia,* 3:236; the number of houses for 1760 is also recorded in James Mease, *Picture of Philadelphia . . .* (Philadelphia, 1811), but no source for the figure is given. The number of taxable inhabitants in the city in 1741 is given in Watson, *Annals of Philadelphia,* 3:235–36, and has been calculated for 1756 from the tax list of that year reprinted by Hannah Benner Roach, comp., "Taxables in the City of Philadelphia, 1756," *Pennsylvania Genealogical Magazine,* 22 (1961): 3–41. The ratio of taxables to inhabitants and houses to inhabitants, the basis for establishing crude population levels for 1740 and 1755, has been derived from Sam Bass Warner's recent calculation of the city's population in 1775: *The Private City: Philadelphia in Three Periods of Its Growth* (Philadelphia, 1968), 12, 225–26.

30. The data in Table 4 are based on estimates that 30% of the slave population were under 12 and 5% over 50 in 1767 and that these ratios changed steadily for the next eight years by which time those under 12 composed 15% and those over 50, 7.6% of the slave population. The total population of Philadelphia is taken from estimates presented in Gary B. Nash and Billy G. Smith, "The Population of Eighteenth-Century Philadelphia," *Pennsylvania Magazine of History and Biography,* 99 (1975), 366.

31. Rush to Granville Sharp, May 1, 1773, in L. H. Butterfield, ed., *Letters of Benjamin Rush,* 1 (Princeton, N.J., 1951), 81.

32. Fifty-three slaves, all belonging to Quakers, were emancipated in 1776. These manumissions and others by non-Quakers are recorded in Papers of Manumission, 1772–1790, C27 and C28, Philadelphia Quarterly Meeting (Orthodox), Pennsylvania Department of Records, Philadelphia, and in some cases are also listed in Manumission Book A, Papers of the Pennsylvania Abolition Society, Hist. Soc. of Pa. Slave children who were promised their freedom when they reached adulthood are not included in this number.

33. The constables' returns of 1775 for Chestnut and Mulberry wards indicate that adult male and female slaves were living together in only 5 of 55 slaveowners' houses.

34. "Observations on the Increase in Mankind," in Labaree et al., eds., *Franklin Papers*, 4:231.

35. *Calculations on American Population; with A Table for estimating the annual Increase . . . in the British Colonies . . .* (Boston, 1775), 13.

36. Southwark, for which no constables' reports are extant, is not included in the calculations for the city. For the New York data, see n.27. In Connecticut in 1774, 32.1% of the population were under ten years of age. *A Century of Population Growth*, 168–69. In Bristol, R.I., in the same year 27.6% of the males and 26.9% of the females were in this age bracket. John Demos, "Families in Colonial Bristol, Rhode Island: An Exercise in Historical Demography," *William and Mary Quarterly*, 3d Ser., 25 (1968): 53.

37. Fifty-eight children of ages one to nine are listed in the constables' reports. A few more were undoubtedly among those for whom ages were not given. The baptismal records of the Anglican church reveal that between 1767 and 1775, 63 black infants, 50 belonging to slaves and 13 belonging to freedmen, were baptized. We can be sure that some of these died in infancy, which explains why the count on the constables' returns is lower than this figure. The demographic decline inherent in such an age structure is made clear in E. A. Wrigley, *Population and History* (New York, 1969), 23–28, 62–76; T. H. Hollingsworth, *Historical Demography* (London, 1969), 98–102, 345–49; and Michael Drake, *Population and Society in Norway, 1735–1865* (Cambridge, 1969), 42–46, 157.

38. Edward Raymond Turner, "The Abolition of Slavery in Pennsylvania," *PMHB*, 36 (1912): 132. On Sept. 8, 1719, the commissioners of the County of Philadelphia exacted rent from Peter, a free black, living on a lot in Philadelphia owned by "the City and County." Journal of the Proceedings of the Commissioners of the County of Philadelphia, 1718–52, Philadelphia City Archives, City Hall.

39. Register Book of Christ Church: Marriages, Christenings and Burials, 1 (Jan. 1, 1719, to March 1750); 2 (March 1750 to Dec. 1762), passim, Hist. Soc. of Pa.

40. *Pennsylvania Gazette*, Mar. 5, 1750/1.

41. Zilversmit, *First Emancipation*, 79–80; [Society of Friends], *A Brief Sketch of the Schools for Black People . . .* (Philadelphia, 1867) cited in Du Bois, *Philadelphia Negro*, 84.

42. Register Books of Christ Church, 2 (1750–62); 3 (1763–1810), *passim*, Hist. Soc. of Pa.

43. The 1774 tax assessors' reports, which indicate rents received by houseowners leasing their property to others, show 17 free black householders. I have found no way to determine whether the assessors identified all black renters or to calculate the size of their families and the number of free blacks renting rooms.

44. Lemuel Shattuck, "On the Vital Statistics of Boston," *American Journal of the Medical Sciences,* 2d Ser., 1 (1841), 371.

45. In 1775, 58 of 423 slaveowners (13.7%) held only slaves under twelve or over fifty years of age. Eight years earlier a somewhat larger number probably held only slaves too old or not old enough to be counted as assessable property. Prospective slave buyers preferred slaves not yet physically mature, perhaps because they were more tractable or adaptable to a new master. In 1767, when the era of large slave importations was ending, the age structure of the slaves was probably somewhat lower and the percentage of slaveowners holding nontaxable slaves somewhat higher. For a discussion of the desirability of young slaves see Wax, "Demand for Slave Labor in Pa.," *Pa Hist.,* 34 (1967), 337. Indicative of this preference was Thomas Willing's request for "A Parcell of healthy [Negro] Boys about 10-12 years old [which] will undoubtedly sell to good advantage." Willing to Coddrington Carrington, Sept. 3, 1756, Willing and Morris Letter Book, 221, Hist. Soc. of Pa.

46. In the Middle Ward of Philadelphia in 1774, according to a recent analysis, almost 23% of the taxpayers lived with other families. Warner, *Private City,* 15, Table 3.

47. *Some Considerations on the Keeping of Negroes, Part Second* (1762), in Phillips P. Moulton, ed., *The Journal and Major Essays of John Woolman* (New York, 1971), 237. Woolman wrote the second part of his widely circulated essay during the period when the slave trade in Pennsylvania was at its height, completing the manuscript in Nov. 1761. Ibid., 195. Another Friend, Thomas Nicholson, wrote in 1767 of his concern that slaveowning proved "a Snare to Friends' Children by being made use of as Nurseries to pride, Idleness and a Lording Spirit, over our Fellow Creatures." "On Keeping Negroes," manuscript dated June 1, 1767, Society Miscellaneous Collection, Box 11-A, Hist. Soc. of Pa.

48. I am indebted to James T. Lemon of the University of Toronto for this information, compiled from the manuscript tax returns of Chester and Lancaster counties at Chester County Courthouse, Chester, Pa., and Lancaster County Courthouse, Lancaster, Pa.

49. The 1773 figures have been compiled from tax lists in Hazard *et al.,* eds., *Pa. Archives,* 3d Ser., 12 and 17. The number of taxables is tabulated in Samuel Hazard, ed., *The Register of Pennsylvania . . . ,* 4 (Philadelphia, n.d.), 12.

50. Compiled from the 1767 tax assessors' reports, excluding Southwark.

51. Southwark is not included in these totals for Philadelphia County, but see n.53.

52. Strassburger and Hinke, *Pennsylvania German Pioneers,* 1:xxix, and Dickson, *Ulster Emigration,* Appendix E.

53. The figures have been adjusted to include Southwark with the city and to reflect the approximate number of servants and slaves not included in the tax lists because their age excluded them as taxable property in the assessors' reports. Servants between the ages of fifteen and fifty were taxable. The constables' returns of 1775 show that 27% of the servants were under fifteen or over fifty years old. I have raised the number of servants listed in the tax reports to account for these "missing" servants.

54. In 1783, when the city's population had grown to about 34,000, the number of servants and slaves had dropped to about 725. This decline may have been caused primarily by a stoppage in the importation of servants during the Revolutionary years and the concurrent release from servitude of all those indented before the war. The 1783 figure is extrapolated from the number of servants and slaves of taxable age on the tax assessors' lists for that year (data for Mulberry Ward are missing). I am indebted to John Daly of the Philadelphia City Archives for providing the 1783 data.

55. The figures for Boston are taken from James A. Henretta, "Economic Development and Social Structure in Colonial Boston," *WMQ,* 3d Ser., 22 (1965): 85, n.18.

56. The Philadelphia County figures are derived from the 1767 tax list. The Chester and Lancaster county figures are taken from Alan Tully, "Patterns of Slaveholding in Rural Southeastern Pennsylvania, 1720–1758" (paper given at meeting of the Association for the Study of Negro Life and History, Oct. 18, 1970).

57. Evidence that slaves were employed extensively as artisans is confirmed by advertisements in the Philadelphia newspapers of this period. In a two-year period bracketing the 1767 tax list, the *Pa. Gaz.* carried a number of advertisements listing slaves who were qualified as carpenters, millers, distillers, bakers, shipbuilders, blacksmiths, sailmakers, and manager of a bloomery. In one advertisement four black sailmakers were offered for sale with the note that "as the sailmakers here are stocked with Negroes, they will be ready at any time for what other market may have a call for them." Ibid., May 19, 1768. See also Leonard Price Stavisky, "Negro Craftsmanship in Early America," *American Historical Review,* 54 (1949): 315–325; Zilversmit, *First Emancipation,* 35–40; and Wax, "Demand for Slave Labor in Pa.," *Pa. Hist.,* 34 (1967): 335–36.

58. Wax, "Demand for Slave Labor in Pa.," *Pa. Hist.,* 34 (1967): 334–35; Jesse Lemisch, "Jack Tar in the Streets: Merchant Seamen in the Politics of Revolutionary America," *WMQ,* 3d Ser., 25 (1968): 375, n.19; and Harold D. Langley, "The Negro in the Navy and Merchant Service—1798–1869," *Journal of Negro History,* 52 (1967): 273–86, provide a few references to seagoing slaves.

59. The early activities of individual Quaker opponents of slavery are best described in Drake, *Quakers and Slavery,* 1–47, and Davis, *The Problem of Slavery,* 291–326.

60. Drake, *Quakers and Slavery,* 48–67, and Sydney V. James, *People*

Among Peoples: Quaker Benevolence in Eighteenth-Century America (Cambridge, Mass., 1963), 130–40.

61. The Quaker slaveholders have been identified primarily from the following sources: birth, death, and marriage records for the Philadelphia Monthly Meeting, as compiled in William Wade Hinshaw, ed., *Encyclopedia of American Quaker Genealogy* (Ann Arbor, Mich., 1936–50); "A Directory of Friends in Philadelphia, 1757–1760," Pemberton Papers, 14, Hist. Soc. of Pa., printed in *PMHB*, 16 (1892): 219–38; Philadelphia Monthly Meeting, Membership Lists, 1759–62 and 1772–73; and Papers of Manumission, 1772–90, C27 and C28, Philadelphia Quarterly Meeting (Orthodox), Pa. Dept. of Recs. Not included in the total of 88 are 7 slaveowners disowned by the Society of Friends between 1760 and 1767, and 4 slaveowners for whom identical names were found in both Quaker and Anglican records.

62. Pemberton to Joseph Phipps, Dec. 13, 1762, Dreer Collection, Hist. Soc. of Pa., quoted in Wax, "Quaker Merchants and the Slave Trade," *PMHB*, 86 (1962): 159.

63. Philadelphia Yearly Meeting Minutes, 1747–79, 174–75, quoted in Wax, "Negro Slave Trade in Colonial Pa.," 31.

64. The most recent consideration of the Germantown petition is J. Herbert Fritz, "The Germantown Anti-Slavery Petition of 1688," *Mennonite Quarterly Review*, 33 (1959): 42–59. On Sauer see William R. Steckel, "Pietist in Colonial Pennsylvania: Christopher Sauer, Printer, 1738–1758" (Ph.D. diss., Stanford University, 1950), 116.

65. It is also possible that the German immigrants, perhaps the most ethnocentric of all Philadelphians before the Revolution, were too anti-Negro to buy slaves. I am indebted to Richard S. Dunn for this suggestion.

66. At the time of the first federal census in 1790, 239 slaves remained in Philadelphia. U. S. Department of Commerce, Bureau of Census, *Heads of Family at the First Census of the United States Taken in the Year 1790: Pennsylvania* (Washington, D.C., 1908), 10.

5

THE FAILURE OF FEMALE FACTORY
LABOR IN COLONIAL BOSTON

Writing in the 1790s, Alexander Hamilton and Tench Coxe, two of the promoters of American industrialism, offered the female poor of the northern cities a way out of indigency. Poor women and children, counseled Hamilton, "are rendered more useful by manufacturing establishments." Coxe added that "the portions of time of housewives and young women which were not occupied with family affairs could be profitably filled up" by intermittent labor in "the manufactories." Both of these early advocates of American industrialism saw women and children as the human material out of which a new American economy could be built.[1] But the idea was far from new. It was merely a refurbished version of a plan put into effect in Boston nearly a half century before by the little known United Society for Manufactures and Importation, later renamed the Society for Encouraging Industry and the Employment of the Poor.

As the latter name hints, it was not entrepreneurial capitalism that brought the first American factory into being in Boston; nor was economic diversification on the minds of Boston's leaders; or an attempt to free women from confining domestic roles.[2] It was poverty in frightening proportions and the concomitant escalating costs of poor relief that ushered in America's first experiment in factory production. And a momentous experiment it was, marking the beginning of a century-long rocky series of attempts to restructure the organization and rhythm of urban work. We label the process "the industrial revolution," but this is far too grandiloquent a term to describe the small, fumbling attempts at exploiting the labor of impoverished women and children in the northern seaport towns at the end of the colonial period.

We may say, at the risk of oversimplification, that it was war that put the first American woman into the first American factory. New England had always carried the brunt of the wars against the French in

This essay first appeared in *Labor History*, 20 (1979): 165–88. Minor alterations have been made in the text and the footnotes.

North America, and Boston, as the maritime center and the chief staging ground for most of the expeditions against the Papist enemy, had borne especially heavy burdens. While in Philadelphia and New York the legislatures avoided war taxes by authorizing only a few companies of provincial troops, Massachusetts sent large numbers of its men off to die of starvation and disease in futile Caribbean amphibious assaults against Spanish bases in 1740–41, in the massive attack against Louisbourg in 1745, and in frontier fighting along the French-Canadian border. The colony's losses were staggering. Historians have made only tentative efforts to count up the fatalities, but William Douglass, surveying the human wreckage in 1748 at the end of King George's War, believed that nearly one-fifth of the province's adult males lost their lives. Even if we cut this casualty estimate in half, we are left with a literal decimation of the province's income earners, especially those in the lower class where recruitment was concentrated. Reports of the widowing of Boston's population indicate the magnitude of the town's losses. In 1742, when a census was taken, town officials reported 1,200 widows, "one thousand whereof are in low circumstances." If these figures are accurate, then a staggering 30 percent of the town's married women had no spouses to contribute to the support of their households. Three years after the war ended the tax assessors reported that Boston contained 1,153 widows "of which at least half are very poor."[3]

The social derangement caused by Boston's extraordinary contribution to the war effort can also be seen in the rapid decline of taxable polls during this period. They fell from 3,395 in 1738 to 2,972 in 1741, to about 2,660 in 1746. This loss of more than 700 taxables represented a stripping from the tax rolls of persons now too poor to pay anything into the public coffers. Before the attack on Louisbourg, some critics predicted that if Governor William Shirley's grand strategy failed, as they expected, "such a shock would be given to the province that half a century would not recover us to our present state." Ironically, the expedition had triumphed but in succeeding brought such human and financial devastation that the victory was lamented for years thereafter. The glory of bringing French Catholic power to its knees was slight comfort for hundreds of Boston families that had to reflect upon the victory in homes that were fatherless, husbandless, and dependent on charity for food and fuel. By war's end, Boston's economy had faltered badly, poor taxes had reached an all-time high, and town officials were desperately trying to cope with the unparalleled numbers of indigent residents, among whom widowed women and their dependent children were the most numerous.[4]

Various attempts were made to find remedies for the plight of the poor. The children of the poor were bound out to financially secure families. The dispossessed were warned out of town as they tramped into the city from outlying areas after the war. The affluent were exhorted to greater charitable contributions. Heartrending appeals for provincial tax relief were sent to the legislature. But none of these measures, though they may have helped, could solve the problem. So in the end, men turned from the benevolent desire to help the poor to the idea that the poor should help themselves.

The roots of such an approach to poverty are very tangled. New England Puritans, like their Elizabethan forbears, had always maintained a hearty distaste for the dependent poor, especially those who were thought to prefer public alms to hard work and self-support. Cotton Mather put the matter plainly in 1695 when he wrote that "for those that Indulge themselves in *Idleness,* the Express Command of God unto us, is *That you should Let them Starve.*"[5]

But by the 1740s it had become clear that the problem in Boston was not one of able-bodied persons who refused work, but persons for whom no work was available. On a very small scale, Boston had faced this problem as early as 1656, and by 1700 the selectmen had taken a tentative step toward a practice extensively employed in England— creating work-relief programs for the poor so that they would earn their own keep in facilities provided and supervised by public authorities.[6]

Many English writers had by this time abandoned an earlier view that economic recessions and depressed wages were the main causes of indigency and began to blame the poor themselves for their plight. The lower class, it was said, was naturally lazy and would work only when forced to do so by hunger and extreme poverty. Thus, it was argued, lawmakers who passed relief statutes with the best of intentions only cultivated dependency and encouraged sloth. William Petty, one of the most respected economic writers of the late seventeenth century, even promoted a scheme for perpetually maintaining an artificial famine by storing food in government granaries. Kept at the edge of starvation, the laboring classes would develop an urge to work that was constitutionally absent in them.[7]

Out of this new climate of thought came the public workhouse movement. By 1723, when workhouses were operating in almost every sizable English town, thousands of impoverished persons were taken off out-relief and forced from their homes. Taken to the workhouses, they were set to spinning flax, weaving linen, and picking oakum. It was hoped that through hard labor the poor would pay for their own support and in the process gain a taste for the rewards of industry and frugality. The workhouse would benefit the middle and upper classes by reducing the poor rates; it would aid the poor by reprogramming them for a more satisfactory way of life. Some English writers also recommended transferring the management of the poor to private corporations owned by investors who might turn a profit from appropriating the labor of the indigent, even as they rehabilitated them. The English workhouse became a cultural artifact of the early eighteenth century, an institution arising from a moral analysis of poverty and committed to reducing the taxpayers' load in maintaining the impoverished. John Bellers, a Quaker merchant of London, dignified these workhouses with the name of "colleges of industry" and a number of other authors with whom Bostonians were familiar, including Henry Fielding, William Temple, William Petty, Charles Davenant, and Bernard Mandeville, also promoted the new system.[8]

In 1735, with poverty spreading, Boston undertook its first major experiment in working the poor. The town meeting decided to build a separate workhouse where the able-bodied poor would be segregated, relieved, and rehabilitated. Slowly over the next few years private subscriptions were solicited, about £900 sterling in all, and by 1739 the brick Workhouse on the Common opened its doors. Nineteen months later, an inspection committee reported that expenses had exceeded income by £466 to £360 sterling and that forty-eight adults and seven children were employed in the house, mostly picking oakum, carding, and spinning. In 1742, thirty-six persons were in the house and the number from that point on does not seem to have exceeded fifty.[9]

Obviously, the overseers were not going to cure Boston's poverty problem by institutionalizing about 5 percent of the town's distressed persons. But why were so few persons ordered to the Workhouse, which had attracted 126 donors and gained the approval of the town meeting and provincial legislature? The answer cannot lay in the incommodiousness of the building, for it was one of the largest structures in Boston. Two stories high and 140 feet long, it was capable of holding scores of impoverished, unemployed persons.[10] The difficulty, apparently, was that Boston's poor resisted being taken from their homes. In 1740, a visitor remarked that the overseers of the poor were "very tender of exposing those that had lived in a handsome manner; and therefore give them good relief in so private a manner, that it is seldom known to any of their neighbors." This statement provides us with a clue as to why the Workhouse failed. Many of the poor were widows with young children. Many of them had lived decently, if not "handsomely," in the past. Hence, it is not difficult to understand that they would rebel at the notion of giving up their lodgings, however cramped and cold, and repairing to the Workhouse where poverty was compounded with indignity and their ties with friends and relatives, as well as neighborhood life, would be broken.[11]

The most unfortunate of Boston's impoverished—the aged, sick, crippled, and insane without families to care for them—had no choice but to go to the Almshouse, as did about one hundred Bostonians each year in the 1740s. Another forty or fifty persons could be induced to go to the Workhouse, especially if they did not have children or had been apprehended for prostitution or other crimes. But most of Boston's poor women regarded themselves above such treatment and preferred to starve at home even if the authorities decided to cut off out-relief and ordered them to the Workhouse. These persons refused to brook the strict regimen of the Workhouse, with its rules against free coming and going and its provisions for bread and water diets for "wanton and lascivious Behavior." Moreover, they must have found it ungenerous that the selectmen allowed them only one penny out of every shilling they earned—and that "to be disposed of by the Overseers for their greater Comfort." Alarmed at the spiralling cost of relief and affronted by the challenge to order and harmony that hundreds of pauperized and idle townspeople evoked, Boston's leaders erected a substantial building that they could not fill. The workhouse experiment failed because it underestimated the stubbornness of ordinary people, who had ways of defending themselves against attempts to alter their way of life.[12]

By 1748, Boston's leaders were ready to make another attempt to deal with the widowed poor and their dependent children. If they would not trade their mean lodgings for the workhouse, perhaps they could be persuaded to go to a "manufactory" during the day where their labor would contribute to their own support and lighten the taxpayer's burden. Thus was born the United Society for Manufactures and Importation. Its subscribers intended to put the unemployed poor to work, halt the rise of property taxes, and perhaps even make a profit off the cheap labor of poverty-stricken women and children.[13] Public authorities had been unable to make the dependent poor self-supporting; now private hands were to have a try.

The supporters of the Society for Manufactures were drawn from the ranks of Boston's most successful merchants and entrepreneurs. They concluded that of the various kinds of work that might be done by women and children, spinning and weaving were the most feasible. This notion was especially attractive because Massachusetts annually imported from England cloth worth thousands of pounds. The production of cloth by the poor, it was thought, not only would end idle pauperism and reduce taxes but also would improve the province's balance of trade by cutting back on imports. And hopefully, it would turn a profit for the Society's investors. But what kind of cloth? Woolens seemed not to be the answer because, although they were widely used, sheep grazing was only marginally profitable in New England and it took considerable craft skill, certainly skill beyond the capacities of a shifting, casual labor force, to produce the worsted materials favored by city people in contrast to the rough homespuns country folk found adequate for their needs.[14] Linen was the alternative and had much to recommend it. Flax grew well from the middle colonies northward to New Hampshire and linen was also widely imported—to the value, according to contemporary estimates, of £20,000 to £60,000 per year. Thirty years before, a group of Scotch-Irish immigrants had demonstrated the art of spinning flax in Boston and set off a mild "spinning craze." These Ulster immigrants had remained only briefly in Boston before setting out for the New Hampshire frontier where they founded the town of Londonderry and soon proved that linen could be profitably produced.[15] More important, linen production had been promoted in Ireland since the late seventeenth century and was now regarded there as the sure-fire method of curing urban poverty. Here, then, seemed to be the answer to the bundle of problems that had beset the town. As the successors to the United Society later pronounced, the "palliatives" of poor relief would be replaced by "a lasting and permanent Scheme, that may be expected to reach to Root of this Malady."[16]

Despite these optimistic hopes, nothing went easily for the organizers of the manufactory. The initial call for investors in 1748 brought only thirty-six subscribers and about £200 sterling—some indication of the chariness that many felt about the prospects of success. Linen weavers and loom builders could not be found in Boston and had to be advertised for abroad.[17] Nor were spinners available, for contrary to the conventional understanding of historians, urban women and children who could spin were the exception rather than the rule.[18] It took until December 1750 to lease a building, set up "sundry looms," and open several free spinning schools where pauper children were to be taught the art of the distaff and wheel.[19] By this time the United Society had reorganized and changed its name to the more benevolent sounding Society for Encouraging Industry and the Employment of the Poor.

To stir up enthusiasm for the opening of the manufactory, the Society published an extraordinary pamphlet on November 2, 1750. It had a cumbersome title—*A Letter from Sir Richard Cox, Bart. To Thomas Prior, esq.; Shewing from Experience a sure Method to establish the Linnen-Manufacture, and the Beneficial Effects it will immediately produce*—but inside the covers was an exciting tale of poverty and progress. Sir Richard was none other than the grandson of the former Lord Chancellor of Ireland, and his tract, published in Dublin and reprinted in London in 1749, described a fifteen-year experiment to bring prosperity and peace to the vale of tears he found on the River Bandon, where the two tiny towns of Kinsale and Bandon-bridge lay. Cox had been horrified in 1733 to find that the natives of his inherited estate "had contracted such a Habit of Idleness" that they would not work and that their children had imbibed "their pernicious Example." Naked beggars roamed the streets, people lived from hand to mouth, houses tumbled down in disrepair, and hope was nowhere to be found.

A well-meaning man, Sir Richard vowed to alter this dismal situation. Thus, he embarked on an industrial experiment, turning his estates into a social laboratory and studying human motivation until he found the formula for putting everyone to work, from the oldest members of the community down to little children who had just "quit their Leading-Strings." It had taken time, but by 1749, when Sir Richard published the pamphlet, Kinsale and Bandon-bridge were thriving towns where prosperity and contentment had replaced poverty and despair. The key to it all was the manufacture of linen.[20]

The pamphlet, like most promotional tracts, was somewhat fanciful, for what is known about the history of the Bandon River villages in the mid-eighteenth century does not entirely confirm Richard Cox's description of economic progress. But the promoters of the manufactory in Boston were not concerned with accuracy. They had convinced themselves that linen production would solve Boston's problems and they were doubtless glad to find such a glowing account of its success elsewhere. They had received it fortuitously from an old hometown boy, Benjamin Franklin, who had sent it to friends in Boston shortly after receiving it from his London scientific correspondent, Peter Collinson.[21] The pamphlet was quickly reprinted in Boston with a preface explaining that "The Circumstances of this Province, and those of Ireland, tho' not altogether similar, are in so many Respects alike. . . ." They trusted, said the Society's offices, that the public would be swayed to support the manufactory, now almost ready to open.

The public that needed to be swayed, of course, was composed of the unemployed and impoverished members of the community. It is not probable that very many of them read the *Letter from Sir Richard Cox,* but it is likely that most were privately urged by the Overseers of the Poor and the clergy to contribute themselves to the experiment. Their response was not gratifying. A few months after the manufactory opened its doors in 1751, notices appeared in the papers describing the sermon that Joseph Sewall preached at a public meeting of the Society. "It is earnestly wished by all Lovers of their Country," it was pleaded, that the poor "would exert themselves at this Time" by working in the manufactory. "Great Numbers of Persons," if they would step forward, might now be "useful both to themselves and the publick, who have heretofore been a dead Weight upon . . . this poor Town." Six months later the Society reported that 5,000 yards of linen per year was now being produced, two-thirds of it by women working for the Society. Though the number of yards produced looks impressive at first glance, it is in fact what about three weavers supplied by thirty spinners could produce annually. It was a pathetic output for a town whose pauper population approached one thousand souls.[22]

At the very time when the Society was reporting its limited progress in putting the indigent of Boston to work, smallpox struck the town. It descended so severely on the lower class that it "entirely destroyed the Linnen Manufacture." The Society's officers were determined to continue the experiment, however, for their town was deep in a commercial recession that compounded all its other troubles. At the root of this decay was the decline of shipbuilding—a keystone of the town's economy. At the end of the Anglo-French War in 1748 shipbuilding was struck by what one citizen called "a galloping consumption." This was the result not only of a decline in orders that accompanied the return of peace but the rise of satellite ports in eastern Massachusetts as shipbuilding centers.[23]

Added to the loss of shipbuilding was an exodus of butchers, bakers, tanners, distillers, and glovers. According to the selectmen, many of these artisans fled the city because of onerous tax rates passed during the war and maintained in the postwar period in order to support a growing number of poor. Poverty bred poverty, for as the number of poor who had to be maintained grew, officials levied heavier taxes upon those who themselves were struggling to make ends meet. "Unless the heavy Burthen be lightened," complained town officials in 1758, "there will be no such Town as Boston."[24] In this situation many artisans apparently decided to try their luck in outlying towns where tax rates were far lower. The loss of many substantial taxpaying families only increased the burden on those who remained, leaving the selectmen to bray pathetically that adverse conditions had "carried away from us many of Our most Industrious, frugal and provident Inhabitants, who have left us a number of thoughtless Idle and Sottish Persons, who have very soon" become public charges.[25]

Operating amid these adversities, the Society redoubled its efforts when the smallpox epidemic passed. Several hundred spinners resumed their work and four or five looms hummed away. Newspaper accounts printed encouraging comments.[26] Simultaneously, the Society's officers launched a campaign for subscriptions to erect a large new building and enlisted some of Boston's most prestigious ministers, including Samuel Cooper at Brattle Street Church and Charles Chauncy of the First Church, in the cause. The latter argued that because of the Society's praiseworthy efforts "some hundreds of Women and Children have ... been kept at Work, whereby they have done a great deal towards supplying themselves with Bread, to the easing the Town of its Burthen in providing for the poor." Now was the time for wealthy Bostonians to come to the aid of their town by subscribing as much as possible toward building the new manufactory. Cooper, who was Boston's most accurate reflector of the growing economic philosophy of self-interest, made a naked appeal to the pocketbooks of the affluent. Nobody, he wrote, was "actuated by a kind of mad good Nature" that led him to devote himself "to the Gratification of others, without any concern or Relish for his own private Happiness." But Bostonians could simultaneously indulge their natural and legitimate "self-love" and support a public cause because the manufactory was designed to "advance our private interest" by lowering taxes and turning a profit while giving employment to the idle. Chauncy also looked the profit motive in the eye: "The only proper Question is, whether this is, a likely Scheme, under proper Cultivation, to counter-balance with Advantage, the Expence necessary in order to its taking Effect."[27]

Ministerial urgings, however, could unlock less than £200 sterling of Boston's mercantile wealth. Some merchants may have feared that textile production would cut into trade profits, for cloth was a major import item. Others may have questioned whether the manufactory could operate at a profit, and they could point to the Society's own report, in March, 1752, that the operation was £500 in debt. Cooper also hinted at financial problems in 1753 when he urged the well-to-do not to weary of "doing well" in subscribing to the new building fund and predicted a "fair Prospect of *reaping*" in the future.[28]

Unable to attract enough private capital, the Society's officers turned to government and got the response they sought. In March, 1753 the Town Meeting voted to lend £130 sterling toward the construction of a new building and in June, Boston's representatives persuaded the General Court to impose a luxury tax on coaches, chariots, and other wheeled vehicles for five years in order to raise £1125 sterling more. Newly capitalized, the Society started afresh. Construction on a large building began in the spring of 1753 and the Linen Manufactory House on Tremont Street was ready by fall. To whip up enthusiasm for its opening, the Society staged a spinning exhibition on the Common in August. "Near 300 Spinsters, some of them 7 or 8 years old and several of them Daughters of the best Families among us," reported the *Boston Gazette*, ". . . made a handsome Appearance on the Common." High upon a stage erected for the occasion sat a number of weavers, one at work at his loom.[29]

All of the bright hopes that the Linen Manufactory would rid Boston of its poverty problem were shattered within a few years after the new facility opened its doors. Boston's leading ministers continued to give annual promotional sermons and the number of looms in operation rose from nine in 1753 to twenty-one in 1757. But by 1758 operations at the Manufactory were grinding to a halt. When Thomas Barnard gave the annual sermon in September of that year, he noted that economic affliction was still growing in Boston and that the thousands of men being recruited for the French and Indian War would create an even greater need for putting women to work. His sermon ended on a plea that reveals that the linen chimera was about to end. He urged the Society's members to continue their work even "tho' you should lose on the Balance," for their losses would be recompensed in lower poor taxes and the knowledge that they were helping to banish idleness.[30] But nobody was listening. In the next year the General Court, which had been unable to meet the cost of the new manufactory from the luxury tax receipts (doggedly resisted by the wealthy) ordered the building sold at auction in order to recover the costs. But who would buy a linen factory that would not work? No bids were made and all the province could do was lease a part of its white elephant to two Boston weavers, John and Elisha Brown, who wanted to run their own textile enterprise.[31] Not until the British troops eyed it as a barracks in 1768 could anyone think of a use for the Linen Manufactory.

Why had the Linen Manufactory failed? Cheap labor, sufficient capital, and technology were the prime factors that had led to success in Scotland and Ireland and all seemed available in Boston. It was not for lack of money to erect a large building and equip it with looms, spinning wheels, hackling and bleaching equipment, and other necessary items that the Manufactory closed its doors in 1759. Nor was it for lack of labor, for weavers were obtained and hundreds of women and children taught to spin. During its existence, in fact, the Society produced more than 17,000 yards of cloth. Yet the enterprise failed financially because it could not produce linen as cheaply as it could be imported. In part, this may have been because, as the Society claimed, government subsidies were not provided as in Ireland. There were also the problems of synchronizing labor and procuring ample supplies of flax.[32] But much of the answer to the Manufactory's failure lies in the resistance of the supposed recipients of the Society's efforts. As in the case of the workhouse, the majority of women and children were reluctant to toil in the Manufactory. They would spin at home, working as time allowed to produce what they could within the rhythm of their daily routine and accepting small piecework wages. But removal to an institutional setting, even for daytime labor, involved a new kind of labor discipline and separation of productive and reproductive responsibilities that challenged deeply rooted values. "The factory system," E. P. Thompson reminds us, "demands a transformation of human nature, the 'working paroxysms' of the artisan or outworker must be methodised until the man is adapted to the discipline of the machine." Boston's women, of course, were not asked to adjust to power-driven machinery. But in creating a methodical, day-long work situation, the Society was asking them to transform not only their traditional irregular work habits but to rearrange their maternal responsibilities in order to leave the home for work.[33]

To understand how extensively routinized labor in the manufactory might change the work experience of laboring-class women we need to apprehend how they previously contributed to the family economy. This is extraordinarily difficult, for we are operating not only in a vacuum of secondary literature concerning the work experience of pre-industrial American women in urban areas but are faced with a dearth of evidence on the day-by-day working life of the wives and daughters of artisans and laborers. But we do know from studies in England and France in this period that laboring-class women typically supplemented their husbands' wages because, in an economy where large numbers of people regularly lacked an adequate supply of food, this was absolutely necessary. Servanthood and manufactory labor were the two types of work most frequently performed by young, unmarried women in Europe, but married women resisted factory labor, preferring domestic manufacturing, especially spinning at home. Spreading rapidly in eighteenth-century European towns, domestic spinning helped the laboring poor to establish a viable family economy while at the same time allowing "women to fulfill what they defined as their primary role, their family duties."[34]

We cannot transpose the European experience directly to Boston; but the wider context of the urban work experience of eighteenth-century women does provide insights into the world of Boston's women. As the wives of artisans, mariners, and laborers, they had probably always contributed to the family economy by helping in their husbands' shops, taking in washing, serving as seamstresses for middle- and upper-class families, and doing daytime domestic labor in the houses of the well-to-do. After the 1720s, when the economic security of laboring-class families was steadily undermined, supplemental income from wives and older daughters probably became even more imperative. Domestic service may have been particularly important because, unlike Philadelphia, Newport, Charleston, and New York, Boston lacked the substantial labor pool of female slaves and indentured servants who performed household work in those cities. New York in 1756 had 695 female slaves over sixteen years of age and 443 under that age—a total of 1,138 slave women to serve a white population of 10,768. Philadelphia in 1767 had about 600 female slaves and indentured servants for a white population of about 18,500, and families of means also had at their command a substantial pool of free, unmarried immigrant women who entered the city each year. Boston, by contrast, received only a trickle of poor Scots-Irish and German immigrants and contained only 301 black females and 16

Indian females in 1765 for a white population of 14,672.[35] Much of
the demand for domestic labor, it seems certain, must have been filled
by young, unmarried women and by the wives of lower-class men,
especially if they were childless.

Older women with young children may have taken in boarders as a
second major way of supplementing the family income. There is a striking difference in the number of people per house in Boston and in the
other port towns in this period, and we can infer from this either that
Boston families were larger or that many householders rented rooms
and furnished board to transients, unmarried mariners, and other families from the ranks of the laboring poor. In 1741 Boston had 9.53
persons per house and in 1765, 9.26 persons. This contrasts sharply
both with Philadelphia, where there were 6.51 inhabitants per house in
1749 and 6.26 in 1760, and with New York, where there were 6.72
persons per house in 1753.[36] All of the data available to us indicate that
the birthrate in Boston was lower than in the other northern ports, for
the mid-century wars took a fearful toll on a generation of young males,
leaving a surplus population of young women whose child-bearing potential was cut short by the loss of a husband or who remained single
and childless altogether for lack of marriageable men. Hence, it is reasonable to conclude that the large number of persons per house in
Boston, which exceeded the New York and Philadelphia averages by
about 50 percent, primarily represents the taking in of single boarders
and even families. For many Boston women, especially widows, this
may have been the primary means of providing a family income.

Both in daytime domestic service and in maintaining boarders Boston's poor widows, who represented the major problem for the admin-
istrators of poor relief, had previously been able to combine maternal
responsibilities with intermittent work, which brought a modest income
but had to be supplemented with out-relief. Factory labor, however,
required a workplace that was far less amenable to the discharge of
women's familial responsibilities. Even when children of seven years
and older were taken to the factory to assist in preparing flax for
spinning, the problem of managing younger children remained. Spinning in the home could fit into the maternal work life of the woman; in
the factory it could not.

Evidence of resistance to the new work system is mostly indirect.
No records are extant that show how many spinners and weavers
worked in the Manufactory, although something may be inferred from
the fact that in 1757 there were twenty-one looms and sixty spinning
wheels in the building. Hundreds of spinners had been trained in the
previous years and twenty-one looms would have required yarn from
the wheels of several hundred of them. Many, it appears, had accepted

the Society's suggestion that they work at home, or, to reverse the causality, had obliged the Society to accept this modification of the original plan. Even so, the pre-epidemic production level, which was hardly impressive, was not being met in early 1753, and later that year it was reported that almost as many people were spinning for themselves as for the Society. Boston's poor would spin and weave, but they were less than enthusiastic about doing it within the confines of the Society's manufactory house. With their initial plan falling apart, the Society began offering free house rent and firewood to those who would weave linen cloth in their homes.

Over the next few years, Boston's poor turned away from the Society. By 1760, according to the Society's records, twice as much cloth had been produced over the previous nine years for "Private persons" as for the Society, a reversal of the situation in the opening years of the experiment. Several merchants began to purchase privately produced cloth, and apparently most of the poor preferred to produce for the merchants as their domestic responsibilities allowed, rather than work for or in the Manufactory. A decade after the Manufactory failed, a town committee concluded that "the carrying on this Business in private families (as by experience has been found in Scotland & Ireland as well as among ourselves) where the spinning and weaving are done when they [the women] have no other Employ" was the only way to put textile production on a viable footing. If they had been "fully supported" by wages, women and children might have been induced to go to the Manufactory. But since they could not live on the wages offered, about seven shillings per week for spinners, they preferred to stay at home, working at their wheels in their free time, selling their yarn to independent weavers, and counting on private and public relief to supplement their meager income.[37]

The resistance of these women is all the more remarkable given the pressure they were under from the town's leading figures, who were intent on making the Linen Manufactory succeed. This upper-class determination is most revealingly articulated in the sermons given at the annual meetings of the Society. Some of eastern Massachusetts' best known clergymen—Charles Chauncy, John Barnard, Samuel Cooper, Thomas Barnard, Thomas Prince, Joseph Sewell, and Ebenezer Pemberton—gave these sermons, which were often prefaced with descriptions of the plight of the poor. Once expressed, however, sympathy was quickly followed by admonitions that the idle poor could no longer expect the town to support them. Years before, when economic opportunity was waning in Boston, Cotton Mather advised the poor to endure their poverty quietly, pray for those whose benefactions eased their distress, and "be willing to go to Heaven by the way of an Almshouse,

when GOD shall assign you such a lodging. . . ."[38] Now the message
from above became even harsher: work in the Manufactory was being
provided and the poor must accept it or expect to starve. In a sermon
preached at the launching of the Society's new subscription drive in
August, 1752, Chauncy took as his text the Christian Law: "Thus we
commanded you, that if any would not work, neither should he eat."
He decried "the Swarms of Children, of both Sexes, that are continually
strolling and playing about the Streets of our Metropolis, cloathed in
Rags and brought up in Idleness and Ignorance"; he decried the "lazy
and indolent, who are both healthy and strong"; he warned against
giving money to the idle poor, because charity of this kind, far from
helping, would be "a great Hurt to a Community." Samuel Cooper
reiterated the emerging ideology that public out-relief or private charity
for widows and their children was money "worse than Lost." The only
justifiable charity, he pronounced, was that which was directed toward
"an Employment for honest Poverty, [that] chases away moaping Idleness, and meager Want; and introduces cheerful Industry and smiling
Plenty in their Stead."[39]

Inherent in these strictures was the threat of cutting off public
relief and discouraging private charity, thus forcing impoverished
women to adapt themselves to factory labor or go hungry. But such
finger-wagging at the poor, though it may have cheered propertied
Bostonians who welcomed any work program that would bring taxes
down, met with considerable resistance among the lower class. Widowed women had little reason to subscribe to the notion that they
were "lazy" or "idle" or lived parasitically on "promiscuously" distributed charity or that their children needed to be "trained up, not
only to endure but to love a constant Employment." Such allegations
must have been deeply resented by those whose misfortunes were not
of their own making. Many of them had recently contributed husbands to a Canadian expedition that had been sponsored by the
governor and the wealthy merchants of the town in the face of
widespread resistance. Now they heard it charged that their idle children would soon graduate "from picking of sticks to picking of
Pockets" and thus must be taken to the Manufactory to learn more
suitable habits. It is clear from the declining production of cloth in
the Linen Manufactory and its complete failure by 1759 that lower-
class women stubbornly resisted the new ideology and institutions of
poor relief. The most vulnerable, to be sure, submitted to the new
factory work discipline. Impecunious migrants entering Boston, such
as Henry Neal, his wife, and children, were hustled off to the Manufactory by the overseers of the poor and did not resist. Nor, perhaps,
did young lower-class women, who could find no marriage partners

in a town where the sex ratio had been badly skewed by war casualties. But many poor women refused to submit to a work routine that disrupted their way of life and split the dual functions of laboring-class women—work and family—into separate spheres. Samuel Cooper's argument that factory labor would not only inculcate industriousness but would add something "to the innocent Gaiety and Sprightliness of Childhood" was not well received, we may imagine, in most lower-class Boston homes.[40]

Boston leaders had undertaken the first experiment in the American colonies in routinized labor involving large numbers of people in a single workplace outside the home. But the Linen Manufactory, the embryo of capitalistic industrial factories, was conceived more in desperation at the rising tide of poverty than in entrepreneurial striving. As in England, authorities in Massachusetts had moved beyond many countries in agreeing implicitly that people should not be allowed to starve. Now they reached out in their frustration at mid-century to grasp at a straw that had floated across the Atlantic.

Something of the ambivalence of Boston's authorities toward the new system of poor relief can be seen in the halting manner in which the Manufactory operated. In sermon literature the clergy castigated "idleness" but they did not charge, as so frequently was the case in England, that it was voluntary. Yet once an opportunity to work had been provided, the clergy warned that widows and children must take their places in the cloth-making scheme and accept part of the responsibility for their indigency. Otherwise, public and private charity would be cut off.

Despite this hectoring, women resisted. Their recalcitrance, moreover, may have been fed by the reluctance of the overseers of the poor to suspend out-relief for those who were Boston born and bred. They had no compunctions about acting severely with the strolling poor who entered Boston, but with their own people they were far less ruthless than authorities in English towns. Appalled at conditions that they supposed applied only to European cities, they could not bring themselves to deny aid to women who would not submit to factory work for meager wages. It was this lack of coercion by elected officials that allowed most of Boston's widows and children to remain in their homes, spinning as time allowed within their familial routines. At the same time, neither the town nor the province was willing to continue subsidizing an industrial experiment that had failed to produce a profit. So the Linen Manufactory collapsed. Boston's leaders had found a way of making work for the poor and unemployed but had not discovered how to adapt the work to the needs and values of those who were to do it.

NOTES

1. Quoted in Mary Ryan, *Womanhood in America From Colonial Times to the Present* (New York: Franklin P. Watts, 1975), 102. Victor S. Clark noted this "direct descent from the Boston Society of American industrial corporations, particularly those engaged in making textiles." *The History of Manufactures in the United States, Vol. 1: 1607–1860* (New York: McGraw Hill, 1929), 183.

2. Some of the alternative interpretations of the movement toward women's factory labor in Europe are perceptively discussed in Joan W. Scott and Louise A. Tilly, "Women's Work and the Family in Nineteenth-Century Europe," *Comparative Studies in Society and History*, 17 (1975): 36–64.

3. Otis Little, *The State of the Trade in the Northern Colonies Considered...* (Boston, 1749), 8; William Douglass, *Summary, Historical and Political...* (2 vols.; London, 1760), 1:356, 510n, as printed in *Boston Independent Advertiser*, Feb. 8, 1748; William H. Whitmore, et al., *Reports of the Record Commissioners of Boston* (39 vols.; Boston, 1880–1902), 15:369 (hereafter *Bos. Town Rec.*); *Boston Gazette*, Aug. 27, 1751, gives the total white population as 14,190. The rise of widowhood is also reflected in the inventories of estate. From 1736 to 1745, 11.7 percent of the decedents were widows but this climbed in the next two decades to 14.9 and 17.5 percent respectively. Since lower-class women are under-represented in the inventories and since some lag can be expected before widows of King George's War would die, it seems likely that at least 25 percent of the town's adult women were widows. The inventories are in Suffolk County Courthouse, Boston.

4. For a table of taxable polls see Gary B. Nash, "Urban Wealth and Poverty in Pre-Revolutionary America," *Journal of Interdisciplinary History*, 6 (1976): 564; Thomas Hutchinson, *The History of the Colony of Massachusetts-Bay*, quoted in George A. Rawlyk, *Yankees at Louisbourg* (Orono: Univ. of Maine Press, 1967), 37.

5. *Durable Riches* (Boston, 1695); also see Mather, *Concio and Populum* (Boston, 1721), quoted in Stephen Foster, *Their Solitary Way: The Puritan Social Ethic in the First Century of Settlement in New England* (New Haven: Yale Univ. Press, 1971), 135, 137. Foster's discussion of poverty (127–52) in Boston and attitudes toward it is the best available.

6. In 1656, a group of subscribers privately raised money to buy materials with which to set unemployed youths to work (Foster, 147). In 1700, the selectmen spent £500 (£390 sterling) for a "Stock to set the poor on work" (*Bos. Town Rec.*, 8:3). The work program in 1700 was the outcome of a law passed in the previous year for "setting the Poor to work in workhouses." (Albert B. Hart, ed., *The Commonwealth History of Massachusetts*, 4 vols. [New York: States History Co., 1928], 2:266–67).

7. William Petty, *Economic Writings*, edited by Charles Hull (Cambridge: Univ. Press, 1899), 1:274–75. Also see Dorothy Marshall, "The Old Poor Law, 1662–1795," *Economic History Review*, 8 (1937): 38–47.

8. A. W. Coats, "Economic Thought and Poor Law Policy in the Eighteenth Century," *Economic History Review*, 2d Ser., 13 (1960–61): 46–50;

Sidney and Beatrice Webb, *English Local Government From the Revolution to the Municipal Corporations Act, I: The Parish and the County* (London: Longmans and Co. 1906). For Bellers, see John Bellers, *Proposals for raising a College of Industry* (London, 1695), and *Essays about the Poor, Manufacturers, Trade, Plantations, and Immorality . . .* (London, 1699).

9. *Bos. Town Rec.* 12:104–05, 111, 114, 116, 156, 159–62, 165–68, 172; Carl Bridenbaugh, *Cities in the Wilderness: Urban Life in America, 1625–1742* (New York: Knopf, 1955; orig. ed., 1938), 393; Foster, 147–48. The fullest account of the Workhouse is in Stephen Edward Wiberly, Jr., "Four Cities: Public Poor Relief in Urban America, 1700–1775," (unpublished Ph.D. diss., Yale Univ., 1975), 88–98; *Bos. Town Rec.* 12:273 for financial report. The 1742 count is in Massachusetts Historical Society *Collections*, 3d Ser. 1, (Boston, 1846), 152. Even in 1768, when poverty expenditures were even greater, there were only forty persons in the Workhouse (Carl Bridenbaugh, *Cities in Revolt: Urban Life in America, 1743–1776* [New York: Knopf, 1971; orig. ed., 1955], 320.)

10. *Bos. Town Rec.*, 12:159–60. According to a census taken in 1756, the Almshouse, which was completed in 1686 and was not nearly as large as the new Workhouse, held 148 inmates in 33 rooms. City of Boston, Indentures, 1734–1757, City Clerk's Office, City Hall, Boston. A list of 126 subscribers to the Workhouse fund is in *Bos. Town Rec.*, 12:180–83. John Kern, "The Politics of Violence: Colonial American Rebellions, Protests, and Riots, 1676–1747" (unpublished Ph.D. diss., Univ. of Wisconsin, 1976), 233–34, identifies many of the subscribers as prerogative men.

11. "Bennett's History of New England," *Proceedings of the Massachusetts Historical Society*, 5 (Boston, 1862), 116–17; Wiberly, who has analyzed the admissions records of the Almshouse and Workhouse, shows that women and children out-numbered men about three or four to one (94–95).

12. *Bos. Town Rec.*, 12:234–41, for the rules of the Workhouse; Wiberly emphasizes that the Workhouse was a financial failure, costing the town more per indigent than out-relief (95–97).

13. In its promotional pamphlet, *The Society for Encouraging Industry . . . Articles of Incorporation . . . with a List of Subscribers* (Boston, 1748, reprinted 1754) it was pointed out that "the most immediate Advantage" to be gained by the scheme "is that which will arise" when "Many Thousands of the poor are taught to support themselves." A corollary benefit was that the price of labor—"so much and justly complained of"—will fall. A. P. Usher believed that the Society's name and their expressions of concern for the plight of the poor "were mostly an indirect way of expressing an ambition to make good use of cheap labor" (Hart, *Commonwealth History of Mass.*, 2:408). The most extensive published account, which is antiquarian but filled with useful documentary material, is William R. Bagnall, *The Textile Industries of the United States . . .* (Cambridge, Mass.: Riverside Press, 1893), 28–37.

14. In 1754, it was claimed that sheep were not widely raised in Massachusetts because of the long winters (*The Society for Encouraging Industry . . .* [Boston, 1754], 1) but Usher disputes this (*Commonwealth History of*

Mass., 2:407) and he is supported by the 1735 tax valuation which counted 130,001 sheep of at least one year's age. (Leonard Labaree, William B. Willcox, et al., *The Papers of Benjamin Franklin* [New Haven: Yale Univ. Press, 1959–], 3:440).

15. Edward L. Parker, *The History of Londonderry*. . . (Boston: Perkins and Whipple, 1851), 36–39, 48–50. The author does not indicate when the linen industry began but implies that the Londonderry settlers brought their wheels and looms with them. The linen production was apparently carried out as a home industry.

16. *Society for Encouraging Industry . . . ,* 3. For the growth of the Irish linen industry, see George O'Brien, *The Economic History of Ireland in the Eighteenth Century* (Dublin: Maunsel and Co., 1918), 189–207; and W. H. Crawford, "The Rise of the Linen Industry," in L. M. Cullen, ed., *The Formation of the Irish Economy* (Cork: 1969).

17. Bagnall, *Textile Industries,* 29–31. The Society was directly violating a 1749 act of Parliament which made the enticement of manufacturing artisans a criminal offense (David J. Jeremy, "British Textile Technology Transmission to the United States: The Philadelphia Region Experience," *Business History Review,* 47 [1973]: 25–26).

18. It is usually assumed that eighteenth-century women learned spinning and weaving as a matter of course. Edith Abbott, an authority on the subject, says that in the "latter half of the eighteenth century many women were regularly employed spinning at home for purchasers who were really commission merchants"; that "the most important occupations for women . . . before the establishment of the factory system were spinning and weaving"; and that, although "it is impossible to make any estimate of the number of women who did such work . . . it is quite safe to say that spinning for the household was a universal occupation for women . . ." (Abbott, *Women in Industry: A Study in American Economic History* [New York: D. Appleton & Co., 1900], 19–20). But such statements are based primarily on the assumption that English practice was carried to America. The extensiveness of household spinning and weaving varied widely in the colonies. In rural areas they were probably extensive. But the absence of wheels and looms in the thousands of surviving Boston household inventories and the discussions about the need to establish spinning schools in 1718 and 1750 makes this clear. In 1720, a town-appointed committee recommended the founding of seven spinning schools for children, offered £300 (£126 sterling) on interest-free loan to anyone who would undertake to start such schools, and found no takers. In 1721 Daniel Oliver, a wealthy merchant, erected a spinning school at his own expense but little came of it (Bagnall, *Textile Industries,* 17–18). In 1750, the Society advertised that "several Spinning Schools in this Town" would be opened shortly and children would be taught free (*Boston Evening Post,* Dec. 17, 1750).

19. Edward Winslow, "The Early Charitable Organizations of Boston," *New England Historical and Genealogical Register,* 44 (1890), 100–103 reprints the initial list of subscribers, but incorrectly gives 1735 as the year when the United Society for Manufactures and Importation was established. This

error is noted in Bagnall, 29. For importing Irish weavers and the opening of the Manufactory, see *Boston Evening Post*, July 9, 1750, Dec. 10, 1750. The United Society may have leased a part of the Workhouse, for the Manufactory was located, according to the Dec. 10 notice, on the Common "below the seat of Thomas Hancock," which fits the location of the Workhouse. The Company's records show that the North School and two private houses were rented (Ezekiel Price Papers, #314, 317, Mass. Historical Society, Boston).

20. *A Letter from Sir Richard Cox . . .* (Boston, 1750). The quoted passages are from pp. 7 and 16. Cox neglected to state that the impoverishment of many Irish towns was attributable to the Woolen Act of 1699, which placed prohibitive tariffs on woolens imported from Ireland to England. This accomplished the desired effect of crushing the Irish woolen industry, which was eventually replaced by linen manufacturing. For Cox, see *Dictionary of National Biography*, Leslie Stephens and Sidney Lee, eds., 4 (London, 1917), 1339–40.

21. *Papers of Franklin*, 5:233n–34n. According to Collinson, Franklin "proposed the same Plan to some Ingenious publick spirited Friends." I assume Collinson referred to friends in Boston, for Philadelphia had no sizeable poverty problem at this time. The Bostonians, of course, already had a linen production scheme underway.

22. *Boston Gazette*, Aug. 27, 1751; *Report of the Committee for the Society of Encouraging Industry . . .* (Boston, 1752). According to the Society's records, "1 loom will Employ 10 Spinners." Price Papers, #319. In March 1753 the Society claimed that 200 children had been taught to spin but their output must have been meager (*Boston Evening Post*, Feb. 26, 1753). I have found no good statistics on the output of linen weavers but E. P. Thompson reports that a farming weaver could produce 8½ or 9 yards per day, and Richard Cox, who awarded prize money to the most productive weavers in his village, reported 45 yards per week in 1747, 74 yards per week in 1748, and 121 yards per week in 1749. Three weavers, producing 32 yards per week each, would yield 5,000 yards in a year. Thompson, "Time, Work-Discipline, and Industrial Capitalism," *Past and Present*, #38 (1967): 71; *Letter from Sir Richard Cox*, 26–28.

23. William Douglass, *Summary, Historical and Political . . .* (2 vols.; London, 1760), 1:540; *Bos. Town Rec.*, 14:221. In 1756 the selectmen claimed in a petition to the General Court that during one year in the recent past 14,000 tons of shipping had been built whereas after the war shipbuilding output fell to less than 3,000 tons. Petition of Town of Boston, Feb. 11, 1756, Massachusetts Archives, 117:67–68, Statehouse, Boston.

24. *Bos. Town Rec.*, 14:220–22; Petitions of the Town of Boston, Feb. 11, 1756 and April 1758, Mass. Archives, 117:55–68, 395–96.

25. *Bos. Town Rec.*, 14:239–40. By the end of the epidemic only 174 of 15,684 inhabitants had not been infected, either through inoculation or involuntarily. More than 10 percent of the uninoculated sick had died and it seems probable that these were concentrated in the lower class where resistance to inoculation was strongest. John Duffy, *Epidemics in Colonial America* (Baton Rouge: Louisiana State Univ. Press, 1953), 59–60.

26. *Bost. Evening Post,* Feb. 26, 1753.

27. *Boston Post-Boy,* Feb. 12, 1752; Charles Chauncy, *The Idle-Poor Secluded from the Bread of Charity by the Christian Law* (Boston, 1752), 18–19; Samuel Cooper, *A Sermon Preached in Boston, New England, Before the Society for Encouraging Industry* . . . (Boston, 1753), 12–23.

28. Price Papers, #311–13, 317; from 1753 to 1759 the Society raised another £900 sterling in donations and subscriptions; *Report of the Committee of the Society* . . . (Boston, 1752); Cooper, *A Sermon Preached,* 34.

29. *Bos. Town Rec.,* 14:234–35; *Mass. Acts and Resolves,* 3:680–82. Most of the £2,246 expended in purchasing land and erecting the Manufactory House was advanced by Thomas Gunter, a Roxbury merchant, who was to be repaid from luxury tax receipts; "An account of the cost of the Linen Manufactory House. . . ." Mass. Archives, 59:391–94, Statehouse, Boston, shows that most artisans and suppliers were paid in September, 1753. See also *Boston Gazette,* Aug. 14, 1753, quoted in Richard B. Morris, *Government and Labor in Early America* (New York: Harper Torchbooks, 1965), 517. The public spinning exhibition and the attempt to induce lower-class women to spin by using upper-class daughters as examples of this kind of civic duty were taken straight from Richard Cox's description of his Irish linen experiment.

30. Barnard, *A Sermon Preached before the Society* . . . (Boston, 1758). In an appendix to the sermon, the "Committee of the Society" repeated the old pitch that linen production was unusually well suited for Boston's problem, for the "greatest Part of the Labour is done by Women and Children, who have no other Employment and can therefore work cheaper at this." They closed with a final plea for contributions so that the poor could "maintain themselves by their Industry, instead of their being maintain'd by others in Idleness, the Pest of Society, and the Mother of every Vice."

31. By early 1756, the Society had received only £312 sterling from the carriage tax. Wiberly, 100. Gunter's involvement and subsequent attempts to recover his money can be followed in a series of petitions to and actions by the General Court in Mass. Archives, 59:281–294, 427–28, 431, 441–42, 452–57, 494–99, 509–10, and *Massachussetts House Journals,* 35:56–57, 249, 262, 314; 36:48. Elisha Brown had been hired by the Society to supervise operations in the early 1750s (Price Papers, #317).

32. Ibid., #314, 318; *Bos. Town Rec.,* 16:226–27; Thomas Barnard, in *A Sermon Preached* . . . (Boston, 1758), 23, admitted that linen was cheaper to import than weave domestically but asked his auditors to reject "the stale Objection, of the Cheaper Importation of Linen" in view of the social advantages to be gained. In their initial petition to the General Court for a provincial subsidy, the Committee of the Society wrote at length on the subsidies in Ireland that had launched the linen-weaving industry there.

33. E. P. Thompson, "Time, Work-Discipline, and Industrial Capitalism," 56–97, examines this problem brilliantly, although without distinguishing the special problems pertaining to women's work; Thompson, *The Making of the English Working Class* (London: Gollancz, 1963), 362.

34. Patricia Branca, "A New Perspective on Women's Work: A Comparative Typology," *Journal of Social History,* 9 (1976): 133. I have also been guided by Olwen Hufton, "Women and the Family Economy in Eighteenth-Century France," *French Historical Studies,* 9 (1975): 1–22; Mary Lynn McDougall, "Working-Class Women During the Industrial Revolution, 1780–1914," in Renate Bridenthal and Claudia Koonz, eds., *Becoming Visible: Women in European History* (Boston: Little, Brown, Co., 1977), 255–79; Theresa M. McBride, "The Long Road Home: Women's Work and Industrialization," in *ibid.,* 280–95; and Elizabeth H. Pleck, "Two Worlds in One: Work and Family," *Journal of Social History,* 10 (1976): 178–95.

35. New York: Evarts B. Greene and Virginia D. Harrington, *American Population Before the Federal Census of 1790* (Gloucester, Mass.: P. Smith, 1966), 101; Philadelphia: Gary B. Nash, "Slaves and Slaveowners in Colonial Philadelphia," *William and Mary Quarterly,* 3rd Ser., 30 (1973): 246, for the total number of slaves and servants, one-third of whom were female; Boston: J. H. Benton, Jr., *Early Census Making in Massachusetts, 1643–1765 with a Reproduction of the Lost Census of 1765 . . .* (Boston: C. E. Goodspeed, 1905), following 71.

36. The census of 1765, cited in n.35 above, indicates 1,676 houses in the city. In 1742 there were 1,719 houses. *Boston Town Rec.,* 14:369–70. The ratios are taken from Lemuel Shattuck, *Report of the Committee of the City Council Appointed to Obtain the Census of Boston for the Year 1845* (Boston, 1846), 54. The ratio in New York has been calculated by extrapolating the population for 1753 from the censuses of 1749 and 1756 and dividing by the number of houses in 1753 as specified by Thomas Pownall, the governor of Massachusetts, in Lois Mulkearn, ed., *T. Pownall, A Topographical Description of the Dominions of the United States of America . . .* (Pittsburgh: Univ. of Pittsburgh Press, 1949), 44. For Philadelphia I have used the house count as given in John K. Alexander, "The Philadelphia Numbers Game: An Analysis of Philadelphia's Eighteenth-Century Population," *Pennsylvania Magazine of History and Biography,* 98 (1974): 324, and the population figures calculated in Billy G. Smith, "Death and Life in a Colonial Immigrant City: A Demographic Analysis of Philadelphia," *Journal of Economic History,* 37 (1977): 865.

37. The Society reported that 489 yards had been woven for them and 340 yards for private persons ("Report of the Committee of the Society . . . ," *Boston Evening Post,* Feb. 19, 1753). In the quarterly report a year earlier, the Society noted that 1,772 yards had been produced, more than twice as much (*Report of the Committee for Encouraging Industry . . . Feb. 1752* [Boston, 1752]); *Boston Evening Post,* Feb. 19, 1753; Cooper, *A Sermon Preached,* 33; Memorial of Andrew Oliver et al. to the Governor and Council, May 1753, Mass. Archives, 59:381–83; Price Papers, #318. John Hancock and John Barrett were buying cloth procured from independent weavers and were thus competing directly with the manufactory (*ibid.,* #329). In 1752, 72 percent of the cloth woven was for the Society (*Report of the Committee . . . Feb. 1752); Bos. Town Rec.,* 16:226–27. The Society's records show that spinners could process

100 pounds of flax per year and were paid 3 shillings, 9 pence (Massachusetts money) per pound (Price Papers, #322). This works out to 7.2 shillings a week (4.8 shillings sterling), not enough to buy food for even one person.

38. Mather, *Some Seasonable Advice unto the Poor* . . . (Boston, 1712). The sermon was reprinted in 1726.

39. Chauncy, *The Idle-Poor Secluded from the Bread of Christian Charity*, 9–17; also see Chauncy, *Industry and Frugality Proposed as the Surest Means to make Us a Rich and Flourishing People; And the Linen Manufacture Recommended As tending to promote These among Us* (Boston, 1753), especially 10; Cooper, *A Sermon Preached*, 23. Some of the older ideology regarding the poor, charging the rich with responsibility for alleviating the distress of the unfortunate, still persisted. The *Boston Gazette* (Aug. 27, 1751) reprinted an essay on poor relief from the *New York Gazette* in 1751 that urged people of means to buy from artisans and shopkeepers who had fallen upon hard times, even if it meant paying a bit more, and to sell the necessities of life to the poor below the prevailing rates.

40. Chauncy, *Industry and Frugality Proposed* . . . , 10; *Bos. Town Rec.*, 19:38; Cooper, *A Sermon Preached*, 33.

6

THE TRANSFORMATION OF
URBAN POLITICS,
1700–1764

THAT COLONIAL POLITICS were highly factional and unstable is a familiar theme in early American history. Like pieces of colored glass in kaleidoscopic arrangement, it is said, factions came and went, shifting with time, place, circumstances, and the personalities of leaders. But rarely, according to the historical studies of recent decades, did these groupings develop the organizational machinery, the coherence, the continuity, or the political sophistication of the political parties which emerged in the aftermath of the American Revolution.[1]

Historians have attempted primarily to unravel the legislative history of these factional struggles, especially as they pitted representative assemblies against royal or proprietary governors and officeholders, and to invest these contests with either economic or ideological significance. Thus scholars know a great deal about struggles over parliamentary privileges, the power of the purse, and control of the courts. Historians have passed through almost a century of argument which has cyclically explained political contention as a clashing of rival social and economic groups or, alternatively, as a Whiggish struggle against prerogative government. But for all of this investigation, little is known about the actual practice and style of electoral politics in the first two-thirds of the eighteenth century.

By taking political factionalism as given, playing down the issues dividing factions, and shifting the analysis from the motivations of political groups, it is possible to focus on the practice of factional politics and on the kind of political ethos or culture which was emerging in the period before 1765. An examination of three cities which would become instrumental in the coming of the Revolution—Boston, New

---

This essay first appeared in the *Journal of American History*, 60 (1973): 605–32. Minor alterations have been made in the text and the footnotes, and the date in the title has been slightly changed.

York, and Philadelphia—yields compelling evidence that in the six decades before the Stamp Act crisis a "radical" mode of politics was evolving in the urban centers of colonial life.[2] This "transformation" involved activation of previously quiescent lower-class elements; the organization of political clubs, caucuses, and tickets; the employment of political literature and inflammatory rhetoric as never before; the involvement of the clergy and the churches in politics; and the organization of mobs and violence for political purposes. Although many of these innovations were managed by and for political elites and not intended to democratize colonial political life, the effect was to broaden the spectrum of individuals actively involved in public affairs and to produce a political culture that was far from deferential, increasingly antiauthoritarian, occasionally violent, and often destructive of the very values which the political elite wished to preserve.

At election time in 1726, a prominent Quaker merchant in Philadelphia wrote an English friend that "we have our Mobs, Bonfires, Gunns, Huzzas . . . Itinerations and processions too—Trains made up (as 'tis said) not of the Wise, the Rich or the Learned, for the Gentleman while he was Governour took care to discard all Such. . . ."[3] In this description Issac Norris expressed his dismay that Governor William Keith, who no longer felt obliged to serve the interests of his employer, the widow of William Penn, had cultivated the support of a stratum of society that the "wise, Rich and Learned" believed had no place in the political process. Since 1723, in fact, Keith had been mobilizing support among lower-class workingmen in Philadelphia and newly arrived German and Scotch-Irish immigrants.

Elitist politicians and proprietary supporters complained bitterly of "Sir William's town Mob" and the governor's "sinister army," lamented that elections were "mobbish and carried by a levelling spirit," and charged that the "common People both in town & Country" were "blown up even to a degree of madness."[4] Of the 1726 elections Norris wrote that Keith had "perambulated" the city, "Popping into ye dramshops tiff & alehouses where he would find a great number of modern statesmen & some patriots settling affairs, cursing some, praising others, contriving laws & swearing they will have them enacted *cum multis aegis. "* Worse still, Keith's electoral victory was celebrated by an exuberant procession, "mostly made of Rabble Butchers porters & Tagrags—thus triumphantly has he made his Gradations Downward from a Government to an Equal with Every plain Country Member."[5]

Keith's attempt to build a broader political base in order to gain control of an assembly dominated by Quakers was not the first attempt in Philadelphia to develop new sources of political support to defeat an entrenched opponent. Two decades before, David Lloyd had accomplished a substantial shift of political power by expanding the politically relevant strata of Pennsylvania society and activating a part of the community that had played an insignificant role in politics. Though his real goal was to shield Pennsylvania from proprietary authority, not to shift the center of political gravity downward, Lloyd found that—given the power of the proprietary group—it was mandatory to establish a new base of political support.[6]

This technique of mobilizing the politically inert became increasingly more important to eighteenth-century political life. For the Pennsylvania Quakers, who had overcome earlier disunity and formed a strong anti-proprietary party, the problem was how to maintain influence in a society where they were fast becoming a minority. For the proprietary party, the problem was how to develop popular sources of support in order to overcome Quaker domination of the assembly. Thus both factions, led by men of high position and reputation, nervously began to eye the Germans who were streaming into the colony after 1715. Neither the Quaker-dominated anti-proprietary or "Assembly" party nor the Anglican-based proprietary party welcomed the inundation of German immigrants who were regarded by Englishmen of both groups as crude, alien, and too numerous. But both factions cultivated their support. That the Quakers continued to control the assembly throughout the half-century preceding the Revolution, despite their fading numerical importance, was attributable largely to their success in politicizing the Germans, who were more interested in farming than legislative assemblies but found themselves dragged into the thicket of politics.[7]

With even greater misgivings, the proprietary party courted the German community, which by the 1750s represented about 40 percent of the population in Pennsylvania. In private discourse and correspondence its leaders continued to regard the Germans as "an uncultivated Race" of uncouth peasants, incapable, as one put it, "of using their own Judgment in matters of Government. . . ."[8] But political requirements conquered social and ethnic reservations, and, while proprietary leaders could describe the Germans in 1750 as "more licentious and impotent of a just government than any others" and "a body of ignorant, proud stubborn Clowns," they worked hard to split the German vote, as they had been doing since about 1740.[9] This drive for German support yielded only meager rewards in the political battles of the mid-1750s, but by 1764 the proprietary campaign was crowned with success. Benjamin Franklin and Joseph Galloway attributed their loss in the hotly contested election of that year to the "Dutch vote" which had swung against them.[10] Proprietary leaders would have preferred to exert political leverage from power bases where men were appointed out of regard for their background, accomplishments, and standing in the community—the council, city corporation, College of Philadelphia, hospital, and Library Company.[11] But gradually—and reluctantly—proprietary politicians learned to seek support from groups which they would have preferred to regard as inadmissible to political life. The problem of challenging the legislative strength of their opponents could not otherwise be solved.

Just as members of the proprietary party learned to overcome their scruples with regard to involving Germans in the political process, they learned to swallow reservations about soliciting the support of lower-class mechanics and laborers. Galloway, a Quaker party stalwart, took great delight in pointing out that the "Gentlemen of the best fortune" in the proprietary party, who in their public statements spoke for hierarchy and order in all affairs, "thought it not mean or dishonourable to enter the Houses of the Lowest Mechanics to solicit their Opposition" to the Militia Act of 1756.[12] By 1764 these artisans would become all-important in the attempts of the proprietary party to defeat their opponents.

In New York a similar process was taking place, although attempts to mobilize a broad-based electorate were not as continuous. Jacob Leisler was perhaps the first to seek support among those whom by traditional thinking were better left outside the political arena. Leisler also relied upon the support of the Dutch who would continue to play a crucial role in electoral politics throughout the prerevolutionary period. Unlike the Germans in Philadelphia, however, the Dutch were well represented at all levels of the social structure and were well integrated into the social and economic fabric of New York City at the beginning of the eighteenth century.

Only a few years after Keith so effectively organized the artisanry of Philadelphia, the fires of political contention in New York, banked briefly after the Leislerian era by the adroit management of Governor Robert Hunter, grew hot enough to convince upper-class leaders that they must delve to deeper strata in society to develop political support. The heavy-handed aggrandizement of power by Governor William Cosby and a decisive defeat in the assembly elections of 1727 were enough to convince the Morris party that they must play the game of tavern politics if they hoped to prevail. The city elections of 1733 and 1734, which among other things led to the trial of John Peter Zenger for seditious libel, reflected this new appeal to workingmen and the Dutch in the city.[13] That both sides could play the same game is evident in the attempts of Stephen De Lancey and Francis Harrison, members of the governor's inner circle, to carry the aldermanic election in the South Ward in 1734 by sending a troop of English soldiers from Fort George to the polls; and in the remarkable invitations of Governor Cosby himself, as Cadwallader Colden noted indignantly, to "many of low rank to dine with him such as had never pretended or expected so much respect."[14] These attempts at political mobilization were carried even further in 1737, if Colden can be believed. Describing the municipal elections he wrote: "The sick, the lame, and the blind were all carried to vote. They were carried out of Prison and out of the poor house to vote. Such a struggle I never saw and such a hurra[h]ing that above one half of the men in town are so hoarse that they cannot speak this day. The pole lasted from half an hour after nine in the morning till past nine at night."[15]

The ambition and energy of the De Lancey brothers, Stephen and Oliver, pushed the process a step further during the next decade. In their hatred of Governor George Clinton, who held office in New York from 1743 to 1753, the De Lanceys carefully cultivated the support of the large mechanic population in the city—an attempt, as Clinton complained, "to overturn his Majesty's Goverment by wresting the Power out of the Hands of His Officers, and placing it in a popular faction."[16] To the imperious Colden the sight of rich assembly candidates courting workingmen conjured up the remembrance that "true roman virtue was allmost totally extinguished before their great or rich men went about to court the common people for their votes." Colden hoped the "lower rank" in New York would not become "so low & weak as to take it as favour to be call'd by their names by rich men & to be shook by the hand," as had happened centuries ago while the Roman Empire was crumbling.[17]

Charges by elitists such as Colden and Clinton that opponents were attempting to rule by "meer popular influence" or were attempting "to instigate the passions of the lowest rank of people to the most wicked purposes" must be approached with caution.[18] But analysis of the three assembly elections of the 1760s indicates that the work of politicizing the laboring class had proceeded far enough to make it all but impossible to win electoral contests without the support not only of the skilled artificers, who often owned considerable property, but also the unskilled laborers, cartmen, mariners, and boatmen.[19] It is also important to note that the factional fighting that went on from the late 1720s through the 1760s sent all leaders scurrying after the Dutch vote. The Morris party did its best to cultivate the Dutch at the beginning of this period, as did the De Lancey faction at mid-century.[20] In the mid-1750s when New York was inflamed by the controversy over King's College, both sides recognized that the support of the Dutch was crucial and exhausted all means to obtain it. The inability of William Livingston and his partisans to win a large part of the Dutch vote explains more than anything else the shattered hopes of the Presbyterian faction in its attempt to prevent the Anglicans from obtaining a charter for the college.[21] The effect of this competition for Dutch support was to split an ethnic bloc which early in the century had been virtually unified at the polls.[22]

In Boston the process of activating the inactive proceeded along somewhat different lines but in the same direction. Unlike Philadelphia and New York, Boston had a population that was ethnically homogeneous. Throughout the colonial period factional leaders appealed for the support of a mass of English voters only lightly sprinkled with Scotch and Irish. Boston was also different in that ever since an armed crowd had mysteriously gathered in April 1689 to command the streets of Boston and force Edmund Andros into exile, its citizens, at all levels of society, had been far less quiescent than their counterparts in other urban centers. This may be partially explained by the effect on the political life of the city which the town meeting fostered.[23] In Boston, as in no other city, open debate was heard and decisions were made by majority vote on many issues, ranging from passing a bylaw "to prevent playing football in the streets" to voting £10 to Susana Striker for a kidney stone operation for her son, to taxing inhabitants for the erection of public buildings, poor relief, schoolteachers' salaries, and other expenses.[24] And whereas in New York and Philadelphia only a small number of municipal officers were elected, in Boston the voters installed not only selectmen, sheriffs, assessors, and constables, but surveyors of hemp, informers about deer, purchasers of grain, haywards, town criers, measurers of salt, scavengers, viewers of shingles, sheepreeves, hogreeves, sealers of leather, fenceviewers, firewards, cullers of stave hoops, auditors, and others.[25]

Thus in terms of a politically minded and active lower rank, Boston had already developed by the early eighteenth century what other urban centers haltingly and sporadically moved toward in the half-century before 1765. Governor Cosby of New York pointed up this difference in 1735 when he charged the Morris faction, which was working the streets of New York to stir up opposition, with copying "the example and spirit of the Boston people."[26]

But if the clay with which leaders of political factions worked was of a somewhat different consistency in Boston, the problems of delving deeper in society to ensure political victory were essentially the same. Thus the "soft money" faction led by Elisha Cooke, Oliver Noyes, Thomas Cushing, and William Clark "turned to the people as the only possible base of political strength in Boston and took it upon [themselves] to organize politics and elections in the town with unprecedented vigor and attention" in the 1720s.[27] In the following decade, when a series of economic issues in Boston came to a head, and in the 1740s, when the second currency crisis ripened, exceptional measures were again taken to call upon those not included in the ranks of respectability. "Interested Men," complained Peter Oliver in 1749, had "set the Canaille to insult" Thomas Hutchinson for his leadership of the conservative fiscal movement.[28] In this way political leaders recruited the support of lower-class artisans and mechanics whose bodies provided a new kind of political power, as demonstrated in three mob actions of the 1740s in Boston directed by men of stature in the community, and whose votes provided the margin of victory in the increasingly frequent contested elections.[29]

To engage in political mobilization, factional leaders found they had to pursue a course which ran against the grain of their social philosophy. Given the widely shared belief in maintaining rank and order in all human affairs and the rationalist view that only the cultivation of the mind raised man above his naturally depraved state, it was to be expected that the gentility would look upon courting the favor of "the lesser sorts" or involving them in politics as a reckless policy containing the seeds of anarchy. To activate the multitude was to energize precisely that part of society which was ruled by passion—the baser impulses in human nature—rather than by reason. The letters and reports of leaders in Boston, New York, and Philadelphia are filled with allusions to "the rabble," "the unthinking multitude," and the dangers of exciting "the passions" of the populace. Although these fears resonated most strongly in conservative quarters, they were shared by popular leaders such as Livingston and Franklin, who were also concerned with preserving social hierarchy and respect for authority. It was more difficult, of course, for those with a more rigid and authoritarian outlook to reconcile the eighteenth-century rationalist philosophy with the necessity of campaigning for votes and adopting the techniques of popular politics. But when political necessity called, they too learned to set aside ingrained social principles. The best that could be hoped for was that somehow the support of unassimilated or lower-class elements could be engaged without altering the structure of values by which such groups deferred to elitist politicians. Men at the top had embarked upon a radical course of political recruitment while hoping that these stratagems would not have radical effects.

Because all factions felt the necessity of broadening the political base, the dynamics of politics changed markedly. In a society in which the people at large acquiesced in the rule of the upper stratum, and in which social, economic, and political leadership were regarded as indivisible, political decisions could be made quietly and privately. Elites would be held in check, of course, by periodic tests of confidence administered by the propertied part of the community. But when the upper layer of society split into competing factions, which were obliged to recruit the support of those previously inert or outside the political process, then politics became open, abusive in tone, and sometimes violent.

New techniques of political organization were required. Men began to form political "tickets," as happened in Pennsylvania as early as 1705, in Boston at the end of the 1720s, and in New York as early as 1698. Leaders of the more conservative factions usually resisted this move in the direction of popular politics. Philadelphia conservatives James Logan and Norris, for example, decried the use of tickets that obliged the voter to "have eight men crammed down his throat at once."[30] The use of tickets was also accompanied by written balloting and the introduction of the caucus—closed at first—to nominate a slate of candidates. Thus Quaker leaders in the 1720s loudly declaimed Keith's "Electing-Club" in Philadelphia.[31] But within a few decades the anti-Quaker proprietary leaders would be complaining bitterly that the Quakers used their yearly meeting, which met during the week before assembly elections, as a political caucus—a practice condemned in 1755 as "the finest Scheme that could possibly be projected for conducting political Intrigues, under the Mask of Religion."[32] Yielding to the realities of political life, the proprietary leaders in 1756 adopted the tactics of their opponents and even outdid the Quaker party by calling for open rather than private caucuses. A notice in the *Pennsylvania Gazette* summoned the electorate to the Philadelphia Academy for an open-air, on-the-spot primary election. Ideological consistency was abandoned as Quaker party writers condemned the innovation in the next issue of the newspaper, only to be attacked by the aristocratic proprietary spokesman who defended the rights of the freeholders "to meet in a peaceable Manner to chuse their Representatives."[33] Seeing a chance for electoral success in the Quaker opposition to war appropriations, the proprietary leaders put scruples aside and resorted to tactics that heretofore had offended their sense of political propriety.

In Boston popular politics came under the control of perhaps the best-organized caucus in the English colonial world. So far as the limited evidence indicates, the Boston caucus was organized about 1719 and functioned intermittently for about four decades before splitting into the North End Caucus and the South End Caucus. The Boston caucus nominated candidates for the city's four seats in the General Court and proposed selectmen and other town officials at the annual elections. Operating in the taverns, it perfected a network of political influence through affiliations with the independent fire companies, the Merchants' Club, and other social organizations.[34]

In New York the devices of popular politics were less in evidence than in Philadelphia or Boston because New York did not have annual assembly elections and employed viva-voce voting rather than the written ballot. Though a secret balloting law had been "long desired by . . . Friends to Liberty in this City," according to a political writer a few years before the Revolution, such a law had never passed.[35] Nonetheless, popular politics took a long stride forward in 1739 with the replacement of the private nomination of assembly candidates by public nominating meetings. As Carl Becker noted more than half a century ago, this change constituted a recognition on the part of political leaders that "great numbers constituted as good a political asset as great names."[36] The origins of this innovation may be traced back to the work of the Morris-Alexander-Smith coalition against Governor Cosby in the early 1730s, although the first solid evidence of the open caucus is found in 1739 when the New York *Gazette* reported that "a great number of the freeholders and freemen of the . . . city have agreed and resolved to choose the following persons to represent them. . . ."[37]

An even more significant element in transforming politics from a private to a public affair was the use of the press. Although the political press had been used extensively in seventeenth-century England, it was not widely employed in colonial politics until the 1720s. Before that an occasional pamphlet had directed the attention of the public to a controversial issue. But such early polemical efforts as Joseph Palmer, *The Present State of New England* (Boston, 1689), or Thomas Lloyd, *A Seasonable Advertisement to the Freemen of this Province* . . . (Philadelphia, 1689), were beamed at the General Court or the assembly, though their authors probably hoped also to cultivate the support of the populace at large. "Campaign literature"—direct appeals to the freemen at election time—was rare in Boston before 1710, in Philadelphia before 1720, and in New York before 1730. But as issues became more heated and politicians discovered the need to reach a wider audience, the resort to the press became a fixed part of political culture. In Philadelphia, for example, where only five pieces of political literature had appeared in the first quarter of the century, the public was bombarded with forty-six pamphlets and broadsides between 1725 and 1728. Bostonians in 1721 and 1722 could spend their evenings in tavern discussions of any of the twenty-eight argumentative tracts on the currency crisis that appeared in those years. In New York, where the political press was somewhat more restrained in the prerevolutionary period than in Boston or Philadelphia, the Morris-Cosby struggle for power brought twenty-seven pamphlets from the presses between 1732 and 1734, when only an occasional piece had appeared before.[38]

By the 1740s the printed word had become an indispensable part of campaigning. In every contested election pamphleteers industriously alerted the public to the awful consequences that would attend a victory by the other side. When the excise bill was under consideration in 1754, seventeen pamphlets appeared in the streets of Boston to rally public support against it.[39] The King's College controversy in New York kept the city's two printers busy with the publication of several dozen efforts.[40] In Philadelphia the Paxton Massacre was argued pro-and-con in at least twenty-eight pamphlets, and in the election contest that followed in the fall of 1764 no less than forty-four pamphlets and broadsides were published, many with German editions.[41] A rise in polemical literature and election appeals is also evident in colonial newspapers which were increasing in number in the eighteenth century.[42]

This increase in the use of the press had important implications, not merely because of the quantity of political literature but also because the pamphlets and newspaper screeds were intended to make politics everyone's concern. The new political literature was distributed without reference to social standing or economic position and "accustomed people of all classes, but especially of the middling and lower estates, to the examination and discussion of controversial issues of all sorts."[43] Thus, those whom even the most liberal politicians would not have formally admitted to the political arena were drawn into it informally.

The anguished cries of politicians about the dangerous effects of this new polemical literature give a clue to the ambivalent feelings which the elite held in regard to the use of the press. An optimist like Franklin looked upon fiery pamphlets and newspaper fusillades as instruments "to prepare the Minds of the Publick,"[44] but most men assumed that man easily succumbed to his basest instincts and that the unthinking multitude, which included a vast majority of the population, was moved by passion rather than reason. Guided by these views, most leaders could not help but look upon exhortatory literature as a threat to the social order. Conservative politicians frequently attacked what they called irresponsible attempts "to inflame the minds of the people" or "to breed and nourish Discontent, and to foment Faction and Sedition."[45] And yet by the 1750s, and often before, even the most conservative leader could not resist the resort to the press, even though it might contradict his social philosophy. Men such as James De Lancey, who earlier had lamented its use, were eagerly employing the press by mid-century. Their opponents could only shake their heads in dismay—charging that attempts were being made to propagate "Clamour & Slander" and to turn the heads of "ignorant people & others who are not well acquainted with the publick affairs"—and then take up the pen themselves.[46] In Philadelphia it was the proprietary party, espousing social conservatism and constantly warning about the anarchic and leveling designs of Quaker politicians, that raised the art of pamphleteering to new levels of sophistication in the 1750s. No one in Philadelphia could quite match the imperious William Smith for statements about the necessity of the ordered, deferential society; but no one did more to make the abusive pamphlet a part of the eighteenth-century political arsenal.[47]

Given this increasing reliance upon the press, it was inevitable that the professional pamphleteer would emerge as a new figure in politics. Isaac Hunt, David James Dove, and Hugh Williamson of Philadelphia were only three of a group of political writers who earned their pay by devising new ways of touching the fears and aspirations of the electorate through deception, innuendo, and scurrility. The professional pamphleteer, in the hire of elitist politicians, symbolized the contradiction between the new political stratagems and the old social outlook.[48]

Not only a quantitative leap in political literature but also an escalation of rhetoric made the use of the press a particularly important part of the new politics. As political literature became institutionalized, the quality of language and the modes of argumentation changed markedly. In the early eighteenth century pamphleteers exercised restraint, appealing to the public judgment and the "best interest of the country." Perhaps mindful of the revolutionary potential of the printed word, authors couched their arguments in legalistic terms. For example, in Boston, during the exchange of pamphlets on the currency crisis in 1714, hundreds of pages were offered to the public, but readers encountered nothing more virulent than charges that the opposition view was "strange and Unaccountable," "intolerable," "unreasonable and unjust," or that writers on the other side were guilty of "bold and wilful Misrepresentation." But by 1754 the anti-excise pamphleteers were raising images in the public mind of "Little pestilent Creature[s]," "dirty miscreants," and unspeakably horrible creatures ready to "cram [their] . . . merciless and insatiable Maw[s] with our very Blood, and bones, and Vitals" while making sexual advances on wives and daughters.[49] In Philadelphia, Keith's political campaigns in the 1720s introduced a genre of literature that for the first time directly attacked men of wealth and learning. "According to my experience," wrote David Lloyd, "a mean Man, of small Interest, devoted to the faithful Discharge of his Trust and Duty to the Government, may do more good to the State than a Richer or more Learned Man, who by his ill Temper and aspiring Mind becomes an opposer of the Constitution by which he should act."[50] This was egalitarian rhetoric which inverted the social pyramid by rejecting the traditional notion that the maintenance of social order and political stability depended on vesting power in men of education and high status.

But this kind of language was a model of restraint compared to mid-century political vitriol. In newspapers and pamphlets, contending elites hurled insults at each other and charged their opponents, to cite one example from Philadelphia, with "Inveterate Calumny, foul-mouthed Aspersion, shameless Falsehood, and insatiate Malice. . . ."[51] New York also witnessed a change in rhetorical style as pamphleteers substituted slander and vituperation for reasonsed discourse. The Anglican clergy was left no semblance of integrity in the attacks of the Livingston faction during the King's College controversy. In phrases that made Zenger's New York *Journal* seem polite by comparison, readers were told of the "ghastly juggling . . . and insatiate Lust of Power" of the Anglican clergymen and learned of "our intended Vassal-age," the "Seduction of Priest-craft," and "clerical Rubbish and Villainy."[52]

In effect, the conservatives' worst fears concerning the use of the press were being confirmed as the tactics of printed political discourse changed from attacking the legality or wisdom of the opposition's policies or pleading for the election of public-minded men to assailing the character and motives of those on the other side. The effect of the new political rhetoric was self-intensifying as each increase in the brutality of language brought an equivalent or greater response from the opposition. Gradually the public was taught to suspect not simply the wisdom or constitutional right of one side or the other, but the motives, morality, and even sanity of its leaders. The very high-placed individuals to whom the rank-and-file were supposed to defer were being exposed as the most corrupt and loathsome members of society.

In mob activity and threats of violence the radicalization of politics can be seen in its most dramatic though not its most significant form. It is well to make a distinction between spontaneous disorders expressive of deeply felt lower-class grievances and mob activity arranged and directed by political leaders to serve their own purposes. A connection existed between the two kinds of activity since political elites, witnessing random lower-class disorder, did not fail to note the effectiveness of collective force; and lower-class elements, encouraged or even rewarded by political leaders for participating in riotous activity, undoubtedly lost some of their awe and reverence for duly constituted authority, gaining a new sense of their own power.[53]

Mobs expressing class grievances were less common in the colonial cities than in rural areas, where land disputes and Indian policy were major sources of conflict throughout the eighteenth century.[54] The food rioting that was a persistent factor in the history of European cities of this period was almost unknown in Boston, New York, and Philadelphia.[55] Far more common was the sporadic violence directed at individuals identified with unpopular causes. Cotton Mather, who went unappreciated by a large part of Boston's population throughout his lifetime of religious and political eminence, had his house fire-bombed in 1721.[56] In 1749 Thomas Hutchinson, long identified with hard-money policies, watched ruefully as his house burned to the cheers of the mob while the fire company responded with a suspicious lack of speed.[57] James Logan and his wife spent a night under the bed when the mob bombarded their stately house with stones, convincing Logan that law and order in Philadelphia was as shattered as his window panes.[58] This kind of violence, along with unofficially sanctioned riots such as the annual Pope's Day battles between North End and South End in Boston, reflected the general abrasiveness of life in the eighteenth century and the frailty of law enforcement in the cities.[59]

Far more significant was violence inspired and controlled by the elite. This was often directed at imperial officers charged with carrying out unpopular trade or military policies. Thus Boston was more or less in the hands of the mob for three days in 1747, after the commander of the British fleet in the harbor ordered his press gang to make a nocturnal sweep through the streets. The mob, wrote Governor William Shirley, "was secretly Contenanc'd and encourag'd by some ill minded Inhabitants and Persons of Influence in the Town. . . ."[60] The garrisoning of troops in New York City led to "constant violence" and the efforts of crown officials to block illegal trade with the enemy was forcibly resisted in 1759 by the city's merchants who employed waterfront mobs to do their work.[61] But mobs were also used in internal political struggles that did not involve imperial policy. In Boston in the 1730s, when the issue of a public market dominated municipal politics, a band of night raiders sawed through the supports of the market houses in the North End and later demolished another building. When Governor Jonathan Belcher vowed to see justice done, letters circulated in the town claiming that 500 men stood ready to oppose with force any attempt to intervene in the case.[62] In Philadelphia, Keith's "town mob," as his detractors called it, was sufficiently enlivened by their election victory in 1726 to burn the pillory and stocks—the symbols of authority and social control.[63] Two years later a dispute over a vacant assembly seat led to a campaign of intimidation and assault on Quaker members of the assembly by Keith's partisans. The Quakers complained that such "Indecensies [were] used towards the Members of Assembly attending the Service of the Country in *Philadelphia,* by rude and disorderly Persons," that it was unsafe to meet any longer in Philadelphia.[64] When the assembly met in the following spring, it faced an incipient insurrection. Keith's mob, according to James Logan, was to apply "first to the Assembly and then storm the Government," knocking heads, plundering estates, and putting houses to the torch, if necessary, to get what it wanted.[65] Only the hasty passage of an act authorizing the death penalty for riot and insurrection seems to have averted violence.

In 1742 Philadelphia was shaken by a bloody election-day riot. It was a prime example of the elite's willingness to employ the mob.[66] Even before election day, rumors circulated that the Quaker party intended to maintain its majority in the assembly by steering unnaturalized Germans to the polls and that the proprietary party meant to thwart this attempt by engaging a pack of toughs. The rumors had substance. When the leaders of the two political factions could not agree on procedures for supervising the election, heated words and curses were exchanged; and seventy sailors wielding clubs and shouting "down with the plain Coats & broad Brims" waded into the Quaker crowd assembled before the courthouse.[67] When the Quaker leaders retreated inside, the sailors filled the air with a hailstorm of bricks. A counterattack was launched by Germans and younger Quakers, who momentarily forgot their pacifist principles. "Blood flew plentifully around," the proprietary secretary reported.[68] Conducting investigations later, the Quaker assembly concluded that the riot had been engineered by the leaders of the proprietary party. Though some historians have disputed this, two of the proprietor's chief officials in Pennsylvania privately admitted as much.[69]

Although mob violence was probably not nearly so widespread in the colonial cities as in London, the leaders of all factions were sensitive to the power that the mob possessed. Few colonial leaders wanted to democratize society or shift political power downward in the social order. But locked in competition with other upper-class groups, they found it necessary to expand the politically relevant sector of society by encouraging the common people to participate in direct political action.

It would be a mistake to believe that political mobs were passive instruments manipulated by the elite. Though lower-class economic and social grievances only rarely achieved ideological expression in this period, the men who worked by night in Boston or Philadelphia surely gained a new sense of their own power. The urban artisan or laborer discovered that he was not only a useful but also often an essential part of politics. As early as 1729, James Logan sensed the implications of deploying "the multitudes." "Sir William Keith," he wrote, "was so mad, as well as wicked, most industriously to sett up the lowest part of the People; through a vain expectation that he should always be able to steer and influence them as his own Will. But he weakly forgot how soon the minds of such People are changed by any new Accident and how licentious force, when the Awe of Government . . . is thrown off, has been turned against those who first taught them to throw it off."[70]

Another important facet of the "new politics" of the prerevolutionary decades was the growing involvement of religious leaders in politics, something nearly all leaders deplored but nonetheless exploited. Of course religious leaders had never been isolated from political life in the early history of the colonies; but such efforts as they made to influence public affairs were usually conducted discreetly and privately. When clergymen published pamphlets on political subjects, they did so anonymously. The common assumption that it was inappropriate for clergymen to mix religion and politics was clearly articulated in 1722 when Cotton Mather and John Wise were exposed as two of the principal controversialists in the heated currency debate in Massachusetts. "Some of our Ecclesiasticks of late," wrote an anonymous pamphleteer, "have been guilty of too officious a meddling with State Affairs. To see a Clergy-man (Commedian-like) stand belabouring his Cushion and intermixing his Harrangue with THUNDERBOLTS, while entertaining his peaceable Congregation with things whereof he is . . . Ignorant . . . how ridiculous is the Sight and the Sound."[71] Such attacks on clerical involvement in politics would continue throughout the prerevolutionary period. But by mid-century church leaders were beginning to shed their anonymity and to defend their right to engage in "preaching politics," as Jonathan Mayhew put it in Boston in 1750.[72]

To some extent this politicization of the clergy can be attributed to the Great Awakening, for amid the evangelical fervor of the early 1740s "religious controversies and political problems were blended in a unique pattern of interaction."[73] But perhaps more important was the fact that by the 1740s the fires of political contention were growing hotter, impelling factional leaders to enlist the services of religious leaders. In Philadelphia, the issue of war and defense appropriations in 1748, not the Great Awakening, brought the first full-scale exchange on a secular question between opposing denominational spokesmen. In a dozen signed pamphlets Presbyterian and Quaker leaders such as Gilbert Tennent and Samuel Smith carried out a public dialogue on the necessity of military defense—a battle of words that thrust the clergy into the political arena.[74]

No more dramatic representation of a politicized clergy can be imagined than the jailing of the Anglican ecclesiastic William Smith by the Pennsylvania assembly in 1758. Writing anonymously, Smith had published two open-handed attacks on the Quaker party in 1755 and 1756 as part of the proprietary party's offensive against the Quaker-dominated assembly. He continued his assaults in 1757 and 1758 in the *American Magazine* and the *Pennsylvania Journal*. Determined to halt these attacks, the assembly charged Smith and one of his fellow writers with libel. During the course of a long trial and subsequent appeals to

England, Smith carried out his duties and political ambitions from the Philadelphia jail.[75]

The clergy's increasing involvement in politics had a second dimension which was closely related to the Great Awakening. One of the side effects of the revivalist movement was an expansion of political consciousness within the lower reaches of society. The average city dweller developed a new feeling of autonomy and importance as he partook of mass revivals, assumed a new power in ecclesiastical affairs, and was encouraged repeatedly from the pulpit to adopt an attitude of skepticism toward dogma and authority. Doctrinal controversy and attacks on religious and secular leaders became ritualized and accepted in the 1740s.[76] It was precisely this that caused high-placed individuals to charge revivalists with preaching levelism and anarchy. "It is . . . an exceeding difficult gloomy time with us . . . ," wrote William Rand from Boston; "Such an enthusiastic, factious, censorious Spirit was never known here. . . . Every low-bred, illiterate Person can resolve Cases of Conscience, and settle the most difficult Points of Divinity, better than the most learned Divines."[77] Such charges were heard repeatedly during the Great Awakening, revealing the apprehension of those who trembled to see the "unthinking multitude" invested with a new dignity and importance. Nor could the passing of the Great Awakening reverse the tide, for this new sense of power did not atrophy with the decline of religious enthusiasm, but remained as a permanent part of the social outlook of the middle and lower strata of society.

The October 1764 elections in Philadelphia provide an opportunity to observe in microcosm all of the radicalizing tendencies of the previous three-quarters of a century. The city had already been badly shaken by the Paxton Boys, who descended on the capital to press demands for frontier defense and to take the lives of a group of Christian Indians, who were being sheltered by the government in barracks at Philadelphia. This exercise in vigilante government led to a Quaker-Presbyterian pamphlet war. Against this background the Quaker party decided to organize the October assembly elections around a campaign to replace proprietary with royal government.[78]

By the spring of 1764 the move to place Pennsylvania under royal government was underway, and political leaders in both camps were vying for popular support. Proprietary aristocrats, suppressing their contempt for the urban working class, made strenuous efforts to recruit artisan support and, for the first time, placed three ethnic candidates— two Germans and one Scotch-Irish—on their eight-man assembly slate. "The design," wrote a party organizer, "is by putting in two Germans to draw such a Party of them as will turn the scale in our Favor. . . ."[79] The success of these efforts can be measured by the conversion to the proprietary cause of Carl Wrangel and Henry Muhlenberg, the Lutheran church leaders in Philadelphia, and Christopher Sauer, Jr., and Heinrich Miller, the German printers. By the end of the summer all of these men were writing or translating anti-Quaker pamphlets for distribution in the German community.[80]

The efforts of the proprietary party to search in the lower social strata for support drove Franklin and the assembly party to even greater lengths. In early April, Franklin called a mass meeting and sent messengers house-to-house to turn out the largest possible audience. The featured speaker was Galloway, who delivered an "inflammatory harangue" about the evils of proprietary government.[81] This was the opening shot in a campaign to gather signatures on a petition pleading for the institution of royal government. In the concerted drive to obtain signatures, according to one critic, "Taverns were engag'd, [and] many of the poorer and more dependent kind of labouring people in town were invited thither by night, the fear of being turn'd out of business and the eloquence of the punch bowl prevailed on many to sign. . . ."[82] The town was saturated with polemical literature, including 3,000 copies of the assembly's biting message to the proprietor and their resolves for obtaining royal government. Franklin and Galloway published pamphlets designed to stir unrest with proprietary government, and Quakers, according to one observer, went door-to-door in pairs soliciting signatures for the royal government petition.[83] John Penn, the nephew of the proprietor, was shocked that Franklin's party went "into all the houses in Town without distinction," and "by the assistance of Punch and Beer" were able to procure the signatures of "some of the lowest sort of people" in the city.[84]

It was only a matter of time before the proprietary party, using fire to fight fire, circulated a counter-petition and far outstripped the efforts of Franklin and Galloway to involve the populace in politics. Everyone in Philadelphia, regardless of religion, class, or ideological predisposition, found himself courted by the leaders of the two political factions.[85] Never in Pennsylvania's history had the few needed the many so much.

As the battle thickened, pamphleteers reached new pinnacles of abusiveness and scurrility. Franklin was reviled as an intellectual charlatan who begged and bought honorary degrees, a corrupt politician intimately acquainted "with every Zig Zag Machination," a grasping, conniving, egotistical climber, and a lecherous old man who promoted royal government only for the purpose of installing himself in the governor's chair.[86] His friends responded by labeling an opposition pamphleteer "a Reptile" who "like a Toad, by the pestilential Fumes of his virulent Slabber" attempted "to blast the fame of a PATRIOT" and describing William Smith, leader of the opposition, as a "consumate

Sycophant," an "indefatigable" liar, and an impudent knave with a heart "bloated with *infernal Malice*"and a head full of *"flatulent Preachments."*[87] As for the Presbyterians, they were redesignated "Piss-Brute-arians (a bigoted, cruel and revengeful sect)" by a Franklin party pamphleteer who later reached the apogee of scatalogical polemics when he suggested that now was the time for Smith, president of the college and a director of the hospital, to consummate his alliance with the pamphleteer David Dove, who "will not only furnish you with that most agreeable of all Foods to your Taste, but after it has found a Passage through your Body . . . will greedily devour it, and, as soon as it is well digested, he will void it up for a Repast to the Proprietary Faction: they will as eagerly swallow it as the other had done before, and, when it has gone through their several Concoctions, they will discharge it in your Presence, that you may once more regale on it, thus refined."[88] One shocked outsider wrote to a friend in Philadelphia: "In the name of goodness stop your Pamphleteer's Mouths & shut up your presses. Such a torrent of low scurrility sure never came from any country as lately from Pennsylvan[i]a."[89]

Religious leaders were also drawn into the campaign. A rural clergyman related that the proprietary leaders had convinced Presbyterian and Anglican ministers in Philadelphia to distribute petitions requesting the preservation of proprietary government. "The Presbyterian ministers, with some others," he lamented, "held Synods about the election, turned their pulpits into Ecclesiastical drums for politics and told their people to vote according as they directed them at the peril of their damnation. . . ."[90] Church leaders such as Tennent, Francis Allison, and Muhlenberg wrote political pamphlets or sent circular letters on the election to every congregation in the province. St. Peters and Christ Church were the scenes of pre-election rallies as denominational groups assumed an unprecedented role in politics.[91] A "Gentlemen from Transylvania" charged that Philadelphia's Anglican leaders had "prostituted their Temples . . . as an Amphitheatre for the Rabble to combat in. . . ."[92]

Inflammatory rhetoric, a large polemical literature, the participation of the churches in politics, mobilization of social layers previously unsolicited and unwelcome in political affairs, all combined to produce an election in which almost everybody's integrity was questioned, every public figure's use of power was attacked, and both sides paraded themselves as true representatives of "the people." The effects were dramatic: a record number of Philadelphians turned out for the election. The polls opened at 9 A.M. and remained open through the night as party workers on both sides shepherded in the voters, including the infirm and aged who were carried to the courthouse in litters and chairs. By the next morning, party leaders were still seeking a few additional votes. Not until 3 P.M. on the second day were the polls closed.[93] When the returns were counted, both Franklin and Galloway had lost their seats to men on the proprietary ticket.[94] Franklin did not doubt that he had been defeated by defecting Germans and propertyless laborers "brought to swear themselves intituled to a Vote" by the proprietary leaders.[95] A bit of post-election doggerel caught the spirit of the contest: "A Pleasant sight tis to Behold / The beggars hal'd from Hedges/ The Deaf, the Blind, the Young the Old: / T' Secure their priveledges / They're bundled up Steps, each sort Goes / A Very Pretty Farce Sir: / Some without Stockings, some no Shoes / Nor Breeches to their A—e Sir."[96]

Although the election represents an extreme case and was affected by factors unique to the politics of proprietary Pennsylvania, it reflected a trend in the political life of other cities as well. Political innovations, involving a new set of organizational and propagandistic techniques, a vocabulary of vituperation, resort to violence, attacks on authority and social position, and the politicization of layers and groups in society that had earlier been beyond the political pale, had transformed the political culture of each of these cities in the half-century before 1764.

The extent of these changes can be measured, though imperfectly, by charting electoral participation.[97] In Boston, where the population remained nearly static at about 15,000 from 1735 to 1764, and the number of eligible voters declined markedly between 1735 and 1750 before beginning a slow upward climb, the number of voters participating in General Court elections showed a significant rise.[98] Although voter turnouts fluctuated widely from year to year, a series of peaks in 1732, 1748, 1757, 1760, and 1763 brought the number of voters from 650 in 1732 to 1,089 in 1763—a 66 percent increase during a period of population stagnation. It is also significant to note that from 1764 to 1775 the General Court elections in Boston never drew as many voters as in the years 1760 and 1763, or, for that matter, as in 1758.[99] These data throw doubt on traditional interpretations of the "democratization" of politics accompanying the Revolutionary movement, if we mean by that term the involvement of more people in the electoral process or the extension of the franchise.

In the city and county of Philadelphia a similar rise in political participation can be traced. Four years in which knowledgeable observers remarked on vigorous campaigning and heavy voter turnouts were 1728, 1742, 1754, and 1764.[100] Table 1 indicates the uneven but generally upward drift of political participation as the eighteenth century progressed. Extant voting statistics for the city of Philadelphia, exclusive of the surrounding areas of Philadelphia County, are obtainable for only a few scattered years, but a comparison of 1751 and 1764, both years of extensive political activity, shows a rise in voting participation from 40.9 to 54.5 percent of the taxable inhabitants.[101] In 1765, when the proprietary and anti-proprietary parties waged another fierce struggle around the issues raised in the campaign of 1764, the percentage of taxable inhabitants voting in the county and city of Philadelphia increased to 51.2 and 65.1 percent. Never again in the prerevolutionary decade would involvement in the electoral process be so widespread, not even in the hotly contested special assembly elections for the city of Philadelphia in April 1776.[102] These figures suggest that the barometric pressure of political culture was on the rise during the half-century preceding the Stamp Act crisis and may, in fact, have reached its pinnacle in the early 1760s.[103]

Table 1.

Year	Taxables	Voters	Percent of Taxables Voting
1728	2,963	971	32.8
1742	5,240	1,793	34.2
1754	6,908	2,173	31.4
1764	8,476	3,874	45.7

That an increasing percentage of qualified voters was participating in electoral politics not only by casting their votes but also by taking part in street demonstrations, rallies, and caucuses was emblematic of the changing political culture of the cities. Upper-class leaders, contending for political advantage, had mobilized the electorate and introduced new techniques and strategies for obtaining electoral majorities. Most of these leaders had little taste for the effects of this new kind of politics and perhaps none of them wished to bring political life to the kind of clamorous, unrestrained exercise in vitriol and slander that prevailed in Philadelphia in 1764 and 1765. But piecemeal they had contributed to a transformed political culture which by the 1760s they could only precariously control.

The transformation of politics was not restricted to the cities.[104] But it proceeded most rapidly in the urban centers of colonial life because it was in cities that men in power could influence large numbers of people; that printing presses were located and political literature was most widely distributed; that population density made possible the organization of clubs, mass meetings, and vociferous electioneering tactics; that numerous taverns provided natural nerve centers of feverish political activity; that disparities of wealth were growing most rapidly;

and that new attitudes and behavioral patterns first found ideological expression. The countryside was far from immune to the new style of politics and a new political culture, but distances and population dispersion created organizational and communication problems which were far harder to solve than in urban places.

But change occurred everywhere, rendering an older mode of politics obsolete. Internal, local, and intraclass as well as interclass struggles in colonial society had transfigured politics, creating almost by inadvertence a political culture which by 1764 already contained many of the changes in political style and behavior usually associated with the Revolutionary period.[105]

NOTES

1. Bernard Bailyn, *The Origins of American Politics* (New York, 1968); Jack P. Greene, "Changing Interpretations of Early American Politics," in Ray A. Billington, ed., *The Reinterpretation of Early American History: Essays in honor of John Edwin Pomfret* (New York, 1968), 151–84.

2. Eighteenth-century writers employed the term "radical" only infrequently; and when they did, they meant "root" or "basic." Thus Samuel Davies looked for an *"outpouring of the Spirit"* as the "grand, radical, all-comprehensive blessing" in 1757; and "Plain Dealer," writing from Philadelphia in 1764, asserted that the cause of Pennsylvania's troubles "is radical, interwoven in the Constitution, and so become of the very Nature of Proprietary Governments." See Alan Heimert, *Religion and the American Mind from the Great Awakening to the Revolution* (Cambridge, Mass., 1966), 13; [Hugh Williamson], *Plain Dealer #2* (Philadelphia, 1764), 7. The term is used here to mean not only basic but also basic in its tendency to shift power downward in a society where politics had heretofore been corporate and elitist in nature.

3. Isaac Norris to Jonathan Scarth, Oct. 21, 1726, Letter Book, 1716–1730, Isaac Norris Papers (Historical Society of Pennsylvania, Philadelphia).

4. Thomas Wendel, "The Keith-Lloyd Alliance: Factional and Coalition Politics in Colonial Pennsylvania," *Pennsylvania Magazine of History and Biography,* 92 (July 1968): 298, 296n, 301.

5. Norris to Scarth, Oct. 21, 1728, Letter Book, 1716–1730, Norris Papers. Eight years later, commenting on the residual effects of William Keith's politics, Norris would write with displeasure that the "usual care was taken to bring in Crowds of Journeymen & such like in opposition." Norris to his son, Oct. 2, 1734, Copy Book of Letters, 1730–1735, ibid.

6. Gary B. Nash, *Quakers and Politics, Pennsylvania, 1681–1726* (Princeton, 1968), 294–99.

7. Arthur D. Graeff, *The Relations Between The Pennsylvania Germans and The British Authorities (1750–1776)* (Philadelphia, 1939); Dietmar Rothermund, *The Layman's Progress: Religious and Political Experience in Colonial Pennsylvania, 1740–1770* (Philadelphia, 1961); Glenn Weaver, "Benjamin

Franklin and the Pennsylvania Germans," *William and Mary Quarterly*, 14 (Oct. 1957): 536–59; John J. Zimmerman, "Benjamin Franklin and the Quaker Party, 1755–1756," ibid., 17 (July 1960): 291–313.

8. Graeff, *Pennsylvania Germans*, 61–63.

9. James Hamilton to Thomas Penn, Nov. 8, 1750, Official Correspondence, 5:88, Penn Family Papers (Historical Society of Pennsylvania, Philadelphia); [William Smith], *A Brief State of the Province of Pennsylvania*, . . . (London, 1755), 40. By 1764 William Smith would be defending the "industrious Germans" from what he claimed were Benjamin Franklin's reference to them—after they defected from Franklin's party in large numbers—as "a wretched rabble." Leonard W. Labaree and others, ed., *The Papers of Benjamin Franklin* (24 vols., New Haven, 1959–), 11:505. The attempts of the proprietary party to recruit the German vote in the early 1740s can be followed in the letters of the party leaders, James Allen and Richard Peters, to John Penn and Thomas Penn, Official Correspondence, 3, Penn Family Papers.

10. Labaree and others, ed., *Papers of Benjamin Franklin*, 11:397; Weaver, "Franklin and the Pennsylvanian Germans," 550.

11. G. B. Warden, "The Proprietary Group in Pennsylvania, 1754–1764," *William and Mary Quarterly*, 21 (July 1964): 367–89.

12. [Joseph Galloway], *A True and Impartial State of the Province of Pennsylvania: Containing an Exact Account of the Nature of Its Government, the Power of it Proprietaries, and Their Governors . . . also the Rights and Privileges of the Assembly and People . . .* (Philadelphia, 1759), 61.

13. Stanley N. Katz, *Newcastle's New York: Anglo-American Politics, 1732–1753* (Cambridge, Mass., 1968), 68–70, 83–85; Bailyn, *Origins of American Politics*, 108–11.

14. Nicholas Varga, "New York Politics and Government in the Mid-Eighteenth Century," (doctoral dissertation, Fordham University, 1960), 397; *The Letters and Papers of Cadwallader Colden* (9 vols., New York, 1918–1937), 9:298.

15. *Letters and Papers of Cadwallader Colden*, 2:179 (punctuation added).

16. Quoted in Katz, *Newcastle's New York*, 175.

17. *Letters and Papers of Cadwallader Colden*, 4:214; 3:313–14, 318–19.

18. Ibid., 3:390, 319. In 1740 Clinton accused Oliver De Lancey of working "openly and in all companyes, and among the lower rank of people" to defeat the governor's friends. Clinton to Duke of Bedford, June 12, 1750, in John R. Brodhead and others, eds., *Documents Relative to the Colonial History of the State of New York* (15 vols., Albany, 1853–87), 6:571.

19. Roger J. Champagne, "Liberty Boys and Mechanics of New York City, 1764–1774," *Labor History*, 8 (Spring 1967): 124–31; Milton M. Klein, "Democracy and Politics in Colonial New York," *New York History*, 40 (July 1959): 238–39; Milton M. Klein, "Politics and Personalities in Colonial New York," ibid., 47 (Jan. 1966), 5–10.

20. Katz, *Newcastle's New York*, 84; Milton M. Klein, "The American

Whig: William Livingston of New York" (doctoral dissertation, Columbia University, 1954), 450. Historians have neglected the role of the Dutch in New York City politics, although they comprised about 35 percent of the electorate in the 1760s.

21. Klein, "American Whig," 402. See also Beverly McAnear, "American Imprints Concerning King's College," *Papers of the Bibliographic Society of America*, 44 (Fourth Quarter 1950): 315.

22. The extent to which ethnic bloc voting broke down in the eighteenth century is dramatically apparent in a comparison of surnames on the 1701 and 1761 poll lists that give the names of the electors for each candidate. All the percentages are higher on the 1761 breakdown because voters were choosing four representatives from a slate of six candidates whereas in the 1701 election (three wards only) voters were choosing one of two candidates. For the 1701 list, see *Minutes of the Common Council of the City of New York, 1675–1776* (8 vols., New York, 1905), 2:163–78. For the 1761 list, see *A Copy of the Poll List of the Election for Representatives for the City and County of New York which election began on Monday the 23rd day of January and ended on Friday the 27th day of the same month in the year of our Lord . . .* (New York, 1880). The author is indebted to Joyce Goodfriend for an analysis of surnames.

	1701 Percentage of		1761 Percentage of	
	English Vote	*Dutch Vote*	*English Vote*	*Dutch Vote*
Candidate 1	73.7	11.5	83.1	85.0
Candidate 2	93.2	13.5	72.1	73.4
Candidate 3	94.1	24.4	59.0	76.1
Candidate 4	26.3	88.5	68.3	57.9
Candidate 5	6.8	86.5	60.4	55.7
Candidate 6	5.9	75.6	55.4	54.3

23. See G. B. Warden, *Boston, 1689–1776* (Boston, 1970), 28–33.

24. William H. Whitmore and others, eds., *Reports of the Record Commissioners of Boston* (39 vols., Boston, 1880–1902), 8:12, 23; 12:passim.

25. In New York elections were held for the aldermen and assistants of the municipal corporation and for assessors, collectors, and constables. In Philadelphia the municipal corporation was self-perpetuating, but sheriffs, commissioners, assessors, and coroners were elected annually.

26. Katz, *Newcastle's New York*, 83–84.

27. Warden, *Boston*, 92.

28. Douglas Adair and John A. Schutz, eds., *Peter Oliver's Origin & Progress of the American Revolution: A Tory View* (San Marino, Calif., 1961), 32.

29. Eighteenth-century elections were by no means always contested. One measure of politicization is the frequency of contested elections. A few prelimi-

nary statistics for Boston may be illustrative. Defining a contested election as one in which the candidate was opposed and lost at least 25 percent of the vote, one can trace a rise in oppositional politics from the 1720s (when voting statistics for General Court elections are first regularly available) through the 1750s.

Boston Election Contests

Decade	Number of Contested Seats
1720–29	14/45 (31.1%)
1730–39	23/48 (47.9%)
1740–49	25/45 (55.0%)
1750–59	24/40 (60.0%)

30. Edward Armstrong, ed., *The Correspondence between William Penn and James Logan* (2 vols., Philadelphia, 1870–1872), 2:188, 336, 427.

31. Norris to Joseph Pike, Oct. 28, 1728, Letter Book, 1716–30, Norris Papers; *A Modest Apology for the Eight Members . . .* (Philadelphia, 1728).

32. [William Smith], *A Brief State*, 26; Peters to Thomas Penn, Aug. 25, Nov. 17, 1742, Letter Book, 1737–50, Richard Peters Papers (Historical Society of Pennsylvania, Philadelphia).

33. *Pennsylvania Gazette*, Sept. 12, 19, 1756. See also William R. Steckel, "Pietist in Colonial Pennsylvania: Christopher Sauer, Printer, 1738–1758" (doctoral dissertation, Stanford University, 1949), 233–44.

34. G. B. Warden, "The Caucus and Democracy in Colonial Boston," *New England Quarterly,* 43 (March 1970): 19–33.

35. New York *Gazette,* Jan. 8, 1770; Bernard Friedman, "The New York Assembly Elections of 1768 and 1769; The Disruption of Family Politics," *New York History,* 46 (Jan. 1965): 17–18.

36. Carl L. Becker, "The History of Political Parties in the Province of New York, 1760–1776," *Bulletin of the University of Wisconsin,* 2 (1909–10): 18.

37. Quoted in Carl L. Becker, "Nominations in Colonial New York," *American Historical Review,* 6 (Jan. 1901): 272. Another important aspect of popular politics was the proliferation of clubs which became both social and political organisms. These operated in all the cities from early in the eighteenth century and seem to have increased rapidly in the third quarter of the century. By the 1750s cultural and civic groups such as Franklin's Junto in Philadelphia, the Library Society in New York, and fire companies in all cities had also been highly politicized, much to the dismay of some of their founders.

38. The pamphlets were identified in Charles Evans, *American Bibliography* (14 vols., Chicago and Worcester, Mass., 1903–59); and Clifford K. Shipton and James E. Mooney, *National Index of American Imprints Through 1800: The Short-Title Evans* (2 vols. [Worcester, Mass.], 1969).

39. Paul S. Boyer, "Borrowed Rhetoric: The Massachusetts Excise Controversy of 1754," *William and Mary Quarterly,* 21 (July 1964): 328–51.

40. See McAnear, "American Imprints Concerning King's College," 301–39.

41. Many, although by no means all, of the pamphlets are reprinted in John R. Dunbar, ed., *The Paxton Papers* (The Hague, 1957), or discussed in J. Philip Gleason, "A Scurrilous Colonial Election and Franklin's Reputation," *William and Mary Quarterly*, 18 (Jan. 1961): 68–84.

42. The sheer bulk of this literature grew rapidly in the second quarter of the century, though tapering off in New York and Boston thereafter. Election day sermons are not included in the figures for Boston.

Number of Pamphlets

Decade	Boston	New York	Philadelphia
1695–1704	6	5	2
1705–14	12	3	2
1715–24	40	0	2
1725–34	28	32	43
1735–44	37	13	15
1745–54	38	26	15
1755–64	26	19	109

43. Carl Bridenbaugh, "The Press and the Book in Eighteenth–Century Philadelphia," *Pennsylvania Magazine of History and Biography*, 65 (Jan. 1941): 5. Although it is difficult to determine precisely who read—or was affected by—this literature, it is clear that for a few pounds an interested politician could supply every eligible voter in a city such as Philadelphia with a copy of an election polemic. One to three thousand copies of election pamphlets such as these were often printed in Philadelphia. Of equal significance, election pamphlets and broadsides were commonly read aloud at the polls.

44. Labaree and others, eds., *The Papers of Benjamin Franklin*, 7:374. Franklin came close to changing his mind concerning the beneficial effects of the political press when he became the target of a savage pamplet offensive in 1764.

45. For example, see *A View of the Calumnies lately spread in some Scurrilous Prints against the Government of Pennsylvania* (Philadelphia, 1729).

46. James De Lancey, *The Charge of the Honourable James De Lancey, Esqr. Chief Justice of the Province of* New York, *To the Gentlemen of the Grand-Jury for the City and County of* New York, *on Tuesday the 15th of* October, 1734 (New York, 1734); James De Lancey, *The Charge of the Honourable James De Lancey Esq; Chief Justice of the Province of* New York, *to the Gentlemen of the Grand-Jury for the City and County of* New York, *on Tuesday the 15th Day of* January, Annoq; Domini. 1733 (New York, 1734); *Letters and Papers of Cadwallader Colden*, 4:122, 161.

47. Writing to the proprietor in 1755, Smith confessed that "The Appeal to the public was against my Judgment." Another proprietary leader, Peters, had written earlier that "I never knew any good come to the honest & right side of the Question in the Province by Publick Papers." See Paul A. W. Wallace, *Conrad Weiser, 1696–1760, Friend of Colonist and Mohawk* (Philadelphia, 1945), 115.

48. Almost nothing has been written on the professional pamphlet writers of the colonial period, many of whom seem to have been schoolteachers. For a sketch of David James Dove, which indicates how willingly he changed sides in the factional struggles in Pennsylvania, see Joseph Jackson, "A Philadelphia Schoolmaster of the Eighteenth Century," *Pennsylvania Magazine of History and Biography*, 35 (No. 3, 1911): 315–32.

49. Boyer, "Borrowed Rhetoric: The Massachusetts Excise Controversy of 1754," 341–44.

50. *A Vindication of the Legislative Power* (Philadelphia, 1725).

51. *Pennsylvania Journal*, April 22, 1756. The charges were made against Smith in return for "the Vomitings of this infamous Hireling" whose attacks on Franklin "betoken that Redundancy of Rancour, and Rottiness of Heart which render him the most despicable of his Species." Ibid.

52. Thomas Gordon, *The Craftsman* (New York, 1753), iii–xiii, xxv, xxvi.

53. Pauline Maier has shown that the prerevolutionary mob was usually anti-imperial or designed to extend rather than attack authority. See Pauline Maier, "Popular Uprisings and Civil Authority in Eighteenth-Century America," *William and Mary Quarterly*, 27 (Jan. 1970): 3–35. But she has ignored the role of the mob in provincial politics and, by focusing exclusively on the quasi-legal activity of mobs, overstates the acceptance of mob activity.

54. There are few parallels in the history of the colonial cities to the forays of the White Pine rebels in Massachusetts, the land rioters in New York and New Jersey in the 1740s, and the Paxton Boys in Pennsylvania. For accounts of these movements, see Joseph J. Malone, *Pine Trees and Politics, The Naval Stores and Forest Policy in Colonial New England, 1691–1775* (Plymouth, England, 1964); Irving Mark, *Agrarian Conflicts in Colonial New York, 1711–1775* (New York, 1940); Donald L. Kemmerer, *Path to Freedom: The Struggle for Self-Government in New Jersey, 1703–1776* (Princeton, 1940); Theodore Thayer, *Pennsylvania Politics and the Growth of Democracy, 1740–1776* (Philadelphia, 1953); and Brooke Hindle, "The March of the Paxton Boys," *William and Mary Quarterly*, 3 (Oct. 1946): 461–86.

55. For a comparative view of the mob, see Gordon S. Wood, "A Note on Mobs in the American Revolution," *William and Mary Quarterly*, 23 (Oct. 1966): 635–42; and William A. Smith, "Anglo-American Society and the Mob, 1740–1775" (doctoral dissertation, Claremont Graduate School, 1965).

56. *The Diary of Cotton Mather, 1709–1724,* Massachusetts Historical Society Collections (8 vols., Boston, 1900–1912), 8:657–58.

57. Warden, *Boston*, 140.

58. James Logan to James Alexander, Oct. 23, 1749, Letter Book, 1748–50, James Logan Papers (Library Company of Philadelphia).

59. R. S. Longley, "Mob Activities in Revolutionary Massachusetts," *New England Quarterly*, 6 (Mar. 1933): 102–3.

60. Maier, "Popular Uprisings," 4–15; Charles H. Lincoln, ed., *The Correspondence of William Shirley: Governor of Massachusetts and Military Commander in America, 1731–1760* (2 vols., New York, 1912), 1:406.

61. Julius Goebel, Jr., and T. Raymond Naughton, *Law Enforcement in Colonial New York: A Study in Criminal Procedure (1664–1776)* (New York, 1944), 194; Milton M. Klein, "The Rise of the New York Bar: The Legal Career of William Livingston," *William and Mary Quarterly*, 15 (July 1958): 348.

62. Warden, *Boston*, 121–24; Carl Bridenbaugh, *Cities in the Wilderness: The First Century of Urban Life in America, 1625–1742* (New York, 1938), 352.

63. Patrick Gordon to John Penn, Oct. 17, 1726, Official Correspondence, 1, Penn Family Papers.

64. Gertrude MacKenney, ed., *Votes and Proceedings of the House of Representatives of the Province of Pennsylvania, Pennsylvania Archives* (Eighth Series) (8 vols., Harrisburg, Pa., 1931–35), 3:1908. See also *The Proceedings of some Members of Assembly, at Philadelphia*, Apr. 1728 vindicated from the unfair *Reasoning* and unjust *Insinuations* of a certain *Remarker* (Philadelphia, 1728).

65. Logan to John, Richard, and Thomas Penn, Apr. 24, 1729, Official Correspondence, 2:55, Penn Family Papers.

66. For two interpretations of the riot, see Norman S. Cohen, "The Philadelphia Election Riot of 1742," *Pennsylvania Magazine of History and Biography*, 92 (July 1968): 306–19; and William T. Parsons, "The Bloody Election of 1742," *Pennsylvania History*, 36 (July 1969): 290–306.

67. Richard Hockley to Thomas Penn, Nov. 1, 1742, Official Correspondence, 3, Penn Family Papers.

68. Peters to the Proprietors, Nov. 17, 1742, Letter Book, 1737–50, Peters Papers.

69. Hockley to Thomas Penn, Nov. 1 and Nov. 18, 1742, Official Correspondence, 3:241–43, Penn Family Papers; Peters to Thomas Penn, Nov. 17, 1742, Letter Book, 1737–50, Peters Papers.

70. Logan to John, Richard, and Thomas Penn, Apr. 24, 1729, Official Correspondence, 2:55, Penn Family Papers.

71. Andrew McF. Davis, *Colonial Currency Reprints, 1682–1751* (4 vols., Boston, 1910–11), 2:134.

72. Quoted in Heimert, *Religion and the American Mind*, 15.

73. Rothermund, *Layman's Progress*, 82.

74. The debate can be followed in a series of pamphlets published in 1748. See, for example, William Currie, *A Treatise on the Lawfulness of Defensive War* (Philadelphia, 1748); Gilbert Tennent, *The Late Association for Defence, Encourag'd, or the Lawfulness of a Defensive War* (Philadelphia, 1748); and John Smith, *The Doctrine of Christianity, As Held by the People Called Quakers, Vindicated: In Answer to Gilbert Tennent's Sermon on the Lawfulness of War* (Philadelphia, 1748).

75. William Renwick Riddell, "Libel on the Assembly: a Prerevolutionary Episode," *Pennsylvania Magazine of History and Biography*, 52 (No. 2, 3, 4, 1928): 176–92, 249–79, 342–60; William S. Hanna, *Benjamin Franklin and Pennsylvania Politics* (Stanford, 1964), 134–37; Leonard W. Levy, *Freedom of*

Speech and Press in Early American History; Legacy of Suppression (New York, 1963), 53–61.

76. Rothermund, *Layman's Progress,* 55–60, 81–82; Heimert, *Religion and the American Mind,* 27–58, 239–93. The process was not confined to the cities. See Richard L. Bushman, *From Puritan to Yankee: Character and the Social Order in Connecticut, 1690–1765* (Cambridge, Mass., 1967).

77. [William Rand], *The Late Religious Commotions in New-England Considered . . .* (Boston, 1743), p. 18.

78. Hindle, "The March of the Paxton Boys," 461–86; Hanna, *Benjamin Franklin and Pennsylvania Politics,* 154–68; James H. Hutson, "The Campaign to Make Pennsylvania a Royal Province, 1764–1770," *Pennsylvania Magazine of History and Biography,* 94 (Oct. 1970): 427–63; 95 (Jan. 1971): 28–49.

79. Samuel Purviance, Jr., to James Burd, Sept. 10, 1764, Vol. 1, Shippen Family Papers (Historical Society of Pennsylvania, Philadelphia). James Pemberton, a Quaker leader, wrote that the proprietary leaders engaged in "unwearied Endeavors . . . to prejudice the minds of the lower class of the people" against Franklin. James Pemberton to John Fothergill, Oct. 11, 1764, James Pemberton Papers (Historical Society of Pennsylvania, Philadelphia).

80. Hutson, "Campaign to Make Pennsylvania a Royal Province," 452; Theodore Tappert and John W. Doberstein, trans. and eds., *The Journal of Henry Melchior Muhlenberg* (3 vols., Philadelphia, 1942–45), 2:91, 99–102, 106–7, 123.

81. John Penn to Thomas Penn, May 5, 1764, Official Correspondence, 9:220, Penn Family Papers; John Dickinson, *A Reply to a Piece called the Speech of Joseph Galloway, Esquire* (Philadelphia, 1764), 32–33.

82. Dunbar, ed., *Paxton Papers,* 369; Huston, "Campaign to Make Pennsylvania a Royal Province," 437–52.

83. William Bingham to John Gibson, May 4, 1764, Shippen Papers.

84. John Penn to Thomas Penn, May 5, 1764, Official Correspondence, 9:220, Penn Family Papers.

85. Autograph Petitions, 1681–1764, Penn Family Papers.

86. Labaree and others, eds., *Papers of Benjamin Franklin,* 11:380–84.

87. Quoted in ibid., 11:384; Gleason, "A Scurrilous Colonial Election and Franklin's Reputation," 82.

88. [Isaac Hunt], *A Letter From a Gentleman in Transilvania To his Friend in* America *giving some Account of the late disturbances that happen'd in that Government, with some Remarks upon the political revolutions in the Magistracy, and the Debates that happened about the Change* (Philadelphia, 1764); [Isaac Hunt], *A Humble Attempt at Scurrility* (Philadelphia, 1765), 36–37.

89. Quoted in Gleason, "A Scurrilous Colonial Election and Franklin's Reputation," 82n.

90. Quoted in Guy Soulliard Klett, *Presbyterians in Colonial Pennsylvania* (Philadelphia, 1937), 256.

91. Thayer, *Pennsylvania Politics,* 97; Klett, *Presbyterians in Pennsylvania,* 256–57; Rothermund, *Layman's Progress,* 126–30; Thomas Stewardson,

contributor, "Extracts from the Letter-Book of Benjamin Marshall 1763–1766," *Pennsylvania Magazine of History and Biography*, 20 (No. 2, 1896): 207–08.

92. [Hunt], *A Letter from a Gentleman in Transilvania*, 10.

93. Tappert and Doberstein, eds., *Journals of Henry Melchior Muhlenberg*, 2:122–23; William B. Reed, *Life and Correspondence of Joseph Reed* (2 vols., Philadelphia, 1847), I, 36–37; William Logan to John Smith, Oct. 4, 1764, John Smith Papers (Historical Society of Pennsylvania, Philadelphia); Labaree and others, eds., *Papers of Benjamin Franklin*, 11:390–91. Benjamin Newcomb has studied the election and concluded that the Stamp Act roiled Pennsylvania politics and consequently brought about a dramatic increase in electoral participation. See Benjamin H. Newcomb, "Effects of the Stamp Act on Colonial Pennsylvania Politics," *William and Mary Quarterly*, 23 (Apr. 1966): 257–72. The Stamp Act, however, was hardly mentioned in the outpouring of pamphlets accompanying the election of 1764, which revolved around the move for royal government.

94. Tappert and Doberstein, eds., *Journals of Henry Melchior Muhlenberg*, 2:123; Reed, ed., *Life and Correspondence of Joseph Reed*, 1:36–37. For the results of the city elections, see Isaac Norris, "Journal, 1764" (Rosenbach Foundation, Philadelphia).

95. Labaree and others, eds., *Papers of Benjamin Franklin*, 11:434. The charge that "the riotous Presbyterians" had deprived Franklin of his seat in the assembly by "Illicit Arts and contrivances" was also communicated to the English ministry. Peter Collinson to Lord Hyde, Oct. 11, 1764, Peter Collinson-Bartram Papers (American Philosophical Society, Philadelphia).

96. *The Election Medley* (Philadelphia, 1764).

97. Despite the extensive literature on the subject, the extent of the franchise, particularly in the cities, is by no means certain. Robert E. Brown estimates that 56 percent of the adult males were eligible for the vote in Boston but later revises this upward to 75 percent or higher on the basis of literary evidence and inference. Robert E. Brown, *Middle-Class Democracy and the Revolution in Massachusetts, 1691–1780* (Ithaca, 1955), 50, 58, 96. For Philadelphia the estimate is 75 percent. Chilton Williamson, *American Suffrage from Property to Democracy, 1760–1860* (Princeton, 1960), 33–34. For New York, Milton Klein argues that "virtually all the white adult males" *could* obtain the franchise. Klein, "Democracy and Politics in New York," 235. Roger Champagne and Beverly McAnear show that about 65–70 percent of the adult males *were* qualified to vote. Champagne, "Liberty Boys and Mechanics of New York City," 125–29; and Beverly McAnear, "The Place of the Freeman in Old New York," *New York History*, 21 (Oct. 1940): 418–30. The number of eligible voters in the cities probably never exceeded 75 percent of the taxables, and this percentage seems to have been declining in the eighteenth century as urban poverty and propertylessness increased. Williamson indicates that in Philadelphia in 1774 only 1,423 of 3,124 adult males (about 45 percent) were taxed for real or personal property. Williamson, *American Suffrage*, 33. Of course it is possible that many who were ineligible still voted, as was almost certainly the case in Philadelphia.

98. Precise population graphs for Boston cannot be devised, but the stagnant population level and the decrease in the number of taxables after 1735 seems firmly established by the scattered census materials and the references to the number of taxables for a number of years in the Selectmen's Records. See Warden, *Boston*, 127–29; Bridenbaugh, *Cities in the Wilderness*, 303n; Carl Bridenbaugh, *Cities in Revolt: Urban Life in America, 1743–1776* (New York, 1955), 5, 216; and *Boston Town Records*, 14:13, 100, 280.

99. *Reports of the Record Commissioners of Boston*, vols. 8, 12, 16, 18. Scattered vote counts are available for the pre-1717 period for selectmen elections and town meetings.

100. Voters in Philadelphia participated in two assembly elections each October, one for the eight representatives for Philadelphia County and one for two "burgesses" from the city. Thus they were doubly represented in the assembly. These elections were usually held on successive days. Voting statistics are from newspapers, private correspondence, and Isaac Norris, "Journals." The number of taxables for the four years has been extrapolated from the known number of taxables for the years 1720, 1734, 1740, 1741, 1760, and 1767.

101. Isaac Norris, "Journals, 1764." For another set of totals for Philadelphia County, which vary slightly, see Benjamin Franklin Papers, 69:97 (American Philosophical Society, Philadelphia). The 1765 figures are from ibid., 98, and are reprinted in Labaree and others, eds., *Papers of Benjamin Franklin*, 12:290–91n.

102. See David Hawke, *In the Midst of a Revolution* (Philadelphia, 1961), 13–31.

103. Voting statistics for New York City, where assembly elections were far less frequent, have been found for only two years in the period before 1765. But when combined with statistics for the elections of 1768 and 1769, it appears that in New York the peak of political participation before the Revolution may also have been reached in the early 1760s. See Klein, "Democracy and Politics in Colonial New York," 237.

104. For example, see Kenneth A. Lockridge, *A New England Town, The First Hundred Years: Dedham, Massachusetts, 1636–1736* (New York, 1970), 93–164; and Edward M. Cook, Jr., "Social Behavior and Changing Values in Dedham, Massachusetts, 1700 to 1775," *William and Mary Quarterly*, 27 (Oct. 1970): 546–80.

105. For the view that the radicalization process should be associated with the post-1763 period, see Merrill Jensen, "The American People and the American Revolution," *Journal of American History*, 57 (June 1970): 5–35.

RESHAPING SOCIETY
IN THE REVOLUTIONARY ERA

☆ ☆ ☆ ☆ ☆ ☆ ☆ ☆ ☆ ☆ ☆ ☆ ☆

7

URBAN WEALTH AND POVERTY IN
PREREVOLUTIONARY AMERICA

I THOUGHT OFTEN of the happiness of new England," wrote Benjamin
Franklin in 1772, "where every man is a freeholder, has a vote in
public affairs, lives in a tidy, warm house, has plenty of good food and
fewel, with whole cloaths from head to foot, the manufacture perhaps
of his own family. . . ."[1] But less than two decades earlier, already
caught in a trough of unemployment and economic depression that
would plague the town through the rest of the colonial period, the
Boston Overseers of the Poor reported that "the Poor supported either
wholly or in part by the Town in the Alms-house and out of it will
amount to the Number of about 1000. . . ." Poor relief in Boston,
claimed the town officials, was double that of any town of similar size
"upon the face of the whole Earth."[2]

Writing from Philadelphia in 1756, Mittelberger exclaimed: "Even
in the humblest or poorest houses, no meals are served without a meat
course." Yet just a few years before, Quaker John Smith wrote in his
diary, "It is remarkable what an Increase of the number of Beggars
there is about this town this winter." "This is the best poor man's
country in the world," pronounced several visitors to Philadelphia in
the two decades before the Revolution. But the managers of the Philadelphia almshouse were obliged to report in the spring of 1776 that of
the 147 men, 178 women, and 85 children admitted to the Almshouse,
only a few blocks from where the Second Continental Congress was
debating the final break with England, "most of them [are] naked,
helpless, and emaciated with Poverty and Disease to such a Degree, that
some have died in a few Days after their Admission."[3]

These comments and reports illustrate how widely contemporary
opinion varied concerning the degree of egalitarianism, the extent of
poverty, and the chances for humble colonists to succeed in pre-

---

This essay first appeared in the *Journal of Interdisciplinary History*, 4 (1976): 545–84.
Minor alterations have been made in the footnotes, and the appendix has been omitted.

revolutionary society. This is one reason why social historians are setting aside literary sources in order to examine previously unused data that will give a more precise and verifiable picture of how the structure of wealth and opportunity was changing in colonial America, and how alterations in the social profile were causally linked to the advent of the revolutionary movement.

Their efforts, especially as they pertain to the urban centers of colonial life, have achieved only modest success. They have not gone much beyond Bridenbaugh's impressionistic description of the cities, written almost three decades ago, and Henretta's mid-1960s analysis of Boston.[4] And even these enticing contributions are shrouded in uncertainties. Bridenbaugh presented only scattered data indicating that the colonial cities faced a growing problem in alleviating the distress of the poor in the half-century after 1725. Henretta, analyzing two tax lists separated by almost a century, attempted to show that significant changes had occurred in the social structure and distribution of wealth in Boston. His data, however, did not allow him to pinpoint when and for what reasons these changes occurred. At present, then, there is reason to believe that the cities of prerevolutionary British America became more stratified as they grew larger and more commercialized; that they contained a growing proportion of property-less persons; and that they developed genuinely wealthy and genuinely impoverished classes.[5] Although some social historians have been finding that colonial society was assuming structural features commonly associated with European communities, economic historians have been examining statistics on shipbuilding, trade, and wealthholding, and concluding that the American economy was expanding and vibrant throughout the late colonial period. They argue that although the colonists did not benefit equally from this prolonged growth, nearly everybody's standard of living rose. "Even if there were distinct levels of economic attainment in colonial society," writes McCusker, "and even if we find that the secular trend in the concentration of wealth created an increasing gulf between the rich and the poor over the years separating 1607 and 1775, the fact remains that not only were the rich getting richer but the poor were also, albeit at a slower rate."[6]

In order to understand the internal sources of revolutionary sentiment in the 1760s and 1770s, we must resolve this apparent confusion as to how population growth and economic development affected provincial society. Especially for the northern cities, which became the focal point of revolutionary agitation, we need to determine the degree and timing of changes in prerevolutionary social structure and wealthholding; whether the poor were growing proportionately or disproportionately to population increase; whether the level of care for the impoverished was improving, deteriorating, or remaining steady; whether the lot of the lower and middle classes was sinking or rising, both in relative and absolute terms; whether increases in social stratification affected social mobility and, if so, at which levels of society; and, finally, how these changes were linked, if at all, to the transformation of urban politics and the onset of the Revolution. This essay cannot provide final answers to any of these questions; that will require the labor of many historians over a period of years. Instead, I wish to present new data that challenge some of the generally accepted notions regarding urban social and economic development. They are suggestive of the unexplored connections between social change and revolutionary politics in the colonial cities.

We can begin with simple questions: How was the wealth of northern urban communities divided in eighteenth-century America and how was this changing? Secular trends in the distribution of wealth can be measured in two ways: by comparing tax lists over time, and by analyzing the inventories of estate that were made for thousands of deceased adults in the colonial cities. Tax records must be used with caution because what was taxed in one city was not necessarily taxed in another; because large numbers of free adult males were not included in the tax lists, especially in the last few decades of the colonial period; and because tax lists, based on a regressive tax system, grossly underestimated the wealth of many individuals, particularly those in the top quarter of the wealth structure. But tax lists did generally include a vast majority of wealth-owners in the urban population, and if allowances are made for the distortions in them, they can be used to ascertain long-range trends.[7]

Inventories of estate, conversely, allow for more refined insights into secular changes in the colonial economy, for they alone offer a continuous data for urban populations. They also suffer potentially from one major defect—their representativeness in respect to both age and social class. Inventories exist for less than 50 percent of deceased heads of household in Boston and a somewhat smaller proportion of Philadelphians. Moreover, it has been widely suspected that the estates of the wealthier colonists were inventoried more frequently than those of their poorer neighbors. It must also be remembered that the inventories reveal the wealth of persons at the ends of their lives and are thus age-biased.[8] But if the age and class biases are taken into account the inventories are an extraordinarily valuable source for studying social change. Unlike tax lists they are available for every year, and thus allow us to determine how changes in the economy were affecting not only the relative wealth, but also, more importantly, the absolute wealth held at each level of society.

The data in Table I show a general correspondence in the changing patterns of taxable wealth distribution in three cities. Although different in their religious, ethnic, and institutional development, Boston, New York, and Philadelphia seemed to follow roughly parallel paths insofar as their wealth structures were affected by growth and participation in the English mercantile world. The wealth profile of the three cities varied only slightly in the late seventeenth century, even though Boston and New York were founded a half-century before Philadelphia, and even though Boston was half as large again as the other cities. Similarly, the configurations of wealth in New York in 1730 and Philadelphia in 1756 are not very different, with the Schutz coefficient of inequality[9] corresponding almost exactly (Tables I and 2). On the eve of the Revolution, taxable assets were divided among Bostonians and Philadelphians in much the same manner, even though Boston's population had stagnated after 1730 while Philadelphia continued to grow rapidly until the Revolution.[10]

These tax lists confirm what some historians surmised even before the advent of quantitative history—that the long-range trend in the cities was toward greater concentration of wealth.[11] At every level of society, from the poorest taxpayer to those who stood in the ninth decile, city dwellers, by the end of the colonial period, had given up a share of their economic leverage to those in the top tenth. Moreover, a

Table 1. Wealth Distribution in Three Northern Cities, 1687–1774

	Boston 1687	Phila. 1693	N.Y. 1695	N.Y. 1730	Phila. 1767	Boston 1771	Phila. 1774
0–30	2.6	2.2	3.6	6.2	1.8	0.1	1.1
31–60	11.3	15.2	12.3	13.9	5.5	9.1	4.0
61–90	39.8	36.6	38.9	36.5	27.0	27.4	22.6
91–100	46.3	46.0	45.2	43.7	65.7	63.4	72.3
91–95	16.1	13.2	13.2	14.2	16.2	14.7	16.8
96–100	30.2	32.8	32.0	25.4	49.5	48.7	55.5
Schutz Coeffic.	.49	.43	.46	.44	.61	.58	.66

SOURCES: The Boston tax list, 1687, *BRC*, 1: 91–133; the 1771 valuation list, Massachusetts Archives, 82:92–147, State House, Boston. (These include 169 persons in 1687 and 631 in 1771 who were listed with no assessable wealth.) The New York tax list, 1695, *Collections of the New-York Historical Society* (New York, 1911–1912), vols. 43–44; 1730, New York City Archives Center, Queens College, Flushing, N.Y. (Harlem has not been included since the occupations of its inhabitants were not then urban in character.) For Philadelphia, 1693, *Pennsylvania Magazine of History and Biography*, 8 (1884): 85–105; 1767, Van Pelt Library, University of Pennsylvania, Philadelphia; 1774, Pennsylvania State Archives, Harrisburg, Pennsylvania. (1767 and 1774 include Southwark, an adjacent district, the residents of which by mid-eighteenth century were primarily mariners, merchants, and artisans associated with shipbuilding.)

close examination of this uppermost layer reveals that even those in the 91 to 95 percentile were not important beneficiaries of this process. In Boston their share of the wealth was actually less in 1771 than in 1687. In Philadelphia their position in 1774 was only slightly better than it had been in 1693. The only impressive gains were made by those in the top 5 percent of society. Into the hands of these men fell all of the relative economic power yielded from below over a century's time. By the eve of the Revolution their share of the taxable wealth in Boston had grown from 30 to 49 percent and in Philadelphia from 33 to 55 percent. Those in the lower half of society were left with only 5.1 percent of the taxable wealth in Boston and 3.3 percent of the wealth in Philadelphia.[12]

Because only a few tax lists from the first half of the eighteenth century have survived, it is still not possible to speak with authority concerning the precise timing of this redistribution of wealth. The data in Table I show that New York's wealth was more evenly distributed in 1730 than in 1695, suggesting that if the New York pattern prevailed in the other ports, then the major redistribution came late in the colonial period. But the more equal division of resources in New York in 1730 is partly accounted for by the fact that the largest assessment in that year was for an estate of £670, whereas in 1695 several estates were assessed at more than £2,000, thus bending the distribution curve considerably in the direction of inequality. A tax list for Philadelphia in 1756, which on first glance appears to indicate a long-range trend toward equalization of wealth, confirms the point that these lists must be used with caution in order to avoid confusing real changes with changes in the manner of assessment. As shown in Table 2, the distribution of wealth on the Philadelphia tax list of 1756 is far more even than in 1693 or in 1767, apparently indicating a long-range growth toward equality in the

Table 2. Philadelphia Wealth Distribution in 1756

	As Assessed on Tax List	Minimum Wealth Adjusted	Minimum Wealth Adjusted and Single Men Included
0–30	11.4	1.7	1.6
31–60	16.4	15.7	14.0
61–90	32.6	37.3	37.8
91–100	39.6	45.3	46.6
91–95	14.2	12.2	12.6
96–100	25.4	33.1	34.0
Schutz Coeffic.	.35	.44	.45

SOURCE: *Pennsylvania Genealogical Magazine,* 20 (1961): 10–41.

first half of the eighteenth century, and then a dramatic reversal in the next ten years. Two crucial characteristics of the 1756 list nullify this conclusion, however. First, the list omits all single persons, who ordinarily would have been assessed a head tax and counted in the lowest wealth bracket. Secondly, the minimum assessment was levied at £8, whereas, on the 1767 and 1774 assessment lists for the provincial tax, the minimum assessments were £2 and £1 respectively.[13] Both of these artificialities create a wealth distribution curve that reflects far greater equality than actually existed. Table 2 shows the division of wealth after taxpayers in the lowest assessment category (£8) have been revalued so as to correspond to the 1767 pattern, and after the number of taxables has been increased by 11 percent and these single men have been counted in the lowest assessment bracket.[14] These adjustments, which make the various Philadelphia lists more comparable, place the wealth configurations of 1693 and 1756 in close correspondence, and thus suggest that the major change in wealth distribution came during and after the Seven Years' War. But we simply lack sufficient data on the tax-inscribed urban populations of the first half of the eighteenth century to make conclusive statements on the timing involved.

Probate records, which, unlike tax lists, are available for every year, generally confirm this long-range picture of change, but yield a more precise picture of the timing. The distribution of wealth in Philadelphia and Boston, as recorded in nearly 4,400 inventories of estate, fluctuated widely in the eighteenth century; but the overall trend was strongly toward a less even division of resources (Table 3 and Figures 1–3).[15] In the lower 60 percent of society, the grasp of ordinary people on the community's wealth, which was never large, deteriorated substantially, while those in the top tenth, comprising the elite, significantly consolidated their favored position.

It would be unwise to extract too much meaning from these data as to the exact timing of economic changes, for the inventories reflect wealth at the end of colonists' lives rather than the economic outlook in any particular year. But the inventories corroborate the thesis suggested by the tax data, that a major aggrandizement of wealth occurred at the top of society, especially within the uppermost 5 percent.[16] This seems to have occurred somewhat earlier in Boston than in Philadelphia (insofar as the distance between mean and median wealth is a measurement of inequality), as one might expect given the earlier development of the New England port. By 1735, when Boston had nearly reached the limit of population growth in the colonial period, the major changes in the wealth structure had already taken place. Thereafter a ragged pattern emerges from the data. In Philadelphia, the population of which surpassed Boston's in the early 1760s and continued to grow for the rest of

Table 3. Distribution of Inventoried Personal Wealth in Boston and Philadelphia, 1685–1775: Percentage of Inventoried Estates

	1684–99	1700–15	1716–25	1726–35	1736–45	1746–55	1756–65	1766–75
				Boston				
Low								
0–30	3.3	2.8	2.0	1.9	1.8	1.8	1.4	2.0
31–60	13.9	9.8	7.7	7.4	8.4	8.3	6.0	7.6
61–90	41.6	32.9	28.6	25.1	30.2	34.7	25.1	29.3
91–100	41.2	54.5	61.7	65.6	58.6	55.2	67.5	61.1
High								
91–95	15.3	14.6	13.2	11.4	12.2	15.9	15.5	14.7
96–100	25.9	39.9	48.5	54.2	46.4	39.3	52.0	46.4
Number of Inventories	304	352	314	358	318	532	390	390
				Philadelphia				
Low								
0–30	4.5	4.9	3.9	3.7	2.6	1.5	1.1	1.0
31–60	16.5	16.9	11.1	11.9	9.3	5.5	6.0	4.7
61–90	42.6	37.0	38.1	30.6	36.8	22.9	32.4	24.4
91–100	36.4	41.3	46.8	53.6	51.3	70.1	60.3	69.9
High								
91–95	14.7	16.3	15.7	13.0	20.7	13.8	16.5	14.1
96–100	21.7	25.0	31.1	40.2	30.6	56.3	43.8	55.8
Number of Inventories	87	138	113	154	144	201	279	318

the colonial period, the degree of inequality increased steadily, from the settlement of the city in 1682 through the 1740s, and then fluctuated, as in Boston, in the three decades before the Revolution.

In spite of the difficulties in interpreting the timing of change, it is clear that by the end of the colonial period the top 5 percent of the inventoried decedents had more than doubled their proportion of the assets left at death in Philadelphia (from 21.7 to 55.8 percent) and almost doubled it in Boston (from 25.9 to 46.4 percent). Almost every other part of the population left smaller shares of the collective wealth, with those in the bottom half absorbing the greatest proportionate losses.

The data on wealth distribution can lead only so far toward an understanding of eighteenth-century social change. First, it is apparent that the growth of the port cities, and their participation in a series of international wars, provided important new opportunities for the accumulation of wealth on a scale not possible in the seventeenth century.

The creation of colonial fortunes by as few as 2–3 percent of the city dwellers was sufficient to alter the indices of inequality by significant amounts.[17] In this sense, tax and probate data only confirm what architectural and social historians have traced in studying the erection of urban mansions and country seats befitting a genuinely wealthy class.[18] Secondly, the tax and probate records provide striking evidence that the process of growth and commercialization was creating cities where those in the lower layers of society possessed few taxable assets and virtually no hold on the community's resources. The fact that fully half of Boston's inventoried decedents after 1715 left less than £40 personal wealth and £75 total wealth, while the bottom quarter left only about half this amount, should temper the enthusiasm of those who have argued that colonial communities enjoyed a state of changeless prosperity down to the eve of the Revolution.[19]

To get beyond the limitations of these sources we must turn to records of poor relief for a fuller understanding of how and when the social anatomy of the prerevolutionary cities changed. As in the case of tax and probate records, these materials yield reluctantly to analysis. A casual reading of the Boston town records, for example, tempts one to conclude that the period of greatest distress for the lower class of that city began in the late 1730s and peaked in the early 1750s. A report of the selectmen in early 1736 reported that "the maintenance of the Poor of the Town is a very great and growing charge" and noted that whereas in 1729, £944 had been spent on poor relief, the outlays in 1734 had more than doubled, reaching £2,069. Three years later, the overseers reported that "our Town-charges to the Poor this Year amounts to about £4,000."[20] What purported to be a fourfold increase in expenditures in eight years, however, turns out on closer examination to be about a threefold increase. Massachusetts was caught in a spiraling inflation during this period and the Overseers, in appealing to the legislature for tax relief, did a bit of inflating of their own. The actual expenditures, converted to English sterling, were £245 in 1729 and £760 in 1737.[21]

Sixteen years later, in 1753, the town petitioned the legislature that poor relief had risen alarmingly to "over £10,000 a year ... besides private Charity."[22] Because they were reporting their expenditures in "old tenor"—the severely depreciated Massachusetts paper money that had been called in two years before and disallowed after 1751—this figure must be converted to actual expenditures of about £900 sterling. Although this was a substantial increase over a fifteen-year period during which the population grew about 25 percent, it was not nearly so great as that which occurred in the next two decades. Poor relief costs rose rapidly between 1751 and 1765, and thereafter, when the city's population remained static at about 15,500, drifted still higher.[23] From annual sterling expenditures of £23–31 per thousand population in the period from 1720 to 1740, poor relief rose to £50 per thousand in the 1740s, £77 in the 1750s, and then skyrocketed to £158 in the early 1770s (Table 4). In New York and Philadelphia poor relief expenditures also began a rapid ascent in the late colonial period, although impoverishment on a large scale began a half-generation later than in Boston. In both cities expenditures of less than £50 sterling per thousand population (which may be taken as a rough measure of public funds needed to support the aged, infirm, orphaned, and incurably ill in the cities during times of economic stability) were required in the period prior to the Seven Years' War.[24] But New York and Philadelphia followed the path of Boston in the third quarter of the century. By the twilight of the colonial period both cities were spending about three times per capita the amount needed to support the poor in the 1740s.

Statistics on rapidly rising expenditures for the relief of the poor cannot by themselves demonstrate that poverty was enshrouding the lives of a rapidly growing part of the urban communities. These data might reveal that public authorities were not supporting a rapidly growing class of poor but were simply becoming more generous in their support of occasional indigency or, alternatively, that the responsibility for poor relief was shifting from private charities to public relief. Neither of these explanations is supportable. Charitable organizations, including ethnic and occupational friendly societies, proliferated after 1750, taking up some of the burden of poor relief. There are also indications that the churches substantially increased their aid to the indigent in the late colonial years.[25] As for the actual numbers of the poor, the records of the overseers of the poor in the three cities, including statistics on admissions to almshouses and workhouses, demonstrate that public officials were coping with greatly swollen poor rolls. In attempting to support more and more penniless, jobless city dwellers, their major concern was to devise measures for reducing the cost of caring for the destitute under their charge rather than to upgrade the quality of relief. The erection of large almshouses and workhouses, accompanied by the phasing out of the more expensive out-relief system, was the general response to this problem.[26]

New York and Philadelphia reported inconsequential numbers of persons admitted to their almshouses before the middle of the century. In New York, where an almshouse was not built until 1736, the churchwardens and vestrymen distributed relief to only forty persons or so each year between 1720 and 1735. Most of these were the crippled, sick, aged, or orphaned. By building an almshouse in 1736, which admitted only nineteen inmates in its first year, New York was able to

Table 4. Poor Relief in Three Northern Seaports

	Boston			Philadelphia			New York		
	Population	Av. Ann. Expend. (Sterl.) £	Expend. per 1,000 Popul. £	Population	Av. Ann. Expend. (Sterl.) £	Expend. per 1,000 Popul. £	Population	Av. Ann. Expend. (Sterl.) £	Expend. per 1,000 Popul. £
1700–10	7,500	173	23	2,450	119	48	4,500		
1711–20	9,830	181	18	3,800			5,900	249	32
1721–30	11,840	273	23	6,600			7,600	276	25
1731–40	15,850	498	31	8,800	471	49	10,100	351	21
1741–50	16,240	806	50	12,000			12,900	389	21
1751–60	15,660	1204	77	15,700	1083	67	13,200	667	39
1761–70	15,520	1909	123	22,100	2842	129	18,100	1667	92
1771–75	15,500	2478	158	27,900	3785	136	22,600	2778	123

reduce the cost of caring for the poor and to keep annual expenditures under £400 sterling until almost mid-century.[27] The Philadelphia Overseers of the Poor reported that before the 1760s the inmates of the small almshouse, built in 1732, rarely exceeded forty in number, with about the same number of outpensioners. Expenditures on the eve of the Seven Years' War were about £600 sterling per year with another £350 sterling expended by the Pennsylvania Hospital for the Sick Poor.[28] By the most liberal estimates, the number of townspeople receiving out-relief or cared for in almshouses did not exceed nine per thousand population in New York and Philadelphia before the Seven Years' War.[29]

In Boston, where the population before mid-century outstripped that of the other two cities by a ratio of about five to three, the shadow of poverty appeared somewhat earlier. As early as 1734 the almshouse held 88 persons and by 1742 the number had risen to 110. In 1756 a room-by-room census listed 148 persons cramped into thirty-three rooms.[30] The number of those supported on out-relief grew even faster, according to a petition in 1757, which estimated that about one thousand Bostonians were receiving poor relief, either as inmates of the almshouse or as outpensioners.[31] If this report is accurate, the rate of those receiving public relief had reached sixty-two per thousand population in Boston before the onset of the Seven Years' War.

In the third quarter of the century poverty struck even harder at Boston's population and then blighted the lives of the New York and Philadelphia lower class to a degree entirely unparalleled in the first half of the century. In New York, where the population increased by about half in the third quarter of the century, the rate of poverty jumped fourfold or more. Because the records of the vestrymen and churchwardens for this period have been lost, it is not possible to chart this increase with precision. But a report in the New York *Weekly Gazette* leaves little doubt that change had occurred rapidly after the late 1740s, when New York was still spending less than £400 sterling per year for relief. On March 1, 1771, the *Gazette* reported that 360 persons were confined in the New York almshouse, and during the next twelve months 372 persons were admitted, leaving a total of 425 persons jostling for space in the overcrowded building. Another report in early 1773 revealed that during one month out-relief had been distributed to 118 city dwellers, suggesting that by 1773 a minimum of 600, and perhaps as many as 800, lower-class New Yorkers were too poor to survive without public assistance.[32] Within one generation the rate of poverty had climbed from about nine per thousand to between twenty-seven and thirty-six per thousand.

For Philadelphia it is possible to be much more precise about the timing and extent of change. As late as 1756 Philadelphia rarely supported as many as 100 indigent persons, at an expense of about £600 sterling. But in the winter of 1761–62 the old system of poor relief broke down as cold weather, rising food and firewood prices, the resumption of Irish and German immigration, and a business depression all combined to place nearly 700 persons in distress.[33] For the next five years the Overseers of the Poor struggled with a poverty problem which in its dimensions was entirely beyond their experience. They raised the poor rates, conducted charity drives, and petitioned the legislature for aid in building a new almshouse. "Into rooms but ten or eleven feet square," they reported in 1764, "we have been obliged to put five or six beds" while housing an overflow in a nearby church. By 1766 the almshouse population had swelled to 220.[34]

In despair at their attempts to grapple with the growing poverty problem, the city in 1766 turned over its poor-relief system to a group of civic leaders, most of them Quaker merchants. By legislative act the privately incorporated Contributors to the Relief and Better Employment of the Poor were authorized to build a new almshouse and workhouse, curtail out-relief, and use poor-tax revenues for escorting the itinerant poor out of the city, while setting the able-bodied resident poor to work at weaving, oakum picking, and cobbling in the workhouse.[35] But from 1768 to 1775 the poverty problem only worsened. An average of 360 persons were admitted annually to the new "Bettering House," and by 1775 the Contributors to the Relief of the Poor warned that they had insufficient funds to maintain the city's destitute, even though they had raised the poor rates to the highest in the colony's history.[36] Including those already in the Bettering House at the beginning of each year, an average of 666 Philadelphians lived a part of their lives each year in this public shelter. Two blocks away about 350 poor persons each year were receiving aid in the Pennsylvania Hospital for the Sick Poor, established in 1751 to restore to health those who might otherwise have left impoverished spouses and children to the public charge.[37] In the decade before the Revolution, the rate of poverty in Philadelphia jumped to about fifty per thousand inhabitants—a fivefold increase in one generation.

In Boston, where poverty had become a serious problem earlier than in New York and Philadelphia, the last twenty years of the colonial period were marked by great hardship. While the city's population stagnated, admissions to the almshouse climbed rapidly: 93 per year from 1759 to 1763; 144 per year from 1764 to 1769; and 149 per year from 1770 to 1775. When added to those already in the almshouse at the beginning of each year, these new inmates brought the almshouse population in the winter months to about 275–300.[38] These figures would probably have soared still higher except for the space limitations of the house and the inability of the town to finance the building of a larger structure. Instead, Boston continued to support large numbers of townspeople on out-relief, whereas New York and Philadelphia relied increasingly on the expedient of committing the poor to large alms-houses and workhouses. The records of Samuel Whitwell, a Boston overseer of the poor, reveal that in the years 1769 to 1772 about 15 percent of the householders in his wards were on out-relief—a far higher percentage than in New York or Philadelphia.[39] If Whitwell's wards are representative of the city as a whole, than at least 500 to 600 Bostonians were receiving out-relief as the colonial period closed, in addition to 300 others in the almshouse.

To prevent the rolls of the poor from swelling still further, Boston's Overseers of the Poor systematically warned out of the city hundreds of sick, weary, and hungry souls who tramped the roads into the city in the eighteenth century. To be "warned out" did not mean to be evicted from Boston. Instead it was a device, dating back to King Philip's War in 1675 when refugees from outlying towns had streamed into the city, for relieving the town of any obligation to support these newcomers if they were in need, or should become so in the future. Migrants warned out of Boston could vote, hold office, and pay taxes; but they could not qualify for poor relief from the city coffers which they helped to fill.[40]

The many thousand entries in the Warning Out Book of the Boston Overseers provides confirmation that the third quarter of the eighteenth century was a period of severe economic and social dislocation. From 1721 to 1742 an average of about 25 persons per year had been warned out of the city. The Warning Out Book reveals that from 1745 to 1752 the number climbed to 65 per year, and then from 1753 to 1764 the number tripled again to about 200 persons per year. In the prerevolutionary decade newcomers denied entitlement to poor relief rose to just over 450 per year.[41]

It is not possible to ascertain the condition of all of these migrants as they reached Boston in rapidly increasing numbers after the outbreak of the Seven Years' War. But many of them appear to have been disabled veterans; others seem to have been part of the rapidly growing population of jobless, propertyless, drifting persons thrown up by the churning sea of economic dislocation in the early 1760s, when the end of wartime military contracting and the departure of free-spending British military personnel brought hard times to all of the cities. Only 6 of the 50 adult males warned out of Boston can be found on the 1771 tax list, and all of them were among the bottom tenth of the city's tax-payers. Of 234 adult males warned out in 1768 only 21 were listed three years later on the tax list, and again all of them fell into the lowest tenth of the wealth structure. It must be assumed that all of the others died, moved on again, or were simply too poor even to be included on the tax list.

By looking at the characteristics of those warned out of Boston in different years, one can gain further appreciation of the change overtaking New England society in the third quarter of the century. Before mid-century, when those entering Boston in quest of opportunity averaged about sixty-five per year, most of the migrants were married couples and their children (Table 5). But during the Seven Years' War the character of the migration began to shift. Married men and women continued to seek out Boston; but single men and women also filled the roads into the city whereas before the war their numbers had been insignificant. From 7 percent of the total migrating body in 1747 they became 25 percent in 1759 and 43 percent in 1771.[42]

Table 5. Migration into Boston, 1747–71

	1747	1759	1771
Single men	3.0%	8.5%	23.4%
Single women	4.0	16.8	20.0
Widows and widowers	7.9	8.9	4.4
Married couples	33.6	27.4	27.5
Children	51.5	38.4	24.7
Total Number	101	190	320

The wrenching changes that filled the almshouses and workhouses to overflowing, drove up poor rates, redistributed wealth, and crowded the roads leading into the seaboard cities with destitute and unemployed persons in the generation before the Revolution also hit hard at the broad stratum of society just above those whose names appear in almshouse, hospital for the poor, out-relief, and warning out lists. These people—shoemakers rather than laborers, ropemakers rather than mariners, shopkeepers rather than peddlers—were adversely affected in great numbers in Boston beginning in the mid-1740s and in Philadelphia and New York a dozen years later. They have been entirely lost from sight, even from the view of historians who have used tax lists to analyze changing social conditions, because their waning fortunes rendered them incapable of paying even the smallest tax when the collector made his rounds.

In Boston this crumbling of economic security within the lower middle class can be traced in individual cases through the probate records and in aggregate form in the declining number of city "taxables" (Table 6). In a population that remained nearly static at about 16,000 from 1735 to the Revolution, the number of rateable polls declined from a high of more than 3,600 in 1735, when the city's economy was

Table 6. Rateable Polls in Boston, 1728–71

Year	Population	Polls	Percent
1688	5,900	1,499	25.4
1728	12,650	c3,000	23.7
1733	15,100	c3,500	23.2
1735	16,000	3,637	22.7
1738	16,700	3,395	20.3
1740	16,800	3,043	18.1
1741	16,750	2,972	17.7
1745	16,250	2,660	16.4
1750	15,800	c2,400	15.2
1752	15,700	2,789	17.8
1756	15,650	c2,500	16.0
1771	15,500	2,588	16.7

at its peak, to a low of about 2,400 around mid-century. This loss of more than a thousand taxable adults does not represent a decline in population but the declining fortunes of more than one thousand householders—almost one-third of the city's taxpaying population. The selectmen made clear that this reduction of the town's taxable inhabitants was caused by an increase in the number of people who had fallen to the subsistence level or below. As early as 1753 they reported that about 220 persons on the tax ledgers were "thought not Rateable . . . for their Poverty, besides many Hundreds more for the same reason not Entered in those Books at all." By 1757, at a time when the number of taxable inhabitants had decreased by more than a thousand, they pointed again to this thinning of the tax rolls. "Besides a great Number of Poor . . . who are either wholly or in part maintained by the Town, & so are exempt from being Taxed, there are many who are Rateable according to Law either for their Polls or their Tenements that they occupy or both, who are yet in such poor Circumstances that Considering how little business there is to be done in Boston they can scarcely procure from day to day daily Bread for themselves & Families." One can only estimate how numerous these persons were, but if the number of Bostonians receiving partial or full support from public relief funds reached as high as a thousand in the prerevolutionary generation, as previously estimated, then some 400 other taxpayers may have been living close enough to the subsistence line to have had their taxes abated.[43]

Hard times also struck the laboring classes in Philadelphia, although somewhat later than in Boston. City tax collectors reported to the county commissioners the names of each taxable inhabitant from whom they were unable to extract a tax. The survival of the county commissioners' minutes for the period 1718 to 1776 allows for some precision in tracing this decline.[44] Thousands of entries in the journals chronicle the plight of persons labeled "insolvent," "poor," "runaway," "sickly," or simply "no estate." Taken together these journal entries portray the history of economic distress in Philadelphia during the pre-revolutionary generation. As indicated in Table 7, these Philadelphians constituted a growing part of the taxpaying population. Representing less than thirty per thousand taxables in the period before 1740, they increased to about sixty to seventy per thousand in the years from 1740 to 1760, and then to one out of every ten taxpayers in the prerevolutionary decade.

Table 7. Indigent Taxables in Philadelphia, 1720–75

Years	Average Number of Taxables	Average Number per Year Relieved of Taxes	Percentage
1720–29	1,060	26	2.5
1730–39	1,450	45	3.1
1740–49	1,950	140	7.2
1750–59	2,620	161	6.1
1760–69	3,260	351	10.8
1770–75	3,850	407	10.6

By returning to the probate records it is possible to obtain a rough measurement of how all of these trends were affecting people at each level of society in the cities. So far as the individual was concerned—the mariner in Philadelphia or the cabinetmaker in Boston, for example—the distribution of wealth may have had little meaning. Most eighteenth-century city dwellers probably had only an impressionistic understanding of the relative economic power held by each layer of society and the way in which this was changing. The rich were getting richer, some spectacularly so, while the number of poor grew—that much was undoubtedly clear. But for most city people the preeminent concern was not the widening gap between lordly merchants and humble mechanics but how much they could earn, whatever their occupation, and what it would buy. Regardless of his wealth relative to those at the top of society, the cooper, baker, carpenter, and small shopkeeper had a palpable understanding of how far his income would go in putting food on the table, furniture in the house, and clothes on the backs of his children. Moreover, he was in a position to understand how his standard of living compared to his neighbors, others in his occupational group, and those who had stood in his rank in urban society a decade or so before.

It is precisely these factors that the inventories of estate reveal when studied collectively. The data displayed in Table 8 and Figures 1 and 2 show that Bostonians who at death occupied places in the bottom half of inventoried decedents left markedly smaller estates in the eighteenth century.[45] At the end of the colonial period mean inventoried wealth among these city dwellers was hardly half of what it had been in the late seventeenth century. Since the standard of living was extremely modest even in the best of times for these families, this decline must have proved especially difficult. Although the wealth of those dying between 1745 and 1755 was increasing, laboring-class householders never attained the level that had prevailed in the period from 1685 to 1710. In the prerevolutionary decade, three out of every ten inventoried personal estates ranged between £1 and £26 sterling and total estates between £1 and £43 sterling—a level of wealth that indicated a lifetime spent accumulating little more than working tools, clothes, and a few household furnishings.[46] At the bottom of this group were men like mariner James Black, nameless in the historical record except for an inventory listing three coats, four jackets, a chest, and a quadrant, with a total worth of £5.2.0 Massachusetts currency. At the top of this group, stood men like tavern-keeper Francis Warden whose estate, worth £30.10 in Massachusetts currency in 1766, consisted mostly of plain house furnishings, embellished by an occasional "luxury" item such as one silver spoon or a "hand clock" worth one pound.[47]

Not until one examines Boston inventories in the top 40 percent of decedents can evidence be found that the eighteenth century provided opportunities for leaving more property than was possible for the same stratum of late seventeenth-century society. About six out of ten Bostonians in this group owned a house and their inventories reveal that most of them could afford pewter on the table, books in the parlor, mahogany furniture, and often the purchase of a slave or indentured servant. Their estates also decreased in value in the early eighteenth century, though not nearly so much as those below them. After about 1740 their fortunes rose appreciably, as shown in the ranges of wealth in Table 8.

It was primarily within the upper tenth of society that Bostonians were able to maintain or better the position of their counterparts from previous years. Even the elite, composed primarily of merchants and large land investors, was not immune to the prolonged period of economic instability, as the jagged lines in Figures 1 and 2 indicate.[48] Most of the peaks on those charts indicate the fortunes of spectacularly successful men such as merchants Peter Faneuil, Charles Apthorp, and Samuel Waldo. It is noticeable that peaks in personal wealth descend

Table 8. Range of Personal Wealth (£ Sterling) in Boston and Philadelphia Inventories

	1685–99	1700–15	1716–25	1726–35	1736–45	1746–55	1756–65	1766–75
0–30								
Boston	2–70	1–33	1–23	1–17	1–23	1–27	1–19	1–26
Boston[a]	2–86	1–55	1–33	1–26	1–34	1–50	1–31	1–43
Phila.	5–79	5–93	5–60	3–63	5–68	1–56	1–65	4–57
31–60								
Boston	72–206	34–102	24– 78	17– 65	20– 78	28–102	20– 67	27– 77
Boston[a]	87–292	56–215	34–143	27–132	35–173	51–177	32–146	44–212
Phila.	79–246	94–189	64–222	65–180	69–189	56–183	65–252	57–229
61–90								
Boston	207– 711	103–454	79–318	66–273	79– 301	103– 583	68– 397	78– 409
Boston[a]	307–1,151	217–736	146–653	138–690	174– 720	179– 984	149– 758	215–1,249
Phila.	252– 625	189–577	222–744	189–539	231–1,085	184–1,022	252–1,914	229–1,530
91–100								
Boston	728–2,634	460– 4,078	356–6,422	275–9,046	305–5,496	592– 3,389	405– 6,538	422– 3,095
Boston[a]	1,155–3,417	742–11,007	660–7,362	714–9,606	769–7,557	1,005– 5,609	769–15,614[b]	1,293– 5,138
Phila.	666–1,978	585– 2,556	752–4,618	589–5,751	1,165–4,510	1,057–16,000	1,945–22,621	1,530–36,624

[a]Boston inventories including real wealth.
[b]Excluding Samuel Waldo with inventoried wealth of £53,265.

Figure 1.   Mean Inventoried Personal Wealth in Boston

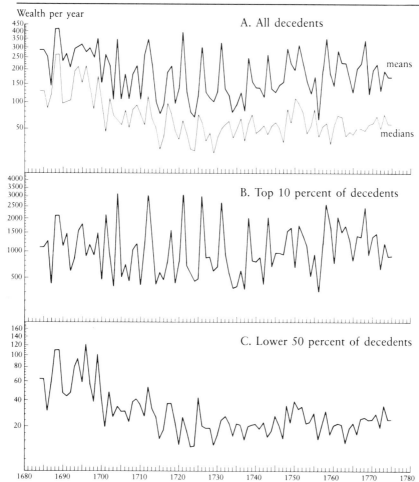

after 1720, which may indicate that the executors of some of Boston's wealthiest men, as was the case with Thomas Hancock, were able to shield their estates from probate. But more likely, these descending peaks reflect Boston's declining position among the American entrepôts in the English mercantile system.[49] Nonetheless, those in the top tenth of Boston's inventoried decedents were far better able to maintain their standard of living than the rest of the townsfolk in the first half of the eighteenth century.

In Philadelphia, where population growth continued throughout the colonial period and where only short-lived economic recessions struck before the 1760s, people at every level of society left considera-

Figure 2. Mean Inventoried Real and Personal Wealth in Boston

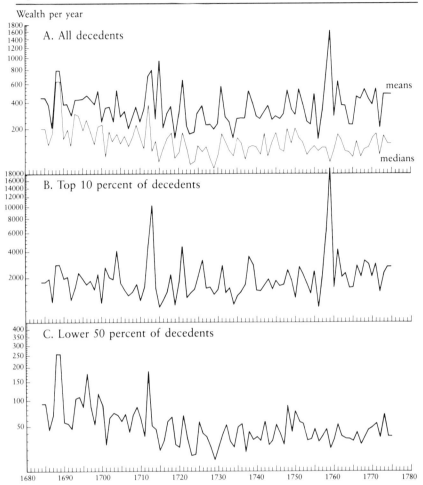

Wealth per year

A. All decedents

means

medians

B. Top 10 percent of decedents

C. Lower 50 percent of decedents

bly greater wealth than their counterparts in Boston. There is little doubt that Philadelphia as a whole was more prosperous than Boston after about 1735. Those in the lower half of Philadelphia society, primarily less-skilled artisans, merchant seamen, and laborers, left personal estates several times as large as Bostonians of their rank. But in spite of the growth of the city and the rapid development of the Pennsylvania interior in the eighteenth century, these people found themselves struggling to maintain the standard of living of their predecessors, though the decline in their inventoried wealth was minor by comparison to Boston. It must also be noted that the somewhat larger estates left by the lower half after 1750 are deceptive because price inflation raised commodity prices about 50 percent between 1745 and 1775 and thus wiped out most of the gains that are indicated on Figure 3 by the peaks in 1751, 1756, and 1767, and, overall, by the slightly upward trend after 1747.[50]

Among the upper 40 percent of Philadelphians, and especially among the top tenth, sustained urban growth brought greater material rewards as the colonial period drew to a close. This marks a real difference between the two cities. Unlike their Boston counterparts, the merchants, lawyers, land speculators, shopkeepers, and some master artisans in the Quaker city were able to accumulate much larger estates as the eighteenth century progressed. These gains were modest for those from the sixtieth to eightieth percentile. But within the ninth decile the estates of decedents nearly doubled on average between the beginning and end of the colonial period. Among the top tenth, the mean estate more than tripled. Furthermore, those at the pinnacle of Philadelphia society accumulated truly impressive estates in the twilight of the colonial era. In Boston the uppermost wealthholders from 1685 to 1745 consistently outstripped Philadelphia's elite. But after Philadelphia's economy eclipsed Boston's in the 1740s, the Quaker city's magnates, capitalizing on the rapid growth of marketable agricultural surpluses from the hinterland and the war-contracting that shifted to the middle colonies in the Seven Years' War, left fortunes that far exceeded the estates of affluent Bostonians. From 1746 to 1775 only three Boston inventories recorded personal estates of £6,000 sterling or more. Thirty-one Philadelphia inventories exceeded £6,000 sterling and many climbed above £15,000.

Several important conclusions can be drawn from this evidence. First, changes in the *share* of wealth held at different levels of society do not necessarily reflect how city dwellers in a particular stratum were faring in terms of absolute wealth. The mean personal estate of men in the bottom half of Philadelphia's decedents grew somewhat in the last twenty-five years of the colonial period, but this wealth represented a shrinking proportion of the city's inventoried assets because their estates had advanced less rapidly than those above them (Table 2 and Figure 3C). Conversely, Bostonians in the upper tenth controlled a growing proportion of inventoried wealth between 1700 and 1735 even though their estates were shrinking appreciably during this period (Table 2 and Figure 1B and 2B). Secondly, although the long-range trend in the redistribution of wealth was similar in Philadelphia and Boston, the actual experiences of people in the same stratum differed widely between the two cities. Philadelphians had their economic problems, including trade recessions in the mid-1720s and late 1740s. But they suffered neither the extreme fluctuations that characterized Boston's economic environment, nor the half-century of currency deprecia-

Figure 3.   Mean Inventoried Personal Wealth in Philadelphia[a]

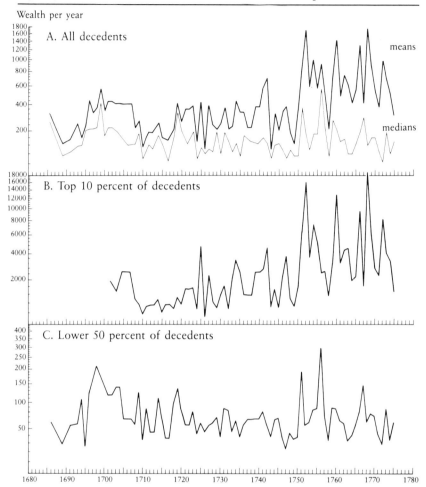

[a]The number of inventories for the years before 1701 is insufficient to provide data points for 3B. In 3C the data before 1701 have been aggregated at two- and three-year intervals when necessary to provide a minimum of five inventories for each data point.

tion that cut into the material well-being of most Bostonians but seems to have had its most devastating effects on the laboring classes. Philadelphia was a city in which the statistical probability of duplicating the success of Benjamin Franklin was extraordinarily small for those beginning at the bottom. But the deterioration of earning power in Philadelphia did not extend so far up in the social ranks as it did in Boston and did not erode the economic security of those in the bottom two-thirds of society as extensively as in the New England port.[51] The inventoried estates of Bostonians in the bottom 60 percent of society fell by more than half in the first half of the eighteenth century; in Philadelphia the decline was about 25 percent. In Boston only men in the top 20 percent died at the end of the colonial period with larger estates than similarly placed men of the late seventeenth century. In Philadelphia every one in the top 50 percent of society left more personal wealth after 1756 than had men of this rank a half century before.

Thirdly, contrary to the theory of economic development advanced by most economists of capitalist societies, the concentration of wealth in the hands of the entrepreneurial class did *not* benefit all ranks of society.[52] In fact, the upper-class consolidation of wealth between 1685 and 1775 was accompanied by the erosion of real assets held at death by those in the lower four-fifths of Boston society and the lower 60 percent of Philadelphia society. Though examples of spectacular individual ascent from the bottom could be found in both cities, the chances of success at any level of society below the upper class seem to have been considerably less in the eighteenth century than before. We will need life-cycle analyses for all the port towns before any firm conclusions can be reached concerning changes in opportunity for movement off the bottom, but the probate data and the records of poor relief make a presumptive case that for most city dwellers, including many shopkeepers and professionals as well as laboring people, the dominating fact of eighteenth-century life, as wealth was becoming more concentrated, was not material success but economic stasis.

Taken together, these data on wealth distribution, inventoried wealth, poor relief, warnings out, and tax forgiveness indicate that life in the seaport cities was changing profoundly in the eighteenth century. These changes were manifested in the growth of poverty after 1740 that was chronic enough to embrace at least one-fifth of the heads of household by the eve of the Revolution. They were evidenced in the general weakening of economic leverage of the artisan and shopkeeper class and the fall from taxable status of large numbers of these people. They were apparent in the augmentation of power in the hands of merchants, lawyers, and land speculators—a consolidation of wealth that took most visible form in the building of lavishly appointed city houses and the increase in four-wheeled carriages, usually attended by liveried slaves, which rolled through the city streets at a time when the poorhouses were bulging with inmates. This restructuring of colonial society was highly visible to rich and poor alike.[53]

The causes of this transformation can only be tentatively explored in this essay. It will require a mammoth investigation of shifts in the operation of the Atlantic economy and the links between the mercantile cities and the agricultural hinterlands before we will comprehend what was occurring in these seaboard centers of colonial life. But two factors seem to hold special explanatory potential in unraveling the economic and social mechanisms at work. First, the pressure of population on land, already explored by a number of historians, seems to have severely restricted opportunity in older agricultural areas. This factor may have set hundreds of people from the small inland towns on the road to the coastal cities after the 1740s and may have held there, especially in Philadelphia and New York, hundreds of new immigrants who otherwise would have sought their fortune on the frontier. Compounding the seriousness of this rural dislocation was the role which stiffening Indian resistance to further land encroachments played in the third quarter of the century. The Cherokee, Delaware, and Shawnee resistance movements of 1758–61, and Pontiac's pan-Indian movement of 1763–65, may hold explanations for the bottling up of the new immigrants who flooded into the colonies from northern Ireland and Germany after the Seven Years' War.[54]

Secondly, the cycle of wartime boom and postwar recession, which occurred almost once a generation between the late seventeenth century and the Revolution, seems to have had an unusually disfiguring effect on urban societies. International conflict made merchant princes out of military contractors in all three northern cities. In Boston, for example, Andrew and Jonathan Belcher profited mightily from Queen Anne's War. A generation later, another conflict—King George's War—brought great wealth to Benjamin Colman, Thomas Hancock, Benjamin Hallowell, and others. The same was true in New York and Philadelphia where the Seven Years' War enriched merchants such as Charles Ward Apthorp, William Bayard, Oliver DeLancey, David Franks, John Baynton, and Joseph Fox. But at the same time, these wars left in their wake hundreds of broken and impoverished war veterans from the Canadian expeditions and privateering voyages, and hundreds of destitute war widows. Equally important, financing the wars required the imposition of heavy new taxes, which fell with severity upon the lower and middle classes. Added to this, urban artisans and laborers found that commodity prices rose rapidly, especially after 1760, while their wages failed to keep pace.[55]

The case of Boston is especially illuminating. The Cartagena and Louisburg expeditions of 1743–45, whatever they may have done for Yankee self-esteem, imposed heavy taxes on the middle and lower classes, drained the provincial treasury, and left hundreds of families in Boston fatherless and husbandless. Eight years later Boston's leaders were still lamenting the staggering burden which the war had imposed.[56]

Compounding the postwar problems was the growth of satellite ports such as Salem, Newburyport, and Marblehead in the second quarter of the century. Growing rapidly, they chipped away at the mainstays of Boston's economy—shipbuilding, the carrying trade in fish, and distilling. As Boston's selectmen explained in a series of petitions to the General Court for tax relief, the loss of shipbuilding contracts led to a decline in the trade of coopers, bakers, tanners, tallow-chandlers, victuallers, and many others. Shipbuilding in 1747–48, they reported, produced 10,140 tons (in several earlier years it had exceeded 14,000 tons). But in 1755–56, only 2,162 tons emerged from the Boston shipyards. Distillers reported a 50 percent decline in their volume, skinners declared a drop in skins dressed yearly from about 30,000 to 6,000 between 1746 and 1756; and at one point in the late 1740s twenty-five of the town's thirty butchers took their business elsewhere. "We are in a low impoverished condition," wrote Charles Chauncy in 1752, in attempting to promote a linen manufactory, which, for a brief time, was seen as a way of employing "some hundreds of Women and Children" so that they might do "a great deal towards supplying themselves with Bread, to the easing of the Town of its Burthen in providing for the poor."[57] Capping Boston's difficulties was inflation, which had been a problem since about 1715 but reached crisis proportions in the late 1740s. The erosion of purchasing power, in an era when prices rose much faster than laboring men's wages, may have been one of the major factors in the decline of inventoried wealth in the lower two-thirds of society. The runaway inflation was finally halted in 1750 with the calling in of paper money and a drastic devaluation, but laboring Bostonians, rightly or wrongly, felt the cure struck particularly hard at them.[58]

The onset of the Seven Years' War brought temporary relief to the city as war contracts, enlistments, and spending by British soldiers sparked a commercial revival. But the return of prosperity was short-lived. With the end of the American phase of the war in 1760 came a serious bottoming out of the economy and the beginning of a depression that hit the city hard in the 1760s. The beginning of the postwar depression coincided with natural disaster. In March 1760, the worst fire in colonial history consumed the houses, stores, and possessions of 377 Bostonians. That 218 of these fire victims were described as poor is one indication of how widespread poverty had become in the town.[59]

In the aftermath of the Seven Years' War Boston's economic malaise spread to New York and Philadelphia. The Quaker city had been the main port of entry for German and Scottish-Irish immigrants since the 1720s and, in the twenty years before the outbreak of the final Anglo-French conflict in North America, an average of more than a dozen ships per year disgorged passengers. But as late as the mid-1750s the city's almshouse contained no more than sixty inmates, a good indication that those who chose to remain in Philadelphia were easily absorbed into the economy. After the reopening of the oceanic road to the colonies following a wartime hiatus from 1755 to 1760, however, the arriving Rachel Rhumburgs, Daniel O'Neals, and Patrick McGuires found high prices, few jobs, and foreboding talk of deteriorating relations between colonists and native Americans in the areas of new settlement. The wartime boom, which had sent per capita imports of British goods soaring to an all-time high, turned with shocking swiftness into a postwar recession. Merchants who had overextended their credit in building up large inventories of goods found themselves bankrupt; ships lay idle, leaving hundreds of mariners without employment; and money was scarce, particularly after the restrictive Currency Act of 1764. Five years after the bubble of wartime prosperity broke, a Philadelphia doctor, whose work in the poor German and Irish neighborhoods of Mulberry Ward put him in intimate touch with the lower class, wrote of the continuing depression: "Our tradesmen begin to grow clamourous for want of employment [and] our city is full of sailors who cannot procure berths. Who knows," he added prophetically, "what the united resentments of these two numerous people may accomplish."[60]

In New York, the prosperous center of British military activities and colonial privateering exploits during the Seven Years' War, the postwar recession, combined with price inflation, also struck with severity. "Everything is tumbling down, even the traders themselves," explained John Watts, one of the chief beneficiaries of military contracts.[61] Three years later, "A Tradesman" complained of the "dismal Prospect before us! a long Winter, and no Work; many unprovided with Fire-Wood, or Money to buy it; House-Rent and Taxes high; our Neighbours daily breaking their furniture at Vendue in every Corner." During the remainder of the colonial era, the economy in New York, as in Philadelphia, was buffeted by violent fluctuations. The chief victims, wrote one New Yorker in 1767, were "the poor industrious tradesmen, the needy mechanic, and all men of narrow circumstance." New York, like the other cities, rallied briefly in the early 1770s, but the prosperity of an earlier era was never recovered.[62]

Before we can go much farther in our understanding of the dynamics of urban colonial society it will be necessary to explore a number of questions. To what extent did Anglo-American business cycles affect the economy at large and various occupational and social groups in particular? Did the movement toward a wage-labor market, where indentured servants and slaves were replaced in the northern cities by free workers who could be hired and fired at the employer's will, create a new class of urban poor? Precisely how did the international wars of the eighteenth century affect the structure of opportunity in the seaboard cities?

To what extent did Indian resistance against further land encroachments in the interior lead to an increase of migration into the cities, in a
kind of eastward movement, in the late colonial period? Was occupational specialization and the exposure of a growing part of the urban
workforce to the increasingly severe fluctuations of a market economy
making entry into some crafts more difficult? How was the burden of
price inflation, in Boston between about 1715 and 1750 and in New
York and Philadelphia from 1745 to 1775, distributed among urban
dwellers? Finally, was poverty in the city a transitional state, endured
for brief periods by newcomers and recently freed indentured servants
who then went on to better things; or, alternatively, was it becoming a
way of life for an increasing number of city dwellers? From the data
presented above come indications rather than clear-cut answers to these
questions. But the evidence of considerable economic distress and
thwarted aspirations in the late colonial period is compelling.

If it can be assumed that the urban people of the 1760s responded
not only to high principles enunciated in revolutionary pamphlets, but
also to the conditions of their lives, then this evidence suggests that we
need a new assessment of the forces that brought the Revolution into
being. Those "mindless mobs," so roundly dismissed at the time for their
inability to act except out of passion, may not have been so incapable of
determining how their life chances had been affected in the decades
before 1776. Accordingly, careful attention must be paid to the printed
attacks on the wealthy that appeared with increasing frequency in newspapers and tracts in the late colonial period. "Poverty and discontent
appear in every Face (except the Countenances of the Rich)," stormed a
pamphleteer in Boston in 1750. The author went on to remark that it was
no wonder that a handful of merchants, who had fattened themselves on
war contracts and through manipulating the unstable money market,
could "build ships, Houses, buy Farms, set up their Coaches, Chariots,
live very splendidly, purchase Fame, Posts of Honour" and so forth while
the bulk of the population languished. Was it equitable, asked a writer in
the *New-York Gazette* in 1765, "that 99, rather 999, should suffer for
the Extravagance or Grandeur of one? Especially when it is considered
that Men frequently owe their Wealth to the impoverishment of their
Neighbours?" Was supporting the poor an act of charity or simple justice, asked another New York writer in 1769, reminding his audience
that "it is to the meaner Class of Mankind, the industrious Poor, that so
many of us are indebted for those goodly Dwellings we inhabit, for that
comfortable Substance we enjoy, while others are languishing under the
disagreeable Sensations of Penury and Want."[63]

Understanding how life in the cities was changing may also render
far more comprehensible political factionalism in the late colonial pe-

riod and the extraordinary response to the attempts at imperial reform
initiated after the Seven Years' War. The rise of radical leaders such as
James Otis and Samuel Adams in Boston, for example, cannot be separated from the years of economic difficulty, spreading poverty, and the
limited chances of advancement that so many people in the city experienced. Nor can the widespread support of revolutionary radicals in
New York and Philadelphia be understood without reference to the new
conditions in the cities at the end of the colonial period. In this sense,
understanding whether Otis was clinically mad is less important than
perceiving that in his venomous attacks on the wealthy, powerful, aristocratic, in-bred Hutchinsonian circle, the members of which had repeatedly demonstrated their insensitivity to lower-class Bostonians, Otis
had struck a resonant chord. When a conservative writer attacked Otis
and his colleagues in 1763 as "the darling idols of a dirty, very dirty,
witless rabble commonly called the little vulgar," he was not unmindful
of the prior attacks by Otis on those in Boston who "grind the faces of
the poor without remorse, eat the bread of oppression without fear, and
wax fat upon the spoils of the people."[64] When the Stamp Act riots
came, it was entirely appropriate from the lower-class point of view
that the initial targets should be the luxuriously appointed homes of
Andrew Oliver, Benjamin Hallowell, and Thomas Hutchinson, the last
detested by the lower class since the late 1740s as the architect of a
merciless deflationary policy that in the long run may have benefited the
mechanic and shopkeeping class but was seen at the time as primarily
beneficial to the rich. Rich men began burying their treasures and sending valuable possessions to the homes of poorer friends, indicating that
Governor Francis Bernard was close to the mark in concluding that the
Boston crowd was engaged not only in a political response to new
imperial regulations but also in "a war of plunder, of general levelling,
and taking away the distinction of rich and poor."[65]

   Much more work must be done before firm pronouncements can
be made about linkages between the changing dynamics of urban
societies and the onset of the revolutionary movement. The challenge
at hand is not to make simplistic connections between the decline of
mean inventoried wealth and the advent of revolutionary sentiment
or between the rise of urban poverty and the beginnings of the imperial crisis. It is far from certain that rapid social change brings social
unrest, or even that those who suffer the most are the first to rise
against the causes of their suffering. What is needed, rather, is a
deeper understanding of how changing social and economic circumstances, beginning in the early eighteenth century and accelerating in
the last generation of the colonial period, eroded the allegiance of
many urban dwellers to the British mercantilistic system and also to

their own internal social systems. The collapse of the Atlantic economy at the end of the Seven Years' War, coming near the end of a long period of urban change, seems to have shaped the way these people thought about the future far more profoundly than has been recognized. Nobody before the 1760s thought to associate economic dislocation in Boston, or the rise of poverty in New York, with a mercantile system that provided a handsome flow of credit and cheap manufactured goods, as well as military protection. But the economic shocks beginning at the end of the Seven Years' War began to focus thought in an entirely new way—both in reference to participation in the British mercantile world and in regard to the internal structuring of urban society, where elements of the elite were increasingly being viewed as conscienceless aggrandizers of wealth and power. It is the large body of evidence, indicating how the conditions of life and the promise for the future were changing in the cities, that makes far more comprehensible than a purely ideological interpretation can do, both the creation and reception of revolutionary sentiment.

NOTES

1. Albert Henry Smyth (ed.), *The Writings of Benjamin Franklin*, (New York, 1907), 5:362–63.
2. William H. Whitmore et al. (eds.), *Reports of the Record Commissioners of Boston* (Boston, 1885), 14:240, 302 (hereafter, *BRC*).
3. Gottlieb Mittelberger (Oscar Handlin and John Clive [eds.]), *Journey to Pennsylvania* (Cambridge, Mass., 1960), 49; Albert C. Myers (ed.), *Hannah Logan's Courtship* (Philadelphia, 1904), 152; Report of the Contributors to the Relief and Employment of the Poor, in *Pennsylvania Gazette*, May 29, 1776.
4. Carl Bridenbaugh, *Cities in the Wilderness: Urban Life in America, 1625–1742* (New York, 1938); Bridenbaugh, *Cities in Revolt: Urban Life in America, 1743–1776* (New York, 1955); James A. Henretta, "Economic Development and Social Structure in Colonial Boston," *William and Mary Quarterly*, 22 (1965): 75–92.
5. For a general formulation of changing social structure see Jackson Turner Main, *The Social Structure of Revolutionary America* (Princeton, 1965). Main makes no detailed analysis of any particular community over time and is therefore unable to delineate the dynamics and extent of change. There are a growing number of studies of land- and wealth-holding in New England towns and Chesapeake counties, but the seaboard cities have thus far escaped analysis.
6. John J. McCusker, "Sources of Investment Capital in the Colonial Philadelphia Shipping Industry," *Journal of Economic History*, 32 (1972):146–57; James F. Shepherd and Gary M. Walton, "Trade, Distribution and Economic Growth in Colonial America," ibid., 128–45; Alice Hanson Jones, "Wealth Estimates for the American Middle Colonies, 1774," *Economic Development and Cultural Change*, 18 (1970), esp. 127–40; idem, "Wealth Esti-

mates for the New England Colonies about 1700," *Journal of Economic History*, 32 (1972): 98–127, esp. 105–7.

7. Some of the difficulties in using tax lists are discussed in James T. Lemon and Gary B. Nash, "The Distribution of Wealth in Eighteenth-Century America: A Century of Change in Chester County, Pennsylvania, 1693–1802," *Journal of Social History*, 2 (1968): 2–7. The primary distortions in the tax lists are that (a) certain important forms of urban wealth, including mortgages, bonds, book debts, and ships, were usually not taxed; (b) large numbers of persons, too poor to pay a tax, were omitted from the lists, especially in the late colonial period; (c) tax assessments tended to represent a smaller percentage of actual wealth as they moved from the bottom to the top of the social scale; (d) urban tax lists did not include land held outside the city, usually by the wealthy. All of these biases tend in the same direction—toward minimizing the actual concentration of wealth. As the wealth of the urban elite increased in the eighteenth century, the distortion grew larger; thus the changes indicated in the following analysis of tax data should be regarded as minimally stated.

8. For a discussion of these biases and their correction see Gloria L. Main, "Probate Records as a Source for Early American History," *William and Mary Quarterly*, 32 (1975): 89–99; idem, "The Correction of Biases in Colonial American Probate Records," *Historical Methods Newsletter*, 8 (1974): 10–28; Daniel Scott Smith, "Underregistration and Bias in Probate Records: An Analysis of Data from Eighteenth-Century Hingham, Massachusetts," *William and Mary Quarterly*, 32 (1975): 100–110.

9. The Schutz coefficient, which measures relative mean deviation, is a widely used single-number indicator of inequality (0 = perfect equality; 1.0 = perfect inequality).

10. The Boston list of 1771 is actually an evaluation of various forms of property and thus differs from the Philadelphia tax assessors lists of 1767 and 1772 in three important respects. First, the Boston list includes important forms of wealth not included on the Philadelphia list, such as ships, stock in trade, the value of commissions in merchandise, and money at interest. Since all these forms of wealth were concentrated in the upper class, the Boston distribution is more accurate than the Philadelphia distribution, which does not take account of these categories. Secondly, on the Boston list, houses and land (valued at one year's rent) are assigned to "such persons as shall appear to have been the actual tenants thereof upon the first day of September last." Thus Boston's renters, who made up about 60% of the taxable inhabitants, were valued with the property of their landlords, distorting the distribution toward greater equality than actually existed. Thirdly, the Boston list excludes nearly 1,000 potentially taxable adults who were omitted because of "age, infirmity, or extreme poverty." This represents about 25–30% of the taxable population in Boston, whereas in Philadelphia about 7% of the taxable population was exempted in 1767 and about 10% in 1774. In both cities, but especially Boston, these omissions skew the distribution toward greater equality than actually existed. Although there is no way to weigh these biases mathematically, it can be presumed that the second and third factors tend to cancel out the first in the

Boston list of 1771; and that in all tax lists for the colonial period the degree of wealth inequality is understated. The quotations above are from the Massachusetts tax law of 1771 in Ellis Ames and Abner C. Goodell (eds.), *The Acts and Resolves, Public and Private, of the Province of Massachusetts Bay* . . . (Boston, 1886), 5:104, 156–59.

11. See esp., James Truslow Adams, *Provincial Society, 1690–1763* (New York, 1927); Virginia D. Harrington, *The New York Merchant on the Eve of the Revolution* (New York, 1935); Bridenbaugh, *Cities in Revolt.*

12. Because the Boston lists of 1687 and 1771 are not strictly comparable, these figures must not be regarded as measurements of actual wealth structures, but simply as indicators of the direction and approximate degree of change.

13. In Pennsylvania, when the rate of taxation was 3 or 4 pennies per £ of assessable estate, as in the case of the poor tax, county tax, lamp and watch tax, or paving tax, the assessors set the minimum valuation at from £8 to £12. For the far heavier provincial tax, levied after 1754 at a rate of 18 pence per £ of assessable estate, the minimum assessments were lowered to £1 or £2. This, in itself, suggests the difficulty that laboring-class Philadelphians were having in coping with the heavy provincial taxes after 1754.

14. In five tax lists drawn between 1767 and 1775, and in a tax list for three wards in 1754, the percentage of Philadelphians assessed a head tax varied between 10.0 and 13.3% of the total taxable population.

15. Boston real estate has been excluded from the data on wealth distribution in order to obtain comparability with the Philadelphia data where inventories only occasionally included real estate. The distribution of real wealth in Boston closely approximated that of personal wealth.

16. It would be preferable to chart the Schutz coefficient of inequality annually to determine the timing of change, but the number of inventories is not large enough to allow this. The distance between the annual mean and median wealth of all decedents, which is a rough measurement of the degree of inequality, is displayed in Figures 1A, 2A, and 3A. For a discussion of these problems, see Russell R. Menard, P. M. G. Harris, and Lois Green Carr, "Opportunity and Inequality: The Distribution of Wealth on the Lower Western Shore of Maryland, 1638–1705," *Maryland Historical Magazine*, 69 (1974): 168–84.

17. A comparison of the graphs of mean wealth for the top 10% and all decedents (Figures 1A, 1B, 1C) demonstrates the power of the uppermost stratum to define the trendline for the society at large.

18. See, for example, Nicholas B. Wainwright, *Colonial Grandeur in Philadelphia: The Houses and Furniture of General John Cadwalader* (Philadelphia, 1964); Malcolm Freiberg, *Thomas Hutchinson of Milton* (Milton, Mass., 1971); Bridenbaugh, *Cities in Revolt*, chap. 6 on "Urban Elegance."

19. See, for example, Jones, "Wealth Estimates for the American Middle Colonies," 119–40; Bernard Bailyn, *The Ordeal of Thomas Hutchinson* (Cambridge, Mass., 1974), 97.

20. Jan. 1, 1735/36, *BRC*, 12:121–22; 178; 14:13.

21. All values, which in the inventories are given in Massachusetts and Pennsylvania currency, have been converted to sterling. I have used the conver-

sion figures given in *Historical Statistics of the United States, Colonial Times to 1957* (Washington, D.C., 1960), 773, and filled in the missing years from the price per ounce of silver cited in the inventories for these years. For Philadelphia, the yearly sterling equivalents for Pennsylvania currency are taken from Anne Bezanson, Robert D. Gray, and Marian Hussey, *Prices in Colonial Pennsylvania* (Philadelphia, 1935), 431.

22. *BRC*, 14:240.

23. Several sources have been collated to determine the annual expenditures on the Boston poor from public tax monies. Beginning in 1754 the town records give an annual report of the treasurer on disbursements to the Overseers of the Poor. These reports continue, with a few interruptions, to 1775. The Overseers of the Poor Account Book, 1738–69, Massachusetts Historical Society, Boston, includes monthly expenditures for the poor and sporadic records, mostly for the 1750s, on disbursements for the workhouse. The expenditures for 1727, 1729, 1734, 1735, and 1737 are given in *BRC*, 12:108, 121–22, 178. For the period from 1700 to 1720 I have estimated poor relief costs at one-third the town expenses (given yearly in *Boston Town Records*), the ratio that prevailed in the five years between 1727 and 1737 when poor-relief expense figures are given.

24. The figures for New York have been reconstructed from the Minutes and Accounts of the Church Wardens and Vestrymen of the City of New York, 1696–1715, New-York Historical Society; and Minutes of the Meetings of the Justice, Church Wardens, and Vestrymen of the City of New York, 1694–1747, New York Public Library. The salary of the clergymen for the Society for the Propagation of the Gospel, which was included in these expenditures, has been subtracted from the yearly totals. The New York records after 1747 have apparently not survived, but the level of expenditures on the eve of the Revolution was reported by the vestrymen and churchwardens in a petition to the Continental Congress in May 1776. Peter Force, *American Archives*, 4th Ser., 6 (Washington, D.C., 1846), 627. Also see Raymond A. Mohl, "Poverty in Early America, A Reappraisal: The Case of Eighteenth-Century New York City," *New York History*, 50 (1969): 5–27. The sources for the Philadelphia data, which are extremely scattered, are given in Nash, "Poverty and Poor Relief in Prerevolutionary Philadelphia," *William and Mary Quarterly*, 33 (1976): 3–30.

25. Bridenbaugh, *Cities in Revolt*, 126–28, 321–25; Nash, "Poverty and Poor Relief," 23–24. To take one example, the charitable expenditures of the Philadelphia Society of Friends, during an era when their membership was not growing, rose from an annual average of £38 in the 1740s and 1750s to £95 annually in the fifteen years before the Revolution. Monthly charity disbursements are given in the Minutes of the Monthly Meeting of Women, Friends of Philadelphia, vol. F2, Friends Record Center, Philadelphia.

26. David J. Rothman, *The Discovery of the Asylum: Social Order and Disorder in the New Republic* (Boston, 1971). Chap. 1 analyzes this change but associates it primarily with the early nineteenth century.

27. Churchwardens and Vestrymen's Accounts, New-York Historical Society; Mohl, "Poverty in Colonial New York," 8–13.

28. Report of the Board of Managers, Nov. 3, 1775, Records of the Contributors to the Relief and Employment of the Poor, Almshouse Managers Minutes, 1766–78, City Archives, Philadelphia. For expenditures, see Nash, "Poverty and Poor Relief," 3–9.

29. Population figures from New York have been calculated from a series of censuses in the eighteenth century. Evarts B. Greene and Virginia D. Harrington, *American Population before the Federal Census of 1790* (New York, 1932), 95–102. The Philadelphia data are constructed from a series of house censuses and lists of taxable inhabitants given in John F. Watson, *Annals of Philadelphia, and Pennsylvania . . .* (Philadelphia, 1857), 3:235–36. See also John K. Alexander, "The Philadelphia Numbers Game: An Analysis of Philadelphia's Eighteenth-Century Population," *Pennsylvania Magazine of History and Biography,* 98 (1974): 314–24; Nash and Billy G. Smith, "The Population of Eighteenth-Century Philadelphia," ibid., 99 (1975): 362–68. The Boston population figures are taken from John B. Blake, *Public Health in the Town of Boston, 1630–1822* (Cambridge, Mass., 1959), 247–49.

30. BRC, 12:121–22; Lemuel Shattuck, *Report to the Committee of the City Council Appointed to Obtain a Census for Boston for the Year 1845* (Boston, 1846), 4; "A List of Persons, Beds, &c in the Alms House, Aug. 1756," in City of Boston, Indentures, 1734–51, City Clerk's Office, Boston, vol. 1.

31. BRC, 14:302. For another discussion of poverty in Boston see Stephen Foster, *Their Solitary Way: The Puritan Ethic in the First Century of Settlement in New England* (New Haven, 1971), 144–52.

32. *New-York Gazette,* Feb. 11, 1771, Mar. 30, 1772; *New-York Gazette and Weekly Mercury,* Mar. 15, 1773.

33. *Pennsylvania Gazette,* Jan. 7, 1762; Minutes and disbursement book, Records of the Committee to Alleviate the Miseries of the Poor (1762), Wharton-Willing Collection, Historical Society of Pennsylvania.

34. Nash, "Poverty and Poor Relief," 9–14; Gertrude MacKinney (ed.), *Votes and Proceedings of the House of Representatives of the Province of Pennsylvania, Pennsylvania Archives,* 8th Ser. (Harrisburg, 1935), 7: 5506, 5535–36.

35. Nash, "Poverty and Poor Relief," 14–16.

36. Almshouse Managers Minutes, 1768–78, give monthly figures on admissions and discharges from the almshouse and workhouse. For the 1775 warning see Board of Managers report, Nov. 3, 1775, ibid.

37. For the early history of the hospital, see William H. Williams, "The 'Industrious Poor' and the Founding of the Pennsylvania Hospital," *Pennsylvania Magazine of History and Biography,* 98 (1973): 431–43. Admission and discharge records, from which these figures have been drawn, are in Attending Managers Accounts, 1752–81, Pennsylvania Hospital Records (microfilm), American Philosophical Society, Philadelphia.

38. Figures compiled from Admission and Discharge Book, 1758–74, Records of the Boston Overseers of the Poor, Massachusetts Historical Society.

39. "Accounts of Payments to the Poor, April, 1769–March 1771, Wards

2 and 12," Records of the Boston Overseers of the Poor. In Philadelphia, the account book of Thomas Fisher, Overseer of the Poor for Lower Delaware Ward in 1774, shows aid to only 7.2% of the taxables. Boston made three attempts between 1748 and 1769 to employ the able-bodied poor in a cloth factory, but all of them failed.

40. Josiah Benton, *Warning Out in New England, 1656–1817* (Boston, 1911), 5–52, 114–16.

41. Bridenbaugh, *Cities in the Wilderness*, 392, "Persons Warned Out of Boston, 1745–92," Records of the Boston Overseers of the Poor.

42. This analysis is based on a study of persons warned out of Boston in 1747, 1759, and 1771. The Warning Out Book gives the relationship of each person in the family group. A full study of the entries in the Warning Out Book, including the place of origin of the migrants, would enlarge our understanding of economic and social dislocation during this period. For a suggestive study see Douglas Lamar Jones, "The Strolling Poor: Transiency in Eighteenth-Century Massachusetts," *Journal of Social History*, 8 (1975): 28–54. After the Seven Years' War, Philadelphia relied increasingly on transporting poor migrants out of the city. The names of these deportees are scattered through the minutes of the Overseers of the Poor, 1768–74, and in the *Minutes of the Common Council of the City of Philadelphia, 1704–76* (Philadelphia, 1847), passim.

43. *BRC*, 14:13, 100, 280; G. B. Warden, *Boston, 1689–1776* (Boston, 1970), 128, 325n; Shattuck, *Report to the Committee*, 5; *BRC*, 12: 178; 14:302.

44. The manuscript volumes of the County Commissioners' Minutes from 1718 to 1766 are in City Archives, Philadelphia. Another volume, for 1771 to 1774, is at Historical Society of Pennsylvania, and the succeeding volume, extending to Aug. 21, 1776, is in Tax and Exoneration Records, Pennsylvania State Archives, Harrisburg.

45. A graph of mean inventoried wealth for the lowest three deciles would indicate an even more pronounced downward trend than for the bottom five deciles. Because of the small number of inventories in the early years, the Philadelphia data have been clustered at three- and two-year intervals from 1684 to 1694. Until 1701 the number of inventories is too small to permit plotting the uppermost 10%.

46. In order to extract the fullest meaning from these data, yearly mean wealth has been displayed for the bottom half and top tenth of decedents (Figures 1–3), while the ranges of wealth in four strata (lower, middle, and upper thirty percentiles, plus the uppermost tenth) have been grouped by decades (Table 8). Means, medians, and ranges can be constructed for any grouping of years, but the timing of change is most readily discernible when short periods of time are used. Data on the range of wealth at various levels of society, however, are too cumbersome to present annually. For a discussion of these problems see Menard et al., "Opportunity and Inequality."

47. Inventory of James Black, Jan. 10, 1770, Suffolk County Probate Records, 68:464, Suffolk County Courthouse, Boston; Inventory of Francis Warden, Oct. 3, 1766, ibid., 65:377.

48. Most of the extreme peaks in Figures 1–3 are explained by the invento-

ries of exceptionally wealthy men. An extreme case, which makes the point clearly, is the peak in 1759 on Figures 2A–B. The estate of Samuel Waldo, a wealthy merchant and land speculator, was inventoried in this year. Waldo's fortune totaled £1,425 sterling in personal wealth and £51,840 sterling in real estate. His personal estate was fairly typical of the top 10% of Boston decedents and therefore caused no sharp upward movement on Figure 1B. But the extensive landholdings caused a sharp rise in the graph of mean total wealth among the top 10% of decedents and also among all decedents. I have rejected the use of "trimmed means" suggested by Gloria L. Main ("The Correction of Biases," 16–19, 27–28) because in the cities the accumulation of great wealth, though infrequently on the scale of Waldo's, was an important characteristic of the social structure.

49. See Main, "The Correction of Biases," 16, for an argument that the rich of Dedham avoided probate in the eighteenth century. Although the estates of some wealthy Bostonians were not probated, I have found no evidence that the wealthy are underrepresented in the Boston Inventories. On Boston's decline see Jacob M. Price, "Economic Function and the Growth of American Port Towns in the Eighteenth Century," *Perspectives in American History,* 8 (1974): 138–49.

50. For commodity price inflation see Bezanson et al., *Prices in Colonial Pennsylvania,* chap. 12.

51. The data presented here bear on the material estates of groups of people and not on opportunity for individuals at different levels of society at different points of time. Although some inferences can be made regarding changes in opportunity, we need life-cycle analyses for each of the cities before firm conclusions can be made regarding social mobility. I have made an initial effort toward this end in "Up From the Bottom in Franklin's Philadelphia," *Past & Present,* 77 (1977): 57–83.

52. See, for example, W. W. Rostow, *The Process of Economic Growth* (New York, 1959), 292–96.

53. For the imitation of English aristocratic life in Philadelphia, see Wainwright, *Colonial Grandeur;* Margaret B. Tinkcom, "Cliveden: The Building of a Colonial Mansion," *Pennsylvania Magazine of History and Biography,* 88 (1964); Carl and Jessica Bridenbaugh, *Rebels and Gentlemen: Philadelphia in the Age of Franklin* (New York, 1942), chap. 6. The *Wöchenliche Philadelphische Staatsbote* reported in Dec. 1767 that fifty German city dwellers were walking the streets with their children crying for bread. Starving Germans, sometimes with naked children, were reported in the city in 1772. See O. Seidensticker, *Geschichte der Deutschen Gesellschaft von Pennsylvanien* (Philadelphia, 1876), 149–52.

54. Philip J. Greven, Jr., *Four Generations: Land and Family in Colonial Andover, Massachusetts* (Ithaca, N.Y., 1970); Charles S. Grant, *Democracy in the Connecticut Frontier Town of Kent* (New York, 1961); Kenneth Lockridge, "Land, Population, and the Evolution of New England Society, 1630–1790," *Past & Present,* 39 (1968): 62–80; Rowland Berthoff and John M. Murrin, "Feudalism, Communalism, and the Yeoman Freeholder: The American Revolution Considered as a Social Accident," in Stephen G. Kurtz and James H.

Hutson (eds.), *Essays on the American Revolution* (Chapel Hill, 1973). For information on Indian resistance see David H. Corkran, *The Cherokee Frontier: Conflict and Survival, 1740–1762* (Norman, Okla., 1962); Randolph C. Downes, *Council Fires on the Upper Ohio: A Narative of Indian Affairs in the Upper Ohio Valley until 1795* (Pittsburgh, 1940); C. A. Weslager, *The Delaware Indians: A History* (New Brunswick, N.J., 1972).

55. Bridenbaugh, *Cities in Revolt*, 43–97; Virginia D. Harrington, *The New York Merchant on the Eve of the Revolution* (New York, 1935); William S. Sachs, "The Business Outlook in the Northern Colonies, 1750–75," (unpub. Ph.D. diss., Columbia University, 1957), chap. 2; W. T. Baxter, *The House of Hancock: Business in Boston, 1724–75* (Cambridge, 1945), 92–107; Nash, "Up From the Bottom," 15–22.

56. Warden, *Boston*, 127–34. The lingering effects of the war were discussed by an anonymous writer in the *Boston Independent Advertiser*, Feb, 8, 1748, who claimed that nearly one-fifth of the province's adult males had been lost in the war, and five years later by an anonymous writer in *Industry & Frugality Proposed . . .* (Boston, 1753).

57. Some of the petitions are in *BRC*, 12:119, 198; 14:12, 220–21, 238–40, 280; and in Massachusetts Archives, 67:55–68, 395–96. For Boston's economic difficulties, also see Price, "American Port Towns," 140–49; James G. Lydon, "North Shore Trade in the Early Eighteenth Century," *American Neptune*, 28 (1968): 261–74; Charles Chauncy, *The Idle-Poor Secluded from the Bread of Charity by the Christian Law* (Boston, 1752).

58. For the decline of purchasing power see Andrew McF. Davis, *Currency and Banking in the Province of Massachusetts-Bay* (New York, 1901), 378. In 1739 William Douglass analyzed the effect of currency depreciation on workingmen's budgets, showing that a carpenter whose daily wages had risen from five to twelve shillings from 1712 to 1739 was earning, by the later date, only the equivalent of 3s 4d in buying power at current prices. *Discourse Concerning the Currencies of the British Plantations . . .* (Boston, 1740), 22–23. Malcolm Freiberg, "Thomas Hutchinson and the Province Currency," *New England Quarterly*, 30 (1957): 190–208.

59. Warden, *Boston*, 149–52; "List of Losses by Fire, 1760," Manuscript Division, Boston Public Library; *BRC*, 29:89–100; Baxter, *House of Hancock*, 150–59.

60. German ship arrivals are given in Ralph Beaver Strassburger and William John Hinke, *Pennsylvania German Pioneers: A Publication of the Original Lists of Arrivals in the Port of Philadelphia from 1727 to 1808,* (Norristown, Pa., 1934), 1:xxix. Immigration from Northern Ireland is traced in R. J. Dickson, *Ulster Emigration to Colonial America, 1718–75* (London, 1966), Appendix E; Arthur L. Jensen, *The Maritime Commerce of Colonial Philadelphia* (Madison, Wis., 1963), 118–22; Harry D. Berg, "The Economic Consequences of the French and Indian War for the Philadelphia Merchants," *Pennsylvania History*, 13 (1946): 185–93; Joseph A. Ernst, *Money and Politics in America, 1755–75: A Study in the Currency Act of 1764 and the Political Economy of Revolution* (Chapel Hill, 1973), 102–3. Benjamin Rush to Ebenezer Hazard,

Nov. 8, 1765, in L. H. Butterfield (ed.), *Letters of Benjamin Rush* (Princeton, 1951), pt. 1, 18.

61. To Scott, Pringle, Cheap, and Co., Feb. 5, 1764, quoted in Ernst, *Money and Politics in America,* 90. See also the descriptions of business failures and hard times in "To my Countrymen, the Inhabitants of the Province and City of New-York," *New-York Gazette or Weekly Post-Boy,* Aug. 26, 1762; Harrington, *New York Merchant,* 313–20. For the effect of economic cycles on one merchant see Philip L. White, *The Beekmans of New York in Politics and Commerce, 1647–1870* (New York, 1950), chap. 12.

62. *New-York Journal,* Dec. 17, 1767. "Probus," in *New-York Journal,* Nov. 19, 1767. See also Ernst, *Money and Politics,* 251–60; Harrington, *New York Merchant,* 316–51.

63. Vincent Centinel (pseud.), *Massachusetts in Agony; or, Important Hints to the Inhabitants of the Province: Calling aloud for Justice to be done to the Oppressed . . .* (Boston, 1750), 3–5, 8, 12–13. *New-York Gazette,* July 11, 1765, quoted in Bernard Friedman, "The Shaping of the Radical Consciousness in Provincial New York," *Journal of American History,* 56 (1970): 794. *New-York Gazette or Weekly Post-Boy,* Nov. 13, 1769; also ibid., Dec. 24, 31, 1767, Jan. 7, 21, 1768. I have attempted a fuller analysis of the growing attack on the wealthy in my essay "Social Change and the Growth of Prerevolutionary Urban Radicalism," in Alfred Young (ed.), *The American Revolution: Explorations in the History of American Radicalism* (DeKalb, Ill.: Northern Illinois University Press, 1976).

64. *Boston Evening Post,* Mar. 14, 1763; *Boston Gazette,* Jan. 11, 1762, Supplement.

65. Bernard to the Board of Trade, Aug. 31, 1765, in William Cobbett (ed.), *The Parliamentary History of England* (London, 1813), 16:129–31.

8

SOCIAL CHANGE AND THE GROWTH OF PREREVOLUTIONARY URBAN RADICALISM

Recent studies of the American Revolution have relied heavily on the role of ideas to explain the advent of the American rebellion against England.[1] The gist of the ideological interpretation of the Revolution is that colonists, inheriting a tradition of protest against arbitrary rule, became convinced in the years after 1763 that the English government meant to impose in America "not merely misgovernment and not merely insensitivity to the reality of life in the British overseas provinces but a deliberate design to destroy the constitutional safeguards of liberty, which only concerted resistance—violent resistance if necessary—could effectively oppose."[2] It was this conspiracy against liberty that "above all else . . . propelled [the colonists] into Revolution."[3]

An important corollary to this argument, which stresses the colonial defense of constitutional rights and liberties, is the notion that the material conditions of life in America were so generally favorable that social and economic factors deserve little consideration as a part of the impetus to revolution. "The outbreak of the Revolution," writes Bernard Bailyn, a leading proponent of the ideological school, "was not the result of social discontent, or of economic disturbances, or of rising misery, or of those mysterious social strains that seem to beguile the imaginations of historians straining to find peculiar predispositions to upheaval." Nor, asserts Bailyn, was there a "transformation of mob behavior or of the lives of the 'inarticulate' in the prerevolutionary years that accounts for the disruption of Anglo-American politics."[4] Another historian, whose focus is economic change and not ideas, writes that "whatever it might have been, the American Revolution was not a rising of impoverished masses—or merchants—in search of their share of the wealth. The 'predicament of poverty,' in Hannah Arendt's

---

This essay first appeared in Alfred F. Young, ed., *The American Revolution: Explorations in the History of American Radicalism* (DeKalb, Ill.: Northern Illinois University Press, 1976), 3–36. Minor alterations have been made in the text and the footnotes.

phrase, was absent from the American scene"—so much so that even though the "secular trend in the concentration of wealth created an increasing gulf between the rich and the poor over the years separating 1607 and 1775, the fact remains that not only were the rich getting richer but the poor were also, albeit at a slower rate."[5]

One of the purposes of this essay is to challenge these widely accepted notions that the "predicament of poverty" was unknown in colonial America, that the conditions of everyday life among "the inarticulate" had not changed in ways that led toward a revolutionary predisposition, and that "social discontent," "economic disturbances," and "social strains" can generally be ignored in searching for the roots of the Revolution. I do not suggest that we replace an ideological construction with a mechanistic economic interpretation, but argue that a popular ideology, affected by rapidly changing economic conditions in American cities, dynamically interacted with the more abstract Whig ideology borrowed from England. These two ideologies had their primary appeal within different parts of the social structure, were derived from different sensibilities concerning social equity, and thus had somewhat different goals. The Whig ideology, about which we know a great deal through recent studies, was drawn from English sources, had its main appeal within upper levels of colonial society, was limited to a defense of constitutional rights and political liberties, and had little to say about changing social and economic conditions in America or the need for change in the future. The popular ideology, about which we know very little, also had deep roots in English culture, but it resonated most strongly within the middle and lower strata of society and went far beyond constitutional rights to a discussion of the proper distribution of wealth and power in the social system. It was this popular ideology that undergirded the politicization of the artisan and laboring classes in the cities and justified the dynamic role they assumed in the urban political process in the closing decades of the colonial period.

It is toward understanding this popular ideology and its role in the upsurge of revolutionary sentiment and action in the 1760s that this essay is devoted. Our focus will be on the three largest colonial cities— Boston, New York, and Philadelphia. Other areas, including the older, settled farming regions and backcountry, were also vitally important to the upwelling of revolutionary feeling in the fifteen years before 1776 and in the struggle that followed. But the northern cities were the first areas of revolutionary ferment, the communication centers where newspapers and pamphlets spread the revolutionary message, and the arenas of change in British North America where most of the trends overtaking colonial society in the eighteenth century were first and most intensely felt.

To understand how this popular ideology swelled into revolution-ary commitment within the middle and lower ranks of colonial society, we must first comprehend how the material conditions of life were changing for city dwellers during the colonial period and how people at different levels of society were affected by these alterations. We cannot fathom this process by consulting the writings of merchants, lawyers, and upper-class politicians, because their business and political corre-spondence and the tracts they wrote tell us almost nothing about those below them in the social hierarchy. But buried in more obscure docu-ments are glimpses of the lives of both ordinary and important people—shoemakers and tailors as well as lawyers and merchants. The story of changing conditions and how life in New York, Philadelphia, and Bos-ton was experienced can be discerned, not with perfect clarity but in general form, from tax, poor relief, and probate records.

The most generally recognized alteration in eighteenth-century ur-ban social structures (discussed in detail in the previous essay) is the long-range trend toward a less even distribution of wealth. Tax lists for Boston, Philadelphia, and New York, ranging over nearly a century prior to the Revolution, make this clear. By the early 1770s the top 5 percent of Boston's taxpayers controlled 49 percent of the taxable assets of the community, whereas they had held only 30 percent in 1687. In Philadelphia the top twentieth increased its share of wealth from 33 to 55 percent between 1693 and 1774. Those in the lower half of society, who in Boston in 1687 had commanded 9 percent of the taxable wealth, were left collectively with a mere 5 percent in 1771. In Philadel-phia, those in the lower half of the wealth spectrum saw their share of wealth drop from 10.1 to 3.3 percent in the same period. It is now evident that the concentration of wealth had proceeded very far in the eighteenth-century cities.[6]

Though city dwellers from the middle and lower ranks could not measure this redistribution of economic resources with statistical preci-sion, they could readily discern the general trend. No one could doubt that upper-class merchants were amassing fortunes when four-wheeled coaches, manned by liveried Negro slaves, appeared in Boston's crooked streets, or when urban mansions, lavishly furnished in imitation of the English aristocracy, rose in Philadelphia and New York.[7] Colonial pro-bate records reveal that personal estates of £5,000 sterling were rare in the northern cities before 1730, but by 1750 the wealthiest town dwellers were frequently leaving assets of £20,000 sterling, exclusive of real es-tate, and sometimes fortunes of more than £50,000 sterling—equivalent in purchasing power to about 2.5 million dollars today.[8] Wealth of this magnitude was not disguised in cities with populations ranging from about 16,000 in Boston to about 25,000 in New York and Philadelphia and with geographical expanses half as large as public university campuses today.

While urban growth produced a genuinely wealthy upper class, it simultaneously created a large class of impoverished city dwellers. All of the cities built almshouses in the 1730s in order to house under one roof as many of the growing number of poor as possible. This was the beginning of a long trend toward substituting confinement in workhouses and almshouses for the older familial system of direct payments to the poor at home. The new system was designed to reduce the cost of caring for a growing number of marginal persons—people who, after the 1730s, were no longer simply the aged, widowed, crippled, incurably ill, or orphaned members of society, but also the seasonally unemployed, war veterans, new immigrants, and migrants from inland areas seeking employment in the cities. These persons, whose numbers grew impressively in the 1750s and 1760s, were now expected to contribute to their own support through cloth weaving, shoemaking, and oakum picking in city workhouses.[9]

Beginning in Boston in the 1740s and in New York and Philadelphia somewhat later, poverty scarred the lives of a growing part of the urban populations. Among its causes were periodic unemployment, rising prices that outstripped wage increases, and war taxes which fell with unusual severity on the lower classes. In Boston, where the Overseers of the Poor had expended only £25–35 sterling per thousand inhabitants in the 1720s and 1730s, per capita expenditures for the poor more than doubled in the 1740s and 1750s, and then doubled again in the last fifteen years of the colonial period. Poor relief rose similarly in Philadelphia and New York after 1750.

In the third quarter of the eighteenth century poverty struck even harder at Boston's population and then blighted the lives of the New York and Philadelphia laboring classes to a degree unparalleled in the first half of the century. In New York, the wartime boom of 1755–60 was followed by postwar depression. High rents and unemployment brought hundreds of families to the edge of indigency. The incidence of poverty jumped more than fourfold between 1750 and 1775. By 1772 a total of 425 persons jostled for space in the city's almshouse, which had been built to accommodate about 100 indigents. In Philadelphia, in the decade before the Revolution, more than 900 persons each year were admitted to the city's institutions for the impoverished—the almshouse, workhouse, and Hospital for the Sick Poor.[10] The data on poor relief leaves little room for doubt that the third quarter of the eighteenth century was an era of severe economic and social dislocation in the cities, and that by the end of the colonial period a large number of urban dwellers were without property, without opportunity, and, except for public aid, without the means of obtaining the necessities of life.

The economic changes that redistributed wealth, filled the almshouses to overflowing, and drove up poor rates, also hit hard at the lower part of the middle class in the generation before the Revolution. These people—master artisans rather than laborers, skilled shipwrights rather than merchant seamen, shopkeepers rather than peddlers—were financially humbled in substantial numbers in Boston beginning in the 1740s and in Philadelphia and New York a dozen years later.

In Boston, this crumbling of middle-class economic security can be traced in individual cases through the probate records and in aggregate form in the declining number of "taxables." In that city, where the population stagnated after 1735, the number of "rateable polls" declined from a high of more than 3,600 in 1735, when the city's economy was at its peak, to a low of about 2,400 around mid-century. By 1771, Boston's taxables still numbered less than 2,600.[11] This decline of more than a thousand taxable adults was not caused by loss of population but by the sagging fortunes of almost one-third of the city's taxpaying population. Boston's selectmen made this clear in 1757 when they pointed out that "besides a great Number of Poor . . . who are either wholly or in part maintained by the Town, & so are exempt from being Taxed, there are many who are Rateable according to Law . . . who are yet in such poor Circumstances that Considering how little business there is to be done in Boston they can scarcely procure from day to day daily Bread for themselves & Families."[12]

In Philadelphia, the decay of a substantial part of the "middling sort" similarly altered the urban scene, though the trend began later and did not proceed as far as in Boston. Taxpayers dropped from the rolls because of poverty represented less than 3 percent of the taxables in the period before 1740, but they increased to about 6 to 7 percent in the two decades beginning in 1740, and then to one in every ten taxpayers in the fifteen years before the Revolution.[13]

The probate records of Boston and Philadelphia tell a similar tale of economic insecurity hovering over the middle ranges of urban society,[14] as spelled out in detail in the previous essay. Among these people in Boston, median wealth at death dropped sharply between 1685 and 1735 and then made a partial but uneven recovery as the Revolution approached. The average carpenter, baker, shopkeeper, shipwright, or tavernkeeper dying in Boston between 1735 and 1765 had less to show for a lifetime's work than his counterpart of a half century before. In Philadelphia, those in the lower ranges of the middle class also saw the value of their assets, accumulated over a lifetime's labor, slowly decline during the first half of the eighteenth century, though not so severely as in Boston. The startling conclusion that must be drawn from a study of nearly 4,500 Boston and Philadelphia inventories of estates at probate is that population growth and economic development in the colonial cities did not raise the standard of living and broaden opportunities for the vast majority of people, but instead conferred benefits primarily upon those at the top of the social pyramid. The long-range effect of growth was to erode the personal assets held at death by those in the lower 75 percent of Boston society and the lower 60 percent of Philadelphia society. Though many city dwellers had made spectacular individual ascents from the bottom, in the manner of Benjamin Franklin of Philadelphia or Isaac Sears of New York, the statistical chances of success for those beginning beneath the upper class were considerably less after the first quarter of the eighteenth century than before. The dominating fact of late-colonial life for many middle-class as well as most lower-class city folk was not economic achievement but economic frustration.

Understanding that the cities were becoming centers of frustrated ambition, propertylessness, genuine distress for those in the lower strata, and stagnating fortunes for many in the middle class makes comprehensible much of the violence, protest, and impassioned rhetoric that occurred in the half-generation before the colonial challenge to British regulations began in 1764. Upper-class colonists typically condemned these verbal attacks and civil disorders as the work of the "rabble," the "mob," the "canaille," or individuals "of turbulent disposition." These labels were used to discredit crowd activity, and historians have only recently recognized that the "rabble" often included a broad range of city dwellers, from slaves and servants through laborers and seamen to artisans and shopkeepers—all of whom were directly or indirectly expressing grievances.[15] Cutting across class lines, and often unified by economic conditions that struck at the welfare of both the lower and middle classes, these crowds began to play a larger role in a political process that grew more heated as the colonial period came to an end.[16] This developing consciousness and political sophistication of ordinary city dwellers came rapidly to fruition in the early 1760s and thereafter played a major role in the advent of the Revolution.

Alienation and protest had been present in the northern cities, especially during periods of economic difficulty, since the early eighteenth century. In Boston, between 1709 and 1713, townspeople protested vigorously and then took extralegal action when Andrew Belcher, a wealthy merchant, refused to stop exporting grain during a bread shortage in the city. Belcher had grown fat on war contracts during Queen Anne's War, and when he chose to export grain to the Caribbean, at a handsome profit, rather than sell it for a smaller profit to hungry townspeople, his ships were attacked and his warehouses emptied by an angry crowd. Rank had no privileges, as even the lieutenant-governor was shot when he tried to intervene. Bostonians of meagre means learned that through concerted action the powerless could become powerful, if only for the moment. Wealthy merchants who would not listen to pleas from the community could be forced through collective action to subordinate profits to the public need.[17]

After the end of Queen Anne's War, in 1713, Boston was troubled by postwar recession and inflation, which cut into the wages of working people. Attempts to organize a land bank in order to increase the scarce circulating medium in Boston were opposed by wealthy men, many of them former war contractors. Gathering around the unpopular governor Joseph Dudley, and his successor, Samuel Shute, these fiscal conservatives blamed the hard times on the extravagant habits of "the Ordinary sort" of people, who squandered their money on a "foolish fondness of Forreign Commodities & Fashions" and on too frequent tippling in the town's taverns.[18] But such explanations did not deceive returning war veterans, the unemployed, or those caught in an inflationary squeeze. They protested openly against men who made their fortunes "by grinding the poor," as one writer expressed it, and who studied "how to oppress, cheat, and overreach their neighbours." "The Rich, Great, and Potent," stormed this angry spokesman, "with rapacious violence bear down all before them, who have not wealth, or strength to encounter or avoid their fury."[19] Although the town meeting voted down the land bank in 1715, it was out of this defeat that the Boston Caucus, the political organization designed to mobilize the middle- and lower-class electorate in the decades to come, arose.[20]

In Philadelphia, economic issues also set the mechanic and laborer against the rich as early as the 1720s. When a business recession brought unemployment and a severe shortage of specie (the only legal circulating medium), leading merchant-politicans argued that the problem was moral in nature. If the poor were unemployed or hungry, they had their own lack of industry and prudence to thank, wrote James Logan, a thriving merchant and land speculator. "The Sot, the Rambler, the Spendthrift, and the Slip Season," he charged, were at the heart of the slump. Schemes for reviving the economy with emissions of paper money were reckless attempts to cheat those who worked for their money instead of drinking their time away.[21]

But, as in Boston, the majority of people were not fooled by such high-toned arguments. Angry tracts appeared on both sides of the debate concerning the causes and cure for recession. Those who favored paper money and called for restrictions on land speculators and monopolizers of the money market made an attack on wealth itself an important theme. Logan found bricks flying through his windows and a crowd threatening to level his house. Meanwhile, he looked on in disgust as Governor William Keith organized a political caucus, encouraged laboring men to participate in politics, and conducted a campaign aimed at discrediting Logan and other wealthy merchants.[22] "It is neither the Great, the Rich, nor the Learned, that compose the Body of any People, and . . . civil Government ought carefully to protect the poor, laborious and industrious Part of Mankind," Keith cautioned the Assembly in 1723.[23] Logan, formerly respected as William Penn's chief proprietary officeholder, a member of council, a judge of the colony's highest court, and Pennsylvania's most educated man, now found himself reviled in widely distributed tracts as "Pedagogus Mathematicus"— an ambitious, ruthless elitist. He and his henchmen, cried the pamphleteers, deserved to be called "petty Tyrants of this Province," "Serpents in the Grass," "Rich Misers," "Phenomena of Aristocracy," "Infringers of our Priviledges," and "Understrappers of Government."[24]

In a striking inversion of the conventional eighteenth-century thinking that only the rich and educated were equipped to hold high political offices, the Keithian faction urged the voters to recognize that "a mean Man, of small Interest, devoted to the faithful Discharge of his Trust and Duty to the Government" was far more to be valued than rich and learned men.[25] For the rest of the decade the anti-Logan forces, organized into political clubs in Philadelphia, held sway at the annual elections and passed legislation to relieve the distress of the lower-class unemployed and middle-class debtors. Members of the Philadelphia elite, such as Logan and merchant Isaac Norris, hated the "new vile people [who] may be truly called a mob," and deplored Keith's "doctrine of reducing all to a level."[26] But they could no longer manage politics from the top. The "moral economy of the crowd," as E.P. Thompson has called it—the people's sense that basic rules of equity in social relations had been breached—had intervened when the rich would do nothing to relieve suffering in a period of economic decline.[27]

When an economic slump beset New York in the 1730s, causing unemployment and an increase in suits for debt, the reaction was much the same as in the other cities. The John Peter Zenger trial of this era is best remembered as a chapter in the history of the freedom of the press. But central to the campaign organized by Zenger's supporters were the indictment of the rich and the mobilization of the artisanry against them. A 1734 election tract reminded the New York electorate that the city's strength—and its future—lay with the fortunes of "Shuttle" the weaver, "Plane" the joiner, "Drive" the carter, "Mortar" the mason, "Tar" the mariner, "Snip" the tailor, "Smallrent" the fairminded landlord, and "John Poor" the tenant. Pitted against them were "Gripe the Merchant, Squeeze the Shopkeeper, Spintext and Quible the Lawyer."[28] In arguments reminiscent of those in Philadelphia a decade before, the Lewis Morris faction counseled the people that "A poor honest Man [is] preferable to a rich Knave." Only by electing men responsive to the needs of the whole community, the Morrisites advised, could New Yorkers arrest the forces that were impoverishing the artisan class while fattening the purses of merchants and moneylenders. The conservative clergy of the city advised working people to pray harder in difficult times, but the Morrisite pamphleteers urged the electorate to throw out of office those "people in Exalted Stations" who looked with disdain upon "those they call the Vulgar, the Mob, the herd of Mechanicks."[29]

Attacks on wealth and concentrated power continued in New York through 1737. The opulent and educated of the city were exposed as self-interested and oppressive men, not the public-minded community servants that conventional political philosophy prescribed. Though the leaders of the Morris faction were themselves men of substantial wealth, and though they never advocated a truly popular form of politics, their attacks on the rich and their organization of artisan voters became imbedded in the structure and ideology of politics.[30]

A decade later, political contention broke out again in New York City and attacks on the wealthy and well-born were revived. To some extent the political factionalism in the period from 1747 to 1755 represented a competition for power and profit between different elements of the elite. DeLanceys were pitted against Coldens, and Alexanders against Bayards, in a game where the stakes were control of land in neighboring New Jersey, the profits of the Iroquois fur trade, and the power of the assembly in opposition to the governor and his clique of officeholders. But as in earlier decades, the success of these intra-elite struggles depended upon gaining support from below. In appealing to the artisans and tradesmen, especially during periods of economic decline, bitter charges surfaced about the selfishness of wealthy men and the social inequities in society which they promoted.[31] Cadwallader Colden's *Address to the Freeholders* in 1747 inveighed against the rich, who did not build their fortunes "by the honestest means" and who had no genuine concern for the "publick spirit." Colden attacked the wealthy, among whose ranks he figured importantly, as tax dodgers who indulged in wanton displays of wealth and gave little thought to the welfare of those below them. "The midling rank of mankind," argued Colden, was far more honest, dependable, sober, and public spirited "in all Countries," and it was therefore best to trust "our Liberty & Property" to them rather than to New York's "rich jolly or swaggering companions."[32]

In Boston, resentment against the rich, focusing on specific economic grievances, continued to find voice in the middle third of the century. Moreover, since the forming of the caucus a generation before, well-coordinated street action channeled the wrath of townspeople against those who were thought to act against the interest of the commonality. In the 1730s an extended debate erupted on establishing a public market where prices and marketing conditions would be controlled. Many Bostonians in the lower and middle strata regarded a regulated public market as a device of merchants and fiscal conservatives to drive small retailers from the field and reap the profits of victualing Boston themselves. Though they lost their cause after a number of bitter debates and close votes at the town meeting in the mid-1730s, these humbler people, who probably included many without a vote, ultimately prevailed by demolishing the public market on Dock Square in 1737.[33] The attack was accompanied by much "murmuring agt the Government & the rich people," lamented Benjamin Colman, an advocate of the regulated market and a member of the conservative faction. Worse yet, "none of the Rioters or Mutineers" could be discovered. Their support was so broad that they promised that any attempt to arrest or arraign the saboteurs would be met by "Five Hundred Men in Solemn League and Convenant," who would resist the sheriff and destroy any other markets erected by wealthy merchants. The timbers of the public market which fell before the night raiders in 1737 showed how widely held was the conviction that only this kind of civil disobedience would "deliver the poor oppressed and distressed People out of the Hands of the Rich and Mighty."[34]

The Land Bank controversy from 1740 to 1742 further inflamed a wide segment of Boston society. Most of the colony, including Boston, favored a land bank which would relieve the economic distress of the period by issuing more paper money and thus continuing the inflationist policies of the last twenty years. In opposition stood a group of Boston merchants, who "had railed against the evils of paper money" for years and now "damned the Bank as merely a more invidious form of the soft money panacea typically favored by the province's poor and unsuccessful."[35] One of their spokesmen, William Douglass, reflected the elitist view by characterizing the dispute as a struggle between the "Idle & Extravagant who want to borrow money at any bad lay" and "our considerable Foreign Traders and rich Men."[36]

Even though the inflationists swept the Massachusetts assembly elections of 1740 and 1741, they could not overcome the combined opposition of Governor Jonathan Belcher, a group of wealthy merchants, and officials in England. In the end, the Land Bank movement was thwarted. The defeat was not lightly accepted or quickly forgotten by debtors and Bostonians of modest means. Three years later, a committee of the Boston town meeting, which had consistently promoted inflated paper currency as a means of relief for Boston's numerous debtors, exploded with angry words at another deflationist proposal of the mercantile elite: "We cannot suppose, because in some extraordinary Times when a Party Spirit has run high there have been some Abuses of Our Liberties and Priviledges, that therefore We should in a Servile Manner give them all up. And have our Bread & Water measured out to Us by those Who Riot in Luxury & Wantonness on Our Sweat & Toil and be told by them that we are too happy, because we are not reduced to Eat Grass with the Cattle."[37]

The crowning blow to ordinary Bostonians came in 1749 when Thomas Hutchinson, the principal architect of the monetary policy favored by the wealthiest merchants, engineered a merciless devaluation of Massachusetts currency as a cure to the continuing inflation, which by now had reduced the value of paper money to a fraction of its face value. With many persons unemployed, with poverty afflicting hundreds of families, and with Hutchinson personifying the military contractors who had reaped fortunes from King George's War (1739–47) while common people suffered, popular sentiment exploded. The newspapers carried a rancorous debate on the proposed devaluation, street fights broke out when the new policy was instituted, and Hutchinson was personally threatened on several occasions.[38] An anonymous pamphleteer put into words the sentiment of many in the city who had watched the gap widen between rich and poor during hard times. "Poverty and Discontent appear in every Face, (except the Countenances of the Rich), and dwell upon every Tongue." A few men, fed by "Lust of Power, Lust of Fame, Lust of Money," had grown rich by supplying military expeditions during the last war and had now cornered the paper money market and manipulated the rates of exchange for English sterling to their own profit. "No Wonder such Men can build Ships, Houses, buy Farms, set up their Coaches, Chariots, live very splendidly, purchase Fame, Posts of Honour," railed the pamphleteer. But such "Birds of prey . . . are Enemies to all Communities—wherever they live."[39]

The growing sentiment in the cities against the wealthy was nourished by the Great Awakening—the outbreak of religious enthusiasm throughout the colonies beginning in the late 1730s. Although this eruption of evangelical fervor is primarily identified as a rural phenomenon, it also had powerful effects in the cities, where fiery preachers such as George Whitefield and Gilbert Tennent had their greatest successes. We have no study as yet of the Great Awakening in the cities, but clues abound that one important reason for its urban appeal was the fact that the evangelists took as one of their primary targets the growth of wealth and extravagance, accompanied by a dwindling of social concern in colonial America. Nowhere was this manifested more noticeably than in the cities.[40]

The urban dwellers who thronged to hear George Whitefield in Philadelphia in 1739 and 1740, and those who crowded the Common in Boston to hear Whitefield and the vituperative James Davenport in the early 1740s, were overwhelmingly from the "lower orders," so far as we can tell. What accounts for their "awakening" is the evangelists' presentation of a personal religion where humble folk might find succor from debt, daily toil, sickness, and want, and might express deeply felt emotions in an equality of fellowship. At the same time, the revivalist preachers spread a radical message concerning established authority. City dwellers were urged to partake in mass revivals, where the social distance between clergyman and parishioner and among worshipers themselves was obliterated. They were exhorted to be skeptical toward dogma and to participate in ecclesiastical affairs rather than bow passively to established hierarchy.[41]

Through the Great Awakening, doctrinal controversy and attacks on religious leaders became widely accepted in the 1740s. In Boston the itinerant preacher James Davenport hotly indicted the rich and powerful and advised ordinary people to break through the crust of tradition in order to right the wrongs of a decaying society. It was the spectre of unlearned artisans and laborers assuming authority in this manner that frightened many upper-class city dwellers and led them to charge the revivalists with preaching levelism and anarchy. "It is . . . an exceedingly difficult, gloomy time with us . . . ," wrote one conservative clergyman from Boston. "Such an enthusiastic, factious, censorious Spirit was never known here. . . . Every low-bred, illiterate Person can resolve Cases of Conscience and settle the most difficult Points of Divinity better than the most learned Divines."[42]

Such charges were heard repeatedly during the Great Awakening, revealing the fears of those who trembled to see the "unthinking multitude" invested with a new dignity and importance. Nor could the passing of the Awakening reverse the tide, for this new sense of power remained a part of the social outlook of ordinary people. In fact, the radical transformation of religious feeling overflowed into civil affairs. The new feeling of autonomy and importance was bred in the churches, but now it was carried into the streets. Laboring people in the city learned "to identify the millennium with the establishment of governments which derived their power from the people, and which were free from the great disparities of wealth which characterized the old world."[43]

The crescendo of urban protest and extralegal activity in the pre-revolutionary decades cannot be separated from the condition of people's lives. Of course those who authored attacks on the growing concentration of wealth and power were rarely artisans or laborers; usually they were men who occupied the middle or upper echelons of society, and sometimes they were men who sought their own gain—installment in office, or the defeat of a competitor for government favors. But whatever their motives, their sharp criticisms of the changes in urban society were widely shared among humbler townspeople. It is impossible to say how much they shaped rather than reflected the views of those in the lower half of the social structure—urban dwellers whose opportunities and daily existence had been most adversely affected by the structural changes overtaking the colonial cities. But the willingness of broad segments of urban society to participate in attacks on narrowly concentrated wealth and power—both at the polls where the poor and propertyless were excluded, and in the streets where everyone, including women, apprentices, indentured servants, and slaves, could engage in action—should remind us that a rising tide of class antagonism and political consciousness, paralleling important economic changes, was a distinguishing feature of the cities at the end of the colonial period.

It is this organic link between the circumstances of people's lives and their political thought and action that has been overlooked by historians who concentrate on Whig ideology, which had its strongest appeal among the educated and well-to-do. The link had always been there, as detailed research into particular communities is beginning to show. But it became transparently clear in the late colonial period, even before England began demanding greater obedience and greater sacrifices in the colonies for the cause of the British Empire. The connection can be seen in New York in the 1760s, where the pleas of the impoverished against mercenary landlords were directly expressed in 1762, and where five years later the papers were pointing out that while the poor had vastly increased in recent years and while many families were selling their furniture at vendue to pay their rent, carriage owners in the city had grown from five to seventy.[44] The link can also be seen in Philadelphia, where growing restlessness at unemployment, bulging almshouses, rising poor taxes, and soaring prices for food and firewood helped to politicize the electorate and drew unprecedented numbers of people to the polls in the last decade of the colonial period.[45]

However, it was in Boston, where poverty had struck first, cut deepest, and lasted longest, that the connection between changing urban conditions and rising political radicalism is most obvious. That it preceded the post-1763 imperial debate, rather than flowing from it, becomes apparent in a close examination of politics in that city between 1760 and 1765.

The political factionalism of these years has usually been seen as a product of the accession of Francis Bernard to the governorship in 1760 and the subsequent appointment of Thomas Hutchinson to the chief justiceship of the colony over the claims of James Otis, Sr., who thought he had been promised the position. Hutchinson, already installed as lieutenant governor, judge of probate, president of the provincial council, and captain of Castle William, now held high office in all three branches of government—executive, judicial, and legislative. The issues, as historians have portrayed them, were plural officeholding, prosecution of the colony's illegal traders under writs of assistance, and, ultimately, the right of England to fasten new imperial regulations on the colony.[46] But running beneath the surface of these arguments, and almost entirely overlooked by historians, were issues that had far greater relevance to Boston's commonality.

For ordinary Bostonians, Thomas Hutchinson had long been regarded as a man who claimed to serve the community at large but devised policies which invariably benefited the rich and hurt the poor. As far back as 1738, Hutchinson had disregarded instructions from the town meeting and pressed the General Court to pass deflationary measures which hurt the pocketbooks of common people, particularly those in debt. Hutchinson continued his hard money campaign in the 1740s. During the 1747 impressment riot, when an angry crowd took control of Boston and demanded the release of some fifty of the town's citizens seized for service in His Majesty's ships, Hutchinson lined up behind the governor in defense of law and order. Alongside other merchants who were chalking up handsome profits on war contracts issued by Governor William Shirley, Hutchinson now stood at the governor's side as his house was surrounded by a jeering, hostile crowd that battered the sheriff and then "swabb'd in the gutter" and locked in the town stocks a deputy sheriff who attempted to disperse them. Hutchinson and his future brother-in-law, Andrew Oliver, joined two other merchants in drafting a report condemning the impressment proceedings as a "Riotous Tumultuous Assembly" of "Foreign Seamen, Servants, Negroes, and Other Persons of Mean and Vile Conditions."[47]

One year later, Hutchinson became the designer and chief promoter of a plan for drastically devaluing Massachusetts currency. Enacted into law in 1749 after bitter debate, the hard money plan was widely seen as a cause of the trade paralysis and economic recession that struck Boston in the early 1750s. Hutchinson's conservative fiscal measure was roundly attacked in the Boston press and specifically criticized for discriminating against the poor. Four months after the Hutchinson plan became law, Boston's voters turned him out of the House. Shortly thereafter, when his home mysteriously caught fire, a crowd gathered in the street, cursing Hutchinson and crying, "Let it burn!" A rump town meeting sardonically elected Hutchinson tax collector, a job which would take him out of his mansion and into the streets where he might personally see how laboring-class Bostonians were faring during hard times.[48]

The animosity against Hutchinson continued during the next decade, because he aligned himself with a series of unpopular issues—the excise tax of 1754, the Albany Plan of the same year, and another devaluation scheme in 1761.[49] More than anyone in Boston in the second third of the eighteenth century, Thomas Hutchinson stood in the common people's view as the archetype of the cold, grasping, ambitious, aristocratic merchant-politician who had lost touch with his humbler neighbors and cared little whether they prospered or failed.

Fanning the flames of rancor toward Hutchinson in the early 1760s was his leadership of a small group of conservative merchants and lawyers, known in the popular press as the "Junto." These men were known not only for fiscal conservatism but for their efforts to dismantle the town meeting system of government in Boston in order to enlarge their power while curbing that of the middle and lower classes. Most of them were friends of the new governor, Francis Bernard, enjoyed appointments in the provincial government, belonged to the Anglican church, and were related by blood or marriage. Among them were Hutchinson, Andrew and Peter Oliver, Eliakim Hutchinson, Charles Apthorp, Robert Auchmuty, Samuel Waterhouse, Charles Paxton, Thomas Flucker, John Erving, Jr., Edmund Trowbridge, and Chambers Russell.

The move to overthrow the town meeting in 1760 had deep roots. In 1715 and again in the early 1730s conservative merchants had argued that Boston should substitute a borough government for the town meeting. Under municipal incorporation, a system of town government widely used in England as well as in Philadelphia, appointed alderman would serve life terms and would elect the mayor. Under such a plan most municipal officers would be appointed rather than elected. The proposal was designed to limit popular participation in government and transfer control of the city to the elite, whose members argued that they would institute greater order and efficiency.[50]

Both earlier attempts to scrap the town meeting had been staunchly attacked by pamphleteers, who warned that such "reforms" would give exorbitant power to men whose wealth and elevated social status were frail guarantees that they would act in the public interest. The gulf between the rulers and the ruled, between the rich and poor, would only increase, they prophesied, and the people would pay a fearful price for abdicating their political rights. Those who favored incorporation, argued a pamphleteer in 1715, despised "Mobb Town Meetings," where the rich, if they wished to participate, had to mingle with less elevated townspeople. They wished to substitute the rule of the few so that "the Great Men will no more have the Dissatisfaction of seeing their Poorer Neighbours stand up for equal Privilege with them." But neither in 1715 nor in the early 1730s could the elite push through their reorganization of town government.[51]

The town meeting continued to rankle those who regarded laboring people as congenitally turbulent, incapable of understanding economic issues, and moved too much by passion and too little by reason to make wise political choices. Governor Shirley expressed this view most cogently after the demonstration against British impressment of Boston citizens in 1747: "What I think may be esteemed the principal cause of the Mobbish turn in this Town is its Constitution; by which the Management of it is devolv'd upon the populace assembled in their Town Meetings . . . where the meanest Inhabitants . . . by their constant Attendence there generally are the majority and outvote the Gentlemen, Merchants, Substantial Traders and all the better part of the Inhabitants; to whom it is irksome to attend." When so many workingmen, merchant seamen, and "low sort of people" could participate in town meetings, the governor lamented, what could be expected but "a factious and Mobbish Spirit" that kept educated and respectable people away?[52]

In 1760, five months before Hutchinson's appointment as chief justice, the conservative "Junto" made another attempt to gain control of the town government. Realizing that common Bostonians could not be gulled into surrendering their political rights, the "Junto" plotted a strategy for swinging the May elections in Boston and sending to the General Court four representatives who would convince the House to pass a law for incorporating Boston. A "Combination of Twelve Strangers," who called themselves "The New and Grand Corcas," warned the populist *Boston Gazette*, were designing to "overthrow the ancient Constitution of our Town-Meeting, as being popular and mobbish; and to form a Committee to transact the whole Affairs of the Town for the future." In order to control the elections, the article continued, the "Junto" would attempt to keep "tradesmen, and those whom in Contempt they usually term the Low lived People," from voting. They would challenge their eligibility at the polls, attempt to buy their votes, and threaten them with arrest and loss of their jobs.[53] As Samuel Adams later remarked, it was obvious that Hutchinson was bent on destroying the "Democratic part" of government.[54] On the eve of the election, the "Committee of Tradesmen," working with the "old and true Corcas," used the press to urge Boston's working people to stand up to these threats. The artisans should "put on their Sabbath Cloathes . . . wash their Hands and faces that they may appear neat and cleanly," spurn the vote-buying tactics of the "Junto," and elect men who represented their interests.[55]

A record number of voters turned out on May 13, 1760, as both factions courted the electorate. The result was indecisive. Royall Tyler, vociferously opposed by the Anglican "Junto," was elected. But Benjamin Prat and John Tyng, who during the preceding year had taken an unpopular stand on sending the province ship to England, lost their seats to two moderates, Samuel Welles and John Phillips, who were supported by the Hutchinsonians. The conservatives had succeeded to this extent in creating a "popular" issue and using it to rally the electorate against two of the Caucus's candidates. It was enough to hearten the Hutchinsonians, who now had reason to anticipate other electoral successes, and to galvanize the anti-Hutchinsonians into redoubling their efforts among Boston's electorate.

In the period immediately after the 1760 election, James Otis made his meteoric rise in the "popular" party in Boston, leading the fight to curb the growing power of the Hutchinsonian circle. The Otis-Hutchinson struggle has usually been interpreted as a fight over the regulation of trade and oligarchic officeholding, or, more recently, as the culmination of a long-standing interfamily competition. In both interpretations Otis appears as a sulphurous orator and writer (either brilliant or mad according to one's views), who molded laboring-class opinion, called the "mob" into action, and shaped its behavior. To a large extent, however, Otis was only reflecting the perceptions and interests of common Bostonians in his abusive attacks on the lieutenant governor and his allies. For two years after the 1760 elections, which were dangerously indecisive from the viewpoint of the "popular" party, Otis filled the *Gazette* with vitriolic assaults on the Hutchinson clique, each fully answered in the conservative *Evening-Post*. Woven into Otis's offensive was the theme of resentment against wealth, narrowly concentrated political power, and arbitrary political actions which adversely affected Boston's ordinary people. But rather than seeing this campaign solely as an attempt to mobilize the artisans and laborers, we should also understand it as a reflection of opinion already formed within these groups. For years Boston's common people had shown their readiness to act against such oppression—in preventing the exportation of grain, in destroying the public market, and in harassing arbitrary officeholders. Otis, keenly aware of the declining fortunes and the resentment of ordinary townspeople, was mirroring as well as molding popular opinion.

In 1763 the Hutchinson circle made another attempt to strike at the town meeting system of politics, which was closely interwoven with the Boston Caucus. Election messages in the *Evening-Post* urged the electorate to "keep the Public Good only in View" while burying "in everlasting Oblivion" old prejudices and animosities. But this much said, the paper ran a scathing "expose" of the Caucus, which read like the confessions of an ex-Communist. Allegedly written by a former member of the Caucus, it explained how Caucus leaders conducted all political affairs behind closed doors and in smoke-filled rooms. Then, "for form sake," the leaders "prepared a number of warm disputes . . . to entertain the lower sort; who are in an ecstasy to find the old Roman Patriots still surviving." All townspeople were invited to speak at these open meetings, it was claimed, but to oppose Caucus leaders was to earn their "eternal animosity" and end forever any chance of obtaining town office. Democracy, as practiced by the Caucus, was nothing but sham, mocked the *Evening-Post* writer.[56]

The attempt to "expose" the Caucus as a dictatorial clique, with little genuine interest in the laboring classes, failed miserably. The Caucus responded by organizing its most successful roundup of voters in Boston's colonial history. On election day, 1,089 voters went to the poll, a number never to be exceeded even in the tumultuous years of the following decade. They drubbed the candidates favored by the Hutchinsonians. James Otis, the leading anti-Hutchinsonian, got the largest number of votes and was installed as moderator of the town meeting—a token of the confidence in which he was held for his openhanded attacks on Hutchinson.[57]

The bitter Otis-Hutchinson fights of the early 1760s, carried on *before* English imperial policy became an issue in Massachusetts, revolved around a number of specific issues, including the replacement of William Bollan as provincial agent, the establishment of an Anglican mission in the shadow of Harvard College, the multiple offices held by Hutchinson and his relatives, the writs of assistance, and other problems. But more fundamentally, the struggle matched two incompatible conceptions of government and society. Developed during the controversies of preceding decades, these conceptions were spelled out in an outpouring of political rhetoric in the early 1760s and in the crystallization of two distinct factions.

James Otis, Samuel Adams, Royall Tyler, Oxenbridge Thacher, and a host of other Bostonians, linked to the artisans and laborers through a network of neighborhood taverns, fire companies, and the Caucus, espoused a vision of politics that gave credence to laboring-class views and regarded as entirely legitimate the participation of artisans and even laborers in the political process.[58] This was not a new conception of the rightful political economy, but a very old one. The leaders of this movement were merely following in the footsteps of earlier popular leaders—from John Noyes to Elisha Cooke to James Allen. The town meeting, open to almost all property owners in the city and responsive to the propertyless as well, was the foundation of this system. By no means narrowly based, the "popular" party included many of the city's merchants, shopkeepers, lawyers, doctors, clergymen, and other well-to-do men. They provided leadership and filled the most important elective offices—overseers of the poor, tax assessors, town selectmen, and delegates to the House of Representatives. Lesser people filled minor offices and voiced their opinions at the town meetings where they were numerically dominant.

For the conservative merchants and lawyers, led and personified by Thomas Hutchinson, the old system spelled only chaos. "Reform" for these men meant paring back the responsibilities of the town meeting, substituting appointive for elective officeholders, restricting the freedom of the press, and breaking down the virulent anti-Anglican prejudice that still characterized the popular party. Like their opponents, members of the "prerogative" party had suffered as Boston's economy stagnated after 1740. But they saw the best hope for reviving the economy in handing over the management of town government to the wealthy and well-born exclusively. To see Otis address the crowd and to witness "the Rage of Patriotism . . . spread so violently . . . thro' town and country, that there is scarce a cobler or porter but has turn'd mountebank in politicks and erected his stage near the printing-press" was their vision of hell.[59]

Between 1761 and 1764 proponents of the "popular" and "prerogative" conceptions of politics engaged in a furious battle of billingsgate that filled the columns of the *Gazette* and *Evening-Post*. It is easy to be diverted by the extreme forms which the scurrility took. Charges of "Racoon," "stinking Skunk," "Pimp," "wild beast," "drunkard," and dozens of other choice titles were traded back and forth in verbal civil war. But more important than this stream of epithets was the deep-seated, class-tinged animosity which the polemical pieces exposed: hatred and suspicion of laboring people on the part of the Hutchinsonians; suspicion and hatred of the wealthy, Anglican, prerogative elite held by the common people.

Thus, Thomas Pownall, the popular governor from 1757 to 1760, was satirized by a conservative for confusing class lines by going aboard ships in Boston harbor to talk with "common people about ship-affairs" and mingling in the streets with the "dirtiest, most lubberly, mutinous, and despised part of the people."[60] The anti-Hutchinsonians, on the other hand, urged Bostonians to oppose "The Leviathan in power [Hutchinson], or those other overgrown Animals, whose influ-

ence and importance is only in exact mathematical proportion to the
weight of their purses."[61] The Caucus, decried a Hutchinsonian, talked
incessantly about the right "for every dabbler in politicks to say and
print whatever his shallow understanding, or vicious passions may suggest, against the wisest and best men—a liberty for fools and madmen
to spit and throw firebrands at those of the most respectable and most
amiable character."[62] In retort, Otis, speaking as a mechanic, poured
out his resentment: "I am forced to get my living by the labour of my
hand; and the sweat of my brow, as most of you are and obliged to go
thro' good report and evil report, for bitter bread, earned under the
frowns of some who have no natural or divine rights to be above me,
and entirely owe their grandeur and honor to grinding the faces of the
poor, and other acts of ill gotten gain and power."[63] In reply, the
conservatives charged anarchy: "The day is hastening, when some who
are now, or, have lately been the darling idols of a dirty very dirty
witless rabble commonly called the little vulgar, are to sink and go
down with deserved infamy, to all posterity."[64] This was doubtful, re-
torted a writer in the *Gazette:* the problem was that the rich were
obsessed with money and "couldn't have the idea of riches without that
of poverty. They must see others poor in order to form a notion of their
own happiness." Thus, in what was once a flourishing town, "a few
persons in power" attempted to monopolize politics, and promoted
projects "for keeping the people poor in order to make them
humble . . . "[65]

This reciprocal animosity and mistrust, suffusing the newspapers
and pamphlets of the late colonial period, reveals the deeply rooted
social tensions that Bostonians would carry into the revolutionary era.
These tensions shaped the ways in which different social groups began
to think about *internal* political goals once the conflict against *external*
authority began. In the end, the Hutchinson faction, looking not to the
future but staring into the distant past, faced an impossible task—to
convince a broad electorate that the very men who had accumulated
fortunes in an era when most had suffered were alone qualified to
govern in the interest of the whole community. Lower- and middle-class
Bostonians had heard fiscal conservatives and political elitists pro-
nounce the same platitudes for half a century. Even now, a generation
before James Madison formally enunciated an interest-group theory of
politics, they understood that each group had its particular interest to
promote and that aristocratic politicians who claimed to work for the
commonweal were not to be trusted. Such men employed the catch-
words of the traditional system of politics—"public good," "community," "harmony," and "public virtue"—to cloak their own ambitions
for aggrandizing wealth and power.[66] The growing inequalities of

wealth in Boston, which could be readily seen in the overcrowded alms-house and flocks of out-reliefers in contrast to the urban splendor of men like Hutchinson and Oliver, were proof enough of that.

Only by understanding the long animosity that the common people of Boston held for Thomas Hutchinson and his clique can sense be made of the extraordinary response to the Stamp Act in Boston in August 1765—the systematic destruction of the houses of Hutchinson and other wealthy and conservative Boston officials—and of the course of revolutionary politics in the city in the years that followed. It is possible, of course, to revert to the explanation of Peter Oliver, who, at the time, argued that "the People in general . . . were like the Mobility of all Countries, perfect Machines, wound up by any Hand who might first take the winch."[67] In this view, the crowd was led by the nose by middle- and upper-class manipulators such as Otis and Samuel Adams, and used to further their own political ambitions. In this Newtonian formulation, the crowd could never be self-activating, for thought and planned action could have their source only in the minds of educated persons.[68]

Such explanations, however, bear no relationship to the social realities in Boston at the time or to the long history of popular protest in the city. Again and again in the eighteenth century the Boston crowd had considered its interest, determined its enemies, and moved in a coordinated and discriminating way to gain its ends through street action. It was frequently supported in this by men higher up on the social scale—men who shielded the crowd leaders from subsequent attempts of the authorities to punish them.[69] Thus, several socioeconomic groups, with interests that often coincided but sometimes diverged, found it profitable to coordinate their actions.

The attacks on Andrew Oliver's house on the evening of August 14, 1765, and on Hutchinson's house twelve days later, were entirely consistent with this pattern of politics. On the evening of August 14, the crowd, led by the shoemaker Ebenezer MacIntosh, culminated a day of protest against the Stamp Act by reducing Oliver's mansion to a shambles. Accompanied by the sheriff, Hutchinson attempted to stop the property destruction. For his trouble, he was driven off with a hailstorm of stones. Less than two weeks later it was Hutchinson's turn. Forcing him and his family to flee, the crowd smashed in the doors with axes, reduced the furniture to splinters, stripped the walls bare, chopped through inner partitions until the house was a hollow shell, destroyed the formal gardens behind the house, drank the contents of the wine cellar, and carried off every moveable object of value except some of Hutchinson's books and papers, which were left to scatter in the wind.

Not a person in Boston, neither private citizen nor officer of the law, attempted to stop the crowd. Its members worked through the night with almost military precision to raze the building, spending three hours alone "at the cupola before they could get it down," according to Governor Bernard.[70]

Historians agree that in destroying the Boston mansions of Oliver and Hutchinson, the crowd was demonstrating against the Stamp Act. Oliver had been appointed Stamp Distributor, and Hutchinson, though he publicly expressed his view that the act was unwise, had vowed to use his authority as lieutenant governor to see it executed. But in conducting probably the most ferocious attack on private property in the history of the English colonies, the crowd was demonstrating against far more than Parliamentary policy. Stamp distributors were intimidated and handled roughly in many other cities. But nowhere else did the crowd choose to destroy property on such a grand scale and with such exacting thoroughness. The full meaning of these attacks can be extracted only by understanding the long-standing animus against the Oliver-Hutchinson circle. Beyond intimidating British officialdom, the crowd was giving vent to years of hostility at the accumulation of wealth and power by the aristocratic, Hutchinson-led prerogative faction. Behind every swing of the ax and every hurled stone, behind every shattered plate and splintered mahogany chair lay the fury of a Bostonian who had read or heard the repeated references to the people as "rabble," and who had suffered economic hardship while others grew rich. The handsome furnishings in the houses of Hutchinson, Oliver, and others that fell before the "Rage-intoxicated rabble," as one young upper-class lawyer put it, provided psychological recompense for those Bostonians who had lost faith that opportunity or equitable relationships any longer prevailed in their city.[71]

The political consciousness of the crowd and its use of the Stamp Act protests as an opportunity for an attack on wealth itself were remarked upon again and again in the aftermath of the August actions. Fifteen houses were targeted for destruction on the night of August 27, according to Governor Bernard, in what he thought had become "a War of Plunder, of general levelling and taking away the Distinction of rich and poor." "Everything that for years past, had been the cause of any unpopular discontent was revived," he explained; "and private resentments against persons in office worked themselves in, and endeavoured to exert themselves under the mask of the public cause."[72] On the same day, the governor warned that unless "persons of property and consideration did not unite in support of government"—by which he meant that a way must be found to employ the militia or some kind of *posse comitatus* to control crowd actions—"anarchy and confusion" would continue in "an insurrection of the poor against the rich, those that want the necessities of life against those that have them."[73] On September 10, two weeks after the destruction of Hutchinson's house, another Boston merchant wrote that "the rich men in the town" were seized with apprehension and "were moveing their cash & valuable furniture,&c" to the homes of poorer friends who were above suspicion.[74]

Seen in the context of three generations of social and economic change in Boston, and set against the drive for power of the Hutchinson-Oliver faction in Massachusetts, the Stamp Act riots provide a revealing example of the "moral economy of the crowd" in the early stages of the revolutionary movement. Members of the Boston "mob" needed no upper-class leaders to tell them about the economic stagnation of the late colonial period that had been affecting their lives and the structure of opportunity in the town. Nor did they need to destroy the homes of Oliver and Hutchinson in order to obtain the promise of these office-holders to hold the Stamp Act in abeyance. Instead, the crowd paid off some old debts and served notice on those whom it regarded as enemies of its interests.[75] It was the culminating event of an era of protest against wealth and oligarchic power that had been growing in all the cities. In addition, it demonstrated the fragility of the union between protesting city dwellers of the laboring classes and their more bourgeois partners, for in the uninhibited August attacks on property, the Boston crowd went much farther than Caucus leaders such as James Otis and Samuel Adams had reckoned or wished to countenance.[76]

In the other cities the growing resentment of wealth, the rejection of an elitist conception of politics, and the articulation of artisan- and laboring-class interests also gained momentum after 1765. These were vital developments in the revolutionary period. Indeed, it was the extraordinary new vigor of urban laboring people in defining and pursuing their goals that raised the frightening spectre of a radicalized form of politics and a radically changed society in the minds of many upper-class city dwellers, who later abandoned the resistance movement against England that they had initially supported and led.

That no full-fledged proletarian radical ideology emerged in the decade before the Revolution should not surprise us, for this was a preindustrial society in which no proletariat yet existed. Instead, we can best understand the long movement of protest against concentrated wealth and power, building powerfully as social and economic conditions changed in the cities, as a reflection of the disillusionment of laborers, artisans, and many middle-class city dwellers against a system that no longer delivered equitable rewards to the industrious. "Is it equitable that 99, rather 999, should suffer for the Extravagance or Grandeur of one," asked a New Yorker in 1765, "especially when it is considered that Men frequently owe their Wealth to the impoverishment of their Neighbors?"[77] Such thoughts, cutting across class lines, were gaining force among large parts of the urban population in the late colonial period. They were directed squarely at outmoded notions that only the idle and profligate could fail in America and that only the educated and wealthy were entitled to manage political affairs.

But the absence of clearly identifiable class consciousness and of organized proletarian radicalism does not mean that a radical ideology, nurtured within the matrix of preindustrial values and modes of thought, failed to emerge during the Revolution. Though this chapter in the history of the Revolution is largely unwritten, current scholarship is making it clear that the radicalization of thought in the cities, set in motion by economic and social change, advanced very rapidly once the barriers of traditional thought were broken down. A storm of demands, often accompanied by crowd action to ensure their implementation, rose from the urban "tradesmen" and "mechanicks": for the end of closed assembly debates and the erection of public galleries in the legislative houses; for published roll-call votes which would indicate how faithfully elected legislators followed the wishes of their constituents; for open-air meetings where laboring men could help devise and implement public policy; for more equitable laying of taxes; for price controls instituted by and for the laboring classes to shield them from avaricious men of wealth; and for the election of mechanics and other ordinary people at all levels of government.[78]

How rapidly politics and political ideology could be transformed, as colonists debated the issue of rebellion, is well illustrated by the case of Philadelphia. In one brief decade preceding the Revolution the artisanry and laboring poor of the city moved from a position of clear political inferiority to a position of political control. They took over the political machinery of the city, pushed through the most radical state constitution of the period, and articulated concepts of society and political economy that would have stunned their predecessors. By mid-1776, laborers, artisans, and small tradesmen, employing extralegal measures when electoral politics failed, were in clear command in Philadelphia. Working with middle-class leaders such as James Cannon, Timothy Matlack, Thomas Young, and Thomas Paine, they launched a full-scale attack on wealth and even on the right to acquire unlimited private property. By the summer of 1776 the militant Privates Committee, which probably represented the poorest workers, became the foremost carrier of radical ideology in Pennsylvania. It urged the voters, in electing delegates for the constitutional convention, to shun "great and overgrown rich men [who] will be improper to be trusted, [for] they will be too apt to be framing distinctions in society, because they will reap the benefits of all such distinctions."[79] Going even further, they drew up a bill of rights for consideration by the convention, which included the proposition that "an enormous proportion of property vested in a few individuals is dangerous to the rights, and destructive of the common happiness, of mankind; and therefore every free state hath a right by its laws to discourage the possession of such property."[80] For four years, in an extremely fluid political scene, a radicalized artisanry shaped—and sometimes dominated—city and state politics, while setting forth the most fully articulated ideology of reform yet heard in America.[81]

These calls for reform varied from city to city, depending on differing conditions, past politics, and the qualities of particular leaders. Not all the reforms were implemented, especially those that went to the heart of the structural problems in the economy. Pennsylvania, for example, did not adopt the radical limitation on property holding. But that we know from hindsight that the most radical challenges to the existing system were thwarted, or enjoyed only a short period of success, does not mean that they are not a vital part of the revolutionary story. At the time, the disaffected in the cities were questioning some of the most fundamental tenets of colonial thought. Ordinary people, in bold opposition to their superiors, to whom custom required that they defer, were creating power and suggesting solutions to problems affecting their daily lives. How far these calls for radical reform extended and the success they achieved are matters that historians have begun to investigate only lately. But this much is clear: even though many reforms were defeated or instituted briefly and then abandoned, political thought and behavior would never again be the same in America.

NOTES

1. See, for example, Bernard Bailyn, *The Ideological Origins of the American Revolution* (Cambridge: Harvard University Press, 1967); Bailyn, *The Ordeal of Thomas Hutchinson* (Cambridge: Harvard University Press, 1974); Pauline Maier, *From Resistance to Revolution: Colonial Radicals and the Development of American Opposition to Britain, 1765–1776* (New York: Alfred A. Knopf, 1972); Richard D. Brown, *Revolutionary Politics in Massachusetts: The Boston Committee of Correspondence and the Towns, 1772–1774* (Cambridge: Harvard University Press, 1970).

2. Bailyn, "The Central Themes of the American Revolution: An Interpretation," in Stephen G. Kurtz and James H. Hutson, eds., *Essays on the American Revolution* (Chapel Hill: University of North Carolina Press, 1973), 12.

3. Bailyn, *Ideological Origins of the Revolution*, 95.

4. Bailyn, "Central Themes of the American Revolution," 12.

5. John J. McCusker, "Sources of Investment Capital in the Colonial Philadelphia Shipping Industry," *Journal of Economic History* 32 (1972): 156–57.

6. For Boston, see James A. Henretta, "Economic Development and Social Structure in Colonial Boston," *William and Mary Quarterly*, 3d ser. 22 (1965): 75–92. The Boston data have been reexamined and compared with similar data from New York and Philadelphia in Gary B. Nash, "Urban Wealth and Poverty in Prerevolutionary America," *Journal of Interdisciplinary History* 6 (1976): 545–84.

7. For the rise of urban affluence, see Carl Bridenbaugh, *Cities in Revolt: Urban Life in America, 1743–1776* (New York: Alfred A. Knopf, 1955), chap. 6. A revealing individual case is studied in Nicholas B. Wainwright, *Colonial Grandeur in Philadelphia: The House and Furniture of General John Cadwalader* (Philadelphia: Historical Society of Pennsylvania, 1964).

8. Wills and inventories for almost 1,400 eighteenth-century Philadelphians are in the Office of the Recorder of Wills, City Hall Annex, Philadelphia. More than twice that number are available for Boston at the Office of the Recorder of Wills, Suffolk County Court House, Boston.

9. Raymond A. Mohl, "Poverty in Early America, A Reappraisal: The Case of Eighteenth-Century New York City," *New York History* 50 (1969): 5–27. The data and conclusions on poverty and poor relief in the following paragraphs are discussed more fully in Nash, "Wealth and Poverty," and Gary B. Nash, "Poverty and Poor Relief in Pre-Revolutionary Philadelphia," *William and Mary Quarterly*, 3d ser. 33 (1976).

10. Data derived from Records of the Pennsylvania Hospital for the Sick Poor, 1751–1828, American Philosophical Society (microfilms); and Records of the Contributors for the Better Relief and Employment of the Poor, 1767–78, City Archives, Philadelphia.

11. William H. Whitmore et al., eds., *Reports of the Record Commissioners of Boston*, 39 vols. (Boston, 1878–1902), 14:13, 100, 280; Lemuel Shattuck, *Report to the Committee of the City Council Appointed to Obtain a Census of Boston for the Year 1845* (Boston, 1846), 5; G.B. Warden, *Boston, 1689–1776* (Boston: Little, Brown, and Co., 1970), 128, 325n.

12. *Record Commissioners of Boston*, 12:178; 14:302.

13. County Commissioners of Philadelphia, Minutes, 1718–66, City Archives, Philadelphia; Minutes, 1771–74, Historical Society of Pennsylvania; Minutes, 1774–76, Pennsylvania State Archives, Harrisburg.

14. The following discussion of probated wealth is drawn from a much fuller treatment in Nash, "Wealth and Poverty."

15. Gordon S. Wood, "A Note on Mobs in the American Revolution," *William and Mary Quarterly* 23 (1966): 635–42; Pauline Maier, "Popular Uprisings and Civil Authority in Eighteenth-Century America," ibid. 27 (1970): 3–35.

16. Jesse Lemisch, "Jack Tar in the Street: Merchant Seamen in the Polit-

ics of Revolutionary America," *William and Mary Quarterly* 25 (1968): 371–407; Warden, *Boston* chaps. 6–8; Gary B. Nash, "The Transformation of Urban Politics, 1700–1765," *Journal of American History* 60 (1973): 605–32.

17. *Record Commissioners of Boston,* 8:99–104; 11:194–97; Warden, *Boston,* 66.

18. *The Present Melancholy Circumstances of the Province* . . . (Boston, 1719); Everett Kimball, *The Public Life of Joseph Dudley: A Study of the Colonial Policy of the Stuarts in New England, 1660–1715* (New York: Longmans, Green and Co., 1911), 161–78.

19. *A Letter to an Eminent Clergy-Man* . . . [Boston, 1721]; see also the series of pamphlets published from 1719 to 1721 reprinted in Andrew McFarland Davis, *Colonial Currency Reprints, 1682–1751,* 4 vols. (Boston: Prince Society, 1910–11), 1:367–452; 2:3–334.

20. Warden, *Boston,* 91–96; Warden, "The Caucus and Democracy in Colonial Boston," *New England Quarterly* 43 (1970): 19–33.

21. Logan, *A Dialogue Showing What's Therein to be Found* (Philadelphia, 1725); in *A Charge From the Bench to the Grand Jury* (Philadelphia, 1723), Logan argued that the high wages demanded by artisans and laboring men were also a cause of the depression.

22. Thomas Wendel, "The Keith-Lloyd Alliance: Factional and Coalition Politics in Colonial Pennsylvania," *Pennsylvania Magazine of History and Biography* 92 (1968): 289–305; Nash, "Transformation of Urban Politics," 606–8.

23. Gertrude MacKinney, ed., *Votes and Proceedings of the House of Representatives of the Province of Pennsylvania, Pennsylvania Archives,* 8th ser. (Harrisburg, 1931–35), 2:1459. For the attack on Logan's house, see Logan to James Alexander, Oct. 23, 1749, Logan Letter Book, 1748–50, Historical Society of Pennsylvania.

24. *The Triumverate of Pennsylvania: In a Letter to a Friend in the Country* (Philadelphia, 1728); also *A Dialogue Between Mr. Robert Rich and Roger Plowman* (Philadelphia, 1725).

25. David Lloyd, *A Vindication of the Legislative Power* (Philadelphia, 1725); the attacks on accumulated wealth and power were continued in [William Keith], *The Observators Trip to America* (Philadelphia, 1725); Keith, *A Modest Reply to the Speech of Isaac Norris* . . . (Philadelphia, 1727); [Keith], *Remarks upon the Advice to the Freeholders* of the Triumvirate . . . (Philadelphia, 1729).

26. Logan to John Penn, Nov. 17, 1729, *Pennsylvania Magazine of History and Biography* 34 (1910): 122–23; Norris to Joseph Pike, Aug. 28, 1728, Norris Letter Book, 1716–30; David Barclay to Thomas Penn, [1727], Penn Papers; Official Correspondence, 2:43, Historical Society of Pennsylvania.

27. Thompson, "The Moral Economy of the English Crowd in the Eighteenth Century," *Past and Present,* no. 50 (1971): 76–136.

28. Timothy Wheelwright [pseud.], *Two Letters on Election of Alderman* [New York 1734].

29. *New-York Journal,* Mar. 18, May 20, July 8, 1734; for a general consideration of New York City politics in this era, see Patricia U. Bonomi, *A*

Factious People: Politics and Society in Colonial New York (New York: Columbia University Press, 1971), 112–34.

30. *New-York Journal*, July 8, 15, 1734; Mar. 3, 1735; May 30, 1737. The fullest discussion of this era is Beverly McAnear, "Politics in Provincial New York, 1689–1761," (Ph.D. diss., Stanford University, 1935), 420–88.

31. Bonomi, *A Factious People*, chap. 5; *New-York Gazette, or the Weekly Post-Boy*, 25 January 1747/48.

32. Colden, *An Address to the Freeholders* (New York, 1747); *New-York Evening Post*, Dec. 21, 1747; *New-York Mercury*, Jan. 7, 21, 1754; *New-York Gazette*, Jan. 14, 1754; *New-York Post-Boy*, Apr. 22, 1754; McAnear, "Politics in Provincial New York," 535–36.

33. Warden, *Boston*, 116–22; Dirk Hoerder, "People and Mobs: Crowd Action in Massachusetts during the American Revolution, 1765–1780," (Inaugural-diss., University of Berlin, 1971), 94–102.

34. Warden, *Boston*, 122; *The Melancholy State of this Province . . .* ([Boston], 1736), 9.

35. Robert Zemsky, *Merchants, Farmers, and River Gods; An Essay on Eighteenth-Century American Politics* (Boston: Gambit, 1971), 118–19; for the Land Bank, see also George A. Billias, *The Massachusetts Land Bankers of 1740* (Orono: University of Maine, 1959).

36. [Douglass], *Postscript To a Discourse concerning the Currencies of the British Plantations in America* ([Boston, 1740]), 59–60.

37. Minutes of the Boston Town Meeting, in Justin Winsor et al., *The Memorial History of Boston*, 3 vols. (Boston, 1880–83), 2:489–90.

38. *Boston Gazette*, Dec. 4, 11, 1749; Jan. 9, Mar. 13, 20, 1750; *Boston Evening-Post*, Dec. 4, 18, 1749; Mar. 12, 19, 1750; *Boston Independent Advertiser*, Sept. 18, 25, 1749; *Boston Weekly News-Letter*, Feb. 1, 1750; Warden, *Boston*, 139–41; Peter Orlando Hutchinson, ed., *The Diary and Letters of His Excellency Thomas Hutchinson*, 2 vols. (London, 1883–86), 1:54. Hutchinson's account of his role in the devaluation is in his *History of the Colony and Province of Massachusetts-Bay*, ed. Lawrence Shaw Mayo, 3 vols. (Cambridge: Harvard University Press, 1936), 2:334–37; 3:6–7. Hutchinson later recounted that his friend, William Bollan, warned him to retire to his summer mansion at Milton in order to avoid being mobbed by his townsmen. Hutchinson to Bollan, Dec. 27, 1765, Massachusetts Archives, 26:187.

39. Vincent Centinel [pseud.], *Massachusetts in Agony: Or, Important Hints To the Inhabitants of the Province; Calling aloud For Justice to be done to the Oppressed . . .* (Boston, 1750), 3–5, 8, 12 13. The best account of Hutchinson's hard money policy and its repercussions in Boston is Malcolm Freiberg, "Thomas Hutchinson and the Province Currency," *New England Quarterly* 30 (1957): 196–206.

40. The best places to begin a study of the urban dimension of the Great Awakening are Alan Heimert, *Religion and the American Mind from the Great Awakening to the Revolution* (Cambridge: Harvard University Press, 1966); and Dietmar Rothermund, *The Layman's Progress: Religious and Political Ex-*

perience in Colonial Pennsylvania, 1740–1770 (Philadelphia: University of Pennsylvania Press, 1961).

41. Rothermund, *Layman's Progress,* 55–60, 81–82; Heimert, *Religion and the American Mind,* 27–58, 239–93. The process of mental transformation was not confined to the cities of course. See Richard L. Bushman, *From Puritan to Yankee: Character and the Social Order in Connecticut, 1690–1765* (Cambridge: Harvard University Press, 1967); and Rhys Isaac, "Preachers and Patriots: Explorations in Popular Culture and Revolution in Virginia, 1774–1776," in Alfred F. Young, ed., *The American Revolution: Explorations in the History of American Radicalism* (DeKalb: Northern Illinois University Press, 1976), 125–56.

42. For Davenport, see *Boston Evening-Post,* Aug. 2, 1742. The response of the frightened Charles Chauncy is quoted in John C. Miller, "Religion, Finance, and Democracy in Massachusetts," *New England Quarterly* 6 (1933): 52–53.

43. Eric Foner, "Tom Paine's Republic: Radical Ideology and Social Change," in Young, ed., *The American Revolution,* 187–232.

44. *New-York Gazette or Weekly Post-Boy,* Aug. 26, 1762; Aug. 13, 20, 1767; *New-York Journal,* Nov. 18, Dec. 17, 24, 31, 1767; Jan. 7, 21, 1768; Pierre Du Simitiere Papers, Historical Society of Pennsylvania, for carriage owners.

45. Nash, "Transformation of Urban Politics." 626–29.

46. The most important contributions are Malcolm Freiberg, "Thomas Hutchinson: The First Fifty Years (1711–1761)," *William and Mary Quarterly* 15 (1958): 35–55; John A. Schutz, *Thomas Pownall, British Defender of American Liberty: A Study of Anglo-American Relations in the Eighteenth Century* (Glendale, Calif.: A.H. Clark Co., 1951); Ellen E. Brennan, *Plural Office-Holding in Massachusetts, 1760–1780: Its Relation to the "Separation" of Departments of Government* (Chapel Hill: University of North Carolina Press, 1945); John J. Waters, Jr., *The Otis Family in Provincial and Revolutionary Massachusetts* (Chapel Hill: University of North Carolina Press, 1968); and Waters and Schutz, "Patterns of Massachusetts Colonial Politics: The Writs of Assistance and the Rivalry between the Otis and Hutchinson Families," *William and Mary Quarterly* 24 (1967): 543–67.

47. Warden, *Boston,* p. 136; *Boston Record Commissioners* 14:127

48. *Boston Gazette,* Jan. 9, 1750; *Boston Weekly News-Letter,* July 7, 1748; *Boston Evening-Post,* Dec. 11, 18, 1749. See also Herman J. Belz, "Currency Reform in Massachusetts, 1749–50," *Essex Institute Historical Collections,* 103 (1967): 66–84; and Freiberg, "Thomas Hutchinson and the Province Currency," 199–206. The election of Hutchinson as tax collector, an office from which he was exempt by law as a member of the governor's council, was reported in *Boston Weekly Post-Boy,* Dec. 25, 1749.

49. In 1759 Hutchinson himself noted the bitter opposition to him in Boston. Hutchinson to Israel Williams, June 14, 1759, Israel Williams Letters, Massachusetts Historical Society, 2:150. The attacks on Hutchinson's 1761 de-

valuation scheme are in *Boston Gazette,* Dec. 21, 28, 1761; Jan. 11, 1762; and [Oxenbridge Thacher], *Considerations on Lowering the Value of Gold Coins* . . . [Boston, 1762]. See also Hugh F. Bell, "A Personal Challenge: the Otis-Hutchinson Currency Controversy of 1761–1762," *Essex Institute Historical Collections* 106 (1970): 297–323.

50. Warden, *Boston,* 73–77, 104–11.

51. *A Dialogue Between a Boston Man and A Country Man* ([Boston], 1715); *Trade and Commerce Inculcated* . . . (Boston, 1731).

52. Charles H. Lincoln, ed., *Correspondence of William Shirley,* 2 vols. (New York, 1912), 1:418–22.

53. *Boston Gazette,* May 5, 12, 1760.

54. Quoted in John C. Miller, *Sam Adams; Pioneer in Propaganda* (Stanford, Calif.: Stanford University Press, 1936), 27.

55. *To the Freeholders of the Town of Boston* (Boston, 1760); *Boston Gazette,* May 12, 1760.

56. *Boston Evening-Post,* Mar. 21, 1763.

57. *Boston Gazette,* May 16, 1763.

58. On the Caucus, see Warden, "The Caucus and Democracy in Colonial Boston"; and Alan and Katherine Day, "Another Look at the Boston 'Caucus,'" *Journal of American Studies* 5 (1971): 19–42.

59. *Boston Evening-Post,* Mar. 7, 1763.

60. Tom Thumb [Samuel Waterhouse], *Proposals for Printing* . . . *by Subscription the History of Vice-Admiral Thomas Brazen* . . . ([Boston], 1760).

61. *Boston Gazette,* Dec. 28, 1761. See also [Oxenbridge Thacher], *Considerations on the Election of Counsellors, Humbly Offered to the Electors* ([Boston], 1761).

62. *Boston Evening-Post,* Mar. 14, 1763.

63. *Boston Gazette,* Jan. 11, 1762, Supplement.

64. *Boston Evening-Post,* Mar. 14, 1763.

65. *Boston Gazette,* Feb. 28, 1763.

66. The best explication of coexisting "antipartisan theory and partisan reality" during this period is in Stephen E. Patterson, *Political Parties in Revolutionary Massachusetts* (Madison, Wis.: University of Wisconsin Press, 1973), chap. 1.

67. Peter Oliver, *Origins & Progress of the American Rebellion: A Tory View,* eds. Douglass Adair and John A. Schutz (Stanford, Calif.: Stanford University Press, 1967), 65. This is a view found in most modern histories of the period.

68. In most of the recent literature of the early revolutionary period in Boston, and especially in John C. Miller, *Sam Adams;* and Hiller Zobel, *The Boston Massacre* (Boston: W.W. Norton and Co., 1970), the crowd is characterized as mindless, manipulable, and antirational. For a discussion of how the crowd is treated in Zobel's book and several other recent works, see Jesse Lemisch, "Radical Plot in Boston (1770): A Study in the Use of Evidence," *Harvard Law Review* 84 (1970): 485–504; and Edward Countryman, "The Problem of the Early American Crowd," *Journal of American Studies* 7 (1973): 77–90.

69. Pauline Maier, "Popular Uprisings and Civil Authority in Eighteenth-Century America," *William and Mary Quarterly* 27 (1970): 3–35; in many ways the Boston crowd resembles the preindustrial "city mob" described by E.J. Hobsbawm in *Primitive Rebels: Studies in Archaic Forms of Social Movement in the 19th and 20th Centuries* (New York: W.W. Norton and Co., 1965), chap. 7. Nothing illustrates better the support which the lower-class participants in crowd action received from those above them than the consistent refusal of the grand jury in Boston to indict rioters.

70. The Stamp Act riots are best described, though analyzed differently, in Edmund S. and Helen M. Morgan, *The Stamp Act Crisis; Prologue to Revolution* (Chapel Hill: University of North Carolina Press, 1953), 160–69; Warden, *Boston*, 165–69; Zobel, *Boston Massacre*, 24–47; and George P. Anderson, "Ebenezer Mackintosh: Stamp Act Rioter and Patriot," *Publications* of the Colonial Society of Massachusetts, 26 (1924–26): 15–64.

71. Josiah Quincy, Jr., *Reports of Cases Argued in the Superior Court . . . Between 1761–1772 . . .* , Samuel M. Quincy, ed. (Boston, 1865), 169.

72. Bernard to the Board of Trade, Aug. 31, 1765, in William Cobbett, ed., *The Parliamentary History of England*, 16 (London, 1813), 129–31.

73. Bernard to Halifax, Aug. 31, 1765, Francis Bernard Papers, 4:158ff, Houghton Library, Harvard University, quoted in Bailyn, *Hutchinson,* 37n.

74. James Gordon to William Martin, Sept. 10, 1765, Massachusetts Historical Society *Proceedings*, 2d ser. 13 (1899–1900): 393.

75. A month after the destruction of his house Hutchinson admitted that some of those who in 1749 and 1750 had "threatened me with destruction" had "retained their rancor ever since and are supposed to have been aiders and abettors if not actors in the late riot." Hutchinson to Henry Seymour Conway, Oct. 1, 1765, Massachusetts Archives 26:155. Four years earlier Hutchinson had noted that his unpopularity was largely attributable to his hard money policy in the late 1740s. Hutchinson to William Bollan, Dec. 14, 1761, ibid, 26:24.

76. Patterson, *Political Parties in Revolutionary Massachusetts,* chap. 3.

77. *New-York Gazette,* July 11, 1765, quoted in Bernard Friedman, "The Shaping of the Radical Consciousness in Provincial New York," *Journal of American History* 56 (1970): 794.

78. The calls for political reform are best treated in J.R. Pole, *Political Representation in England and the Origins of the American Republic* (New York: MacMillan and Co., 1966); for price controls, Hoerder, "People and Mobs: Crowd Action in Massachusetts"; John K. Alexander, "The Fort Wilson Incident of 1779: A Case Study of the Revolutionary Crowd," *William and Mary Quarterly* 31 (1974): 589–612; and Anne Bezanson, "Inflation and Controls During the American Revolution in Pennsylvania, 1774–1779," *Journal of Economic History* 8, Supplement (1948): 1–20.

79. *To the Several Battalions of Military Associators in the Province of Pennsylvania* (Philadelphia, 1776), quoted in Merrill Jensen, "The American People and the American Revolution," *Journal of American History* 57 (1970): 29 Four months later, the radical party in Philadelphia urged the voters "to

chuse no rich men and [as] few learned men possible to represent them in the [state constitutional] Convention." *Pennsylvania Packet,* Nov. 26, 1776. The best accounts of the Privates Committee are in David Hawke, *In the Midst of a Revolution* (Philadelphia: University of Pennsylvania Press, 1961); R.A. Ryerson, "Political Mobilization and the American Revolution: The Resistance Movement in Philadelphia, 1765–1776," *William and Mary Quarterly* 31 (1974): 565–88.

80. *An Essay of a Declaration of Rights* . . . (Philadelphia, 1776), quoted in Jensen, "The American People and the American Revolution," p. 30.

81. The standard account of this process is J. Paul Selsam, *The Pennsylvania Constitution of 1776; A Study in Revolutionary Democracy* (Philadelphia: University of Pennsylvania Press, 1936). Recent work is extending and revising Selsam's analysis; see especially, Ryerson, "Political Mobilization"; Alexander, "The Fort Wilson Incident of 1779"; and the essay on Thomas Paine by Eric Foner, in Young, ed., *The American Revolution,* 187–232.

9

ARTISANS AND POLITICS IN EIGHTEENTH-CENTURY PHILADELPHIA

THE POLITICAL HISTORY of colonial America has only recently begun to take account of the crucial role played by urban artisans in the forging of a revolutionary mentality and a revolutionary movement. Yet the Revolution began in the seaboard towns and then spread outward to the countryside; and within these commercial centers artisans possessed great political potential, composing about half the taxable inhabitants and about the same proportion of the voters. In Philadelphia, the port city to which this study of artisan political consciousness is devoted, 1,682 of the 3,350 taxable males in 1772 were artisans. Their political weight was critical in any contested election in the first two-thirds of the eighteenth century. And in the wake of the Seven Years' War, as the imperial crisis unfolded, they played a dynamic role in the formation of a revolutionary movement in the largest city of British North America. This essay examines the shaping of a highly politicized artisan community in Philadelphia during the eighteenth century and assesses the ambivalent nature of their political stances.

The term "artisan community," of course, is only a phrase of convenience. At no time were artisans a unified body, identifying themselves as a class or a united interest-group. They were divided by occupation, wealth, religion, status, and ideological position. They ranged from impecunious apprentice shoemakers to wealthy master builders. At the lower end of the scale where tailors, shoemakers, and coopers congregated, they had much in common with merchant seamen and porters with whom they commonly shared low wages, uncertain prospects of advancement, and exclusion from the ranks of property-holders. At the upper end where brewers, bakers, sugarboilers, and some construction tradesmen were found, they blended into the ranks

---

This essay first appeared in Margaret Jacob and James Jacob, eds., *The Origins of Anglo-American Radicalism* (London: Allen and Unwin, 1984), 162–82. The British style of spelling and punctuation has been changed and the footnotes have been slightly altered.

of shopkeepers, proprietors, and even real-estate developers. In spite of these differences artisans had much in common—principally their craft skills and a life defined by productive labor.

In the broadest view we can see two seemingly contrary trends at work among eighteenth-century Philadelphia artisans: on the one hand, the spectacular growth of the city—from about 5,000 in 1720 to 25,000 on the eve of the Revolution—caused greater occupational specialization and greater differentiation of wealth within the body of artisans; on the other hand, a greater feeling of common interest, extending across craft lines, occurred in the late-colonial period as many artisans reshaped their views of their relations to other parts of their community and transformed their understanding of their political roles, rights, and responsibilities. Nonetheless, no homogeneous artisan political community emerged, and the radical potential of the mechanics was severely limited because of the wide range of roles occupied by these tradesmen within the eighteenth-century urban economy.

Any inquiry into the political consciousness of the eighteenth-century artisan requires some definition of the mechanics' values and goals, for politics was not an end in itself for laboring men but the actualization, through laws and public policy, of privately held notions of how society should function. No Philadelphia artisan at the beginning of the eighteenth century imagined that he should stand for election to the assembly, shape governmental policy, or challenge the prevailing wisdom that those with social status, education, and wealth were best equipped to manage civil affairs. But artisans did understand their own interests, had deeply held values, and possessed a keen sense of whether social equity and justice prevailed in their community. This was so notwithstanding a long history of upper-class attempts to define them as a part of the "unthinking multitude," the "base herd," and, when they took to the streets, the "vile mob."[1]

In discussing the artisan's mentality it is best to begin with opportunity because that concept is central to the "economic man," is deeply embedded in almost all discussions of early American society, and is of primary importance in understanding the obstacles that stood in the way of artisan political unity. For most urban artisans at the beginning of the eighteenth century opportunity did not mean the chance to accumulate great material wealth or to achieve high social status. Philadelphia's laboring men were coming from societies where intergenerational mobility was, with some exceptions, extremely slow, where sons unquestioningly followed their fathers' trades, where the Protestant work ethic did not beat resoundingly in every breast, and where warding off dire need, rather than acquiring riches, was the primary goal. It was economic security rather than rapid mobility that was uppermost in their minds.

The urban laboring man's constrained sense of what was possible was shaped by the distinctly preindustrial nature of economic life in the port towns of early eighteenth-century America. Work patterns were irregular, dictated by weather, hours of daylight, the erratic delivery of raw materials, and vacillating consumer demand. When the cost of fuel for artificial light was greater than the extra income that could be derived from laboring before or after sunlight hours, who would not shorten his day during winter? When winter descended on the Delaware seaport, business often ground to a halt, for even in the southernmost of the northern harbors ice often blocked maritime traffic. This meant slack time for mariners and dockworkers, just as laborers engaged in well digging, road building, and cellar excavating for house construction were made idle by frozen ground. The hurricane season in the West Indies also forced slowdowns because few shipowners were willing to place their ships and cargoes before the killer winds that prevailed in the Caribbean from August to October.[2] Other urban artisans were also at the mercy of the weather. If prolonged rain delayed the slaughter of cows in the country or made impassable the rutted roads into the city, then the tanner laid his tools aside, and for lack of his deliveries the cordwainer was also idle. The hatter was dependent upon the supply of beaver skins, which could stop abruptly if disease struck an Indian tribe or war disrupted the fur trade. Weather, disease, and equinoctial cycles all contributed to the fitful pace of urban labor—and therefore to the difficulty of producing steady income. Every urban artisan knew "broken days," slack spells, and dull seasons.[3]

While moving to America could not change the discontinuous work patterns of preindustrial European life, it did bring about an adjustment in perception about what was achievable. Braudel tells us that in Europe "the frontier zone between possibility and impossibility barely moved in any significant way, from the fifteenth to the eighteenth century."[4] But it moved in America. Philadelphia's artisans could anticipate more favorable conditions than prevailed in the homelands that they or their parents had left. Unemployment was virtually unknown in the early decades of settlement, labor commanded a better price relative to the cost of household necessities, and urban land was purchased reasonably.[5]

This did not mean that artisans and laborers worked feverishly to ascend the ladder of success. Craftsmen who commanded five shillings a day and laborers who garnered three knew that weather, sickness, and the inconstancy of supplies (and sometimes demand) made it impossible to work more than 250 days a year. This would bring an income of about £35–60, hardly enough to send aspirations spiralling upward. Even if the margin between subsistence and saving was greater than in Europe, it was still thin enough to mean that years of hard work and frugal living usually preceded the purchase of even a small house. Hence, laboring people were far from the day when the failure to acquire property or to accumulate a minor fortune produced guilt or aroused anger against those above them. Most artisans did not wish to become lawyers, doctors, or merchants.[6] Their desire was not to reach the top but to get off the bottom. Yet they expected to earn a "decent competency" and did not anticipate the grinding poverty of the laboring poor everywhere in Europe.

Philadelphia, for three-quarters of a century after its founding, richly nurtured this expectation of economic security and limited mobility. Not everyone succeeded in the early years, but with the exception of a depression in the mid-1720s the city experienced steady growth and general prosperity from 1681 to the late 1750s. From 1685–1753, 55 percent of the artisans whose inventories of estate have survived left personal property worth between £51 and £200 sterling and another 25 percent left in excess of £200—an amount that signifies a very comfortable standard of living.[7] The city to which Franklin came as a printer's apprentice in 1725 was filled with young artisans who ascended steadily, if not quite so spectacularly and stylishly as Poor Richard.[8] Success for so many in the first eight decades of Philadelphia's history cannot but have affected the aspirations of others newly arriving. No wonder that Franklin became the hero of the city's "leather apron men" and that his little booklet, variously entitled *Father Abrahams's Speech, The Way to Wealth,* and *The Art of Making Money Plenty in Every Man's Pocket,* became a bestseller in Philadelphia. It was not, however, a formula for "unlimited acquisition" but rather a comfortable existence "which was the midpoint between the ruin of extravagance and the want of poverty."[9]

A degree of economic ambition, then, was nourished by actual experience with what was possible. By the same token, ambition varied with occupation and to an extent with the particular era we are considering. It must be kept in mind that mechanics varied considerably in terms of income, wealth, and property-ownership, and that this affected their aspirations and, ultimately, the cast of their political thinking. Thus, those at the bottom of the hierarchy of artificers—coopers, tailors, shoemakers, stocking-weavers, and ship-caulkers—had more limited goals than silversmiths, house carpenters, brickmakers, and instrument-makers. This modesty of aspiration at the lower levels of the artisan hierarchy was expressed clearly in 1779 by the shoemakers and tanners of Philadelphia. "For many years," they wrote, the prices of skins, leather, and shoes were so proportioned to each other as to leave the tradesmen a bare living profit; this is evidently proved by this circumstance well known to everybody, that no person of either of these trades, however industrious and attentive to his business, however frugal in his manner of living, has been able to raise a fortune rapidly, and the far greater part of us have been contented to live decently without acquiring wealth; nor are the few among us who rank as men of property, possessed of more than moderate estates. Our professions rendered us useful and necessary members of our community; proud of that rank, we aspired no higher. . . . [10]

The last phrase of the shoemakers' petition—"Our professions rendered us useful and necessary members of our community"—speaks directly to a second important part of the artisan's constellation of values: respectability. Craft pride and a desire to be recognized for contributing to the community were of great importance to them and functioned, as an English historian has said, as "an alternative to wealth as a criterion for social judgement."[11] One of the keys to Franklin's success as an urban organizer was his skill in appealing to this dignity which artisans felt as members of the producing class. For example, in 1747, with the threat of a French attack looming and the assembly dragging its feet on military mobilization, Franklin exhorted the artisans of Philadelphia to organize a voluntary militia. Writing as "A Tradesman," he argued that the "Plain Truth" of the matter was that the artisans had always been at the heart of civic improvements and now must solve for themselves a problem which their upper-class leaders were cravenly evading.[12] The result was the formation of the Associators, who became a symbol of artisan strength and respectability. Called into being by the artisan *par excellence* among them, acting where upper class leaders had failed, and electing their own officers, they never engaged the enemy but nonetheless conferred upon themselves a collective strength and a confirmation of their value to the community.

Throughout the preindustrial period this artisan self-esteem and desire for community recognition jostled with the upper-class view of artisans as "mean," "base," and "vulgar," to invoke the contemporary definitions of "mechanic." When wealthy urban dwellers referred to skilled craftsmen as "meer mechanics" or made generalized statements about laboring people as inferior, ignorant, and morally suspect, they ran squarely athwart of the self-image of artisans, "the meanest" of whom, as one Philadelphian noted in 1756, "thinks he has a Right of Civility from the greatest" person in the city.[13]

In their attempts to gain respectability in the eyes of the community, and in maintaining their self-respect, artisans placed a premium on achieving "independence," or, to put it the other way round, on escaping dependency. At the most primary level economic independence meant the capacity to fend off the need for charity and poor relief. "The ability to maintain oneself by one's labor without recourse to such things as charity" was "a crucial material and psychological dividing-line," writes I. J. Prothero of the preindustrial London artisan, and the same may be said of his Philadelphia counterpart.[14] In Philadelphia this self-maintenance proved attainable for almost every artisan for three generations after Penn's colony was founded. At a higher level economic independence meant making the transition from apprentice to journeyman to master craftsman—the three-step climb from servitude to self-employment. This transition was of critical importance to eighteenth-century artisans because it meant moving upward not only in economic rewards and the freedom to control hours of work, but also in terms of respectability and an autonomous existence outside the workplace that often proved difficult when one's livelihood was dependent upon another man.

Care must be taken in using words such as "autonomy" and "independence" to describe artisan values because these goals were framed by a broader corporate and communitarian outlook. The notion of belonging to a "Trade" carried with it a sense of cooperative workshop labor where master craftsman, journeyman, and apprentice were bound together in service to themselves, each other, and the community. A man was not simply a carpenter or a cooper in Philadelphia, striving independently to make a living; he was also a member of a collective body, hierarchically structured but organized so that all mechanics, theoretically at least, would in time become masters. Men might aspire individually—Franklin could not brook the role of apprentice or journeyman, and competed fiercely with his fellow-printers in Philadelphia once he established his own shop—but this striving was reined in by a collective trade identity and a commitment to the community in which they labored. "When I was a boy," wrote John F. Watson of the late-eighteenth-century artisans, "there was no such thing as conducting their business in the present wholesale manner, and by efforts at monopoly. No masters were seen exempted from personal labor in any branch of business—living on the profits derived from many hired journeymen. . . . "[15]

This traditional outlook, stressing the mutuality of relations between craftsmen at different ranks within a trade and the community responsibilities of the trade itself, was challenged in the eighteenth century by the rise of the *laissez-faire* ethos which celebrated entrepreneurial, atomistic competition and the accumulative spirit.[16] In the older view, labeled the "Moral Economy" by E. P. Thompson, all economic activity carried social responsibilities with it and was necessarily tied to the good of the community.[17] This put limitations on what an artisan was entitled to charge for his product or his labor and even extended to hold "every man accountable to the community for such parts of his conduct by which the public welfare appears to be injured or dishonored, and for which no legal remedies can be obtained."[18] But the newer outlook, the "possessive individualism" which C. B. MacPherson has probed, legitimated unrestrained economic activity. The craftsman, like every member of the community, could charge as much as the market would bear for his goods and services, and his rights to holding property were inviolate.[19] These jarring views surfaced dramatically at moments of economic crisis such as in Philadelphia in 1779 when food shortages and burgeoning inflation put severe pressure on many artisans and laborers. Bitterly opposed to the shipment of grain by the wealthy merchant Robert Morris at a time when bread was in short supply in the city, many artisans argued that Morris's property rights in the vessel were limited by the needs of the community. "We hold," they stated, "that though by the acceptance of wages [the shipbuilders] have not, and cannot have any claim in the property of the vessel, after she is built and paid for, we nevertheless hold, that they and the state in general have a right in the service of the vessel, because it constitutes a considerable part of the advantage they hoped to derive from their labours." This assertion that property was social in origin, carrying with it responsibilities to the commonweal, was the basis upon which they might concede that "the *property* of the vessel is the immediate right of the owner" but "the service of it is the right of the community collectively with the owners."[20]

It is impossible to chart precisely the advance of the new capitalistic mentality and the receding of the old corporate ethic. To some extent, in fact, the two were fused into a "collective individualism" where the values of community-oriented petty-commodity workshop production commingled with the new notions of economic rationality and pursuit of self-interest.[21] Very loosely, one might argue that in times of prosperity the new bourgeois stance dominated the consciousness of artisans, particularly those in the more profitable trades where opportunity for advancement was the greatest, and that in times of economic stress the "moral economy" compelled greater allegiance, especially among the lower artisans whose opportunities were far more circumscribed. Overarching this dialectic was the long-range tendency within many crafts for the bonds of mutuality to fray between masters and journeymen. Eventually the ties would be virtually severed as a class of capitalist entrepreneurs confronted rather than cooperated with a class of perpetually dependent wage-laborers.

With these values of the workplace in mind we can turn to the political life of Philadelphia's mechanics. Here again the ideal was participation in the civic life of the community with the public good the great end to be accomplished. Serving the commonweal, however, depended heavily on the independent exercise of political "will." As the Whig scientists of politics insisted in the eighteenth century, a republican form of government could only exist when its citizens were not cajoled, bribed, or dominated into making political decisions and choices but freely exercised their independent judgment. This concept led directly back to economic independence because it was impossible for a man freely to assert his political will when he was beholden to another for his economic existence. Without economic self-sufficiency, the laboring citizen inevitably fell prey to the political desires of his patron, employer, landlord, or creditor. Economic dependency destroyed true political liberty—the essence of the "Independent Whig."[22]

Such an emphasis on the independent exercise of political will brings us face to face with the concept of deference. In the historical literature of the last generation this is the key concept for laying bare the dynamics of eighteenth-century politics because it provides the mediating device that seemingly reconciles two contrary tendencies in colonial politics: the large propertied element upon whom the vote was conferred and the persistence of the elite management of politics. Deference is the term employed to describe the unquestioning acceptance of an eighteenth-century moral order which consigned laboring people to economic, social, and political subordination. "Deference," writes J. G. A. Pocock, "is the product of a conditioned freedom, and those who display it freely accept an inferior, nonelite, or follower role in a society hierarchically structured."[23]

From deference it is only a step to speaking of cultural hegemony, the notion that the ruling classes are able to obtain and maintain the consent of those subject to them because their rule gains legitimacy even in the eyes of the most oppressed members of society. "By diffusing its own concept of reality, morality, meaning, and common sense through the schools, press, religious bodies, the daily life of the streets, the workplace, and the family" the ruling class fosters the notion that it uses its authority responsibly and for the good of the whole. Ultimately, this idea becomes a more powerful instrument in the hands of those in control than guns or clubs; for, while class or racial conflict is not eliminated, it is largely muted by an acceptance of "the system" at the lower levels of society.[24]

The concepts of deference and cultural hegemony can be usefully employed in studying artisan politics in Philadelphia, but they must be used with care. For example, there is voluminous evidence that upper-class Philadelphians believed in and promoted as "natural" (or even ordained from above) a system of social relations marked by gentle domination from above and willing dependency from below; but there is also evidence that laboring people did not always accept elite rule and cultural authority complaisantly. The key to making sense of the political activities of Philadelphia's artisans in the eighteenth century is to recognize that "a lived hegemony is always a process ... a realised complex of experiences, relationships, and activities, with specific and changing pressures and limits." As Raymond Williams has advised, cultural hegemony, as a form of dominance, "has continually to be renewed, re-created, defended, and modified" because in most historical circumstances it "is also continually resisted, limited, altered, challenged by pressures not at all its own."[25] In other words, there is nothing static and immutable about a hegemonic condition; rather, it is "an institutionally negotiable *process* in which the social and political forces of contest, breakdown, and transformation are constantly in play."[26] It is therefore necessary to identify the fluctuating forces that operated in eighteenth-century Philadelphia in such a way as to alter the class relations and political ties between artisans and those above them in the city who functioned as the cultural standard-bearers and political magnates of their day.

Only twice in the long period from 1682 to 1776 were the basic goals of the artisans deeply threatened by severe economic adversity. On both occasions they quickly challenged the political dominance of Philadelphia's upper-class merchants and professionals. In the severe depression of the 1720s, when a steep decline in shipbuilding, trade, and house construction brought unemployment and harassment for debt to hundreds of artisans, the mechanics provided the main support for an oppositional ideology that stressed the self-interestedness of the wealthy and the necessity of common people organizing in their own behalf. The immediate question around which artisans organized was the issuing of paper money, which they regarded as an antidote to the severe trade slump that affected almost every sector of the city's economy. But political contention soon leaped across this boundary, broadening to include debates on the accountability of representatives to their constituents, the organization of politics, and the nature of the body politic itself.[27]

It was in the early 1720s, as we have seen in previous essays, that Philadelphia's artisans first entered into electoral politics in large numbers and thereby began to sense the power they commanded when they acted collectively. Instruments of a new form of popular politics appeared in the formation of party tickets through caucuses, the recruitment of immigrant German and Scots-Irish voters, direct appeals to the electorate through broadside "advice" where positions on specific issues were announced and the wealthy denounced, outdoor political rallies that welcomed voters and nonvoters alike, political parades and demonstrations, and the formation of tavern-based artisan political clubs.

The cries of the wealthy gentry politicians under attack tell us how thoroughly alarmed they were at the sight and sound of artisans participating in politics on a mass basis. "Ye people head and foot run mad . . . ," wrote Isaac Norris, one of Philadelphia's wealthiest merchants. "All seems topside Turvey. Our publick Speeches tell ye Country & ye World that neither knowledge or riches are advantageous in a Country . . . The Mobb is Hallood on to render obnoxious Every Man who has any proportion of those."[28] Political power was no longer in the hands of "ye Wise, ye Rich or the learned" but had fallen to "Rabble Butchers, porters & Tagrags," and the political arena had shifted from gentlemen's parlors to "dramshops, tiff, & alehouses" where "a great number of modern statesmen & some patriots" could be found "settling affairs, cursing some, praising others, contriving lawes and swearing they will have them enacted cum multis aegis."[29] The practical results were assembly elections in 1721 and 1722 that were "very mobbish and carried by a levelling spirit." They swept from office conservative men of wealth and replaced them with smaller traders and landowners.[30]

The opposition of the merchant-professional elite to paper money was a major factor in the growth of artisan-based politics in this era. Intensifying the hostility of laboring men to the wealthy were the attacks on artisan respectability, led by James Logan, another merchant and proprietary officeholder. Always eager to take up the cudgels in defence of hierarchy, social order, and wealth, Logan argued in publicly distributed pamphlets that the depression of the 1720s was caused mainly by laboring-class perversity. It was idleness and fondness for drink that made men poor and the charging of high wages by artisans that drove away employment. Those who tried "new politics" and invented "new and extraordinary Measures" such as paper money misunderstood the roots of economic distress. The rich were rich because of their "Sobriety, Industry and Frugality"; the poor were poor because of their "Luxury, Idleness and Folly."[31] Logan paid a price for this personal attempt at cultural hegemony. His house was attacked by an angry mob, which tore off the window shutters, bombarded his bedchamber with bricks, and threatened to level one of Philadelphia's most gracious structures.[32] He was publicly attacked in pamphlets for his contempt of the "poorer sort" and for leading a group of Pennsylvanians who wished to recreate, it was charged, "the Old English Vassalage."[33]

The political mobilization of artisans in the mid-1720s and the distinctly undeferential behavior of laboring people shows how quickly the sense of interclass partnership, the basis of hegemonic rule by Philadelphia's solons, could be shattered. Previously, the superior wisdom of the elite, and hence the legitimacy of their rule, had been generally accepted, although Philadelphia's early years had been so filled with contention and its social ranks had been so fluid that no firm legacy of merchant-family political dynasties had been handed down to the 1720s.[34] Now the affective bonds between social ranks were shattered. Nothing was more important in undermining the sense of partnership than the published pronouncements by men such as Logan and Norris that the mechanics themselves were responsible for Philadelphia's economic difficulties because they demanded too much for their labor and squandered their earnings at the taverns. Mercantile opulence was indispensable to the economic health of the community, argued Logan, in an early form of the trickle-down theory, and only the "Sot, the Rambler, the Spendthrift, and Slip Season" found themselves in economic straits.[35] Such comments struck at the artisans' self-respect, their search for independence, and their sense of belonging to an organic society where people of different status were mutually involved in a social partnership. It was plain that those who lived by the labor of their hands had suffered most in the depression. Thus aroused, what had been a politically passive, deferential laboring class at one moment became a politically conscious, highly active body of mechanics at the next moment.

Leadership of the artisans, however, remained in the hands of those near the top of the social hierarchy. The chief pamphleteer for paper money was Francis Rawle, a lesser merchant, and the leader of the political mobilization was none other than the ex-Jacobite Tory placeman, Sir William Keith, appointed by William Penn in 1717 as governor of Pennsylvania but by the early 1720s thoroughly alienated from Penn's widow and her proprietary officeholders led by James Logan. It was Keith who not only endorsed the issuing of paper money in 1722 but also proposed legislation for reducing the interest rate, curbing lawyers' fees and restricting the imprisonment of debtors. By the next year he had organized the first artisans' political group in Philadelphia's history—the "Leather Apron Club"—and for the next few years masterminded the artisan-based political campaigns.[36]

Politics "cum multis aegis" came to an end when prosperity returned to Philadelphia in the 1730s. Now artisans reassumed their former role of acting as a check on the exercise of power by those in the upper ranks through annual assembly and local elections but otherwise leaving public affairs to their betters. They had intervened only when

those with more time (and presumably more learning) to apply to politics abused the trust placed in them by their constituents. But the 1720s
left a legacy to succeeding generations. It included not only the necessity
of laboring-class political mobilization in times of adversity, but also
residual distrust of the wealthy and a suspicion that they did not, as
they claimed, always act for the public good because they were better
educated and therefore, in theory, disinterested.

Finally, the 1720s shattered the belief that in Pennsylvania economic opportunity was limitless and that therefore one man's rise to
wealth was not accomplished at somebody else's cost. Pennsylvanians
had been casting off the European conception of societies containing
fixed quantities of wealth that must be distributed like a pie, so that
when one man's piece was cut larger others had to satisfy themselves
with narrower slices. Now the artisan had learned that in Philadelphia,
too, the aggrandisement of wealth and power by the few could be costly
to the many. The point was driven home in a parable of class relations
spread through the streets near the end of the depression.

> A Mountebank had drawn a huge assembly about him: Among
> the rest, a fat unwieldy Fellow, half stifled in the Press, would
> be every Fit crying out, Lord! what a filthy Crowd is here!
> Pray, good People, give Way a little! Bless me! what a De[vi]l
> has raked this Rabble together? What a plaguey squeezing is
> this? Honest Friend, remove your Elbow. At last, a Weaver
> that stood next him could hold no longer; A Plague confound
> you (said he) for an overgrown Sloven! and who in the
> De[vi]l's Name, I wonder, helps to make up the Crowd half so
> much as your self? Don't you consider (with a P–x) that you
> take up more Room with that Carcass than any Five here? Is
> not the Place as free for us as for you? Bring your own Guts to
> a reasonable Compass (and be B[un]ged) and then I'll engage
> we shall have Room for us all.[37]

During the postdepression generation, from 1730 to the early
1750s, Philadelphia's rapidly expanding economy offered most artisans
the opportunity to achieve their goals of economic security, respectability, and independence. This is indicated in hundreds of deeds recording
acquisition of property by artisans and scores of inventories of estate
showing substantial artisan wealth. In such a climate the inflamed politics of the 1720s subsided and laboring men were content to leave the
management of public affairs in the hands of those above them.[38] This
may be called deference, but we should employ that term only in the
limited sense that artisans saw no need to intervene directly in politics,
other than to cast their ballots, so long as those for whom they voted
were responsive to their needs. Rapid urban growth and full employ-

ment after 1730 restored the atmosphere of interrank solidarity. The artisans, wrote "Brother Chip" some years later, for years had "tamely submitted" to the nomination of all candidates for office in Philadelphia by a "Company of leading Men" who did not permit "the affirmative or negative voice of a Mechanic to interfere."[39]

Yet, while the hegemonic control of the elite had been reestablished it had constantly to contend with the ideal of the independent voter. Pamphleteers such as "Constant Trueman" kept artisan voters alert to the idea that the preservation of political "will" or "independence" required habits of mind that abhorred subservient behavior. "Let me tell you, Friends," wrote Trueman in 1735, "if you can once be frightened by the Threats or Frowns of great Men, from speaking your Minds freely, you will certainly be taught in a very little Time, that you have no liberty to act freely, but just as they shall think proper to Command or Direct; that is, that you are no longer freemen, but Slaves, Beasts of Burden, and you must quietly submit your Necks to the Yoke, receive the Lash patiently let it be ever so Smart, and carry all the Loads they think proper to clap on your Backs, without kicking or wincing."[40] Trueman's admonitions spoke directly to the fact that many artisans, especially those in the service and retail crafts, lived in a world of economic clientage where their economic security was bound up with an employer, landlord, or extender of credit. This, of course, was the antithesis of the ideal world where they would enjoy economic independence; and to the extent that artisans deferred politically to powerful men with economic leverage on them they alienated their political selves because their independent exercise of judgment had been suspended. In Philadelphia, however, the ability of patrons to strong-arm their laboring clients was somewhat muted by the use of the secret ballot.[41]

In the depression that beset Philadelphia at the end of the Seven Years' War the interclass trust that alone could sustain political deference that was based on affective bonds between different social strata melted away. When the postwar commercial depression bottomed out early in 1765, hopes revived for better times. But within a year the Philadelphia Grand Jury reported that many of "the labouring People, and others in low circumstances, who are willing to work, cannot obtain sufficient Employment to support themselves and their Families."[42] Reports of unemployment continued for the next two years, and by the end of 1769 forced sales of property reached an all-time high. An economic revival occurred in 1770, but it was short-lived because within two years a severe contraction of British credit again brought widespread unemployment.[43]

Compounding the difficulties of laboring Philadelphians was the

movement of food prices, which had been rising during the Seven Years'
War. Although they fell modestly between 1765 and 1769, they then
began a climactic five-year climb that elevated the cost of a weighted
nineteen-item laboring man's diet 23 percent between 1769 and 1774.[44]
This punishing upswing caused no *crise de subsistance* in Philadelphia,
but the situation was serious enough to put hundreds of artisans in
difficult straits and for the Philadelphia overseers of the poor to begin
distributing bread to the poor for the first time in the city's history.[45]

The severity of the post-1760 depression can be seen most clearly in
the rapid growth of a large class of indigents in Philadelphia for the first
time in its history.[46] Urban poverty challenged the governing modes of
thought in Philadelphia, shook artisans' confidence in the internal economic system, and intensified class feeling. "He that gets all he can
honestly, and saves all he gets (necessary Expenses excepted)," printer
Ben was fond of saying to his fellow-mechanics, "will certainly become
RICH."[47] Now the inapplicability of this system of moral economics was
made plain. Even for those who escaped poverty in the 1760s in Philadelphia, the impoverishment of so many below them was impossible to
ignore because when indigency befell a large portion of the lowest
laboring ranks, not simply the aged and infirm, it signified sickness in
the entire economic body.

The response of the laboring poor to the new system of poor relief
that was instituted in 1767 in Philadelphia indicates how the respectability as well as the economic security of the lower artisans was undermined
and how strongly they resented this. Faced with ballooning poor-relief
costs, which necessitated heavier taxes, the Assembly agreed to let a
group of Quaker merchants dismantle the old out-relief system and replace it with a Bettering House where the poor would be confined and, it
was said, taught better work habits. The decision to end out-relief drew
the Quaker merchants who managed the Bettering House into a heated
dispute with the overseers of the poor. The overseers, drawn mostly from
the ranks of established artisans, were far closer to the needy in their
neighborhoods and understood the resentment of the non-Quaker poor
who were being driven into a Quaker-dominated institution. Underlying
these upper-class Quaker attempts at moral management was the old
notion that unemployment and poverty were attributable not to structural weakness in the economy but to moral weakness within the laboring class. In effect, these indictments were attacks on laboring-class respectability. As such they were staunchly resisted, not only by the overseers of the poor, but also by the poor themselves. Many of them, the
overseers reported, "declared in a Solemn manner that they would rather
perish through want" than go to the Bettering House, whose very name
was an insult to their struggles for respect and a secure place in society.

Charity was in itself distasteful to laboring Philadelphians, but charity that carried with it an accusation of moral failing was not to be endured.[48]

In the face of the economic ills of the 1760s and 1770s Philadelphia's artisans embarked on the most intense period of organizing in their history. The cordwainers organized a craft guild in 1760, journeymen carpenters established their own company and attempted to set wage-rates a few years later, and tailors drew together in 1771 in order to fix prices at levels that would yield them a decent subsistence. All of this, of course, was taking place in the midst of the gathering storm between the colonies and England. And central to the response of the seaport cities to British attempts to extract greater economic advantages from the North American colonies were three nonimportation movements which drew artisans into the political arena as never before.

All of the instrumentalities of popular politics that had appeared in the 1720s reemerged in the turbulent 1760s. Outdoor political rallies, vitriolic political campaign literature, petition drives, club activity, and attacks on the wealthy as subverters of the community's welfare characterized the elections of 1764 and 1765 when the turnout of voters reached all-time highs in Philadelphia.[49] In the following decade, however, a transformation of mechanic consciousness ushered in a new era of politics. Most striking, artisans began to exert themselves as a separate political entity. This can be traced in the newspaper and pamphlet appeals, beginning about 1767, which were addressed specifically to the mechanic segment of the community as a separate interest. It gathered momentum in 1768 when artisans, attempting to spur foot-dragging merchants to adopt nonimportation, themselves called public meetings, published newspaper appeals, and organized secondary boycotts of importing merchants. Thereafter artisans began to transcend mere craft allegiances and built a political strength which Franklin had anticipated twenty years before when he declaimed that within their separate crafts the mechanics "are like separate Filaments of Flax before the Thread is form'd, without Strength because without Connection, but UNION would made us strong and even formidable," even when opposed by "the *Great* . . . from some mean views of their Own."[50]

Moreover, the 1760s brought into the political arena the younger and poorer artisans, who, for lack of property, were not yet entitled to vote. Pamphlets and broadsides were read by the unenfranchised, outdoor political rallies and street demonstrations were open to all, organizers of petitions gathered signatures from voters and nonvoters alike. By usage, if not by law, the lower artisan became politically conscious and politically active long before the electoral laws conferred the right of "citizen" upon him.

It took until March 1769 for popular pressure to bring Philadelphia's merchants into the nonimportation fold, and by that time the disillusionment with them in the artisan community was widespread. A year later the merchants tried to break free of the agreement, confirming the suspicions of leather-apron men that, whatever the situation in the past, a community of interest no longer existed between mechanic and merchant. Desiring to end nonimportation after drawing down their inventories, the merchants imperiously informed the artisans that they had "no *Right* to give their sentiments respecting an importation" and called the artificers "A Rabble."[51] Here was additional evidence to craftsmen that the partnership between men in different ranks was at an end and that they must work independently for their objectives, even assuming responsibility for defining and enforcing the community's goals.

Artisans were not able to stop the merchants resuming importations in the spring of 1770. This contributed to the feeling that the organic connection between those who labored with their hands and those who did not was broken and hence accelerated the change of artisan consciousness. Jettisoning their reliance on upper-class leadership, such as had not occurred in the 1720s, mechanics called a public meeting of their fellows and formed their own Mechanics Committee. They took another unprecedented step by deciding that they must not only use their votes to elect men above them who were responsive to their needs, but must also now elect men from their own ranks. Their dominance under severe attack, the merchant elite attempted to invoke the old norms: "The Mechanics (though by far the most numerous especially in this Country)," they sputtered, "have no Right to *Speak* or *Think* for themselves."[52]

In the autumn of 1770, for the first time in many decades, an artisan proudly announced himself as a candidate for sheriff. Artisans soon began to fill elected positions as tax assessors and collectors, wardens and street commissioners, and insisted on their right to participate equally with merchants and gentlemen in the nomination of assemblymen and other important officeholders. The day was past, announced "Brother Chip," taking a moniker with special meaning to ships' carpenters, when laboring men would tamely endorse men nominated by the elite. "Chip" occupied still more radical ground by asserting that it was "absolutely necessary" that one or two artisans be elected to the assembly from Philadelphia.[53] Appalled at this crumbling of deference, merchants and other members of the elite hurled "Many Threats, Reflections, Sarcasms, and Burlesques" against the artisans. This did little to deter laboring men because secret balloting went far to keep them immune from economic retaliation by those they offended.[54]

Possessing many votes and inspirited by success in electing their own kind to important offices, the artisans began pressing the legislature in 1772 for laws that would benefit them. They vigorously opposed excise taxes on liquor, called for the weekly publication of full Assembly debates and roll calls on important issues, and demanded the erection of public galleries to end forever "the absurd and Tyrannical custom of shutting the Assembly doors during debate." It was enough to leave some genteel Philadelphians muttering, "It is Time the Tradesmen were checked—they take too much upon them—they ought not to intermeddle in State Affairs—they will become too powerful."[55]

"Intermeddling in State Affairs" was also taking another direction in the 1770s: the *de facto* assumption of governmental powers by committees called into being by the people at large, artisans most numerous among them. Tradesmen had first clothed themselves in such extralegal authority in policing the importation agreement in 1769. In 1774, in the wake of the Boston Port Act, they showed that they were far more unified and aggressive than in the past by putting forward a radical slate of candidates for enforcing the Continental Association that drubbed a slate offered to the electorate by the city's conservative merchants.[56]

The culmination of this heightened artisan consciousness occurred in the final year before independence. A new surge of radicalism, led by middling men such as Thomas Young, James Cannon, Thomas Paine, and Timothy Matlack, and centered in the thirty-one companies of the Philadelphia militia that had been organized in the spring of 1775, produced demands for the most radical reforms yet suggested by the colonists. Curbing the individual accumulation of wealth, opening up opportunity, divorcing the franchise from property ownership, and driving the mercantile elite from power became explicit objectives enunciated in a flood of polemical literature that swept over Philadelphia. "Our great merchants . . . [are] making immense fortunes at the expense of the people," charged a "Tradesman" in April 1775, just before a special assembly election. Sounding the tocsin on economic inequality that English and European republican writers warned against but genteel American Whigs usually saw fit to ignore, "Tradesman" argued that the merchants "will soon have the whole wealth of the province in their hands, and then the people will be nearly in the condition that the East-India Company reduced the poor natives of Bengal to." Men of this kind must be stopped in "their present prospect of making enormous estates at our expense." Invoking the older notion of an organic community, "Tradesman" yearned for the day when their "golden harvests" were brought to an end and "all ranks and conditions would come in for their just share of the wealth."[57]

This acerbic language, hurled across class lines, was delivered anonymously so the writer need not fear retaliation from a landlord, employer, or creditor. It reveals the alternative culture that some artisans sought to create through seizing control of the political process. Three days earlier, in another newspaper, an account appeared that takes us deeper into the hegemonic crisis that was occurring in Philadelphia. "A poor man," it was stated, "has rarely the honor of speaking to a gentleman on any terms, and never with familiarity, but for a few weeks before the election. How many poor men, common men, and mechanics have been made happy within this fortnight by a shake of a hand, a pleasing smile and a little familiar chat with a gentleman: who have not for the seven years past condescended to look at them. Blessed state which brings all so nearly on a level."[58] The account can be read as evidence that the poor man and the artisan had truly internalized the message promulgated from above—that society was best governed when the elite ruled and laboring men deferred. But the barbed tone of the statement and its thinly disguised disdain of the upper class also portrays an urban society where interclass relations were no longer marked by trust, harmony, mutual respect, and a sense of partnership within hierarchy. When we consider such a description of veiled interclass hostility alongside a knowledge of what was actually happening in the streets of Philadelphia in the spring of 1776, where artisans and small traders were taking power from the hands of the old elite, it becomes clear that, while a deferential pose may have still been maintained by the most vulnerable in the society, the old social equilibrium was now in disarray.[59] It could have survived only within an economy where laboring people were able to fulfill their goals of a "decent competency," dignity, and economic independence.

By the autumn of 1775 the Philadelphia militia had become a school of political education much in the manner of Cromwell's seventeenth-century New Model Army. The militia, writes Eric Foner, "quickly developed a collective identity and consciousness, a sense of its own rights and grievances," and "became a centre of intense political debate and discussion."[60] Organizing their own Committee of Correspondence, which included men of no previous political experience such as tailor Frederick Hagener and paperhanger Edward Ryves, the privates began exerting pressure on the Assembly to take a more assertive stand on independence. They also made three radical demands for internal change: first, that militiamen be given the right to elect all their officers, rather than only their junior officers, as the Assembly had specified in the Militia Law; secondly, that the franchise be conferred on all militiamen, regardless of age and economic condition; and, thirdly, that the Assembly impose a heavy financial penalty, proportionate to the size of his estate, on every man who refused militia service, using this money to support the families of poor militiamen.[61]

Though upper-class Whigs might call the militia privates "in general damn'd riff raff—dirty, mutinous, and disaffected," there was no denying the power of these men.[62] Generally from the lowest ranks of the laboring population, as opposed to the master craftsmen who from 1770 to 1774 had gradually gained control of the extralegal committees, they played a major role in the creation of the radical Pennsylvania constitution of 1776. "An enormous proportion of property vested in a few individuals," they advised the Constitutional Convention, "is dangerous to the rights, and destructive to the common happiness of mankind, and therefore every free state hath a right by its laws to discourage the possession of such property." This distinctly uncomplaisant call for a ceiling on wealth was accompanied by the advice that in electing representatives the people should shun "great and overgrown rich men [who] will be improper to be trusted [for] they will be too apt to be framing distinctions in society, because they will reap the benefits of all such distinctions."[63]

The ability of Philadelphia's artisans to organize and assert their collective strength was best exemplified in the move to broaden the franchise. This required breaking through one of the foundations of elite domination—that only property ownership entitled one to political rights. In the other northern cities voices were raised occasionally for the political rights of the propertyless and the poor.[64] But only in Philadelphia, where a combination of artisans, shopkeepers, and small traders captured control of the political process and then were themselves pressured from below by a highly politicised militia composed mainly of lower artisans, was the franchise given to all taxpayers, regardless of whether they owned property. In a society where the proportion of those without property was growing among artisans, this was a break with the past of enormous significance. It swept away "the basic economic presupposition that the ownership of a specified amount of property was an essential guarantee of political competence."[65] Many avid patriots, such as Bostonian John Adams, were aghast at this, for "it tends to confound and destroy all distinctions, and prostrate all ranks to one common level."[66] That, of course, was what the radical architects of Pennsylvania's constitution had in mind.

There emerged in the revolutionary era no perfect crystallization of artisan consciousness or all-craft solidarity. Artisans were still bound in part by allegiance to particular crafts, and, more important, long-range changes in trades such as shoemaking, tailoring, and printing were increasingly separating journeymen from masters. But, most of all, the revolutionary potential of the Philadelphia artisanry was limited by the strong hold that the "liberal" economic outlook held on large numbers of property-owning, modestly prosperous mechanics in the more lucrative trades. Although these men figured powerfully in the nonimportation movements and in the swelling sentiment for independence after 1774, they did not share the radical social perspective that lay behind the insurgency of the lower artisans of the Philadelphia militia. It was here that a genuine counter-ideology, stressing egalitarianism and communitarianism, resonated with greatest force.

The tensions within the artisan population of the city that always lurked behind the appearance of unity on questions such as nonimportation and independence became tragically evident in the price-control crisis of 1779 in Philadelphia. Lower artisans for the most part advocated strict regulation of prices as a way of reinstituting "the moral economy" at a time when inflation was pushing the cost of life's necessaries beyond the reach of ordinary families, many of whom had sacrificed the male head of household to military duty. The majority of upper artisans, however, hewed to the ideology of free trade and *laissez-faire* principles of political economy. They thereby demonstrated how resilient were the bourgeois values of those who had been swept from office in the final days before independence and had been overpowered in the struggle over the Pennsylvania constitution of 1776.[67] This, then, would be one of the legacies of the Revolution in its largest commercial center: a struggle within the artisanry between those who, while united by an ideology of productive labor, were divided on how far political rights should be extended, how far the powers of government should reach in regulating the economy for the public good, and how relations within the workplace should be structured. It was by no means evident at the time, in the midst of the greatest social and political upheavals ever experienced in the Pennsylvania capital, what the outcome of these internal tensions would be. But to virtually every Philadelphia artisan it became apparent that in the course of defining issues that were palpable in terms of their daily existence, and through the process of struggling around these issues, they had gained a new political self-awareness and a new understanding of their role *vis-à-vis* those who stood above them in the social order.

NOTES

1. For contemporary definitions of mechanic and upper-class attitudes toward artisans, see: Carl Bridenbaugh, *The Colonial Craftsman* (Chicago: Phoenix Books, 1961), 155; and Howard B. Rock, *Artisans of the New Republic: The Tradesmen of New York City in the Age of Jefferson* (New York: New York University Press, 1979), 4–8.

2. Joseph J. Kelley, Jr., *Life and Times in Colonial Philadelphia* (Harris-

burg, Pa.: Stackpole Books, 1973), 48. Richard Pares analyzes the effects of weather on the North American–West Indies trade in *Yankees and Creoles: The Trade between North America and the West Indies before the American Revolution* (Cambridge, Mass.: Harvard University Press, 1956), 18. Two excellent accounts of the irregular pace of northern mercantile life are: W. T. Baxter, *The House of Hancock: Business in Boston, 1724–1775* (Cambridge, Mass.: Harvard University Press, 1945), 184–220; and Virginia D. Harrington, *The New York Merchant on the Eve of the Revolution* (New York: Columbia University Press, 1935), 76–125.

3. "The grand complaint with laborers among us," wrote Benjamin Rush in 1769, "is that we do not pay them sufficient prices for their work. A plain reason may be assigned for this; we consume too little of their manufactures to keep them employed the whole year around . . . " (*Letters of Benjamin Rush*, ed. Lyman H. Butterfield, 2 vols. [Princeton, N.J.: Princeton University Press, 1951], v. 1:74–75). The irregularity of work for Philadelphia's artisans lasted into the nineteenth century, as Bruce Laurie explains in "Nothing on Impulse": life styles of Philadelphia artisans, 1820–1850," *Labor History*, v. 15, no. 3 (Summer 1974): 343–44. Much can be learned on the subject from Keith Thomas, "Work and leisure in pre-industrial society," *Past and Present*, no. 29 (Dec. 1964): 50–66, and from E. P. Thompson, "Time, work-discipline, and industrial capitalism," *Past and Present*, no. 38 (Dec. 1967): 56–97.

4. Fernand Braudel, *Capitalism and Material Life, 1400–1800*, trans. George Weidenfeld (New York: Harper Torchbooks, 1973), ix.

5. On wage-price relatives in England and the colonies, see Victor S. Clark, *History of Manufactures in the United States*, v. 1:1607–1860 (Washington, D.C.: McGraw-Hill, 1929), 155–58.

6. Bridenbaugh argues that among artisans the "driving desire" was "to raise themselves and their families above their present level" and to get into the "white-collar class" (*Colonial Craftsman*, 165). It is the second part of this statement to which I take exception.

7. Gary B. Nash, *The Urban Crucible: Social Change, Political Consciousness and the Origins of the American Revolution* (Cambridge, Mass.: Harvard University Press, 1979), Table 5, 397–98.

8. James G. Lydon, "Philadelphia's commercial expansion, 1730–1739," *Pennsylvania Magazine of History and Biography*, 91, no. 4 (Oct. 1967): 401–18. The occupational careers of these men can be followed in part through the deed books, which can be used to chart property acquisition and occupational change. For this period, see Deed Books E-5/7, E-6/7 and E-7/8, City Archives, City Hall Annex, Philadelphia.

9. J. E. Crowley, *This Sheba, Self: The Conceptualisation of Economic Life in Eighteenth-Century America* (Baltimore: Johns Hopkins University Press, 1974), 84.

10. *To the Inhabitants of Pennsylvania in General, and Particularly Those of the City and Neighbourhood of Philadelphia* (Philadelphia, Pa., 1779).

11. Geoffrey Crossick, *An Artisan Elite in Victorian Society: Kentish London, 1840–1880* (Totowa, N.J.: Rowman & Littlefield, 1978), 135.

12. *The Papers of Benjamin Franklin,* ed. Leonard Labaree et al., vol. 3 (New Haven, Conn.: Yale University Press, 1961), 200–201.

13. *Pennsylvania Journal,* Mar. 25, 1756. Fifteen years later the same author, Jacob Duche, would rephrase the notion, writing that "The poorest labourer upon the shore of *Delaware* thinks himself entitled to deliver his sentiments in matters of religion or politics with as much freedom as the gentleman or scholar. . . . For every man expects one day or another to be upon a footing with his wealthiest neighbour;—and in this hope shews him no cringing servility, but treats him with a plain, though respectful familiarity" (*Pennsylvania Packet,* Mar. 30, 1772).

14. I.J. Prothero, *Artisans and Politics in Early Nineteenth-Century London: John Gast and His Times* (Folkestone, 1979), 26.

15. John F. Watson, *Annals of Philadelphia, and Pennsylvania, in the Olden Time . . . ,*3 vols. (Philadelphia, Pa.: Edwin S. Stuart, 1900), vol. 1:240–41. Watson completed his annals in 1842. For an exploration of the preindustrial artisan's collective trade identity, see Robert Sean Wilentz, "Class conflict and the Rights of Man: artisans and radicalism in antebellum New York," Ph.D. dissertation, Yale University, 1979, chap. 2.

16. Joyce O. Appleby, "The social origins of American revolutionary ideology," *Journal of American History,* 64, no. 4 (Mar. 1978):935–58.

17. E. P. Thompson, "The moral economy of the English crowd in the eighteenth century," *Past and Present,* no. 50 (Feb. 1971):76–136.

18. *Pennsylvania Packet,* June 29, 1779.

19. C. B. MacPherson, *The Political Theory of Possessive Individualism: Hobbes to Locke* (Oxford: Clarendon Press, 1962).

20. *Pennsylvania Packet,* Sept. 10, 1779, quoted in Steven Rosswurm, "Arms, culture and class: the Philadelphia militia and the 'lower orders' in the American Revolution, 1765–1783," Ph.D. dissertation, Northern Illinois University, 1979, 419.

21. The phrase is from Yehoshua Arieli, *Individualism and Nationalism in America Ideology* (Baltimore, Md.: Penguin, 1964).

22. [John Trenchard and Thomas Gordon], *Cato's Letters: or Essays on Liberty, Civil and Religious,* 6th ed. (London, 1755), 2:16; 3:207–8. Another way of surrendering one's political will to those with economic power was to accept election-time "bribes" in the form of liquor or other treats, as New York's *Independent Reflector* (William Livington) explained at length in an essay on "Elections and election-jobbers" in 1753. See Milton M. Klein (ed.), *The Independent Reflector,* (Cambridge, Mass.: Harvard University Press, 1963), 278–84.

23. J. G. A. Pocock, "The classical theory of deference," *American Historical Review,* 81, no. 3 (June 1976):516. For theoretical considerations of deference, see: Howard Newby, "The deferential dialectic," *Comparative Studies in Society and History,* 17 (Apr. 1975): 140–62; Edward Shils, "Deference," in J. A. Jackson (ed.) *Social Stratification* (Cambridge: Cambridge University Press, 1968), 104–32; and Erving Goffman, "The nature of deference and demeanour," in his *Interaction Ritual: Essays in Face-to-Face Behaviour*

(Chicago: Aldine, 1967), 47–95. John Alexander challenges the notion that deference was freely given in Philadelphia in "Deference in colonial Pennsylvania and that man from New Jersey," *Pennsylvania Magazine of History and Biography,* 102, no. 4 (Oct. 1978): 422–36.

24. Alan Dawley, "E. P. Thompson and the peculiarities of the Americans," *Radical History Review,* no. 19 (Winter 1978–79): 43.

25. Raymond Williams, *Marxism and Literature* (Oxford: Oxford University Press, 1977), 113–14.

26. Geoff Eley and Keith Nield,"Why does social history ignore politics?" *Social History,* 5 (1980):269.

27. This is examined more closely in Nash, *Urban Crucible,* pp. 148–56; and in Thomas Wendel, "The Keith-Lloyd alliance: factional and coalition politics in Colonial Pennsylvania," *Pennsylvania Magazine of History and Biography,* 92, no. 3 (July 1968): 289–305.

28. Norris to Stephen DeLancey, Feb. 12, 1723, Norris Letter Book, 1716–30, Historical Society of Pennsylvania.

29. Norris to Jonathan Scarth, Oct. 21, 1726, Norris Letter Book, 1716–30, pp. 474–75; James Logan to John Penn, Oct. 17, 1726, Penn Papers, Official Correspondence, v. 1:237, 239, 247, Historical Society of Pennsylvania.

30. James Logan to Henry Gouldney, Feb. 9, 1722/3, *Pennsylvania Archives,* 2nd ser., 7 (Harrisburg, Pa., 1890): 70–71. Five of Philadelphia's wealthiest merchants were swept from office in 1722 and two others lost their seats in the following year.

31. James Logan, *The Charge Delivered from the Bench to the Grand-Jury* (Philadelphia, Penn., 1723).

32. Logan to James Alexander, Oct. 23, 1749, Logan Letter Book, 1748–50, p. 22, Historical Society of Pennsylvania. Logan was recalling an incident that occurred almost twenty-five years before, which indicates how searing the experience must have been to a man who regarded himself as one of Pennsylvania's chief assets.

33. Among the many pamphlets published from 1723–1728 that indicted Logan as arrogant, power hungry, and insensitive to the difficulties of laboring people the fullest is the forty-five-page pamphlet attributed to William Keith, *The Observator's Trip to America; in a Dialogue between the Observator and His Countryman Roger* ([Philadelphia, Pa.], 1726).

34. Gary B. Nash, *Quakers and Politics: Pennsylvania, 1681–1726* (Princeton, N.J.: Princeton University Press, 1968).

35. James Logan, *The Charge Delivered from the Bench to the Grand Jury* (Philadelphia, Pa., 1723); [Logan], *A Dialogue Shewing What's Therein to Be Found* (Philadelphia, Pa., 1725).

36. Nash, *Urban Crucible,* 148–55; Wendel, "The Keith-Lloyd alliance," 289–305.

37. *A Modest Reply to the Speech of Isaac Norris . . .* ([Philadelphia, Penn., 1727]).

38. A detailed account of the placid period of politics, from the end of the depression of the 1720s until the beginning of the Seven Years' War, is given in

Alan Tully, *William Penn's Legacy: Politics and Social Structure in Provincial Pennsylvania, 1726–1755* (Baltimore, Md.: Johns Hopkins University Press, 1977).

39. *Pennsylvania Gazette*, Sept. 27, 1770.

40. Constant Trueman, *Advice to the Free-Holders and Electors of Pennsylvania* ([Philadelphia, Pa., 1739]), 1–2.

41. In the context of nineteenth-century England and Virginia see the valuable discussion by Paul F. Bourke and Donald A. Debats, "Identifiable voting in nineteenth-century America: toward a comparison of Britain and the United States before the secret ballot," *Perspectives in American History*, 9 (1977–78):259–88.

42. *Votes and Proceedings of the House of Representatives of the Province of Pennsylvania*, ed. Gertrude MacKinney, *Pennsylvania Archives*, 8th ser., 7 (Harrisburg, Pa., 1935); 5830.

43. Nash, *Urban Crucible*, 319–20.

44. Billy G. Smith, "The material lives of laboring Philadelphians, 1750–1800," *William and Mary Quarterly*, 3rd. ser., 38, no. 2 (Apr. 1981): 172–75.

45. Minutes of the Overseers of the Poor, 1768–74, City Archives, City Hall Annex, Philadelphia. See especially the entries for Jan. 27, 1772; Mar. 9, Nov. 1, Dec. 13, 1773; Feb. 28, Oct. 17, 1774; Feb. 1, Mar. 1, Apr. 5, 1775.

46. Gary B. Nash, "Poverty and poor relief in pre-revolutionary Philadelphia," *William and Mary Quarterly* 3rd ser., 33, no. 1 (Jan. 1976): 3–30.

47. *Papers of Benjamin Franklin*, 3:308.

48. Nash, *Urban Crucible*, 327–31. The quotation is from Minutes of the Overseers of the Poor, June 15, 1769, City Archives, City Hall Annex, Philadelphia.

49. Gary B. Nash, "The transformation of urban politics, 1700–1765," *Journal of American History*, 60, no. 3 (Dec. 1973): 626–32. By this time—and in fact for several decades before—the level of political literacy and popular participation in politics was far higher in Philadelphia than in English towns of equivalent size. In Birmingham, for example, which had a population of about 24,000 in 1750 and perhaps 30,000 on the eve of the American Revolution, the parliamentary election of 1774 drew a record 405 voters—the high-water mark of "popular articulacy" in this era. Philadelphia by contrast, with about 15,000 inhabitants in 1765 (not including Southwark and the Northern Liberties), drew 1,448 voters to the polls in 1764; 1,798 in 1765. For Birmingham, see John Money, "Taverns, coffee houses, and clubs: local politics and popular articulacy in the Birmingham area in the age of the American Revolution," *Historical Journal*, 14 (1971):33.

50. Nash, *Urban Crucible*, 305–9, 374–75; Charles S. Olton, *Artisans for Independence: Philadelphia Mechanics and the American Revolution* (Syracuse, N.Y.: Syracuse University Press, 1975), 33–41. Franklin's statement about union is from *Plain Truth: or, Serious Considerations on the Present State of the City of Philadelphia, and Province of Pennsylvania* (Philadelphia, Pa., 1747), in *Papers of Benjamin Franklin*, 3:202.

51. *To the Free and Patriotic Inhabitants of the City of Phila. and Pro-*

vince of Pennsylvania (Philadelphia, Pa., 1779), quoted in Olton, *Artisans for Independence*, 43.

52. *Pennsylvania Gazette*, Sept. 27, 1770.

53. Olton, *Artisans for Independence*, 50–52. "Brother Chip" lectured the elite in the *Pennsylvania Gazette*, Sept. 27, 1770.

54. Quoted in Olton, *Artisans for Independence*, 53.

55. *A Trademan's Address to his Countryman* (Philadelphia, Pa., 1772); *Pennsylvania Gazette*, Sept. 22, 1773, quoted in Olton, *Artisans for Independence*, 56.

56. Richard Alan Ryerson, *The Revolution is Now Begun: The Radical Committees of Philadelphia, 1765–1776* (Philadelphia, Pa., University of Pennsylvania Press, 1978), 79–86.

57. *Pennsylvania Packet*, Apr. 30, 1776.

58. *Philadelphia Evening Post*, Apr. 27, 1776.

59. The rapid disintegration of the old elite's political power is most fully analyzed in Ryerson, *Revolution Is Now Begun*.

60. Eric Foner, *Tom Paine and Revolutionary America* (New York: Oxford University Press, 1976), 64.

61. Olton, *Artisans for Independence*, 74; Foner, *Tom Paine*, 65; Ryerson, *Revolution Is Now Begun*, 133–34, 160–62.

62. Quoted in Foner, *Tom Paine*, 63.

63. *An Essay on a Declaration of Rights* . . . (Philadelphia, Pa., 1776); *To the Several Battalions of Military Associators* . . . (Philadelphia, Pa., 1776). For a general discussion of the eruption of egalitarian sentiment, see Foner, *Tom Paine*, 123–26.

64. For example, in New York see *New-York Journal*, Aug. 18, 1774 and June 20, 1776; also Merrill Jensen, *The American Revolution within America* (New York: New York University Press, 1974), 72–74.

65. J. R. Pole, *Political Representation in England and the Origins of the American Republic* (New York: St. Martin's Press, 1966), 273. The issue of broadening the franchise was first raised in Apr. 1776. Olton, *Artisans for Independence*, 76–77; Foner, *Tom Paine*, 125–26.

66. Quoted in Pole, *Political Representation*, 273 n.

67. The price-control crisis of 1779 and the civil strife that accompanied it are covered fully in Foner, *Tom Paine*, 145–82; and John Alexander, "The Fort Wilson incident of 1779; a case study of the revolutionary crowd," *William and Mary Quarterly*, 3rd ser., 31 (Oct. 1974): 589–612.

10

THOMAS PETERS:
Millwright, Soldier, and Deliverer

Historians customarily portray the American Revolution as an epic struggle for independence fought by several million outnumbered but stalwart white colonists against a mighty England between 1776 and 1783. But the struggle for "life, liberty, and the pursuit of happiness" also involved tens of thousands of black and native American people residing in the British colonies of North America. If we are to understand the Revolution as a chapter in their experience, we must attach different dates to the process and recast our thoughts about who fought whom and in the name of what liberties. One among the many remarkable freedom fighters whose memory has been lost in the fog of our historical amnesia was Thomas Peters.

In 1760, the year in which George III came to the throne of England and the Anglo-American capture of Montreal put an end to French Canada, Thomas Peters had not yet heard the name by which we will know him or suspected the existence of the thirteen American colonies. Twenty-two years old and a member of the Egba branch of the Yoruba tribe, he was living in what is now Nigeria. He was probably a husband and father; the name by which he was known to his own people is unknown to us. In 1760 Peters was kidnapped by African slave traders and marched to the coast. His experience was probably much like that described by other Africans captured about this time:

> As the slaves come down . . . from the inland country, they are put into a booth or prison, built for that purpose, near the beach . . . and when the Europeans are to receive them, they are brought out into a large plain, where the [ships'] surgeons examine every part of every one of them to the smallest mem-

This essay appeared under the title "Thomas Peters: Millwright and Deliver," in David Sweet and Gary B. Nash, eds., *Struggle and Survival in Colonial America* (Berkeley and Los Angeles: University of California Press, 1981), 69–85. Minor alterations have been made in the footnotes.

ber, men and women being all stark naked. Such as are allowed good and sound are set on one side, and the others by
themselves; which slaves are rejected are called Mackrons, being above thirty-five years of age, or defective in their lips,
eyes, or teeth, or grown gray; or that have the venereal disease,
or any other imperfection.[1]

It was Peters's lot to be sold to the captain of a French slave ship,
the *Henri Quatre*. But it mattered little whether the ship was French,
English, Dutch, or Portuguese, for all the naval architects of Europe in
the eighteenth century were intent on designing ships that could pack in
slaves by the hundreds for the passage across the Atlantic. Brutality was
systematic, in the form of pitching overboard any slaves who fell sick
on the voyage and of punishing offenders with almost sadistic intensity
as a way of creating a climate of fear that would stifle any insurrection-
ist tendencies. Even so, suicide and mutiny were not uncommon during
the ocean crossing, which tells us that even the extraordinary force used
in capturing, branding, selling, and transporting Africans from one continent to another was not enough to make the captives submit tamely to
their fate. So great was this resistance that special techniques of torture
had to be devised to cope with the thousands of slaves who were
determined to starve themselves to death on the middle passage rather
than reach the New World in chains. Brutal whippings and hot coals
applied to the lips were frequently used to open the mouth of recalci-
trant slaves. When this did not suffice, a special instrument, the *specu-
lum oris,* or mouth opener, was employed to wrench apart the jaws of a
resistant African.

Peters saw land again in French Louisiana, where the *Henri Quatre*
made harbor. On his way to the New World, the destination of so
many aspiring Europeans for three centuries, he had lost not only his
Egba name and his family and friends but also his liberty, his dreams of
happiness, and very nearly his life. Shortly thereafter, he started his own
revolution in America because he had been deprived of what he considered to be his natural rights. He needed neither a written language
nor constitutional treatises to convince himself of that, and no amount
of harsh treatment would persuade him to accept his lot meekly. This
personal rebellion was to span three decades, cover five countries, and
entail three more transatlantic voyages. It reveals him as a leader of as
great a stature as many a famous "historical" figure of the Revolutionary era. Only because the keepers of the past are drawn from the
racially dominant group in American society has Peters failed to find his
way into history textbooks and centennial celebrations.

Peters never adapted well to slavery. He may have been put to
work in the sugarcane fields in Louisiana, where heavy labor drained

life away from plantation laborers with almost the same rapidity as in the Caribbean sugar islands. Whatever his work role, he tried to escape three times from the grasp of the fellow human being who presumed to call him chattel property, thus seeming to proclaim, within the context of his own experience, that all men are created equal. Three times, legend has it, he paid the price of unsuccessful black rebels: first he was whipped severely, then he was branded, and finally he was obliged to walk about in heavy ankle shackles. But his French master could not snuff out the yearning for freedom that seemed to beat in his breast, and at length he may have simply given up trying to whip Peters into being a dutiful, unresisting slave.

Some time after 1760 his Louisiana master sold Peters to an Englishman in one of the southern colonies. Probably it was then that the name he would carry for the remainder of his life was assigned to him. By about 1770 he had been sold again, this time to William Campbell, an immigrant Scotsman who had settled in Wilmington, North Carolina, located on the Cape Fear River. The work routine may have been easier here in a region where the economy was centered on the production of timber products and naval stores—pine planking, barrel staves, turpentine, tar, and pitch. Wilmington in the 1770s contained only about two hundred houses, but it was the county seat of New Hanover County and, as the principal port of the colony, a bustling center of the regional export trade to the West Indies. In all likelihood, it was in Wilmington that Peters learned his trade as millwright, for many of the slaves (who made up three-fifths of the population) worked as sawyers, tar burners, stevedores, carters, and carpenters.

The details of Peters's life in Wilmington are obscure because nobody recorded the turning points in the lives of slaves. But he appears to have found a wife and to have begun to build a new family in North Carolina at this time. His wife's name was Sally, and to this slave partnership a daughter, Clairy, was born in 1771. Slaveowners did not admit the sanctity of slave marriages, and no court in North Carolina would give legal standing to such a bond. But this did not prohibit the pledges Afro-Americans made to each other or their creation of families. What was not recognized in church or court had all the validity it needed in the personal commitment of the slaves themselves.

In Wilmington, Peters may have gained a measure of autonomy, even though he was in bondage. Slaves in urban areas were not supervised so strictly as on plantations. Working on the docks, hauling pine trees from the forests outside town to the lumber mills, ferrying boats and rafts along the intricate waterways, and marketing various goods in the town, they achieved a degree of mobility—and a taste of freedom—that was not commonly experienced by plantation slaves. In Wilmington, masters even allowed slaves to hire themselves out in the town and to keep their own lodgings. This practice became so common by 1765 that the town authorities felt obliged to pass an ordinance prohibiting groups of slaves from gathering in "Streets, alleys, Vacant Lots" or elsewhere for the purpose of "playing, Riotting, Caballing." The town also imposed a ten o'clock curfew for slaves to prevent what later was called the dangerous practice of giving urban slaves "uncurbed liberty at night, [for] night is their day."[2]

In the 1770s, Peters, then in his late thirties, embarked on a crucial period of his life. Pamphleteers all over the colonies were crying out against British oppression, British tyranny, British plans to "enslave" the Americans. Such rhetoric, though designed for white consumption, often reached the ears of black Americans whose own oppression represented a stark contradiction of the principles that their white masters were enunciating in their protests against the mother country. Peters's own master, William Campbell, had become a leading member of Wilmington's Sons of Liberty in 1770; thus Peters witnessed his own master's personal involvement in a rebellion to secure for himself and his posterity those natural rights which were called inalienable. If inspiration for the struggle for freedom was needed, Peters could have found it in the household of his own slave master.

By the summer of 1775 dread of a slave uprising in the Cape Fear area was widespread. As the war clouds gathered, North Carolinians recoiled at the rumor that the British intended, if war came, "to let loose the Indians on our Frontiers, [and] to raise the Negroes against us."[3] In alarm, the Wilmington Committee of Safety banned imports of new slaves, who might further incite the black rebelliousness that whites recognized was growing. As a further precaution, the Committee dispatched patrols to disarm all blacks in the Wilmington area. In July, tension mounted further, as the British commander of Fort Johnston, at the mouth of the Cape Fear River below Wilmington, gave "Encouragement to Negroes to Elope from their Masters" and offered protection to those who escaped. Martial law was imposed when slaves began fleeing into the woods outside of town and the word spread that the British had promised "every Negro that would murder his Master and family that he should have his Master's plantation."[4] For Thomas Peters the time was near.

In November 1775 Lord Dunmore, the royal governor of Virginia, issued his famous proclamation offering lifelong freedom for any American slave or indentured servant "able and willing to bear arms" who escaped his master and made it to the British lines. White owners and legislators threatened dire consequences to those who were caught stealing away and attempted to squelch bids for freedom by vowing to take bitter revenge on the kinfolk left behind by fleeing slaves. Among slaves in Wilmington the news must have caused a buzz of excitement, for as in other areas the belief now spread that the emancipation of slaves would be a part of the British war policy. But the time was not yet ripe because hundreds of miles of pine barrens, swamps, and inland waterways separated Wilmington from Norfolk, Virginia, where Lord Dunmore's British forces were concentrated, and slaves knew that white patrols were active throughout the tidewater area from Cape Fear to the Chesapeake Bay.

The opportune moment for Peters arrived four months later, in March 1776. It was then that he struck his blow for freedom. On February 9 Wilmington was evacuated as word arrived that the British sloop *Cruizer* was proceeding up the Cape Fear River to bombard the town. A month later twenty British ships arrived from Boston, including several troop transports under Sir Henry Clinton. For the next two months the British controlled the river, plundered the countryside, and set off a wave of slave desertions. Peters seized the moment, broke the law of North Carolina, redefined himself as a man instead of a piece of William Campbell's property, and made good his escape. Captain George Martin, an officer under Sir Henry Clinton, organized the escaped slaves from the Cape Fear region into the company of Black Pioneers. Seven years later, in New York City at the end of the war, Peters would testify that he had been sworn into the Black Pioneers by Captain George Martin along with other Wilmington slaves, including his friend Murphy Steel, whose fortunes would be intertwined with his own for years to come.

For the rest of the war Peters fought with Martin's company, which became known as the Black Guides and Pioneers. He witnessed the British bombardment of Charleston, South Carolina, in the summer of 1776, and then moved north with the British forces to occupy Philadelphia at the end of the next year. He was wounded twice during subsequent action and at some point during the war was promoted to sergeant, which tells us that he had already demonstrated leadership among his fellow escaped slaves.

Wartime service places him historically among the thousands of American slaves who took advantage of wartime disruption to obtain their freedom in any way they could. Sometimes they joined the American army, often serving in place of whites who gladly gave black men freedom in order not to risk life and limb for the cause. Sometimes they served with their masters on the battlefield and hoped for the reward of freedom at the war's end. Sometimes they tried to burst the shackles of slavery by fleeing the war altogether and seeking refuge among the trans-Allegheny Indian tribes. But most frequently freedom was sought by joining the British whenever their regiments were close enough to reach. Unlike the dependent, childlike Sambos that some historians have described, black Americans took up arms, as far as we can calculate, in as great a proportion to their numbers as did white Americans. Well they might, for while white revolutionaries were fighting to protect liberties long enjoyed, black rebels were fighting to gain liberties long denied. Perhaps only 20 percent of the American slaves gained their freedom and survived the war, and many of them faced years of travail and even reenslavement thereafter. But the Revolution provided them with the opportunity to stage the first large-scale rebellion of American slaves—a rebellion, in fact, that was never duplicated during the remainder of the slave era.

At the end of the war Peters, his wife Sally, twelve-year-old Clairy, and a son born in 1781 were evacuated from New York City by the British along with some three thousand other Afro-Americans who had joined the British during the course of the long war. There could be no staying in the land of the victorious American revolutionaries, for America was still slave country from north to south, and the blacks who had fought with the British were particularly hated and subject to reenslavement. Peters understood that to remain in the United States meant only a return to bondage, for even as the articles of peace were being signed in Paris southern slaveowners were traveling to New York in hopes of identifying their escaped slaves and seizing them before the British could remove them from the city.

But where would England send the American Black loyalists? Her other overseas possessions, notably the West Indian sugar islands, were built on slave labor and had no place for a large number of free blacks. England itself wished no influx of ex-slaves, for London and other major cities already felt themselves burdened by growing numbers of impoverished blacks demanding public support. The answer to the problem was Nova Scotia, the easternmost part of the frozen Canadian wilderness that England had acquired at the end of the Seven Years' War. Here, amid the sparsely scattered old French settlers, the remnants of Indian tribes, and the more recent British settlers, the American blacks could be relocated. Thousands of British soldiers being discharged after the war in America ended were also choosing to take up life in Nova Scotia rather than return to England. To them and the American ex-slaves the British government offered on equal terms land, tools, and rations for three years.

Peters and his family were among the 2,775 blacks evacuated from New York for relocation in Nova Scotia in 1783. But Peters's ship was blown off course by the late fall gales and had to seek refuge in Bermuda for the winter. Not until the following spring did they set forth again, reaching Nova Scotia in May, months after the rest of the black settlers had arrived. Peters found himself leading his family ashore at Annapolis Royal, a small port on the east side of the Bay of Fundy that looked across the water to the coast of Maine. The whims of international trade, war, and politics had destined him to pursue the struggle for survival and his quest for freedom in this unlikely corner of the earth.

In Nova Scotia the dream of life, liberty, and happiness turned into a nightmare. The refugee ex-slaves found that they were segregated in impoverished villages, given scraps of often untillable land, deprived of the rights normally extended to British subjects, forced to work on road construction in return for the promised provisions, and gradually reduced to peonage by a white population whose racism was as congealed as the frozen winter soil of the land. White Nova Scotians were no more willing than the Americans had been to accept free blacks as fellow citizens and equals. As their own hardships grew, they complained more and more that the blacks underbid their labor in the area. Less than a year after Peters and the others had arrived from New York, hundreds of disbanded British soldier-settlers attacked the black villages—burning, looting, and pulling down the houses of free blacks.

Peters and his old compatriot Murphy Steel had become the leaders of one contingent of the New York evacuees who were settled at Digby, a "sad grog drinking place," as one visitor called it, near Annapolis Royal. About five hundred white and a hundred black families, flotsam thrown up on the shores of Nova Scotia in the aftermath of the American Revolution, competed for land at Digby. The provincial governor, John Parr, professed that "as the Negroes are now in this country, the principles of Humanity dictates that to make them useful to themselves as well as Society, is to give them a chance to Live, and not to distress them."[5] But local white settlers and lower government officials felt otherwise and soon bent the governor to their will. The promised tracts of farm land were never granted, provisions were provided for a short time only, and racial tension soared. Discouraged at his inability to get allocations of workable land and adequate support for his people, Peters traveled across the Bay to St. John, New Brunswick, in search of unallocated tracts. Working as a millwright, he struggled to maintain his family, to find suitable homesteads for black settlers, and to ward off the body snatchers, who were already at work reenslaving blacks whom they could catch unawares, selling them in the United States or the West Indies.

By 1790, after six years of hand-to-mouth existence in that land of dubious freedom, and after numerous petitions to government officials,

Peters concluded that his people "would have to look beyond the governor and his surveyors to complete their escape from slavery and to achieve the independence they sought."[6] Deputized by more than two hundred black families in St. John, New Brunswick, and in Digby, Nova Scotia, Peters composed a petition to the Secretary of State in London and agreed to carry it personally across the Atlantic, despite the fearsome risk of reenslavement that accompanied any free black on an oceanic voyage. Sailing from Halifax that summer, Peters reached the English capital with little more in his pocket than the plea for fair treatment in Nova Scotia or resettlement "wherever the Wisdom of Government may think proper to provide for [my people] as Free Subjects of the British Empire."[7]

Peters's petition barely disguised the fact that the black Canadians had already heard of the plan afoot among abolitionists in London to establish a self-governing colony of free blacks on the west coast of Africa. Attempts along these lines had been initiated several years before and were progressing as Peters reached London. In the vast city of almost a million inhabitants Peters quickly located the poor black community, which included a number of ex-slaves from the American colonies whose families were being recruited for a return to the homeland. He searched out his old commanding officer in the Black Guides and Pioneers and obtained letters of introduction from him. It is also possible that he received aid from Ottobah Cugoano, an ex-slave whose celebrated book, *Thoughts and Sentiments on the Evil and Wicked Traffic of Slavery and Commerce of the Human Species,* had made him a leader of the London black community and put him in close contact with the abolitionists Granville Sharp, Thomas Clarkson, and William Wilberforce. Once in touch with these men, Peters began to see the new day dawning for his people in Canada.

Peters had arrived in London at a momentous time. The abolitionists were bringing to a climax four years of lobbying for a bill in Parliament that would abolish the slave trade forever; and the ex-slave was on hand to observe the parliamentary struggle. The campaign was unsuccessful in 1791 because the vested interests opposed to it were still too powerful. But it was followed by the introduction of a bill to charter the Sierra Leone Company for thirty-one years and to grant it trading and settlement rights on the African coast. That bill passed. The recruits for the new colony, it was understood, were to be the ex-slaves from America then living in Nova Scotia. After almost a year in London, working out the details of the colonization plan, Peters took ship for Halifax. He was eager to spread the word that the English government would provide free transport for any Nova Scotian blacks who wished to go to Sierra Leone and that on the African coast they would be granted at least twenty acres per man, ten for each wife, and five for each child. John Clarkson, the younger brother of one of England's best-known abolitionists, traveled with him to coordinate and oversee the resettlement plan.

This extraordinary mission to England, undertaken by an uneducated, fifty-four-year-old ex-slave, who dared to proceed to the seat of British government without any knowledge that he would find friends or supporters there, proved a turning point in black history. Peters returned to Nova Scotia not only with the prospect of resettlement in Africa but also with the promise of the secretary of state that the provincial government would be instructed to provide better land for those black loyalists who chose to remain and an opportunity for the veterans to reenlist in the British army for service in the West Indies. But it was the chance to return to Africa that captured the attention of most black Canadians.

Peters arrived in Halifax in the fall of 1791. Before long he understood that the white leaders were prepared to place in his way every obstacle they could devise. Despised and discriminated against as they were, the black Canadians would have to struggle mightily to escape the new bondage into which they had been forced. Governor Parr adamantly opposed the exodus for fear that if they left in large numbers, the charge that he had failed to provide adequately for their settlement would be proven. The white Nova Scotians were also opposed because they stood to lose their cheap black labor as well as a considerable part of their consumer market. "Generally," writes our best authority on the subject, "the wealthy, and influential, class of white Nova Scotians was interested in retaining the blacks for their own purposes of exploitation."[8]

So Peters, who had struggled for years to burst the shackles of slavery, now strove to break out of the confinements that free blacks suffered in the Maritime Provinces. Meeting with hostility and avowed opposition from Governor Parr in Halifax, he made the journey of several hundred miles to the St. John valley in New Brunswick, where many of the people he represented lived. There too he was harassed by local officials; but as he spread word of the opportunity, the black people at St. John were suffused with enthusiasm and about 220 signed up for the colony. With his family at his side, Peters now recrossed the Bay of Fundy to Annapolis. Here he met with further opposition. At Digby, where he had first tried to settle with his wife and children some eight years before, he was knocked down by a white man for daring to lure away the black laborers of the area who worked for meager wages. Other whites resorted to forging indentures and work contracts that bound blacks to them as they claimed; or they refused to settle back

wages and debts in hopes that this would discourage blacks from joining the Sierra Leone bandwagon. "The white people . . . were very unwilling that we should go," wrote one black minister from the Annapolis area, "though they had been very cruel to us, and treated many of us
as though we had been slaves."[9]

Try as they might, neither white officials nor white settlers could
hold back the tide of black enthusiasm that mounted in the three
months after John Clarkson and Thomas Peters returned from London.
Working through black preachers, the principal leaders in the Canadian
black communities, the two men spread the word. The return to Africa
soon took on overtones of the Old Testament delivery of the Israelites
from bondage in Egypt. Clarkson described the scene at Birchtown, a
black settlement near Annapolis, where on October 26, 1791, some 350
blacks trekked through the rain to the church of their blind and lame
preacher, Moses Wilkinson, to hear about the Sierra Leone Company's
terms. Pressed into the pulpit, the English reformer remembered that "it
struck me forcibly that perhaps the future welfare and happiness, nay
the very lives of the individuals then before me might depend in a great
measure upon the words which I should deliver. . . . At length I rose up,
and explained circumstantially the object, progress, and result of the
Embassy of Thomas Peters to England."[10] Applause burst forth at frequent points in Clarkson's speech, and in the end the entire congregation vowed its intent to make the exodus out of Canada in search of the
promised land. In the three days following the meeting 514 men,
women, and children inscribed their names on the rolls of prospective
emigrants.

Before the labors of Clarkson and Peters finished, about twelve
hundred black Canadians had chosen to return to Africa. This represented "the overwhelming majority of the ones who had a choice."[11] By
contrast, only fourteen signed up for army service in the British West
Indies. By the end of 1791 all the prospective Sierra Leoneans were
making their way to Halifax, the port of debarkation, including four
from Peters's town of St. John who had been prohibited from leaving
with Peters and other black families on trumped-up charges of debt.
Escaping their captors, they made their way around the Bay of Fundy
through dense forest and snow-blanketed terrain, finally reaching Halifax after covering 340 miles in fifteen days.

In Halifax, as black Canadians streamed in from scattered settlements in New Brunswick and Nova Scotia, Peters became John Clarkson's chief aide in preparing for the return to Africa. Together they
inspected each of the fifteen ships assigned to the convoy, ordering
some decks to be removed, ventilation holes to be fitted, and berths

constructed. Many of the 1,196 voyagers were African-born, and Peters, remembering the horrors of his own middle passage thirty-two years before, was determined that the return trip would be of a very different sort. As the ships were being prepared, the Sierra Leone recruits made the best of barracks life in Halifax, staying together in community groups, holding religious services, and talking about how they would soon "kiss their dear Malagueta," a reference to the Malagueta pepper, or "grains of paradise," which grew prolifically in the region to which they were going.[12]

On January 15, 1792, under sunny skies and a fair wind, the fleet weighed anchor and stood out from Halifax harbor. We can only imagine the emotions unloosed by the long-awaited start of the voyage that was to carry so many ex-slaves and their children back to the homeland. Crowded aboard the ships were men, women, and children whose collective experiences in North America described the entire gamut of slave travail. Included was the African-born ex–Black Pioneer Charles Wilkinson with his mother and two small daughters. Wilkinson's wife did not make the trip, for she had died after a miscarriage on the way to Halifax. Also aboard was David George, founder of the first black Baptist church to be formed among slaves in Silver Bluff, South Carolina, in 1773. George had escaped a cruel master and taken refuge among the Creek Indians before the American Revolution. He had reached the British lines during the British occupation of Savannah in 1779, joined the exodus to Nova Scotia at the end of the war, and became a religious leader there. There was Moses Wilkinson, blind and lame since he had escaped his Virginia master in 1776, who had been another preacher of note in Nova Scotia and was now forty-five years old. Eighty-year-old Richard Herbert, a laborer, was also among the throng, but he was not the oldest. That claim fell to a woman whom Clarkson described in his shipboard journal as "an old woman of 104 years of age who had requested me to take her, that she might lay her bones in her native country."[13] And so the shipboard lists went, inscribing the names of young and old, African-born and American-born, military veterans and those too young to have seen wartime service. What they had in common was their desire to find a place in the world where they could be truly free and self-governing. This was to be their year of jubilee.

The voyage was not easy. Boston King, an escaped South Carolina slave who had also become a preacher in Nova Scotia, related that the winter gales were the worst in the memory of the seasoned crew members. Two of the fifteen ship captains and sixty-five black emigrés died en route. The small fleet was scattered by the snow squalls and heavy gales; but all reached the African coast after a voyage of about two months. They had traversed an ocean that for nearly three hundred years had carried Africans, but only as shackled captives aboard ships crossing in the opposite direction, bound for the land of their misery.

Legend tells that Thomas Peters, sick from shipboard fever, led his shipmates ashore in Sierra Leone singing, "The day of jubilee is come; return ye ransomed sinners home."[14] In less than four months he was dead. He was buried in Freetown, where his descendants live today. His final months were ones of struggle also, in spite of the fact that he had reached the African shore. The provisions provided from England until the colony could gain a footing ran short, fever and sickness spread, the distribution of land went slowly, and the white councilors sent out from London to superintend the colony acted capriciously. The black settlers "found themselves subordinate to a white governing class and subjected to the experiments of nonresident controllers."[15] Racial resentment and discontent followed, and Peters, who was elected speaker-general for the black settlers in their dealings with the white governing council, quickly became the focus of the spreading frustration. There was talk about replacing the white councilors appointed by the Sierra Leone Company with a popularly elected black government. This incipient rebellion was avoided, but Peters remained the head of the unofficial opposition to the white government until he died in the spring of 1792.

Peters lived for fifty-four years. During thirty-two of them he struggled incessantly for personal survival and for some larger degree of freedom beyond physical existence. He crossed the Atlantic four times. He lived in French Louisiana, North Carolina, New York, Nova Scotia, New Brunswick, Bermuda, London, and Sierra Leone. He worked as a field hand, millwright, ship hand, casual laborer, and soldier. He struggled against slavemasters, government officials, hostile white neighbors, and, at the end of his life, even some of the abolitionists backing the Sierra Leone colony. He waged a three-decade struggle for the most basic political rights, for social equity and for human dignity. His crusade was individual at first, as the circumstances in which he found himself as a slave in Louisiana and North Carolina dictated. But when the American Revolution broke out, Peters merged his individual efforts with those of thousands of other American slaves who fled their masters to join the British. They made the American Revolution the first large-scale rebellion of slaves in North America. Out of the thousands of individual acts of defiance grew a legend of black strength, black struggle, black vision for the future. Once free of legal slavery, Peters and hundreds like him waged a collective struggle against a different kind of slavery, one that while not written in law still circumscribed the lives of blacks in Canada. Their task was nothing less than the salvation of an oppressed people. Though he never learned to write his name, Thomas Peters articulated his struggle against exploitation through actions that are as clear as the most unambiguous documents left by educated persons.

NOTES

1. Quoted in Basil Davidson, *The African Slave Trade* (Boston, 1961), 92.

2. *The Wilmington Town Book, 1743–1778*, Donald R. Lennon and Ida B. Kellam, eds. (Raleigh, N.C., 1973), quoted in Jeffrey J. Crow, *The Black Experience in Revolutionary North Carolina* (Raleigh, N.C., 1977), 27–28.

3. Quoted in ibid., 55–56.

4. Quoted in ibid., 57.

5. Quoted in Ellen Gibson Wilson, *The Loyal Blacks* (New York, 1976), 109.

6. James W. St. G. Walker, *The Black Loyalists: The Search for a Promised Land in Nova Scotia and Sierra Leona, 1783–1870* (New York, 1976), 32.

7. Quoted in ibid., 95.

8. Ibid., 121.

9. Quoted in Wilson, *Loyal Blacks*, 209.

10. Quoted in ibid., 205.

11. Walker, *Black Loyalists*, 129.

12. Wilson, *Loyal Blacks*, 218.

13. Quoted in ibid., 230.

14. Walker, *Black Loyalists*, 145.

15. Ibid., 149.

11

FORGING FREEDOM:
The Emancipation Experience in
the Northern Seaports,
1775–1820

O N THE EVE of the American Revolution some 4,000 slaves and a few hundred free blacks lived in Boston, New York, and Philadelphia, the northern seaport capitals of colonial society. Fifty years later nearly 22,000 free blacks and about 500 slaves resided in these same cities, most of the latter in New York. In two generations a large majority of the northern Afro-American population made the transition from bondage to freedom. Although northern slavemasters had neither constructed a strong moral justification for holding slaves nor manifested a powerful economic need for bonded labor, blacks did not scale the barrier between slavery and freedom easily. Instead, they constructed the economic, institutional, and social scaffolding of freedom slowly, usually in the face of open white hostility.[1] Moreover, the transit from slavery to freedom proceeded unevenly, depending on the nature of slavery and the timing of emancipation, as well as the specific economic and demographic conditions of urban life. But everywhere the coming of freedom marked the tranformation of black life, the emergence of new institutions, and the development of a new consciousness.

Once the exhilaration of freedom had been savored, one brute necessity stood above all others for black Americans of the Revolutionary era: finding a livelihood. During the years of actual fighting some blacks solved the problem of maintenance by military service, either with the American or, more typically, the British armies. At war's end,

This essay first appeared under the title "Forging Freedom: The Emancipation Experience in the Northern Seaport Cities, 1775–1820," in Ira Berlin and Ronald Hoffman, eds., *Slavery and Freedom in the Era of the American Revolution* (Charlottesville: University Press of Virginia, 1982), 3–48. Minor alterations have been made in the text and the footnotes.

the necessities of life could no longer be procured through membership in a large, white-directed organization; now every freedman was on his own. Standing alone, freed blacks, both men and women, looked to the coastal towns for economic survival.[2] The urban migration that ensued swelled the black population in Boston, New York, and Philadelphia fourfold between the Revolution and 1820 (Table 1).

Rapid postemancipation urbanization increased the urban bias already charcteristic of black life in the colonial period. The intensive capitalization of a few industries, demand for laborers by artisans, and the desire of status-conscious gentlefolk for black servants had combined to make prerevolutionary bondage a disproportionately urban phenomenon.[3] Thus, New York City, which contained 13 percent of the colony's white population in 1771, was the home of 16 percent of the slave population. Boston, with 6 percent of the white population of Massachusetts in 1765, contained 15 percent of the colony's slaves. Slaves in Pennsylvania were twice as likely to live in Philadelphia as were the colony's white inhabitants in the 1760s (Table 2).

Most urban slaves apparently remained in the cities after gaining their liberty. They were joined there by hundreds of former bondspeople from the countryside who, like their urban counterparts, concluded that the cities offered the best chance for widening their economic opportunities and enriching their social life. In particular they headed for the maritime towns, for black men had long been important on the coasting vessels and overseas ships of colonial commerce, and black women could hope for domestic service in the homes of an increasingly affluent urban upper class. By taking out of the hands of the master class decisions about where blacks lived, emancipation permanently altered the geography of northern black life.

This urban migration was especially pronounced in the first two decades after the Revolution (Table 1), when a large proportion of northern slaves received their freedom. The percentage of Massachusetts free blacks who lived in Boston rose only slowly in this period, but in both New York and Pennsylvania the proportion of the black populace living in the capital city doubled between the early 1770s and 1800 (Table 2).[4] By 1820 Massachusetts blacks were three times as likely to live in Boston as were Massachusetts whites; in New York and Pennsylvania, Afro-Americans were four times as likely as whites to live in the seaport capital (Table 2).

Immigrants from the South augmented the expansion of urban black life in the North. Between the Revolution and 1800 Delaware, Maryland, and Virginia masters manumitted thousands of slaves, many of whom, along with hundreds of fugitive bondspeople, headed northward. For the first time the North Star came to symbolize freedom. As

Table 1. Black Population in Three Northern Cities

Year	Boston				New York				Philadelphia			
	Slave	Free	Total	Decadal increase	Slave	Free	Total	Decadal increase	Slave	Free	Total	Decadal increase
Prerevolutionary[a]	751	60	811	—	3,037	100	3,137	—	672	200	872	—
1790	0	766	766	—	2,369	1,101	3,470	—	273	1,803	2,078	—
1800	0	1,174	1,174	53.3%	2,868	3,499	6,367	83.5%	53	6,379	6,434	209.6%
1810	0	1,484	1,484	26.4%	1,686	8,137	9,823	54.3%	3	9,675	9,678	50.4%
1820	0	1,726	1,726	16.3%	518	10,368	10,886	10.8%	0	10,758	10,758	11.2%

SOURCES: Boston (1765): J. H. Benton, *Early Census Making in Massachusetts* (Boston, 1905), following p. 71; New York (1771): Evarts B. Greene and Virginia D. Harrington, *American Population before the Federal Census of 1790* (1932: reprint ed., Gloucester, Mass., 1966), p. 102; Philadelphia (1775): Gary B. Nash, "Slaves and Slaveowners in Colonial Philadelphia," *William and Mary Quarterly*, 3d ser., 30 (1973): 237. The number of free blacks in each city has been estimated. Population data for 1790 to 1820 taken from the published federal censuses.
[a] Boston, 1765; New York, 1771; Philadelphia, 1775.

Table 2. Percentage of State Population Living in Capital City

Year	Boston		New York		Philadelphia[a]	
	Black	White	Black	White	Black	White
		%		%		%		%		—%		—%
Prerevolutionary[b]	14.7%	6.2%	15.8%	12.5%	—%	—%
1790	14.2	4.6	23.5	9.5	20.3	9.5
1800	18.2	5.7	33.6	9.7	43.8	10.9
1810	22.0	7.1	32.1	9.4	41.7[c]	10.6
1820	25.6	8.2	35.4	8.5	36.6	9.1

SOURCES: Boston (1765): J. H. Benton, *Early Census Making in Massachusetts* (Boston, 1905), following p. 71; New York (1771): Evarts B. Greene and Virginia D. Harrington, *American Population before the Federal Census of 1790* (1932; reprint ed., Gloucester, Mass., 1966), 102; Philadelphia (1775): Gary B. Nash, "Slaves and Slaveowners in Colonial Philadelphia," *William and Mary Quarterly*, 3d ser., 30 (1973): 237. The number of free blacks in each city has been estimated. Population data for 1790 to 1820 taken from the published federal censuses.
[a]Including Southwark, Moyamensing, Passyunk, and Northern Liberties.
[b]Boston, 1765; New York, 1771.
[c]After correcting for apparent error in west Southwark; the census figure of 1,100 has been reduced to 800.

the center of American abolitionism, Philadelphia especially became the destination for a generation of Southern blacks, mostly from the upper South. Because it adjoined three slave states, Pennsylvania "afforded an asylum for their free blacks and runaway slaves."[5] Indeed, by 1800 the Afro-American population of Philadelphia overtook that of New York City, although on the eve of the Revolution it had been less than a quarter as large (Table 1).

For freedmen the possibility of maritime work, either on ships at sea or as stevedores along the wharves, provided a large part of the urban pull. Federal protection certificates, issued to merchant seamen beginning in 1796, indicate that by the beginning of the nineteenth century free blacks composed at least one-fifth of some 2,000 merchant seamen in Philadelphia, making this the city's single most important job opportunity for black freemen.[6] Because they indicate the birthplace of each mariner, these certificates can be used to trace migration into the seaport centers from both the rural North and the upper South.[7] James Phillips, a free black mariner, received his certificate in 1798. Born outside Philadelphia in 1771 to a free black mother and a white father, he had come to the Delaware River port to make a living at sea. Alexander Giles, another free black Philadelphia seaman, had been born in 1777 in nearby Kent County, Delaware. The son of a black freeman, he too migrated to the Pennsylvania capital. Randall Shepherd, the son of a free black laborer in Nansemond County, Virginia, had trekked north and taken up life as a merchant seaman in Philadelphia, where he obtained a certificate in 1798. Henry Bray had been born in Boston in the year of the Massacre. Like his father, he went to sea to make a living but had resettled in Philadelphia in the 1790s. George Gray had tried all three major maritime capitals. Born in New York City, he moved to Boston and then to Philadelphia. Of the fifteen black mariners who shipped out of Philadelphia in 1798 and applied for certificates, only two had been born in that city. Six had migrated from the upper South, four from the Philadelphia hinterland, two from New England, and one had been born in Africa.[8]

Crew lists also reveal the lure of maritime jobs. From a random selection of thirty-seven ships departing Philadelphia in 1803, the place of birth of forty-one black merchant seamen can be ascertained. Only two of these had been born in Philadelphia. Four black seamen came from elsewhere in Pennsylvania and eight from adjoining areas in New Jersey and Delaware. Three were from New York; four claimed New England birthplaces; thirteen hailed from Maryland, Virginia, or South Carolina; four came from Saint-Dominque; and one each had been born elsewhere in the West Indies, in Guinea, and in Portugal.[9] Young black men freed in the hinterlands after the Revolution could have had only faint hope of carving out a life for themselves as independent farmers and landholders. Facing strong racial prejudice and lacking capital to buy land, tools, and livestock, life in the countryside meant becoming one of a growing number of rural transients or hiring out as a day laborer to farmers, ironmasters, or small-town shopkeepers.[10] More and more black men seized the opportunities available in the maritime centers, where they became part of a literally floating proletariat.

The appeal of the city was not solely economic. Alongside greater opportunities for employment stood the many attractions of black community life. In rural areas freed Afro-Americans lived in relative isolation from other black people and therefore were relatively defenseless against white hostility. But in the cities the concentration of free blacks provided some security against a hostile world and meant greater chances to find an acceptable marriage partner, to establish a family, and to participate in the activities of black churches, schools, fraternal societies, and benevolent organizations. The strength of this urban attraction cannot be quantified, but the possibility of developing a black community doubtless made the city even more appealing to black migrants. Every Afro-American in the postrevolutionary generation faced the fact that the abolition of slavery tended to augment rather than dissolve white racial hostility, and the animus was no less virulent in the cities than in rural areas.[11] But the dense network of urban black institutions and a rich community life made it easier to confront racism in the cities than in the countryside.

The timing of emancipation shaped the pattern of the black urban migration. Boston reported no slaves in the first federal census, and in Philadelphia, where a gradual abolition law had been in effect for ten years, enumerators counted only 273 bondspeople. By the turn of the century both cities had become havens for free Afro-Americans. New York, on the other hand, did not pass an abolition law until 1799, and this measure offered no immediate freedom; instead it liberated slave-born children only when they reached the age of twenty-five if female, twenty-eight if male. Consequently, the slave population of New York City continued to increase steadily from the end of the Revolution until about 1800. Indeed, as late as 1790 New York had more slaves than any city in the nation except Charleston, South Carolina. As the remaining center of northern slavery in the early nineteenth century, New York at first attracted less than its share of freedpeople. Although the city's slaveowners released or sold their slaves far faster than their rural counterparts in the rest of the state, the free black population nevertheless grew less rapidly in New York City than in Philadelphia from 1780 to 1800.[12] Migrating blacks found "free" cities more attractive than "slave" ones.

Black migration to the cities after the Revolution was disproportionately female, a fact with important ramifications for every aspect of urban black life. It reversed the sexual imbalance of the colonial urban black population, which had usually numbered about three males for every two females.[13] Although the failure of the federal census to distinguish blacks by gender before 1820 makes this development difficult to chart, in that year females represented 55 percent of Boston's black population, 57 percent of Philadelphia's, and 60 percent of New York's (Table 3). The deficit of males in 1820 applied to all age categories but was particularly pronounced among young adults between fourteen and twenty-five years old (Table 3). This shortage can be explained partially by forced sales of young slaves to the South and partially by kidnapping, a constant danger in all northern cities.[14] In addition, census takers and other enumerators exaggerated this sexual imbalance by ignoring large numbers of young male transients and mariners who spent much of their time at sea.[15] Still, the deficit of young men cannot be denied. More than eighty years ago W. E. B. Du Bois offered perhaps the most important explanation for this sexual imbalance in the urban black population: "The industrial opportunities of Negro women in cities have been far greater than those of men, through their large employment in domestic service. At the same time the restrictions of employments open to Negroes, which perhaps reached a climax in 1830–1840, . . . has served to limit the number of men."[16] Corroboration for his analysis can be found in the sex ratios of free blacks in the rural areas surrounding the port cities. In many such counties in 1820, males outnumbered females in the fourteen to twenty-five age category.[17]

The possibility of maritime work for men and domestic employment for women lay at the root of the free black migration to the cities. But former slaves also availed themselves of a variety of other occupational opportunities. Historians have customarily assumed a degradation of black skills in the emancipation period, as former slave artisans, lacking a master's protection and patronage, were forced as freemen into menial labor.[18] But loss of skill may not in fact have been extensive, since fewer colonial slaves possessed artisan training than historians have sometimes supposed.[19] In any case, it would be a mistake to analyze only the changing occupational status of black men, for the labor of black women was equally important to the survival of black households. Far more than among whites, the black family was an economic partnership in which both husband and wife earned wages in the marketplace economy.

Some indications of the occupational structure of the first generation of free blacks can be derived from the 1795 Philadelphia directory,

Table 3. Population in 1820 by Race, Age, and Sex

	Boston		Other Mass.		New York City		Other N.Y.		Philadelphia		Other Pa.	
Age	Male	Female	Male	Female	Male	Female	Male	Female	Male	Female	Male	Female
Free black												
0–13	190	222	895	747	1,281	1,491	3,916	3,851	1,607	1,635	4,059	3,830
14–25	81	168	599	610	920	1,851	2,091	2,344	866	1,670	2,482	2,393
26–44	344	368	552	536	1,387	1,998	1,960	2,188	1,610	2,026	2,280	2,047
45+	159	194	488	587	606	834	1,297	1,324	538	758	1,362	1,039
Total	774	952	2,534	2,480	4,194	6,174	9,264	9,707	4,621	6,089	10,183	9,309
% of Total	44.8	55.2	50.5	49.5	40.5	59.5	49.0	51.0	43.1	56.9	52.2	47.8
White												
0–9	5,371	5,468	65,622	63,792	15,898	15,983	206,710	200,530	12,947	12,605	162,434	151,105
10–15	2,460	3,008	36,113	35,300	7,066	8,335	97,231	93,569	5,577	6,605	71,443	71,820
16–25	3,619	4,590	56,807	48,215	11,017	13,120	151,334	119,372	11,070	10,885	117,381	90,619
26–44	7,438	6,044	46,916	51,677	14,872	13,701	123,762	116,198	10,574	11,940	81,570	82,405
45+	1,542	2,624	37,126	43,547	6,459	6,369	74,800	66,016	4,506	5,938	59,987	53,654
Total	20,430	21,734	242,584	242,531	55,312	57,508	653,837	595,685	44,674	47,973	492,815	452,603
% of Total	48.4	51.6	50.0	50.0	49.0	51.0	52.3	47.7	48.2	51.8	52.1	47.9

SOURCE: *Census for 1820* (Washington, D.C., 1821).

the first in any of the port cities to designate black heads of household. The directory lists only 105 blacks, 83 men and 22 women, which is only one-sixth as many heads of household as might be expected, given Philadelphia's total black population of about 4,000.[20] Of the men, 41 percent worked in unskilled positions as laborers, sweepers, sawyers, and whitewashers. Those employed in domestic or personal service, mostly as waitingmen and coachmen, composed another 12 percent. Nearly 10 percent were mariners, and this figure should probably be doubled, given what other sources reveal about black participation in the seagoing labor force and the traditional underenumeration of seafarers. But a significant number (Table 4) worked as professionals (5 percent) and artisans (12 percent) or were engaged in retailing or other proprietorial roles as hucksters, carters, bakers, fruiterers, and grocers (21 percent).[21] Among the 22 women, more than a third were retailers and boardinghouse keepers, and half labored as washerwomen. In 1797 a Philadelphia editor confirmed this evidence that a large number of Afro-Americans had found profitable employment and made a satisfactory adjustment to freedom; he found "the most afflictive and accumulated distress amongst the *Irish Emigrants* and the *French Negroes.*"[22]

Twenty-one years after the 1795 enumeration another Philadelphia directory that designated free blacks provided a second snapshot of black occupational structure.[23] The 1816 directory listed nearly 900 blacks with occupations. The male occupations indicate remarkable stability over two decades. There was a slight drift toward retail and proprietorial roles and toward domestic and personal service, and an erosion of professional positions. But mariners and artisans held their own and even increased slightly their proportions among free blacks (Table 4).

While more than half of Philadelphia's black men held positions as laborers, bootblacks, coachmen, sweep masters, wood sawyers, or waiters, many former slaves had found their way into more remunerative and independent occupations. One in five was a small retailer or proprietor, or, in a few cases, a professional. Philadelphia's forty-five black oystermen dominated that business; fifty other blacks were traders, grocers, shopkeepers, fruiterers, victuallers, and milkmen. One in ten listed in the directory worked as a mariner and another one of every eight as a craftsman. Thirty-two black artisans labored in the building trades, eleven in metal crafts, twenty-seven in leather trades, twelve in shipbuilding, and a dozen more in miscellaneous crafts. The transition from slavery to freedom does not appear to have altered dramatically the occupational structure of black society, and most freedpeople continued to work as day laborers and domestic servants. Still, some improved themselves considerably by plying artisan trades or keeping small shops of their own.

Table 4. Occupations of Free Blacks in Philadelphia and Boston

| | Philadelphia (1795) | | | | Philadelphia (1816) | | | | Boston (1829) | |
| | Male | | Female | | Male | | Female | | Male | |
	Number	Percent	Number	Percent	Number	Percent	Number	Percent	Number	Percent
Professional	4	4.8	1	4.5	10	1.2	1	3.1	2	1.1
Retail & proprietorial	17	20.5	8	36.4	180	21.6	8	25.0	55	29.4
Artisan	10	12.0	1	4.5	105	12.6	1	3.1	10	5.3
Mariner	8	9.6	0		82	9.8	0		36	19.3
Unskilled	34	41.0	0		327	39.2	3	9.4	62	33.2
Domestic & personal service	10	12.0	12	54.5	130	15.6	19	59.4	22	11.8
Total	83		22		834		32		187	

SOURCES: Edmund Hogan, *The Prospect of Philadelphia and Check on the Next Directory* . . . (Philadelphia, 1795); *The Philadelphia Directory for 1816* . . . (Philadelphia, 1816); John Daniels, *In Freedom's Birthplace: A Study of the Boston Negroes* (Boston, 1914), 17–19.

Many black men found employment within the fast-growing black neighborhoods of Philadelphia. To even the least skilled worker this must have provided a satisfaction of its own. And even among those who were no longer permitted to practice an artisan skill acquired under slavery, a life of semiskilled or unskilled work for white employers at least left the black waterman, well digger, or whitewasher free to retire each night to his own residence, free to form a family, free to change his residence, free to worship where he chose, and free to seek the company of his brethren.

In analyzing the occupations of black women, whose wages were indispensable to the household budget, city directories and federal census returns are of little use, for they usually reported only those women who were widowed heads of household. But investigations into black life by the Pennsylvania Abolition Society partially fill the void. In 1795 the Society reported that "the Women generally, both married and single, wash clothes for a living."[24] Half a century later, a far more extensive survey of black households showed that of 4,249 adult women, all but 290 (7 percent) were employed. The vast majority performed domestic labor, mostly for white families, as washerwomen, seamstresses, and "dayworkers"; others were cooks, tradeswomen, ragpickers, and proprietors. In total, employed black women outnumbered employed black men by 3,959 to 3,358, which corresponds roughly to the female-male ratio reported in the 1850 census.[25]

The Society's reports make it evident that a large majority of free black women performed domestic wage labor for white households throughout the early nineteenth century. For the black family this provided the additional income necessary for survival. The laboring experience of the black woman had changed little since bondage, for under slavery she had also worked in the homes of the white upper and middle classes. Emancipation did not lessen white demand for black domestic servants but merely converted slave labor into domestic wage labor. But some black women, perhaps one in twenty, now occupied roles formerly held by no slave woman: shopkeeper, fruiterer, baker, boardinghouse keeper, schoolmistress, huckster. If emancipation degraded the work roles of some black men while raising those of others, it elevated the occupations of a few black women, leaving the labor of the vast majority unaltered.[26]

For newly freed blacks, moving to the city was a logical way to prepare for the future and find work, but changing one's name was the most personal and one of the most satisfying aspects of the transition from bondage to freedom. "A new name," writes Ira Berlin, "was both a symbol of personal liberation and an act of political defiance; it reversed the enslavement process and confirmed the free Negro's newly won liberty, just as the loss of an African name had earlier symbolized enslavement."[27]

By analyzing the forenames and surnames of slaves and freed Afro-Americans in the northern cities, two stages in the process of cultural transformation can be observed: first, the creation of a creole culture; second, the symbolic obliteration of the slave past. A generation before the Revolution, when slave importations into northern ports were at an all-time high, African names or Anglicized versions of African names were common. Twenty-two of the 155 slaves indicted for conspiracy in New York in 1741 had African day names—Cuffee, Cajoe, Quash, Quack, and the like—signifying the day of the week on which they were born. A slightly larger number bore classical names—Pompey, Caesar, and Cato were the most popular—and 28 carried place-names, such as London, York, Hanover, Hereford, and Jamaica. Anglo-American names, usually in a shortened form, were the most common, with 47 slaves named Dick, John, Tom, Toby, or Will.[28] What is striking in this mix of cognomens is the frequency of African names and the relative absence of biblical names, which were attached to only 4 percent of the indicted slaves (Table 5).

As slaves adjusted to life in the northern cities, formed conjugal relationships, and bore children, they rapidly adopted Anglo-American cultural ways, especially in comparison to slaves in the southern colonies.[29] On large plantations blacks found the preservation of African customs far easier, because the slave quarters furnished Africans with an arena for cultural autonomy. The urban slave, in contrast, almost always lived amid a white family, and, while a few other slaves sometimes resided in the same domicile, urban blacks constantly intermingled with whites. Strong evidence of rapid northern acculturation before the Revolution can be found in the forenames given to slave children as they were brought before the Anglican church in Philadelphia for baptism.[30] African, geographical, and classical names were far less common than among the New York slave conspirators of 1741, and biblical and English names appeared far more frequently (Table 5). No scholar has been able to determine precisely how these forenames were assigned, but historians have presumed that while the master may have had some role in naming slave children, the parents bore most of the responsibility. To the extent that slaves assumed the right to name their own children, the infrequency of classical and geographical names represented their desire to rid themselves of absurd invocations of the classical past and of names that connoted where the master was from or where he traded. By the same token, the increasing frequency of biblical and English names provides evidence of adaptation to the culture into which their children were being born and would presumably spend their

Table 5. Forenames of Slaves and Free Blacks, 1741–1820

	N.Y. (1741) Men	Phila. parents (1747–74) Men & women	Phila. children (1747–74) Boys & girls	Phila. (1795) Men	N.Y. former slaves (1790–1810) Men & women	Phila. (1816) Men	N.Y. (1820) Men & women	Boston (1820) Men & women
African	14.2%	10.4%	1.9%	0%	1.8%	0.4%	0.4%	1.0%
Biblical	3.9	16.6	19.0	17.1	7.8	20.7	11.1	8.4
Classical	16.1	18.5	2.5	7.3	10.3	2.1	2.5	5.4
Geographical	18.1	2.4	1.9	1.2	0.7	0.5	0.8	1.0
English	30.3	42.7	66.5	70.7	72.5	76.2	80.2	81.7
Qualities	6.5	5.2	1.9	0	1.4	0	0.4	0
Other	11.0	4.3	6.3	3.7	5.5	0	4.5	2.5
Number	155	211	158	82	437	752	243	202

SOURCES: New York (1741): Daniel Horsmanden, *The New York Slave Conspiracy*, ed. Thomas J. Davis (Boston, 1971), 468–73; Philadelphia Parents and Children (1747–74): Register Books of Christ Church: Marriages, Christenings, and Burials: 1 (Jan. 1, 1719, to Mar. 1750), 2 (Mar. 1750 to Dec. 1762), 3 (1763–1810), Historical Society of Pennsylvania: Philadelphia (1795): Edmund Hogan, *The Prospect of Philadelphia and Check on the Next Directory...* (Philadelphia, 1795); New York Former Slaves (1790–1810): Harry B. Yoshpe, "Record of Slave Manumissions in New York during the Colonial and Early National Period," *Journal of Negro History* 26 (1941): 78–104; Philadelphia (1816): *The Philadelphia Directory for 1816...* (Philadelphia, 1816); New York and Boston (1820): Population Schedules of the Fourth Census of the United States, 1820 (microfilm at Federal Archives and Records Center, Laguna Niguel, Calif.).
NOTE: The names for 1820 are taken from the manuscript federal census for that year.

lives. Philadelphia's slaves often passed their own names along to their children if their names were Elizabeth, Sarah, Benjamin, Richard, or John. But they rarely perpetuated such names as London, Toss, Sharp, Cato, Othello, and Dirander; and such African names as Quasheba, Quam, and Cuffee also disappeared (Table 5).

Upon gaining freedom, Afro-Americans took complete possession of the naming process. Aggregate statistics on forenames, compiled from city directories, manumission records, and census returns, demonstrate the psychological importance that blacks attached to affirming freedom and wiping away reminders of the slave past by taking a new name or adding to an old one. Of all the free black men listed in the Philadelphia directory of 1795, only one had retained a place-name (Dublin), and none carried derisive names (such as Mistake, Moody, and Fortune) that had been hung on them by former owners. The frequency of biblical names increased. The same was true of English names but with one significant difference. The diminutive forms that had earlier been so common had been traded in for the full English cognomen: Ben became Benjamin, Will became William, Tom became Thomas.

Within a generation of emancipation the classically derived Cato, Scipio, Caesar, and Pompey had all but disappeared among Philadelphia's free blacks, as had geographical names and names connoting qualities, virtuous or otherwise. African forenames were also rare by 1795, with only an occasional Cuffee or Cuff remaining from the list of old day names. But biblical names were on the rise among blacks, who in many cases had been born free: Abraham, Isaac, Jacob, Daniel, David, and Joseph were common, and black men named Absalom, Aaron, Elijah, Ishmael, or Solomon were scattered throughout the city. However, the most common male forenames in the 1795 listing were John, James, William, and Thomas, and English forenames accounted for three-quarters of all the names of black men in the 1816 directory— striking evidence of the degree of acculturation that had occurred since slave days. In Boston and New York the trend was the same. Slaves freed in New York after the Revolution divested themselves of comical and geographical forenames, African day names died out rapidly, classical names waned, and English and biblical names were increasingly common (Table 5).

Surnames also provide important evidence of how emancipated Afro-Americans extended the boundaries of psychological space as they pursued a new life in the port cities. In slavery most blacks had no surnames or carried the surname of a master. In freedom they took new surnames or chose one for the first time. In this selection process there was a pronounced effort to make complete the break with the former master. Few of the free blacks listed in the Philadelphia directory of 1795 bore the names of their former owners.[31] The same is true in New York, where the surnames of Dutch slaveowners in manumission records were in use only rarely by 1830.[32] Cognomens such as Alburtus, Brinkerhoff, DePeyster, Schermerhorn, Van der Water, and Van Zandt held no appeal for New York's free blacks, who traded them in for names that bore no reminders of the days of bondage.

Many freed Afro-Americans used the choice of a new name to make manifest their transition from slavery to freedom. Freemans, Newmans, Somersets, and Armsteads were scattered through the census returns of all northern cities. Freeman appears with much greater frequency in New York than in Boston or Philadelphia, which may indicate that since New York's free blacks lived in a society where slavery continued for so long after the Revolution, a number of them wanted to declare their liberation unmistakably through a name announcing their new status. Names suggesting artisan skills were also fairly common—Cooper, Mason, and Carpenter, for example—although sometimes this may have been coincidental. Occasionally a former slave would celebrate freedom with etymological flourish, as did Francis Drake and Hudson Rivers in New York and Julius Caesar in Philadelphia. Others took names commemorating turning points or moments of high drama in their lives. The previous name of the slaveborn West Indian sailor who turned up in Philadelphia during the Revolution and signed aboard John Paul Jones's *Bonhomme Richard* remains unknown. But this Afro-American mariner fought lustily in the epic battle against the *Serapis*, losing a leg during the sanguinary fray, and sometime thereafter renamed himself Paul Jones.[33]

But freed Afro-Americans overwhelmingly chose the most common English surnames, such as Johnson, Brown, Smith, Morris, Williams, Jackson, Thompson, and Thomas.[34] The plainest of English names took an uncommon hold on the black consciousness during the renaming process, to an extent that makes it possible to speak of a homogenization of black surnames during the first and second generations of freedom. Of the 910 surnames of blacks in the 1816 Philadelphia directory, five—Brown, Johnson, Jones, Jackson, and Miller—account for 15 percent of the entries, and the 12 most frequently given surnames make up almost one-quarter of all family names, a far more concentrated naming pattern than among whites.[35]

This selection of common white surnames seems to indicate that free blacks wished to minimize the chance that they would be associated, either within the black community or in the view of whites, with the slave past. To assume the name Johnson or Jones or Jackson was as neutral as one could get, and its full meaning can be appreciated only by observing—to take the Philadelphia case—how studiously blacks avoided the names of prominent slaveowning families such as Cadwalader, Wharton, Shippen, and Dickinson.[36] The clustering of common English surnames among blacks also shows how far acculturation had proceeded and perhaps indicates a growing feeling of racial solidarity among freedpeople.[37] The African past had not been forgotten, but in the names by which they established their individual identities northern urban free blacks strove to show that they were both Afro-American and free of slavery's grip.

In leaving thralldom behind, northern free blacks sought to perpetuate or create a family life. They neither easily nor automatically accomplished this. The great disruption of slave family life during the Revolutionary War, the dislocation in the war's aftermath, the postemancipation migration, and the constraints placed on family formation by the poverty that enshrouded freedmen and freedwomen all made the creation of black households a complex, multifaceted process that occurred not instantly but over a period of years, extending through the first generation in freedom. Consequently, emancipated Afro-Americans first extricated themselves from white households; then often combined households, with relatives, friends, and boarders intermingling; and finally, as they were able, established nuclear households. The process preceeded at different rates in the three cities, depending on when slavery ended, but everywhere black family life grew more secure.[38]

Any discussion of the free black family should be prefaced with a few comments on slave family life in the northern cities. First, a majority of slaveowners in Boston and Philadelphia owned only one adult slave, which greatly reduced the possibilities that two-parent slave families could live, work, and raise children together. Of Philadelphia's 905 slaves aged twelve or older in 1767, one-third lived by themselves in the home of their owner, and another third lived with only one other slave.[39] The hundreds of inventories of slaveowner estates recorded in Boston between 1685 and 1775 indicate that nearly two-thirds of all slaves lived by themselves or with one other slave. Multiple slaveholding was more common in Philadelphia, with one-third of all slaves living alone or with one other slave, and two-thirds living in groups of three or more (Table 6).[40] In New York, where slaveholding was more extensive, the presence of two adult slaves in the same white household was more common in the colonial era. But slave units declined in size over the course of the eighteenth century. In 1790 six of every ten slaveowners held only one slave and another two had only two slaves, meaning that most slave children did not live in two-parent households (Tables 6 and 7).[41]

Table 6. Slave Ownership

Number of slaves owned	Boston 1685–1775 Number	Percent	Philadelphia 1685–1775 Number	Percent	New York 1790 Number	Percent
1	337	58.8	87	42.0	601	55.6
2	145	25.3	51	24.6	208	19.2
3	54	9.4	24	11.6	128	11.8
4	19	3.3	14	6.8	66	6.1
5–8	16	2.8	22	10.6	72	6.7
9+	2	0.3	9	4.3	6	0.6
Total	573	99.9	207	99.9	1,081	100.0

SOURCES: Boston (1685–1775): Inventories of Estate, Office of the Recorder of Wills, Suffolk County Courthouse, Boston; Philadelphia (1685–1775): Office of the Recorder of Wills, City Hall Annex, Philadelphia; New York (1790): *Heads of Families at the First Census of the United States . . . New York* (Washington, D.C., 1907).

Despite the barriers to living together, slaves commonly married in all the cities, and fertility rates among black women were similar to those prevailing among white women. In New York, where the best data are available, the child-woman ratio among blacks was the same or higher than among whites in three mid-eighteenth-century censuses and was somewhat lower in 1771.[42] The child-woman ratio in Philadelphia cannot be measured, but the steady procession of slaves who came to Christ Church to be married and who brought their children there for christening provides firm evidence of slave family formation. For example, Richard and Dinah brought their son Salisbury before the church early in 1749. William Allen's slaves, Quaco and Hannah, presented their son Joseph for christening in July 1751, returned with another son, James, in the following year, and brought a daughter, Hannah, to the church in 1755.[43] Between 1742 and 1775 several hundred slave children were christened in a church that included one-third to one-half of the city's slaveowners.

Still, enslaved blacks had to struggle to maintain the sanctity of their family life. Masters not only shattered slave families by sale, but they also bound out slave children, sometimes as young as six years of age. For example, William Masters, one of Philadelphia's largest slaveowners, apprenticed eleven of the seventeen slave children, aged four to sixteen, who had been born to his adult slaves. Both of Bellinda's daughters, aged twelve and seven, were bound out until the age of eighteen, the older daughter to a man in Wilmington, Delaware. Scipio and Chloe had their seven-year-old son and four-year-old daughter at their sides, but three older sons were bound out.[44] In sum, before the

Table 7. Slave Residence in White Households of Boston, New York, and Philadelphia

	Boston 1685–1775		Philadelphia 1685–1775		Philadelphia 1767		New York 1790	
	Number	Percent	Number	Percent	Number	Percent	Number	Percent
Slaves living alone	337	34.5	87	15.8	297	32.8	601	30.7
With 1 other slave	290	29.7	102	18.5	272	30.1	416	21.3
With 2 other slaves	162	16.6	72	13.1	168	18.6	384	19.6
With 3 other slaves	76	7.8	56	10.2	124	13.7	264	13.5
With 4 or more other slaves	112	11.5	234	42.5	44	4.9	290	14.8
Total	977	100.1	551	100.1	905	100.1	1,955	99.9

SOURCES: Boston (1685–1775): Inventories of Estate, Office of the Recorder of Wills, Suffolk County Courthouse, Boston; Philadelphia (1685–1775): Office of the Recorder of Wills, City Hall Annex, Philadelphia; Philadelphia (1767): Tax Assessors Lists for 1767, Van Pelt Library, University of Pennsylvania, Philadelphia; New York (1790): Heads of Families at the First Census of the United States . . . New York (Washington, D.C., 1907).

Revolution slaves in northern cities eagerly sought conjugal relationships, frequently parented children in spite of not living together, but had difficulty in keeping their offspring with them because of the common practices of hiring out and sundering family ties through sale.

With freedom, Afro-Americans began to establish separate households and secure an independent family life. But for many extricating themselves from their master's house proved to be a slow and difficult task. In Boston, where slavery had been completely eradicated by 1790, more than one of every three blacks still resided in a white household at the time of the first federal census, most of them without another black in the same residence.[45] Thirty years later, all but 16 percent of the city's blacks were members of autonomous black households. In Philadelphia, where 13 percent of the city's blacks remained enslaved in 1790, half of the free blacks, many of them emancipated only in the previous few years, still lived in white households. A generation later, at the time of the 1820 census, only one in four did (Table 8).

Economic necessity, which pressed hard on the newly freed, was doubtless the largest factor in keeping emancipated blacks in the households of former masters or obliging them to take live-in domestic jobs in the homes of other whites. The need was probably greatest when a man or woman had no spouse or relatives and was therefore forced to seek the security that service in a white household could provide. A single black, usually a woman, resided in more than half the white households where former slaves remained. The fact that twice as many black women as men continued to live in white households also indicates the demand for live-in domestic servants.[46]

Comparative data for New York confirm the notion that from one-half to two-thirds of northern blacks were able to establish their own households within a few years of gaining freedom, while for the others the process was much slower. In 1790, when New York still had twice as many slaves as free blacks, about 36 percent of the free blacks were living in white households, almost the same proportion as in Boston. Three decades later, when all but 16 percent of Boston's free blacks and all but 27 percent of Philadelphia's had extricated themselves from white households, 38 percent of New York's free blacks still lived among whites, almost the same as thirty years before. Slavery's longer life explains the difference between New York and the other cities. A gradual abolition law was not passed until 1799, and even then it took almost three decades more to end slavery. In 1810, 1,686 blacks remained enslaved in New York City, and many of those who received their freedom in the next decade were probably among the free blacks continuing to reside in white households at the time of the 1820 census.[47] In Boston and Philadelphia, by contrast, the emancipation

Table 8. Household Residence of Free Blacks, 1790–1820

	Boston		New York		Philadelphia	
	1790	1820	1790	1820	1790	1820
In black households	63.2%	83.9%	63.9%	62.3%	49.8%	73.3%
In white households	36.8%	16.1%	36.1%	37.7%	50.2%	26.7%

SOURCES: *Heads of Families at the First Census* (Washington, D.C., 1907–8); Population Schedules of the Fourth Census of the United States, 1820 (microfilm at Federal Archives and Records Center, Laguna Niguel, Calif.).

process began earlier and concluded more rapidly. By the time of the 1820 census, almost all Afro-Americans in the two cities had been free for a generation or more.

Though residence in a white household, often under an indenture lasting seven years or more, was the intermediate step between subservient and autonomous existence for many freed blacks, a large majority of urban blacks lived in black households by 1820 (Table 8). The census returns for that year do not indicate exact family relationships within households, so it is impossible to delineate family composition exactly. But this census did for the first time enumerate black residents by age and sex, thus permitting some tentative generalizations about black household and family formation in the early decades of freedom.

In all three cities more than three-quarters of the black households contained at least one adult male and one adult female. This was true of 76 percent of the black households in Boston, 79 percent in Philadelphia, and 81 percent in New York (Table 9).[48] Single-parent families were even less frequent in black households containing children under the age of fourteen. Such households were overwhelmingly headed by both an adult male and female—in 78 percent of the cases in Boston, 88 percent in Philadelphia, and 82 percent in New York (Table 10). In a sample of 1,407 black children under fourteen years of age in 1820, 92 percent lived in households that included at least one adult male and one adult female (Table 11).

Still, blacks achieved the goal of a nuclear household slowly. In the immediate aftermath of slavery, unable to establish their own separate households but unwilling to continue to reside with whites, blacks often joined together to form large extended or augmented household units.[49] Black families boarded relatives and friends newly arrived from the countryside and emerging from slavery with no assets or knowledge of urban life. Strong evidence exists for this pattern in New York, where emancipation came later than in Boston or Philadelphia, although the pattern was probably present in the other seaport cities as well in the

Table 9. Black Household Types, 1820

	Philadelphia		Boston		New York	
	Number	Percent	Number	Percent	Number	Percent
Nuclear[a]						
With children	157	48.3	70	33.5	66	26.7
Without children	49	15.1	44	21.1	1	0.4
Total	206	63.4	114	54.6	67	27.1
Augmented[b]	50	15.4	44	21.1	132	53.4
Single parent						
Female-headed	30	9.2	18	8.6	24	9.7
Female-headed augmented	9	2.8	14	6.7	22	8.9
Total	39	12.0	32	15.3	46	18.6
Male-headed	2	0.6	1	0.5	1	0.4
Male-headed augmented	1	0.3	0	—	0	—
Total	3	0.9	1	0.5	1	0.4
Nonfamily[c]						
Female-headed	15	4.6	9	4.3	1	0.4
Male-headed	8	2.5	7	3.3	0	—
Total	23	7.1	16	7.6	1	0.4
Grown child plus parent	4	1.2	2	1.0	0	—
Grand total	325	100.0	209	100.1	247	99.9

SOURCE: Population Schedules of the Fourth Census of the United Staes, 1820 (microfilm at Federal Archives and Records Center, Laguna Niguel, Calif.).
[a]A nuclear household is a simple two-parent family (with children) or conjugal unit (without children).
[b]An augmented family is a nuclear type plus kin or non-kin.
[c]A nonfamily type contains one adult or two or more adults of same sex only.

Table 10. Black Household Types with Children under Fourteen, 1820

	Boston		Philadelphia		New York	
	Number	Percent	Number	Percent	Number	Percent
Two-parent	86	77.5	205	88.4	181	81.5
Female-headed	24	21.6	25	10.8	39	17.6
Male-headed	1	0.9	2	0.9	2	0.9
Total	111	100.0	232	100.1	222	100.0

SOURCE: Population Schedules of the Fourth Census of the United States, 1820 (microfilm at Federal Archives and Records Center, Laguna Niguel, Calif.).

Table 11. Number of Black Children under Fourteen in Various Types of Households, 1820

	Boston		Philadelphia		New York		Total	
	Number	Percent	Number	Percent	Number	Percent	Number	Percent
Two-parent	209	85.3	575	90.6	505	95.8	1289	91.6
Female-headed	34	13.9	58	9.1	20	3.8	112	8.0
Male-headed	2	0.8	2	0.3	2	0.4	6	0.4
Total	245	100.0	635	100.0	527	100.0	1407	100.0

SOURCE: Population Schedules of the Fourth Census of the United States, 1820 (microfilm at Federal Archives and Records Center, Laguna Niguel, Calif.).

immediate aftermath of slavery. Thus in 1820 the average black household was far larger in New York than in Philadelphia or Boston: 6.3 persons as compared with 3.9 in Philadelphia and 4.2 in Boston (Table 12). This reflected not a larger number of children in New York black families[50] but the greater number of "extra" people in the household. While most Boston and Philadelphia black families lived in nuclear units by the second decade of the nineteenth century, the majority of black households in New York remained augmented or extended, and the nonfamily type of household virtually nonexistent. In Philadelphia and Boston 7 to 8 percent of the black households were made up of a single male or female or several adults of the same sex. But in New York only one of 247 households in Ward Six was of the nonfamily type. This circumstance, combined with the large number of blacks living in white households relative to the other cities, suggests that the distance from slavery was often still too short for an individual free black to maintain a household of his or her own (Table 9).

Black families generally contained far fewer children than white families. In New York and Boston the number of children per adult woman was more than twice as high for whites as for blacks. In Philadelphia the ratio was 2.7 for whites and 1.6 for blacks.[51] Some of this difference may be accounted for by the extremely high mortality rate among blacks, usually two to three times that of whites.[52] But family limitation was also a factor. In New York, the one city where we have data from the slave period to compare with the 1820 census figures, it appears that the woman-child ratio actually dropped significantly as slaves passed from bondage to freedom.[53]

These various measurements, although crude, make it clear that the stereotypes about the unstable and matrifocal black family after slavery have little basis in fact, at least so far as concerns the seaport cities of the North. In general, these data support Herbert G. Gutman's contention that "black households and family systems were exceedingly complex in the aftermath of emancipation" but that conjugal and nuclear-family relationships predominated.[54] In all three cities, though the timing differed, freed blacks moved toward the establishment of two-parent nuclear households. Boston, farthest from slavery, had the smallest proportion of blacks living in white households in 1820 (one in six) and a high incidence of nuclear families among black householders (three of five). New York, where 45 percent of the black population remained enslaved in 1800 and 5 percent in 1820, had the largest proportion of free blacks living in white households (nearly two of five) and among black householders a dramatically lower incidence of nuclear families. Philadelphia's free blacks, who were between their counterparts in Boston and New York in terms of distance from slavery, were also between the two extremes in terms of the

Table 12. Blacks in Black Households by Age and Sex, 1820

		Males				Females				Average size of household
		0–13	14–25	26–44	45+	0–13	14–25	26–44	45+	
Boston	Number	112	20	189	31	142	44	271	60	4.2
	Percent of total	12.9	2.3	21.8	3.6	16.3	5.1	31.2	6.9	
	Percent of gender	31.8	5.7	53.7	8.8	27.5	8.5	52.4	11.6	
Philadelphia	Number	211	88	159	80	258	149	210	112	3.9
	Percent of total	16.7	7.0	12.6	6.3	20.4	11.8	16.6	8.8	
	Percent of gender	39.2	16.4	29.6	14.7	35.4	20.4	28.8	15.4	
New York	Number	225	136	205	126	241	203	279	131	6.3
	Percent of total	14.6	8.8	13.3	8.1	15.6	13.1	18.1	8.5	
	Percent of gender	32.5	16.7	29.6	18.2	38.3	22.1	30.4	14.3	

SOURCE: Population schedules of the Fourth Census of the United States, 1820 (microfilm at Federal Archives and Records Center, Laguna Niguel, Calif.).

proportion who lived in white households (one of four) and slightly ahead of Boston in the formation of nuclear families. The effort to create autonomous families was one of the remarkable features of Afro-American life in the early years of freedom.

As they worked themselves free of white households and established households of their own, new patterns of black residence began to emerge. In slave days, of course, Afro-Americans had resided with their masters or with those to whom they had been hired out. Since these masters lived in cities that were only gradually becoming segregated by function and class, slaves lived scattered throughout urban areas. In the first decade of freedom this dispersal continued in some measure, because from one-third to one-half of all manumitted slaves continued to live in white households.

In the 1780s, as blacks began forming their own households, they made independent decisions about where to locate. In Philadelphia, to focus on one case, they began clustering in two areas, one old and one new. The old area, in the northern part of the city, was in North and South Mulberry wards, a relatively poor district of the city with a concentration of Irish and German laboring-class families. Located between Arch and Vine streets west of Fourth, North and South Mulberry wards attracted about 29 of the city's 169 black households by 1790. Another 32 families lived in the Northern Liberties, beyond North Mulberry Ward. The other area was almost entirely new. Located in the southern part of the city, it comprised Cedar and Locust wards and the west part of South Ward. As late as 1785 this had been mostly open land, but within a few years contractors began erecting cheap housing to accommodate the city's growing population.[55] By 1790 some 56 black households had established themselves in the area. They appeared as the advance guard of what would shortly become an enormous movement of black Philadelphians into this southern part of the city. Fifty-two other black families were dispersed throughout the rest of the city.[56]

Because new cheaply constructed tenements rented at a lower rate than older but larger dwellings, black Philadelphians moved steadily into the southern section of the city. But another process, the establishment of African churches and schools, also drew blacks. In 1791, Richard Allen and Absalom Jones were laying plans to build a black church at Sixth and Lombard streets, in some measure because Philadelphia's free blacks had been moving into new housing in this section of Cedar Ward. By 1794 two black churches had opened their doors in the same neighborhood. But if the nascent black neighborhood attracted African churches, the churches, once established, became vital centers of black community life, drawing hundreds of black families as they worked their way out of white households into their own residences. St. Thomas's had a membership of 427 one year after its building was completed; by 1813 it had 560 members, while Bethel Church counted 1,272 communicants.[57]

The lure of the black churches can be seen in the changing residential pattern of blacks in Philadelphia.[58] Black families continued to settle in the northern part of the city, many of them perhaps because they had jobs in that part of town. But the black population in Cedar and Locust wards grew much faster, from 265 free blacks in 1790 to 4,191 in 1820. This "Cedar Street corridor" of black life, as Emma Lapsansky styles it, was no black ghetto. While free blacks established residences there in great numbers, they were never a majority in this period. Neighborhoods remained mixed, both racially and occupationally. Yet the development of racial and class segregation had received a strong impetus as builders constructed primarily cheap housing in new parts of the city and black families sought the security and group consciousness that came through residential consolidation.[59]

To the south of Cedar Ward lay West Southwark and Moyamensing. Still not incorporated into the city at this time, they nonetheless were part of the rapid development of the southern part of Philadelphia. Free blacks moved there by the hundreds after 1790, living in "cabins," "sheds," and "mean low box[es] of wood."[60] Especially in Moyamensing the free black population increased dramatically in thirty years, from 27 in 1790 to 1,174 in 1820. All told, this southern sector of the city, composed of Locust and Cedar wards, West Southwark, and Moyamensing, contained three of every five blacks in Philadelphia by 1820. Moreover, among independent black householders the percentage living in this area was even higher.[61]

Some sense of these emerging neighborhoods, where free black families mixed extensively with laboring-class whites, can be gained from looking at city directories. Gaskill Street, which ran from Third to Fifth between Cedar and Lombard streets, had two black families listed in the 1795 directory and three in the directory of 1811. But five years later, twenty-four black families were spread along Gaskill, all but two of them in the block between Third and Fourth streets. Sometimes families doubled up, as did Richard Bennett, shoemaker, John Bahimy, mariner, and Joseph Reed, laborer, at 62 Gaskill. Charles Brown, porter, and Phillis Exeter, washerwoman, shared 88 Gaskill. By 1816 eighteen black families made their residence on Blackberry Alley, running north and south from the Pennsylvania Hospital. Among the heads of household were a carpenter, painter, carter, porter, plasterer, trader, gardener, waiter, coachman, and laborer. Black families made their homes throughout the Cedar Street corridor, especially in the crowded courts and alleys that builders and landlords were developing in the early nineteenth century.[62]

In the organization of black institutions, closely tied to emerging neighborhoods, free Afro-Americans constructed the social, religious, and emotional ligaments of their communities. The black church, as many historians have noted, stood at the center of this process and marked the strongest tie between the distant African past, the more proximate slave past, and the present and future as free persons. "The Negro church," wrote Du Bois, "is the peculiar and characteristic product of the transplanted African. . . . It has preserved, on the one hand, many functions of tribal organization, and on the other hand, many of the family functions. Its tribal functions are shown in its religious activity, its social authority, and general guiding and co-ordinating work; its family functions are shown by the fact that the church is a centre of social life and intercourse."[63]

Two closely related factors led to the organization of the first black churches in northern cities in the 1790s: discriminatory treatment in white churches and "the gradual rise of a community of interest" among the Afro-Americans drawn into the metropolis after emancipation. This separatist church movement drew much inspiration from the indifference of white churches to the social and political injustices that freed blacks confronted at the end of the eighteenth century. It was also grounded in the desire of Afro-Americans for a more evangelical gospel than white churches proffered and in a determination "to arise out of the dust and shake ourselves, and throw off that servile fear, that the habit of oppression and bondage trained us up in."[64] Similarly, in New York and Boston separate black churches emerged not only because of discrimination but also because of "a growing self-reliance and the rise of individual leaders."[65]

To some extent the rise of the independent black church appears to have been triggered as much by concern for the religious care of the dead as by concern for the living. In both Philadelphia and New York free black churches had their origins in the Free African societies established in the late 1780s and early 1790s. In each case one of the society's first acts was to apply for a separate black burial ground.[66] White churches did not permit the mortal remains of black worshipers to be interred in their cemeteries but instead consigned blacks to the Potter's Field or "Stranger's Burial Ground," as it was tellingly called in Philadelphia. This extension to the dead of the racial inequalities among the living may have been especially grievous to Afro-Americans, whose African religious heritage stressed ancestor reverence and thus emphasized dignifying the dead.

To signify their group identity and to separate themselves from whites, blacks—from the beginning—named their churches, schools, and mutual aid associations and fraternal societies "African." In 1787 Philadelphia free blacks established their first independent organization and called it the Free African Society. From it derived the African Methodist Episcopal Church and the African Episcopal Church of St. Thomas. The African Baptist and African Presbyterian churches would follow. Among the benevolent societies established in this early period were the Angolan Society and the Angola Beneficial Association in 1808, the Sons of Africa in 1810, the African Female Benevolent Society (founding date unknown), and the Male African Benevolent Society in 1819.[62] The Quaker school for blacks, founded in 1770, became known as the Friends African School in the 1790s. The first black insurance company, in existence by 1809, was called the African Insurance Company of Philadelphia.[68] In New York the term *African* was also used for almost all the early churches, the first black school, and the first mutual aid societies. In Boston the African Society, founded in 1797, established the African School in 1798 and the African Meeting House in 1805.[69] The frequency of the term in the names of early churches, schools, and benevolent societies, when considered in conjunction with the rapid Anglicization of black personal names in this period, suggests that while free blacks took on common English names as a way of wiping out the slave past, they simultaneously and self-consciously fostered black solidarity by affixing an adjective to their institutions that would unmistakably differentiate them from parallel white institutions.

Establishing independent institutions took time, and the continued enslavement of a sizable portion of the black population delayed the process, partly because the business of obtaining freedom for those still in bondage absorbed the time, money, and energy of those who were free, and partly because it took a generation of freedom for blacks to extricate themselves from white households and establish residences of their own in neighborhoods where black consciousness could thrive. This stifling effect of slavery can be seen in the wide disparity in black institutional development in Philadelphia and New York. The two cities had black populations of roughly the same size in the first quarter of the nineteenth century. But whereas nearly all Philadelphia blacks were free by 1790, it took another generation to extinguish slavery in New York City. Thus by 1813, when Philadelphia blacks had created six black churches with a total membership of 2,366, only two existed in New York, with a membership that cannot have exceeded one-third of Philadelphia's.[70] Similarly, New York's first free black school was founded in 1786 and the second not until 1820. Meanwhile, by 1811 nine black schools were operating in Philadelphia. New York blacks founded their first mutual aid society, the New York African Society for

Mutual Relief, in 1810, while Philadelphia blacks had organized eleven benevolent societies by 1813.[71] Where slavery had been expunged soon after the Revolution, black institutional life thrived; where it lingered, it had a deadening effect even on those blacks who did escape its clutches.

At different rates, black institutions took form in all northern cities. Created out of the massing of free blacks in the cities and the rise of an independent black consciousness, these churches, schools, fraternal societies, and mutual aid associations in turn became part of the magnetic pull of urban life. By the 1820s Philadelphia Afro-Americans had created an institutional life that was richer and more stable than that of the lower-income whites with whom they shared neighborhoods. Since Afro-Americans were "blocked from upward mobility out of the neighborhood," writes Lapsansky, "they wanted institutions that would provide them with a reasonable future there." For whites, by contrast, these increasingly class-segregated neighborhoods were seen as a "brief stopping place" on the way to something better. White gangs were the institution better suited to "a transient constituency," for they required no large expenditures for permanent structures, no "long-range planned activity," and no regular commitments of time.[72] Hence, white churches and fraternal organizations fared poorly in comparison to black institutions in the lower-class wards of Philadelphia in this period, and black institutions became the envy of whites in racially mixed neighborhoods. Oppressed both as an economic class and a racial caste, urban freedmen and freedwomen drew upon a collective black consciousness to form their own network of thriving institutions.

"Sir," thundered South Carolina's Robert Y. Hayne in the famous nullification debate of 1830, "there does not exist on the face of the earth, a population so poor, so wretched, so vile, so loathsome, so utterly destitute of all the comforts, conveniences, and decencies of life, as the unfortunate blacks of Philadelphia, New York, and Boston. Liberty has been to them the greatest of calamities, the heaviest of curses."[73] The words were uttered, of course, to shame the North for its treatment of emancipated slaves and to contrast their condition unfavorably with those still held in bondage in the South. Hayne's indictment truthfully acknowledged the wretched effects of northern racism. White urban dwellers in the North, as Leon Litwack has written, "worked free Negroes severely in menial employments, excluded them from the polls, the juries, the churches, and the learned professions, snubbed them in social circles, and finally even barred them from entering some states."[74] Yet this is not the full story, for it focuses on what was done to freed blacks rather than on what emancipated Afro-Americans did for themselves. Alongside the history of oppression must be placed the history of people striving to live life as fully, as freely, and as creatively as their inner resources and external circumstances would allow. In the northern capitals of American life after the Revolution, emancipated slaves suffered greatly to be sure, but they also formed communities that would not die and created a viable culture of their own.

NOTES

1. This inquiry is not directed at how whites treated blacks in the northern cities after the Revolution, a dismal subject that has been comprehensively treated elsewhere. See, for example, Leon F. Litwack, *North of Slavery; The Negro in the Free States, 1790–1860* (Chicago, 1961); and Winthrop D. Jordan, *White over Black: American Attitudes toward the Negro, 1550–1812* (Chapel Hill, N.C., 1968) 406–26.

2. W. E. B. Du Bois first noted this movement to the cities in his classic study *The Philadelphia Negro: A Social Study* (1899; reprint ed., New York, 1967), 17. Ira Berlin also draws attention to this phenomenon in "The Structure of the Free Negro Caste in the Antebellum United States," *Journal of Social History*, 9 (1976): 300.

3. Parts of southern New York were exceptions. In Ulster, Westchester, Queens, and especially Kings counties the percentage of blacks in the population at the end of the colonial period exceeded that of New York City. See the 1771 census in Evarts B. Greene and Virginia D. Harrington, *American Population before the Federal Census of 1790* (1932; reprint ed., Gloucester, Mass., 1966), 102.

4. The move to the metropolis from the towns around Boston can be seen in the population changes between 1765 and 1820. In the former year Boston had 848 slaves and the surrounding towns 404. By 1790, 766 free blacks lived in Boston and only 189 in outlying towns. Thirty years later, in 1820, Boston's black population stood at 1,484, while 239 blacks lived in the adjacent towns. Thus Boston's share of the regional black population rose from 68 percent in 1765 to 87 percent in 1820 (Oscar Handlin, *Boston's Immigrants* [1941; reprint ed., New York, 1968], p.249, Table 12. I have changed Handlin's figure for the black population of Boston in 1820 to correspond with the 1820 census). The growth of Boston's black population may have been slowed by the city's efforts to discourage immigrating freedpeople, as, for example, in 1800, when the selectmen ordered the expulsion of 235 wayfarers (Arthur O. White, "The Black Leadership Class and Education in Antebellum Boston," *Journal of Negro Education*, 42 [1973]:507).

5. Visiting Committee to Acting Committee, Jan. 8, 1821, Pennsylvania Prison Society Records, Vol. 2, Part A, Historical Society of Pennsylvania, Philadelphia. For the growth of the free black population in the upper South, see Ira Berlin, *Slaves without Masters: The Free Negro in the Antebellum South* (New York, 1974), 29–35.

6. The proportion of blacks in Philadelphia's maritime labor force can be estimated from the ships' crew lists in the Library of Congress. In a sample of

thirty-seven ships leaving Philadelphia in 1803, 24 percent of the mariners were black; on twenty-five ships sailing in 1805, 21 percent (Records of the Port of Philadelphia, Library of Congress. This information has been provided by Billy G. Smith).

7. The origin of the certificates and the information included in them are described by Ira Dye, "Early American Merchant Seafarers," *Proceedings of the American Philosophical Society,* 120 (1976): 331–34.

8. Seamen's Protective Certificate Applications to the Collector of Customs for the Port of Philadelphia, R. G. 36, Nat. Arch. (I am grateful to Billy G. Smith for providing this information.) Of 137 black seamen applying for protection certificates from 1812 to 1815 in Philadelphia, only 15 percent had been born in the city (Dye, "Early American Merchant Seafarers," 351, Table 6).

9. Ships' Crew Lists, R.G. 36, Nat. Arch. (This information has also been provided by Billy G. Smith.) A study of crew lists and protection certificates for New York and Boston would probably reveal a similar pattern. The free blacks of Massachusetts, wrote an early historian of the period, "have generally ... left the country and resorted to the maritime towns" ("Judge Tucker's Queries respecting Slavery, with Doctor Belknap's Answers," Massachusetts Historical Society *Collections,* 1st ser., 4 [1795]: 206).

10. For an evocative study of the impoverishment of free blacks who tried their luck in Chester and Lancaster counties, west of Philadelphia, see Carl D. Oblinger, "Alms for Oblivion: The Making of a Black Underclass in Southeastern Pennsylvania, 1780–1869," in John E. Bodnar, ed., *The Ethnic Experience in Pennsylvania* (Lewisburg, Pa., 1973), 94–119.

11. Jordan, *White over Black,* 403–26.

12. For the persistence of slavery in one New York county, see Carl Nordstrom, "Slavery in a New York County: Rockland County, 1686–1827," *Afro-Americans in New York Life and History,* 1 (1977): 145–66. In 1800, when 55 percent of New York City's black population was free, nearly three-quarters of the 24,920 blacks elsewhere in the state remained in slavery. In some counties more than 90 percent of the black population was still in bondage. For the number of slaves and free blacks in each county, see *Return of the Whole Number of Persons within the Several Districts of the United States* (Washington, D.C., 1801), 32.

13. In Boston in 1765 there were 510 male and 301 female slaves (J. H. Benton, *Early Census Making in Massachusetts* [Boston, 1905], following p. 71). In Philadelphia constables' reports for 1775, male slaves in two wards outnumbered female slaves 33 to 22 (Constables' Reports, 1775, City Archives, City Hall Annex, Philadelphia). New York may have been the exception. In 1771 there were 1,500 male slaves and 1,637 female slaves (Greene and Harrington, *American Population,* 102). By 1786 New York contained 896 male and 1,207 female slaves (ibid., 104). This female predominance may reflect the disproportionately large number of male slaves who gained their freedom fighting with the British during the Revolution and were evacuated in 1783 to Nova Scotia.

14. For kidnapping in Pennsylvania see Edward R. Turner, *The Negro in*

Pennsylvania (1910; reprint ed., New York, 1969), 115–16; for New York see
Rhoda G. Freeman, "The Free Negro in New York City in the Era before the
Civil War," Ph.D. diss., Columbia University, 1966, 65–97; for Boston see
Lorenzo J. Greene, "Prince Hall: Massachusetts Leader in Crisis," *Freedom-
ways* 1 (1961): 238.

15. John B. Sharpless and Ray M. Shortridge, "Biased Underenumeration
in Census Manuscripts: Methodological Implications," *Journal of Urban History* 1 (1974–75): 409–39.

16. Du Bois, *Philadelphia Negro,* 55. Theodore Hershberg also notes this
for a somewhat later period in Philadelphia ("Free Blacks in Antebellum Philadelphia: A Study of Ex-Slaves, Freeborn, and Socioeconomic Decline," *Journal
of Social History,* 5 [1971–72]: 190).

17. For example, in Delaware, Chester, Montgomery, and Bucks counties,
surrounding Philadelphia, there were 794 males and 665 females aged fourteen
to twenty-five and 788 males and 628 females aged twenty-six to forty-four in
1820 (*Census for 1820* [Washington, D.C., 1821], 18–18*).

18. Du Bois, *Philadelphia Negro,* 141–42; Litwack, *North of Slavery,*
153–86. The period after 1820, when Irish immigrants began to flood the
northern cities, marked a tragic new era in the black struggle for an economic
base.

19. Ira Berlin, "Time, Space, and the Evolution of Afro-American Society
on British Mainland North America," *American Historical Review,* 85 (1980):
46–49. Only in Philadelphia are tax lists available for the late colonial period
that indicate the occupations of slaveowners. About half the slaves owned in the
city in 1767 belonged to artisans, mariners, or tavernkeepers, but since some of
these were slave women working as domestic servants and some of the male
slaves owned by artisans were not necessarily trained as craftsmen, it is impossible to know precisely the proportion of male slaves who possessed artisan skills.
My guess, based on information in tax lists and inventories of estate for Boston
and Philadelphia, is about one-quarter. See Gary B. Nash, "Slaves and Slaveowners in Colonial Philadelphia," *William and Mary Quarterly,* 3rd ser., 30
(1973): 249–52, and Merle G. Brouwer, "The Negro as a Slave and as a Free
Black in Colonial Pennsylvania," Ph.D. diss., Wayne State University, 1973,
51–68.

20. Edmund Hogan, *The Prospect of Philadelphia and Check on the Next
Directory . . .* (Philadelphia, 1795). The directory does not include Southwark,
Moyamensing, or the Northern Liberties, where many blacks resided.

21. In the same year the directory was issued, the Pennsylvania Abolition
Society reported that "some of the men follow Mechanick trades and a number
of them are mariners, but the greatest part are employed as Day labourers"
(quoted in Litwack, *North of Slavery,* 154).

22. *Gale's Independent Gazetteer,* Jan. 3, 1797, quoted in John K. Alexander, *Render Them Submissive: Responses to Poverty in Philadelphia, 1760–
1800* (Amherst, Mass., 1980), 78.

23. *The Philadelphia Directory for 1816 . . .* (Philadelphia, 1816).

24. Quoted in Litwack, *North of Slavery,* 154.

25. Du Bois, *Philadelphia Negro,* 142–43. Family income was also supplemented by children's labor. The Pennsylvania Abolition Society survey in 1848 found that 911 children were employed and another 230 were apprentices (*ibid.* 143).

26. No occupational data are available for this period for New York or Boston, but later data that roughly correspond with Philadelphia's indicate that the situation in the three cities did not vary markedly. For a rough occupational breakdown in Boston in 1829, see John Daniels, *In Freedom's Birthplace: A Study of the Boston Negroes* (Boston, 1941), 17–19. For the occupations of New York City's free blacks in 1855, see Freeman, "The Free Negro in New York City," 444–45.

27. Berlin, *Slaves without Masters,* 51–52. On the importance of names in studying consciousness I have been guided by Wilbur Zelinsky, "Cultural Variation in Personal Name Patterns in the Eastern United States," *Annals of the Association of American Geographers,* 60 (1970): 743–69, and Richard Price and Sally Price, "Saramaka Onomastics: An Afro-American Naming System," *Ethnology,* 11 (1972): 342–67. A number of historians of the slave experience have lately ventured into what the Prices call "the art of naming," but their work primarily concerns the plantation South. See, for example, Berlin, *Slaves without Masters,* 51–52; Eugene D. Genovese, *Roll, Jordan, Roll: The World the Slaves Made* (New York, 1974), 443–50; Peter H. Wood, *Black Majority: Negroes in Colonial South Carolina from 1670 through the Stono Rebellion* (New York, 1974), 181–85; and for the most elaborate discussion of naming practices, Herbert G. Gutman, *The Black Family in Slavery and Freedom, 1750–1925* (New York, 1976), 185–256.

28. Daniel Horsmanden, *The New York Slave Conspiracy,* ed. Thomas J. Davis (Boston, 1971), 468–73. Nine of the slaves bore Spanish names and another ten were given what may be called fanciful names—Brash, Braveboy, Fortune, Sterling, Tickle, and Venture, for example. In classifying names I have followed Newbell Niles Puckett's pioneering "Names of American Negro Slaves," in George P. Murdock, ed., *Studies in the Science of Society* (New Haven, Conn., 1937), 471–94.

29. Berlin, "Time, Space, and the Evolution of Afro-American Society," 44–78.

30. Register Books of Christ Church: Marriages, Christenings, and Burials: 1 (Jan. 1, 1719, to Mar. 1750), 2 (Mar. 1750 to Dec. 1762), 3 (1763–1810), Hist. Soc. of Pa.

31. Black surnames in the 1795 directory have been checked against the surnames of slaveowners in the 1772 Provincial Tax Assessment lists, City Arch., City Hall An., Philadelphia.

32. The Dutch surnames of forty slaveowners who freed 105 slaves in New York City between 1800 and 1816 were attached to only 11 of more than 2,000 free black householders in 1830. The Dutch surnames were taken from Harry B. Yoshpe, "Record of Slave Manumissions in New York during the Colonial and Early National Period," *Journal of Negro History,* 26 (1941): 78–104. They have been checked against the surnames of free blacks in 1830 as

listed in Carter G. Woodson, *Free Negro Heads of Families in the United States in 1830* (Washington, D.C., 1925), 91–100.

33. The story of the black Paul Jones is given in the Alms House Census for 1810, Surgical Ward, Records of the Guardians of the Poor, City Arch., City Hall An., Philadelphia. The historic figure that we know as John Paul Jones was actually named John Paul but had taken the name Paul Jones when, in great difficulties, he fled from England to America before the Revolution.

34. It is not clear whether the name Brown was popular because of its color significance. If this was the case, then the fact that Black was seldom chosen requires explanation. Only rarely do the records reveal specific name changes. One case, seemingly typical, was that of Stephen Tancard, a Norfolk, Va., slave who fled his master during the Revolution, was reenslaved in the West Indies, and later jumped ship in Philadelphia, where he assumed the name of Thomas Williams (William Palmer et al., eds., *Calendar of Virginia State Papers*, 11 vols. [Richmond, 1875–93], 4:334–35. I am indebted to Philip J. Schwartz of Virginia Commonwealth University for bringing this case to my attention).

35. The other most common surnames were Williams, Morris, Anderson, Lewis, Butler, Smith, and Davis. The five most common surnames among whites, by contrast, account for only 5 percent of nearly 17,000 family names in the 1816 directory, and the twelve most common surnames add up to only 8 percent of the total. A partial analysis of the names of free black householders in New York and Boston, as given in the 1820 census, indicates the same tendency to assume common English surnames.

36. Among 105 surnames of blacks in the 1795 Philadelphia directory, 22 are the same as those of slaveowners in 1772. But many of these are such common surnames—Brown, Miller, Harris, Johnson, Hill, Moore, Williams, and Green—that the link is probably coincidental. Only two distinctive linkages appear: Hester Vandergrief, a free black woman, was probably the slave of Joseph Vandergrief, and Abraham Ingles was perhaps the slave of John Inglis. Virtually absent among the surnames of blacks were the family names of Philadelphia's upper-class slaveowners in the late colonial period.

37. This evidence of acculturation runs contrary to the undocumented assertions of J. L. Dillard in *Black Names* (The Hague, 1976), 20–25. Dillard argues that both northern and southern patterns in naming were strongly African, but he offers no supporting evidence. His indictment of Elsdon C. Smith, who believes that freedpeople did not use African names as surnames because they "tended to remind them of their former bondage," is unwarranted. Among the several thousand surnames I have examined, I have found African names only rarely: James Coffee (Cuffe?), S. Congo, and Enos Gongo in Philadelphia and Edward Affricane in New York. For Smith's statement see *American Surnames* (Philadelphia, 1969), 275.

38. The following analysis is based on a study of 202 black households in Boston's Ward Six, 243 black households in New York's Ward Six, and 318 black households in Philadelphia's Locust Ward, all listed in the 1820 census. I have used microfilm copies of the manuscript census schedules at the Federal Archives and Records Center, Laguna Niguel, Calif.

39. Nash, "Slaves and Slaveowners," 244, Table 5.

40. This conclusion is based on an examination of the inventories of estate of 573 Boston slaveowners in the Office of the Recorder of Wills, Suffolk County Courthouse, Boston, and the Inventories of 207 Philadelphia slaveowners in the Office of the Recorder of Wills, City Hall An., Philadelphia. There was no significant change in the pattern of slaveholding over time.

41. Calculated from *Heads of Families at the First Census of the United States Taken in the Year 1790: New York* (Washington, D.C., 1908), 116–37. I have excluded Harlem and also the 74 white households which held both slave and free blacks in 1790. Theoretically, a two-parent family could exist only in households with three or more slaves. This was the case in 241 of the 1,050 New York white households where slaves were present in 1790. For a discussion of slave family life in New York City, see Thomas J. Davis, "Slavery in Colonial New York City," Ph.D. diss., Columbia University, 1974, pp. 165–72. For Philadelphia see Merle G. Brouwer, "Marriage and Family Life among Blacks in Colonial Pennsylvania," *Pennsylvania Magazine of History and Biography,* 99 (1975): 368–72.

42. Davis, "Slavery in Colonial New York City," 170–71, Table 7.1.

43. Register Books of Christ Church: Marriages, Christenings, and Burials. Also see Brouwer, "Marriage and Family Life among Blacks," 370–72.

44. William Masters inventory of estate, 1761, Off. of the Rec. of Wills, City Hall An., Philadelphia.

45. For the rapid manumission of slaves in Boston during the Revolutionary era, see Elaine MacEacheren, "Emancipation of Slavery in Massachusetts: A Reexamination, 1770–1790," *Journal of Negro History,* 55 (1970): 289–306. The following analysis is based on data in the 1790 and 1820 censuses. For 1790 I have used *Heads of Families at the First Census of the United States . . .* (Washington, D.C., 1907–8). For 1820 I have used the manuscript census schedules.

46. In Boston black females in white households outnumbered males 142 to 108; in a sample of four wards in Philadelphia, by 555 to 300; and in a sample of two wards in New York, by 502 to 246. The following table shows that in most cases it was single free blacks or small partial families who resided with whites.

Free blacks in white households, 1820

| Number of free blacks in white households | Number of households | | | | | |
| | Boston | | New York | | Philadelphia | |
	Number	Percent	Number	Percent	Number	Percent
1	120	70.6	1,100	55.2	834	63.4
2	35	20.5	508	25.5	317	24.1
3–4	11	6.5	299	15.0	125	9.5
5+	4	2.4	87	4.4	39	3.0
	170	100.0	1,994	100.1	1,315	100.0

47. There were still 518 slaves in Manhattan in 1820 according to the census. Probably most of them were born in the 1790s. In 1817 a second emancipation law was passed, declaring that slaves born before July 4, 1799, would be free on July 4, 1827. This legislation ended slavery in New York. See Freeman, "The Free Negro in New York City," 3–6.

48. These percentages stand in striking contrast to one city of the upper South, Petersburg, Va., where only 43.7 percent of the free black families were double-headed in 1810 and 41.9 percent in 1820 (Suzanne Dee Lebsock, "Women and Economics in Virginia: Petersburg, 1784–1820," Ph.D. diss., University of Virginia, 1977, 22). Theodore Hershberg reports that in the censuses conducted by the Pennsylvania Abolition Society in 1847 and 1856, two-parent households "were characteristic of 78 percent of black families" ("Free Blacks in Antebellum Philadelphia," 190).

49. The census returns do not allow for a distinction between extended and augmented families since exact blood or marital relations between household members are not specified.

50. The child-woman ratio (calculated as the number of male and female children under fourteen years of age divided by the number of women between twenty-six and forty-four years) was 1.1 in Boston, 1.4 in New York, and 1.6 in Philadelphia. Table 3 gives the number of persons in each sex and age category.

51. Calculated from the 1820 census as recapitulated in Everett S. Lee and Michael Lalli, "Population," in David T. Gilchrist, ed., *The Growth of the Seaport Cities, 1790–1825,* (Charlottesville, Va., 1967), 35. Since the white age categories are infant to nine years of age and ten to fifteen, I have combined the number of children up to nine years old with two-thirds of those aged ten to fifteen in order to gain comparability with black children under fourteen. The number of children has been compared to the number of women of twenty-six to forty-four years of age.

52. For black mortality in Philadelphia see *The Present State and Condition of the Free People of Color of the City of Philadelphia* (Philadelphia, 1838), 34–35; for New York see John Duffy, *A History of Public Health in New York City, 1625–1866* (New York, 1968), 260, 580, and 587. Brissot de Warville observed in 1788: "Married Negroes certainly have as many children as whites, but it has been observed that in the cities the death rate of Negro children is higher" (*New Travels in the United States of America, 1788,* ed. Durand Echeverria [Cambridge, Mass., 1964], 232n, quoted in Berlin, "Time, Space, and the Evolution of Afro-American Society," 48n).

53. The ratio of children under sixteen to women sixteen and older in New York City in 1771 was 1.0; in 1820 it was 0.7. For the 1771 data see Greene and Harrington, *American Population,* 102. It is impossible to say how much of this decline is accounted for by different mortality rates among slaves and free blacks, but it seems certain that the mortality rate among blacks must have risen as they moved from upper-class homes in less densely settled areas to crowded lower-class sections of the city after emancipation.

54. "Persistent Myths about the Afro-American Family," in Michael Gor-

don, ed., *The American Family in Social-Historical Perspective*, 2d ed. (New York, 1978), 476.

55. The development of the southern part of the city is detailed in Emma Jones Lapsansky, "South Street Philadelphia, 1762–1854: 'A Haven for Those Low in the World,' " Ph.D. diss., University of Pennsylvania, 1975.

56. The black residential pattern in 1790 has been plotted from the listings of black households in *Heads of Families at the First Census of the United States: Pennsylvania* (Washington, D.C., 1908).

57. Lapsansky, "South Street Philaadelphia," 180–82. For church membership, Du Bois, *Phildelphia Negro*, 199. On the role of the black churches in the creation of neighborhoods where many black families settled, see also Carol V. R. George, *Segregated Sabbaths: Richard Allen and the Rise of Independent Black Churches, 1760–1840* (New York, 1973). In Boston the decision to build the first black church in the west end of town in 1805 hastened the migration of blacks out of the North End (Daniels, *In Freedom's Birthplace*, 22).

58. Between 1790 and 1810 the share of the city's black population living in the northern sector of North and South Mulberry wards and Northern Liberties fell from 25 to 21 percent. During the same period the portion of the black inhabitants living in the southern area of Cedar and Locust wards, Southwark, and Moyamensing (the newest area of black settlement), rose from 29 to 47 percent (calculated from the 1790 and 1810 censuses).

59. Lapsansky, "South Street Philadelphia," 119–40. In Cedar Ward, Locust Ward, and Moyamensing, the areas where black families were most highly concentrated, Afro-Americans represented 27, 24, and 30 percent of the population, respectively, in 1820. For the increasingly class-divided social geography of New York City in this period, see Betsy Blackmar, "Rewalking the 'Walking City': Property Relations in New York City, 1780–1840," *Radical History Review*, 21 (1980): 131–48.

60. The descriptions of housing, taken from contemporary newspaper accounts, are quoted in Alexander, *Render Them Submissive*, 21–22.

61. In many of the more affluent wards of the city, blacks lived primarily in white households. For example, Chestnut, Walnut, and Dock wards contained 514 free blacks in 1820 (5 percent of the city's black population). But only 62 of them, gathered in thirteen families, resided in black households. The large number of free blacks living in white households in wards where there were few independent black households disguises the growing segregation of black and white residences in the city. The same is true for New York and Boston in this period. For a study of growing residential segregation in Philadelphia between 1811 and 1858, see Norman J. Johnston, "The Caste and Class of the Urban Form of Historic Philadelphia," *Journal of the American Institute of Planners*, 32 (1966): 334–49.

62. Lapsansky, "South Street Philadelphia," 141–48, for the rapid deterioration of the recently built lower-class neighborhoods of the "Cedar Street Corridor." For the black families on Gaskill Street in 1811, ibid., 131–32.

63. Du Bois, *Philadelphia Negro*, 201.

64. "The Causes and Motives for Establishing St. Thomas's African Church of Philadelphia," in William Douglass, *Annals of the First African Church in the United States of America* . . . (Philadelphia, 1862), 93–95.

65. Freeman, "Free Negro in New York City," p. 375; Daniels, *In Freedom's Birthplace*, 226; George A. Levesque, "Inherent Reformers—Inherited Orthodoxy: Black Baptists in Boston, 1800–1873," *Journal of Negro History*, 61 (1975): 491–525.

66. George, *Segregated Sabbaths*, 49; Freeman, "Free Negro in New York City," 410.

67. Philadelphia's black organizations and their founding dates are listed in *The Present State and Condition of the Free People of Color of the City of Philadelphia*, 26–27.

68. Nancy Slocum Hornick, "Anthony Benezet and the Africans' School: Toward a Theory of Full Equality," *Pennsylvania Magazine of History and Biography*, 99 (1975): 399–421. The insurance company is noted in J. Thomas Scharf and Thompson Westcott, *History of Philadelphia, 1609–1884*, 3 vols. (Philadelphia, 1884), 3:2117.

69. For free black institutions and their names in New York, see *The Negro in New York: An Informed Social History, 1626–1940*, ed. Roi Ottley and William J. Weatherby (New York, 1967) and Freeman, "Free Negro in New York City," chaps. 9–11. For Boston see Donald M. Jacobs. "A History of the Boston Negro from the Revolution to the Civil War," Ph.D. diss., Boston University, 1968, chaps. 2–3, and George A. Levesque, "Before Integration: The Forgotten Years of Jim Crow Education in Boston," *Journal of Negro Education*, 48 (1979): 113–25.

70. For the black churches in New York and their difficulties, see Freeman, "Free Negro in New York City," pp. 375–405. Even by 1855 New York's black churches had fewer than 2,000 members (ibid., 422). For the Philadelphia church membership figures see Du Bois, *Philadelphia Negro*, 199.

71. On black schools in Philadelphia, see *The Present State and Condition of the Free People of Color*, 39. Philadelphia's black schools were private since blacks were excluded from tax-supported public schools until 1822, contrary to the school laws first passed in 1802. See Harry C. Silcox, "Delay and Neglect: Negro Public Education in Ante-bellum Philadelphia, 1800–1860," *Pennsylvania Magazine of History and Biography*, 97 (1973): 444–64. For black institutions in New York see Daniel Perlman, "Organizations of the Free Negro in New York City, 1800–1861," *Journal of Negro History*, 56 (1971): 181–97. Perlman concludes that fifty Negro organizations were formed between 1800 and 1850. In 1838 in Philadelphia there were eighty mutual aid societies, with 7,448 members, according to a survey by the Pennsylvania Abolition Society (*Present State and Condition of the Free People of Color*, 39).

72. Lapsansky, "South Street Philadelphia," 205–9. On black consciousness, see George A. Levesque, "Interpreting Early Black Ideology: A Reappraisal of Historical Consensus," *Journal of the Early Republic*, 1 (1981): 269–87.

73. Quoted in Litwack, *North of Slavery*, 39.

74. Ibid. It is one of the ironies of this period that southern defenders of slavery, advocates of recolonization, and northern white friends of free blacks, such as the Quakers, tended to describe, each for their own purposes, the plight of urban Afro-Americans in much the same way.

12

"TO ARISE OUT OF THE DUST":
Absalom Jones and the African Church
of Philadelphia, 1785–95

I N AN OPEN FIELD outside of Philadelphia on a sultry afternoon in August 1793, about one hundred white construction tradesmen and two of Philadelphia's most important citizens sat down at long tables "under the shade of several large trees" and consumed a bounteous dinner complete with excellent liqueurs and melons for dessert. They were served by a company of Philadelphia's free blacks. Then the white Philadelphians arose, about fifty blacks took their places, and were waited on at a second sitting of the banquet by "six of the most respectable of the white company." The occasion for this unusual display of racial reciprocity was the raising of the roof for the African Church of Philadelphia, the first free black church in the northern United States. Benjamin Rush, Philadelphia's ebullient doctor, reformer, social activist, and general busybody, toasted "Peace on earth and good will to men" and "May African churches everywhere soon succeed to African bondage." Describing to his wife the outpouring of emotion on that hot afternoon, he wrote: "Never did I witness such a scene of innocent—nay more—such virtuous and philanthropic joy. Billy Grey in attempting to express his feelings to us was checked by a flood of tears." After dinner all the blacks converged on John Nicholson and clasped the hand of the city's entrepreneur par excellence, who had loaned $2,000 for the building of the church. One old man "addressed him in the following striking language: 'May you live long sir, and when you die, may you not die eternally.' " Rush rhapsodized, "To me it will be a day to be remembered with pleasure as long as I live."[1]

Another year would pass before the African Church of Philadelphia opened its doors for religious services; but the interracial banquet in August 1793 already foreshadowed two interlocking developments that marked the entire course of black history in the early national period: first, the efforts of former slaves to construct a foundation for freedom and a community-based fortress from which to fight white hostility and oppression through the establishment of independent black churches; and second, their difficult relations with the benevolent portion of the white community whose patronage was essential to the building of black institutions in this era but whose ingrained racial attitudes and desire to maintain social control often led to misperceptions, withdrawal of support, and sometimes opposition.

To understand the birth of the African Church of Philadelphia we must recreate the situation in which the city's free blacks found themselves in the 1780s. On the eve of the Revolution the city's slave population had been declining rapidly as a result of high mortality and low fertility rates, combined with the virtual cessation of slave importations.[2] War further diminished the black population as many slaves fled with the British when they evacuated the city in the summer of 1778, and many others were sold by their hard-pressed masters, died in the patriot military forces, or simply ran away. By the close of the war only about 900 black Philadelphians remained among the 1,500 or so who had resided in the city in 1767.[3]

Yet a wartime wave of abolitionist sentiment produced thousands of manumissions that reversed this demographic trend. From Philadelphia's hinterland to the west, from Delaware, Maryland, and Virginia to the south, and from New York, New Jersey, and New England to the north and east came a steady flow of dark-skinned former bondsmen and bondswomen, seeking work and the fellowship of other blacks in the premier port city of the North. By 1790 more than 2,100 of them, all but 273 free, lived in the city and its environs. By 1800 their number had swelled to about 6,500, of whom only 55 remained in bondage.[4]

These gathering black Philadelphians, like former slaves in other parts of the country, had to rethink their relationship to American society in the early years of the Republic. Were they Africans in America who might now return to their homelands? Were they Afro-Americans whose cultural heritage was African but whose future was bound up in creating a separate existence on soil where they had toiled most of their lives? Or were they simply Americans with dark skin, who in seeking places as free men and women had to assimilate as quickly as possible into the cultural norms and social institutions of white society? Working out this problem of identity—and choosing strategies for fulfilling the goals they had set— required close attention to the particular locale in which freedmen and freedwomen found themselves or contrived to reach, for the social climate was far from uniform in postrevolutionary America.

Outwardly, Philadelphia beckoned manumitted blacks as a haven from persecution and an arena of opportunity. The center of American Quakerism, it had launched the first abolition society in the country and was the location of the state government that in 1780, in the midst of war, had passed the first abolition act in the new nation. Philadelphia was also a bustling maritime center that promised employment for migrating Afro-Americans, who rarely possessed the capital to become independent farmers and therefore took to the roads leading to the coastal towns in the postwar years. Its drawing power owed something as well to the considerable sympathy among some whites for freed blacks setting out on the road to freedom. Benjamin Rush wrote his English friend and fellow abolitionist Granville Sharp in 1783 that "advocates for the poor Africans" were regarded in the city as fanatics and disturbers of the peace before the war, but "at present they are considered as the benefactors of mankind and the man who dares say a word in favor of reducing our black brethren to slavery is listened to with horror, and his company avoided by every body."[5]

In its internal workings, however, Philadelphia fell far short of the ideal suggested by Rush. The illiterate and often unskilled black men and women who trekked there after the Revolution had to compete for jobs with Irish and German immigrants and did not always find work. Although not disfranchised by law, free blacks were prohibited by white social pressure from voting. Moreover, virtually every institution and social mechanism in the city—religious and secular, economic and social—engaged in discriminatory practices, which flowed like water from the pervasive belief in black inferiority. Against the assumption that blacks were either innately handicapped or had been irreparably degraded by the experience of slavery stood only a minority of white Philadelphians who believed that recently freed slaves could overcome the marks of birth and oppression. Even the Pennsylvania Abolition Society, composed of those in the city most concerned with the future of free blacks, publicized their doubts in a broadside *Address to the Public* in 1789:

> The unhappy man who has long been treated as a brute Animal too frequently sinks beneath the common standard of the human species; the galling chains that bind his body, do also fetter his intellectual faculties, and impair the social affections of his heart; accustomed to move like a meer Machine by the will of a master, Reflection is suspended; he has not the power of Choice, and Reason and Conscious have but little influence over his conduct, because he is chiefly governed by his passion of Fear. He is poor & friendless, perhaps worn out by extreme Labour Age and Disease. Under such circumstances Freedom may often prove a misfortune to himself and prejudicial to Society.[6]

For black wayfarers who found their way to Philadelphia after the Revolution, overcoming patterns of behavior peculiar to slavery became a crucial matter. By its nature slavery assumed the superiority of the master class, and even the most benevolent master occupied a power relationship vis-à-vis his slaves that daily reminded them of their lowly condition. Perhaps few American slaves believed they were inferior human beings, but slavery required them to act so. "Governed by fear," as the Abolition Society put it, they carried into freedom an acute understanding of the tactics of survival, which included an almost instinctive wariness. Moreover, they now had to face the dominant culture, which was far from ready to treat them as equals and continued to demand complaisant comportment from them. We can infer from the fact that almost all the early black institutions in the North described themselves as "African" rather than "Negro" or "colored"—the Free African Society, the African School, the African Church of Philadelphia—that these former slaves identified positively with their ancestral homelands and did not subscribe to the common white characterizations of Africa as a dismal, cultureless environment. But white racism impinged on their lives at every turn, and although not of the virulent form it would assume early in the nineteenth century, it led many blacks to adopt a diffident posture.

Regarding white attitudes as impermeable and recognizing the psychic scars inflicted by slavery, a few former slaves in the North refused to live in American society and returned to Africa. But the small colonization movement of the 1780s that was centered in New England made only a slight impact on black Philadelphians. They overwhelmingly cast their lot with America.[7] Nonetheless, the will to plan rationally, to strive for an independent and dignified existence, to confront racial prejudice, and to work for the future of their children depended upon throwing off the incubus of slavery, an institution that had perpetuated itself by exacting a terrible price for attempts at independent or self-reliant black behavior.

Free blacks also had to confront the contradictory effects of benevolence on their lives. On the one hand, humane Philadelphians, Quakers foremost among them, succored slaves and freedmen and helped them cope with their vulnerability in a racially divided society. On the other hand, benevolence perpetuated feelings of powerlessness and functioned to maintain white social control.

The positive side of benevolence is seen vividly in the work of Anthony Benezet, the wizened, saintly little Huguenot immigrant who dedicated so much of his life to the Negro's cause. "A one-man abolition society," as one historian has called him, Benezet wrote a dozen pamphlets against slavery and the slave trade between 1759 and 1784, founded a school for blacks in 1770, tirelessly devoted himself to it for the rest of his life, and in 1779 personally lobbied with every member of the Pennsylvania legislature to pass the gradual abolition act.[8] When Benezet died in 1784, slaves and free blacks alike turned out en masse to follow his funeral procession to the graveyard, testifying to his work on their behalf.[9]

Benezet's greatest contribution to black Philadelphians lay in his frontal challenge to the deeply rooted doctrine of black inferiority. He urged his pupils to regard themselves as "citizens of the world" and argued doggedly, as early as 1762, that the African environment had produced notable cultures and must not be considered as a place of jungle barbarism. He taught his black students that it was the environment of slavery, not innate condition, that turned Africans in America into degraded and disheartened human beings. In his black school Benezet became convinced that blacks were equal in human potential to whites. "A. Benezet," he wrote of himself, "teacher of a school established by private subscription, in Philadelphia, for many years, had opportunity of knowing the temper and genius of the Africans; particularly of those under his tuition, who have been of many different ages; and he can with Truth and sincerity declare, he has found amongst them as great variety of Talents, equally capable of improvement, as amongst a like number of Whites."[10]

The negative side of benevolence can be seen in the attitudes of many of Benezet's fellow Quakers. The Society of Friends led the way in opposing the slave trade and in manumitting slaves, and they played a major role in establishing the Pennsylvania Abolition Society in 1775, which had to suspend operations during the war. In 1784 Quakers, along with others, revived the organization, and the Philadelphia Monthly Meeting began visiting black families, quietly urging them to a life of industry and morality, and helping those in distress.[11] By the late 1780s the reorganized Pennsylvania Abolition Society was devoting itself primarily to facilitating the private manumission of slaves and exercising stewardship over those who were free—educating them, watching over them, and inculcating in them middle-class values of sobriety, work, morality, and religious faith.

Yet such services were received among blacks at a cost. "There can be no greater disparity of power," writes David Brion Davis, "than that between a man convinced of his own disinterested service and another man who is defined as a helpless object."[12] Even more to the point, Quaker humanitarianism, as Sydney James points out, was never of the sort that was based on a deep sense of the "likeness among all persons." Unlike the spartan-living, humble Benezet, most Quakers held themselves apart from other people, white and black. The Society of Friends, in fact, was the only religious group in Philadelphia that refused to accept blacks as members in the 1780s. Theirs was more a "doctrine of stewardship" than a true humanitarianism, and their efforts on behalf of blacks "partook more of condescension than humanitarianism."[13] Thus Quaker benevolence sometimes perpetuated black dependence, stood in the way of mutual respect between blacks and whites, and hampered autonomous behavior among those emerging from slavery.

Only a few years out of bondage in the 1780s, Philadelphia's free blacks lived in a highly fluid situation, full of possibilities yet also full of difficulties. Included within their gathering ranks were two men who would exert an extraordinary influence on the shaping of Philadelphia's black community, especially in the creation of black churches as the vital center of Afro-American life. In their backgrounds Absalom Jones and Richard Allen shared much. Both were born into slavery, Jones in 1746 and Allen in 1760. Both experienced bondage in its rural and urban forms, having been raised partly in Philadelphia and partly in southern Delaware. Both lived under humane white masters and both prevailed upon their owners to allow them to learn to read and write. Both were touched by religion in their formative years, Allen by Methodism and Jones by Anglicanism. Finally, both persuaded their masters to reward faithful service by allowing them to purchase their freedom in the early 1780s.[14]

When their paths crossed in Philadelphia for the first time, probably in 1786, Allen was Jones's junior in years but much his senior in religious intensity and commitment to the cause of black freedom and equality. In about 1778, bearing only the slave name Richard, Allen had been converted to Methodism by itinerate exhorters in Kent County, Delaware. No small part of his awakening may be related to the abolitionist stance of those he heard. For his freedom, in fact, he might have thanked Freeborn Garretson, the silver-tongued circuit rider who had convinced Allen's master that slaveholders at judgment day were "weighed in the balance and were found wanting." Shortly thereafter, just before his twentieth birthday, Allen's master, Stokey Sturgis, proposed that Richard and his older brother buy their freedom. Taking a surname to signify his status as a free man, Allen spent the next six years interspersing work as a sawyer and wagon driver with months of riding the Methodist circuits from South Carolina to New York and even into the western Indian country. Traveling with some of the leading early Methodist sojourners, he learned to preach with great effect to black and white audiences alike. By the time he arrived, full of zeal, in the Philadelphia area, probably in February 1786, Allen seems to have completed the crucial psychological middle passage by which those who gained freedom in a legal sense procured as well the emotional autonomy that meant they had overcome their dependence upon whites.[15]

No such blinding religious light had filled the mind of Absalom Jones. Born into a prominent merchant-planter family in Sussex County, Delaware, and named simply Absalom, he was taken from the fields into his master's house when he was very young.[16] Removed from the debilitating world of field labor, he gained an opportunity for learning. Absalom later wrote that with pennies given to him from time to time, "I soon bought myself a primer and begged to be taught by any body that I found able and willing to give me the least instruction." Literacy could only have increased the distance between him and those of his age who did not live in the master's house, and hence Absalom became introspective, or "singular," as he termed it. Then in 1762, his master, Benjamin Wynkoop, sold Absalom's mother and six siblings, left his Delaware plantation, and moved to Philadelphia, bringing the sixteen-year-old slave boy with him. The breaking up of his family, though doubtless traumatic, proved to be a turning point in Absalom's life. While bereft of his kin, he had landed in the center of the nascent abolitionist movement in America and in the city where more than anywhere else in prerevolutionary America humanitarian reformers had created an atmosphere conducive to education and family formation among slaves. Thus, while he had to work in his master's shop from dawn to dark, Jones soon prevailed upon Wynkoop to allow him to attend a night school for blacks, probably the one launched in 1758 by the Anglican clergyman William Sturgeon.[17]

In 1770 Absalom married the slave of his master's neighbor, taking vows in St. Peter's Church where the Wynkoop family worshiped. Soon after this, encouraged by the abolitionist sentiment that Quakers and others had spread throughout Philadelphia, he put the tool of literacy to work. After drawing up an appeal for his wife's release, he carried it, with his wife's father at his side, to "some of the principal Friends of this city," asking for their support. "From some we borrowed, and from others we received donations," he later recounted. Thereafter, as war came to Philadelphia, Absalom "made it my business to work until twelve or one o'clock at night, to assist my wife in obtaining a livelihood, and to pay the money that was borrowed to purchase her freedom."[18] It took years to repay the debt. But by 1778 Absalom had apparently discharged his obligations because he was then pleading with his master to allow him to purchase his own freedom. Wynkoop would not consent until October 1, 1784, six years after the first of what Absalom remembered as a series of humble requests and five years after the slave had purchased a house and lot in the city.[19]

It was probably in 1784, upon gaining his release, that Absalom authenticated his freedom to the world by taking the surname Jones. It was a common English cognomen, yet one that *he* had chosen and one that could not be mistaken for the Dutch name of his master, whom he had served until the age of thirty-eight. But he acted as if he bore his master no grudges. Forbearing, even-tempered, and utterly responsible, he continued to work in Wynkoop's store. More than thirty years later, in an obituary for Jones, it was said that his master, Wynkoop, "always gave him the character of having been a faithful and exemplary servant, remarkable for many good qualities; especially for his being not only of a peaceable demeanour, but for being possessed of the talent of inducing a disposition to it in others."[20]

When Allen and Jones met in Philadelphia is not precisely known, but the context of their meeting is clear. Early in 1786 the Methodist elder in the city sent for Allen to preach to the city's growing population of blacks and offered him St. George's Church in which to hold meetings—at 5:00 A.M. in the morning. "Several souls were awakened," Allen remembered years later in relating his life story to his son, "and were earnestly seeking redemption in the blood of Christ." Impressed by the large number of free blacks drifting into the city, and aware that "few of them attended public worship," Allen began supplementing his pre-dawn services at St. George's with daytime meetings on the commons in adjacent Southwark and the Northern Liberties. Soon he had "raised a Society . . . of forty-two members."[21] Among them was Absalom Jones, who had abandoned Anglican services at St. Peter's Church, where his former master still worshiped, in favor of St. George's. Like taking a surname, this was a step in forging a new identity.

Within months of Allen's arrival in Philadelphia, Absalom Jones and two other recently freed slaves, William White and Darius Jennings, had joined the Methodist preacher to discuss forming a separate black religious society. Religion and literacy had helped all these men achieve freedom, so it was natural that, when they looked around them to find the majority of former slaves illiterate and unchurched, they "often communed together upon this painful and important subject in order to form some kind of religious society." Shortly thereafter Allen proposed this "to the most respectable people of color in this city," only to be "met with opposition." Leading white Methodists who heard of the plan objected even more strenuously, using, Allen wrote, "very degrading and insulting language to try to prevent us from going on."[22] Nonetheless, after these deliberations Jones and Allen decided to organize the Free African Society. Founded in April 1787, it was the first black organization of its kind in America.

Organized in the manner of white benevolent societies, which had originated in craft or ethnic consciousness, the Free African Society has often been seen simply as a black mutual aid organization. In his classic study, *The Philadelphia Negro*, W. E. B. Du Bois described it more generously, calling it "the first wavering step of a people toward an organized social life."[23] But even this is too limited. Although mutual aid was its purported goal, the Society was quasi-religious in character; beyond that it was an organization where the people emerging from the house of bondage could gather strength, develop their own leaders, and explore independently strategies for hammering out a postslavery existence that went beyond formal legal release from thralldom.

Initially an organization in which free blacks took the first halting steps toward developing their own leaders and solving their own problems, the Free African Society soon began assuming a supervisory role over the moral life of the black community: it worked to forge a visionary black consciousness out of the disparate human material finding its way to Philadelphia. In September 1787, a visiting committee on which Absalom Jones would serve many times began inspecting the conduct of members through house visits, thus assuming moral stewardship in the community. In May 1790, the Society attempted to lease the Stranger's Burial Ground in order to turn it into a black cemetery under their control. In the next month the Society established "a regular mode of procedure with respect to . . . marriages" and began keeping a book of marriage records. Having assumed quasi-ecclesiastic functions, the Society took the final step in September 1790 when a special committee recommended the initiation of formal religious services, which began on January 1, 1791.[24]

Many of the Society's enlarged functions bore a decided Quakerly stamp, reflecting the influence of Friends on many of the leading members and the Quakers' early involvement with the African Society. In fact, the Society's constitution, written when the aura of the selfless Anthony Benezet still prevailed, specified that "it is always understood that one of the people called Quakers . . . is to be chosen to act as Clerk and Treasurer of this useful institution." In May 1788, when the Society had become too large to meet at Richard Allen's house, it rented a room in the house of Sarah Dougherty, one of Benezet's former students and a teacher at his African School. By January 1789, the Society was meeting at the Quaker African School House in Willings Alley, and it was here that they first convened religious services in 1791.[25]

Richard Allen viewed the Quakerly drift of the African Society with concern. He made no objections when the black organization adopted Quaker-like visiting committees in late 1787, or when they instituted the disownment practices of the Friends the next year. But when the Society in 1789 adopted the Quaker practice of beginning meetings with fifteen minutes of silence, Allen led the withdrawal of "a large number" of dissenters whose adherence to Methodism had accustomed them to "an unconstrained outburst of the[ir] feelings in religious worship."[26] Allen came no more to meetings of the African Society but privately began convening some of its members in an attempt to stop the drift of the organization toward the practices of a religious group whose "detachment and introspection were not without value, but . . . did not seem to speak to the immediate needs of black people as Allen saw them."[27]

The adherence of many free blacks to Methodism is not hard to understand. As the first black historian of the African Church of Philadelphia wrote in 1862, the new Methodist preachers "made no pretensions to literary qualifications, and being despised and persecuted as religious enthusiasts, their sympathies naturally turned towards the lowly, who, like themselves, were of small estimate in the sight of worldy greatness."[28] Moreover, Methodism was far more experiential than other denominations, advocating lay preachers and lay societies, simplifying the liturgy of the Book of Common Prayer, and holding meetings in fields and forests or, in the city, in sail lofts and homes. Also commending Methodism to former slaves were the well-known antislavery views of its founder, John Wesley, and the Methodist discipline and polity worked out in 1784, which attacked slavetrading and slaveholding and barred persons engaged in these practices from holding church offices, as did no other religious group except the Society of Friends.[29]

Perhaps most important, in Philadelphia the passionate preaching of Richard Allen had drawn many blacks to Methodism. Jones and others tried repeatedly to bring Allen back into the bosom of the Free African Society, but when he proved unyielding in his criticisms of their Quakerly innovations, they followed the Friends' procedure of censuring him "for attempting to sow division among us." When this had no effect, they reluctantly declared in August 1789 that "he has disunited himself from membership with us."[30]

Now the mantle of leadership of the Free African Society fell to Absalom Jones. It was the mild-mannered but persistent Jones who made the crucial connections in the white community that launched plans for building a black church. The ties with the Society of Friends were wearing thin by the summer of 1791 because many Quakers objected to the Sunday psalm singing by blacks in the Quaker schoolhouse.[31] But Jones, perhaps understanding the limits of the Quaker connection, had been forging new patronage lines to one of Philadelphia's most influential citizens—the widely connected, opinionated Benjamin Rush. Over the next four years it was Rush who became the Anthony Benezet of the 1790s so far as Philadelphia's free blacks were concerned.

As a young physician before the Revolution, Rush had written a passionate antislavery pamphlet at the urging of Anthony Benezet. But his ardor for the cause cooled during the war. He did not free his own slave and played no active role in the revival of the Pennsylvania Abolition Society in 1784. Then, in a poignant example of transatlantic abolitionist influence, Rush threw himself into the fray in 1787 after reading Thomas Clarkson's recently published *Essay on the Slavery and Commerce of the Human Species,* which in turn had been inspired by Anthony Benezet's *Historical Account of Guinea,* which had convinced Clarkson to devote his life to abolitionism.[32] So thoroughly was Rush converted to the free blacks' cause that he became one of the Abolition Society's most active members, freed his slave, William Gruber, and shortly thereafter wrote Jeremy Belknap, Congregational minister of Boston's Federal Street Church and friend of free blacks in that city, that "I love even the name of Africa, and never see a Negro slave or freeman without emotions which I seldom feel in the same degree towards my unfortunate fellow creatures of a fairer complexion."[33]

By 1791, three years after Rush penned these lines, Jones and a small group of emerging black activists had fixed their sights on building a community, or "union," black church. It was to be formed, Rush wrote Granville Sharp, from "the scattered and unconnected [black] appendages of most of the religious societies in the city" and from an even larger number of blacks "ignorant and unknown to any religious society."[34] Lacking denominational affiliation, it would not be tied to creeds or ordinances governing most white churches. Its goal was black unity in Christian fellowship, and beyond that a concern for the general welfare of the city's blacks. Jones and his group, in fact, proposed to build a black school first and then a church, though the two enterprises were hardly separable in their minds.[35] Their formula was to become the classic one for the black church as it would emerge in the United States, "a pattern of religious commitment that has a double focus—the free and autonomous worship of God in the way Black people want to worship him, and the unity and social welfare of the Black community."[36]

The plan for a union church flowed naturally from the religious services that the Free African Society had been holding. Rush described how "two or three of their own colour conduct the worship, by reading the Scriptures, praying, singing, and occasionally exhorting." The minutes of the Free African Society reveal that "the religious meeting had been ecumenically defined so that approved ministers of all denominations could be invited to conduct services.[37] One who led services frequently—with results that could not have been predicted at the time— was Joseph Pilmore, an English follower of Wesley who had served the newly formed Methodist congregation in Philadelphia before the Revolution. After a ten-year absence in England from 1774 to 1784, Pilmore returned to Philadelphia and was ordained in the American Protestant Episcopal church. When the Free African Society began holding religious services in 1790, Pilmore was serving as assistant rector at St. Paul's Episcopal Church and had recently married the niece of Anthony Benezet, the revered benefactor of Philadelphia's black community. Pilmore's personal warmth and his indifference to color brought thirty-one black couples to St. Paul's for marriage between 1789 and 1794.[38]

Aided by Rush, Jones and his cohorts drew up a plan for the separate black church. Attempting to cast their appeal broadly, they adopted articles of association and a plan of church government "so general as to embrace all, and yet so orthodox in cardinal points as to offend none."[39] The church was to be named the African Church of Philadelphia, and it was under this title, devoid of denominational reference, that the work of raising subscriptions went forward for the next three years. Jones and his group somehow drew Richard Allen back into the fold, and eight leaders were selected to act as the "representatives" of the African Church. In a ringing broadside appeal for support, they argued that a black church would gather hundreds of those who worshiped in none of the white churches of the city because "men were more influenced [by] their moral equals than by their superiors . . . and . . . are more easily governed by persons chosen by themselves for that purpose, than by persons who are placed over them by accidental circumstances."[40]

This democratic argument was accompanied by another that indicated the ideology of racial separation that was being hammered out. "Africans and their descendants" needed their own church, they advised, because of the "attraction and relationship" among those bound together by "a nearly equal and general deficiency of education, by total ignorance, or only humble attainments in religion," and by the color line drawn by custom. All of this argued for the "necessity and propriety of separate and exclusive means, and opportunities of worshiping God, of instructing their youth, and of taking care of their poor."[41] Such a decisive step toward black self-assertiveness signified the pivotal role in the life of emancipated slaves that the black church would assume in an era when the centrality to community life of the white churches, disestablished and fragmented by the Revolution, was diminishing. Black religion, writes Gayraud S. Wilmore, was "never so much a matter of social custom and convention as it has been for white people. It was a necessity." Even at the beginning it was seen that the black church would be "the one impregnable corner of the world where consolation, solidarity and mutual aid could be found and from which the master and the bossman—at least in the North—could be effectively barred."[42]

The first black historian of this enterprise, writing in the 1860s on the basis of oral interviews "with many of the old memebers [of the African Church]—all now gone to their final account," described just this creative striving for dignity and self-generated power. It was, wrote William Douglass, an "age of general and searching inquiry into the equity of old and established customs," a time when "a moral earthquake had awakened the slumber of ages" and caused "these humble men, just emerged from the house of bondage . . . to rise above those servile feelings which all their antecedents were calculated to cherish and to assume, as they did, an attitude of becoming men conscious of invaded rights. . . . "[43]

Having enunciated the concept of a racially separate, nondenominational and socially oriented church, Jones and the seven other trustees began the mundane work of financing its construction. Rush's suggestions for circulating a broadside appeal with subscription papers—a tried and true method of raising money in Philadelphia—had been received by the black leaders, he wrote, "with a joy which transported one of them to take me by the hand as a brother."[44] Rush now enlisted the aid of Robert Ralston, a Presbyterian merchant, who agreed to act as treasurer of the group. The work of circulating the subscription papers began in the fall of 1791. Rush tried to stay in the background, convinced that "the work will prosper the better for my keeping myself out of sight."[45] But he was hardly capable of self-effacement, and word of his role in the plans soon circulated through the city. William White, rector of Christ Church and recently appointed bishop of the Episcopal church in Pennsylvania, accosted Rush in the streets and "expressed his disapprobation to the proposed African church" because "it originated in pride." Leading Quakers also conveyed their displeasure to Absalom Jones, and the Methodists threatened to disown any black Methodist who participated in the undertaking.[46] Paternalistic Philadelphians discovered that helping their black brothers proved more satisfactory than seeing them help themselves.

Such disapprobation from Anglicans (Episcopalians), Quakers, and Methodists, some of whom had been active in the Abolition Society, drove home the lesson that even whites who claimed to befriend free blacks were unwilling to see them move beyond white control. An early historian of black Methodism, reflecting in 1867 on the final separation of Richard Allen from the white Methodist church, dwelt on precisely this point. "The giant crime committed by the Founders of the African Methodist Episcopal Church," wrote Benjamin Tanner, "was that they dared to organize a Church of men, men to think for themselves, men to talk for themselves, men to act for themselves: A Church of men who support from their own substance, however scanty, the ministration of the Word which they receive; men who spurn to have their churches built for them, and their pastors supported from the coffers of some charitable organization; men who prefer to live by the sweat of their own brow and be free."[47]

The opposition of white leaders partially undermined the appeal for building funds. Some modest contributions were garnered, including donations from George Washington and Thomas Jefferson, and Rush's appeals to Granville Sharp to raise money in England brought in a small amount. Rush himself contributed £25.[48] But after six months, with money only trickling in, Jones and Allen decided to take to the streets themselves. Believing "that if we put our trust in the Lord, he would stand by us," Allen recounted, "we went out with our subscription paper and met with great success," collecting $360 on the first day.[49]

Thereafter the going got harder and much of the early optimism began to fade. The initial subscriptions proved sufficient, however, to buy two adjacent lots on Fifth Street, only a block from the statehouse, for $450. But most blacks had only small amounts to contribute from their meager resources, and most whites seem to have snapped their pocketbooks shut at the thought of an autonomous black church. White church leaders, who had initially responded to the idea of a separate black church as a piece of arrogance on the part of a people so recently released from slavery, now began calculating the effect on their own churches. "The old and established [religious] societies," Rush confided to a friend, "look shy at them, each having lost some of its members by the new association." Still, Rush did not waver in his conviction that "the poor blacks will succeed in forming themselves into a distinct independent church."[50]

Whatever their difficulties, the resolve of black Philadelphians to form a separate church was mightily strengthened in the fall of 1792 in one of the most dramatic confrontations in early American church history. A number of black leaders were still attending services at St. George's Methodist Church, where the congregation had outgrown the seating capacity. When the elders decided to expand their house of worship, black Philadelphians contributed money and labor to the effort. Then, on the first Sunday after the renovations were completed, the elders informed the black worshipers who filed into the service that they must sit in a segregated section of the newly built gallery. Allen later recounted:

> We expected to take the seats over the ones we formerly occupied below, not knowing any better. We took those seats; meeting had begun, and they were nearly done singing, and just as we got to the seats, the Elder said, "Let us pray." We had not been long upon our knees before I heard considerable scuffling and loud talking. I raised my head up and saw one of

the trustees, H——M——, having hold of the Rev. Absalom
Jones, pulling him off his knees, and saying, "You must get up,
you must not kneel here." Mr. Jones replied, "Wait until the
prayer is over, and I will get up, and trouble you no more."
With that he beckoned to one of the trustees, Mr. L—— S——,
to come to his assistance. He came and went to William White
to pull him up. By this time prayer was over, and we all went
out of the church in a body, and they were no more plagued by
us in the church.[51]

Many historians, assuming that the incident at St. George's took
place in 1787, even before the Free African Society was formed, have
seen the discriminatory and insulting treatment by the elders of St.
George's as the force that drove Jones and Allen away from an assimila-
tionist position and toward the creation of a separate black church. The
black church, it is argued, had its origins in the racial segregation imposed by whites. But recent research has shown that the confrontation
at St. George's took place in late 1792, more than five years after the
Free African Society was established, several years after separate black
religious services were being held, and many months after Absalom
Jones and others had launched the subscription campaign for a black
church.[52] The St. George's incident did confirm, however, what many
blacks must have suspected—that there would be no truly biracial
Christian community in the white churches of the city. Allen recalled
that after the incident the black leaders renewed their determination "to
worship God under our own vine and fig tree" and "were filled with
fresh vigor to get a house erected to worship God in."[53]

By late 1792, with money coming in very slowly for construction
of the African Church, the black leaders faced the prospect that they
could not raise sufficient funds to build a church on the lots they had
purchased. To their rescue came the unlikeliest of figures—the Welsh
immigrant John Nicholson, who had blazed meteorically onto the
Philadelphia scene after the war as state comptroller and high-flying
speculator in western lands and revolutionary loan certificates. Not
wholly accepted in polite Philadelphia circles, and uninvolved in the
work of the Abolition Society, Nicholson provided what none of the
established Philadelphia elite would offer—a large loan to begin construction. "Humanity, charity, and patriotism never united their claims
in a petition with more force than in the present instance," Rush
wrote to Nicholson in a letter hand carried by William Gray and
Absalom Jones. "You *will* not—you *cannot*" refuse their request "for
the sake of Religion & Christianity and as this is the first Institution
of the kind. . . . "[54]

It took two months more to execute the mortgage and another

month to draw up building contracts.[55] Finally, in March 1793, with reports of continued black rebellion in the French West Indies filtering into Philadelphia, the city's free blacks and some of their white benefactors gathered to see earth turned for the church. A quarter of a century later, Allen remembered the day vividly: "As I was the first proposer of the African Church, I put the first spade into the ground to dig the cellar for the same. This was the first African church or meeting house to be erected in the United States of America."[56]

Before the two-story brick building on Fifth Street could be completed, its humble founders had to endure additional difficulties. Like most visionaries, Jones and his cohorts had planned expansively, designing a church capacious enough to seat 800. The cost estimates for the building ran to $3,560.[57] Even with the $1,000 loan from Nicholson, more money had to be raised. Another kind of black movement for independence paradoxically undermined this attempt. With hundreds of French planters fleeing the Afro-French rebellion in Saint-Dominque and streaming into Philadelphia with French-speaking slaves at their sides, many white city dwellers reneged on their pledges to the African Church in order to help the destitute white slaveholders now taking refuge in their city. When Benjamin Rush sent William Gray to Baltimore to raise money from the parishioners of a church shepherded by a cousin of Rush's wife, he was similarly rebuffed because of the heavy claims made on white philanthropy by the influx of French sugar planters.[58] Philadelphia's free blacks learned that even the most sympathetic white men placed the distress of white slaveowners, even those from outside the United States, ahead of the aspirations of those who had been slaves.

Nicholson again came to the rescue, loaning another $1,000 in mid-August.[59] Ten days later the black leaders staged the roof-raising banquet on the edge of the city. But even as glasses were raised in toast, ill fortune struck again, this time delaying the completion of the church for nearly a year. It came in the form of the worst epidemic of yellow fever in the history of North America. The first victims succumbed late in July 1793; by late August the fever had reached epidemic proportions. With twenty Philadelphians dying daily of the putrid fever, shopkeepers began closing their doors, and all who could afford it commandeered horses, wagons, and carriages to carry their families out of the city. Hardest hit were the laboring poor. Living in crowded alleys and courts where the fever spread fastest, they were too poor to flee, sometimes too poor even to pay for a doctor.[60]

By early September the social fabric of the city was falling to pieces. The work of tending the sick and burying the dead exceeded the capacity of the doctors and city authorities because most nurses, carters, and gravediggers, regarding the disease as contagious, refused to go near the sick, dying, and dead. Husbands fled wives of many years who were in the throes of death, parents abandoned sick children, masters thrust servants into the streets. Mathew Carey, the main chronicler of the catastrophe, wrote that "less concern was felt for the loss of a parent, a husband, a wife or an only child than, on other occasions, would have been caused by the death of a servant, or even a favorite lap-dog."[61] Hundreds perished for lack of treatment, "without a human being to hand them a drink of water, to administer medicines, or to perform any charitable office for them." By mid-September the poor were starving and the dead lay everywhere in the streets, while thousands of middle- and upper-class Philadelphians fled to the countryside.[62]

Into this calamitous breach stepped Philadelphia's free blacks. Benjamin Rush, who played generalissimo of the relief forces, implored Richard Allen in early September to lead his people forward as nurses, gravediggers, and drivers of the death carts. Assuring Allen that the malignant fever "passes by persons of your color," he suggested that this God-bestowed exemption from the disease laid blacks "under an obligation to offer your services to attend the sick."[63]

The Free African Society met on September 5 to consider Rush's request. Much of what had transpired in the last six years might have inclined them to spurn the requests for aid—the humiliating incident at St. George's the year before, the opposition to establishing their own church, and most recently the readiness of those who had signed their subscription lists to beg off in order to aid slaveowning French planters who arrived with their chattel property in tow and then attempted to overturn the state law requiring manumission within six months of any slave brought into the state. But much had also transpired that argued for contributing themselves to the white community's desperate plight— the encouragement they had received in planning their church, the considerable aid of the Abolition Society, and the personal solicitation of Rush, their closest advisor.

A pamphlet written by Absalom Jones and Richard Allen after the epidemic indicates that they saw this as a God-sent opportunity to prove their courage and worth and to show that they could drive anger and bitterness from their hearts. Perhaps they could dissolve white racism by demonstrating that in their capabilities, civic virtue, and Christian humanitarianism they were not inferior, but in fact superior, to those who regarded former slaves as a degraded, hopelessly backward people. The "God who knows the hearts of all men, and the propensity of a slave to hate his oppressor," they wrote, "hath strictly forbidden it in his chosen people." Philadelphia's black Christians would act as the Good Samaritan, the despised man who aided a fellow human in desparate need when all the respected men of the community turned their heads. They would succor those who despised and opposed them because "the meek and humble Jesus, the great pattern of humanity, and every other virtue that can adorn and dignify men, hath commanded [us] to love our enemies, to do good to them that hate and despitefully use us."[64]

On September 6, 1793, Jones and Allen offered their services to the mayor, who immediately placed notices in the newspapers notifying citizens that they could apply to Jones or Allen for aid. "The African Society, intended for the relief of destitute Negroes," wrote the best authority on the epidemic, "suddenly assumed the most onerous, the most disgusting burdens of demoralized whites." They nursed the sick, carried away the dead, dug graves, and transported the afflicted to an emergency lazaretto set up outside the city. Jones, Allen, and William Gray, under instructions from Rush, acted as auxiliary doctors, bleeding patients and administering purges. By September 7, wrote Rush, Jones and Gray were "furnish[ing] nurses to most of my patients." Before the epidemic ran its course, Rush's untutored black assistants had bled more than eight hundred persons, making notes on each case for Rush as they worked through the day. At night they drove the death carts to the cemeteries.[65]

Within two weeks Rush's claims that Negroes were immune to the infectious fever, transmitted by the *Aedes aegypti* mosquito, had proven a ghastly error. Seventy Philadelphians were dying each day, and now blacks were numerous among them. "The Negroes are everywhere submitting to the disorder," Rush wrote on September 26, "and Richard Allen who had led their van is very ill."[66] In the first weeks of October the mortality raged through the half-abandoned city like a brushfire. On October 11 alone 119 died. Still convinced "that it was our duty to do all the good we could to our suffering fellow mortals," Jones, Allen, and the other blacks carried out their gruesome tasks. By the end of the month nearly 12,000 whites, along with the national and state governments, had fled the city, and nearly 4,000 persons, including about 240 blacks, had succumbed to the fever.[67] Not until early November did the epidemic pass.

Work on the African Church, suspended for nearly three months during the yellow fever crisis, resumed in December 1793. By the end of the year workmen had enclosed the building and completed the exterior.[68] It took further fundraising and another six months to complete the interior. In soliciting support in the white community the black leaders may have expected to draw on the credit they had accumulated through their heroic efforts during the terrible days of autumn. But even this altruism had to be defended, for Mathew Carey, the Irish immigrant publisher in the city, publicly vilified the free blacks for opportunistically charging exorbitant fees to nurse the sick and remove the dead. Carey's pamphlet, *A Short Account of the Malignant Fever*, was itself a lesson in deriving profit from mass misery. Selling briskly, it went through four editions between November 14 and December 20. Carey provided a narrative account of the holocaust, discussed the origins of the epidemic (a subject on which Philadelphia's doctors argued vociferously, in private and in print, for the rest of the decade), and appended lists of the dead.[69] But the city's saviors in Carey's account were the rising merchant Stephen Girard and other whites who organized an emergency hospital just outside the city, where they selflessly tended the sick and dying. For the black Philadelphians who drove the death carts, buried the dead, and nursed the sick in the back streets and alleys of the city Carey had few good words.

Carey's *Short Account* drew a shocked response from Jones and Allen.[70] They did not deny that some opportunistic persons "in low circumstances," both white and black, charged extravagant prices to nurse or remove the infected. This was to be expected, "especially under the loathsomeness of many of the sick, when nature shuddered at the thoughts of the infection, and the task was aggravated by lunacy, and being left much alone" with the sick. But Philadelphians should consider such stories, they argued, alongside those of the many blacks who asked no recompense at all, content to take whatever the patient thought proper to give. One old black women, when asked her fee, answered, "A dinner master on a cold winter's day." Ceasar Cranchell, a founding member of the African Society, swore he would not "sell my life for money," even though he should die, which he did in the process of tending sick whites.[71] Jones, Allen, Gray, and most other blacks had remained in the city throughout the biological terror, while nearly 20,000 whites, including Carey, had fled. Assured that they were immune from the disease, black Philadelphians remained in the city, only to learn otherwise; before cold weather ended the scourge, nearly one-tenth of the black population had died, proportionately as great a number as among whites. "Was not this in a great degree the effects of the services of the unjustly vilified black people?" asked Jones and Allen.[72]

Perhaps Carey's cruel remarks on the effort of the free blacks derived from the Irishman's advocacy of the large number of Hibernians flooding into Philadelphia and their competition with former slaves for unskilled and semiskilled job.[73] More germane, however, is that Carey's views did not convince the city's church leaders. To the contrary, by the time the epidemic had passed, the opposition to the African Church, except among the Methodists, seems to have dissolved.

As workmen completed the African church in the spring of 1794, Philadelphia's blacks gathered to make a momentous decision about denominational affiliation, apparently now convinced that without such a legitimizing affiliation they would violate the canons of Christian culture. They may also have believed that affiliation was necessary to guarantee state recognition of their corporate status—without which their church property would be insecure. Whatever the reasons, a "large majority" of the black elders and deacons favored uniting with the Episcopal (formerly Anglican) church, with only Jones and Allen opting for the Methodists.

The majority view is understandable for several reasons. The Methodist church had insulted Philadelphia's blacks just a few years before, and the presiding white elder remained opposed to a separate black church and, remembered Allen, "would neither be for us nor have anything to do with us."[74] Moreover, Methodism, while an evangelical and popular movement, operated under an autocratic ecclesiastical structure wherein its congregants had no voice in the pastoral affairs of their church or in the church's annual conferences.

The Episcopal church, on the other hand, had much to commend it to Philadelphia's free blacks. Its worship had been theologically flexible and tinged with evangelicalism since before the Revolution, and its authority structure was more fluid than that of the Methodists. Many black Philadelphians, both slaves and free persons, had married, worshiped, and christened their children in the city's three Episcopal churches.[75] Furthermore, their two closest white supporters were Episcopalians—Benjamin Rush, who had converted from the Presbyterian church in 1787, and Joseph Pilmore, the former Methodist who, after returning to Philadelphia as an Episcopal priest, had ministered to the Free African Society's religious meetings.

Steadfast in his conviction that "there was no religious sect or denomination that would suit the capacity of the colored people as well as the Methodist," Allen quietly withdrew again. He could not accept the invitation to be the minister of the church. "I informed them," he wrote later, "that I could not be anything else but a Methodist, as I was born and awakened under them, and I could go no further with them, for I was a Methodist, and would leave them in peace and love."[76]

With Allen declining to lead them, the deacons and elders turned to Absalom Jones. He lacked Allen's exhortatory gifts, but his balance, tenacity, education, and dignified leadership qualities all commended him. His "devotion to the sick and dying" during the terrible days of the yellow fever epidemic had also brought him wide recognition in the black community. "Administering to the bodily as well as the spiritual wants of many poor sufferers, and soothing the last moments of many departing souls among his people," it was later written, "he became greatly endeared to the colored race."[77]

With Jones leading them, the elders and deacons of the African Church of Philadelphia began to formalize the union with the Episcopal church in July 1794. The black Philadelphians agreed to "commit all the ecclesiastical affairs of our church to the government of the Protestant Episcopal Church of North America," while at the same time securing internal control of their church—and church property—through a constitution that gave them and their successors "the power of choosing our minister and assistant minister," provided that members were to be admitted only by the minister and church wardens, and specified that the officers of the church—the vestrymen and deacons—were to be chosen by ballot from among members of at least twelve months' standing. Finally, only "men of color, who were Africans, or the descendants of the African race," could elect or be elected into any church office except that of minister and assistant minister. With the help of Benjamin Rush they had contrived a formula for maintaining black control of the church, while allowing for the absence of trained blacks to fill the ministry. They had "declared a conformity to our Church in Doctrine, Discipline and Worship," wrote Bishop William White, but simultaneously they had gained the promise of ordination of their leader, Absalom Jones, while preserving the all-important rights of self-government.[78]

Later in 1794 the African Church—renamed St. Thomas's African Episcopal Church—formally requested Bishop White to qualify Absalom Jones "to act as our minister." The bishop gave permission for Jones to read services, and ten months later the State Episcopal Convention approved Jones's appointment. It did so only after arranging a quid pro quo whereby it waived the Greek and Latin requirement for the ministry in exchange for the stipulation that the African Church forego the right to send a representative to the yearly convention where church policy was set.[79]

On July 17, 1794, the African Church of Philadelphia opened its doors for worship. The published account of the dedication ceremony indicates that most of the white ministerial opposition had melted. "The venerable Clergy of almost every denomination, and a number of other very respectable citizens were present," it was related. James Abercrombie, assistant minister of Christ Church, officiated, and Samuel Magaw, rector of St. Paul's Church, gave the sermon from the text "Ethopia shall soon stretch out her hands unto God." The discourse was from Isaiah: "The people that walked in darkness have seen a great light"—the same epigram that was etched in marble above the church doors.[80] But we may imagine that among the worshipers, those who were black and those who were white derived different meanings from this epigram.

Magaw's sermon stressed the need for gratitude and complaisance on the part of the blacks who crowded the church. They or their fathers, he preached, had come from the heathenish lands of Senegal, Gambia, Benin, Angola, and Congo, and that burden of birth had been increased by the dismal effects of slavery, which "sinks the mind, no less than the body, . . . destroys all principle; corrupts the feelings; prevents man from either discerning, or choosing aright in anything." Having providentially been brought from "a land of Pagan darkness, to a land of Gospel light," these former slaves must now maintain their gratitude to the white Christians who freed them and donated or loaned money to build the church. As for their brethren still in slavery, they should pray—but not take action. He emphasized the need for black passivity and moderation in all things, and warned them to suppress the pride that was on the rise among them. Instead, they should cultivate "an obliging, friendly, meek conversation." Their church, Magaw counseled, in a perfect display of white paternalism, owed its existence to the benevolent action of whites. That it had been born in strife and discrimination and had arisen only when free blacks defied the opposition of white churchmen received no mention.

How did black Philadelphians receive Magaw's message? It must have confirmed among many of them the wisdom of forming a black church, not only to worship God in their own way but as a means of proving themselves and thus achieving equality and real freedom. By setting alongside Magaw's advice the thoughts of Jones and Allen, published a few months before, we can better comprehend the social and psychological struggle in which free blacks were engaged. "You try what you can to prevent our rising from the state of barbarism you represent us to be in," wrote Jones and Allen in their reply to Mathew Carey, "but we can tell you from a degree of experience, that a black man, although reduced to the most abject state human nature is capable of, short of real madness, can think, reflect, and feel injuries, although it may not be with the same degree of keen resentment and revenge, that you who have been and are our great oppressors, would manifest if reduced to the pitiable condition of a slave." This hot indictment of white oppression and denigration of blacks was followed by an insistence on the capabilities of Africans and their descendants, which echoed Benezet's views. "We believe, if you would try the experiment of taking a few black children, and cultivate their minds with the same care, and let them have the same prospect in view, as to living in the world, as you would wish for your own children, you would find them upon the trial, they were not inferior in mental endowments."[81]

One month later, Absalom Jones enunciated the alternative black interpretation of the words from Isaiah—"the people that walked in darkness have seen a great light." The "darkness" through which they had walked was not the land of their birth but slavery. And the "great light" they had now seen was the light of freedom as well as the light of Christianity. In recording the "Causes and Motives" for establishing the African church, written just a month after the church building opened, Jones again expressed the rising tide of black determination to find strategies that would promote strength, security, and a decent existence. They had learned, Jones wrote, "to arise out of the dust and shake ourselves, and throw off that servile fear, that the habit of oppression and bondage trained us up in."[82] In what seems to be a direct reference to the charges of Bishop White about black "pride," Jones continued that they wished "to avoid all appearance of evil, by self-conceitedness, or any intent to promote or establish any new human device among us"; hence they had decided to "resign and conform ourselves" to the Protestant Episcopal Church of North America.[83] Nonetheless, this was to be an autonomous black church, as their constitution spelled out.

Although he did not mention it, Jones might have added that the black "pride" and determination to create their own institutions drew much sustenance from the day-to-day accomplishments of Philadelphia's blacks during the decade that followed the end of the Revolution. Through their ability to establish families and residences, by their demonstrated capacity to sustain themselves as free laborers and artisans, and in their success at conducting themselves morally, soberly, and civilly, they must have proved to themselves the groundless and racist character of the prevalent white view that former slaves were a permanently corrupted people.

The reports of the Pennsylvania Abolition Society and the observations of other Philadelphians bear out the generally successful transition to freedom that blacks made in the city after the Revolution. In 1785 Benjamin Rush reported that "the slaves who have been emancipated among us are in general more industrious and orderly than the lowest class of white people."[84] In 1790 the first federal census taker found only 3 blacks among the 273 inmates of the almshouse and 5 black prisoners among 191 felons in the Walnut Street Prison, indicating a far lower incidence of immiseration and criminality among a people only a few years out of bondage than among the free white population. In 1791 Rush reported that "such is their integrity and quiet deportment that they are universally preferred to white people of similar occupations." Four years later, shortly after the dedication of St. Thomas's, the Abolition Society's survey of black households revealed that more than one-fourth of the free black families owned houses, most "live comfortably," and their behavior, "in point of morality, is equal to those whites who are similarly situated as to employment and means for improvement."[85]

This is not to argue that the transition from slavery to freedom was untrammeled. Philadelphia in the 1790s was full of struggling black sojourners, many with limited skills, who arrived by water and land from every direction. Hundreds of them could not establish independent black households at first, many had to bind out their children, and only a minority rose above a pinched and precarious existence. But their general ability to fashion a respectable life for themselves, giving credence to the arguments of Benezet, helped to galvanize leaders and convince them of their capability to establish separate churches.

As St. Thomas's African Episcopal Church was being completed and its affiliation with the Protestant Episcopal church formalized, Richard Allen continued to pursue his vision of Black Methodism. Successful as a carter, trader, and master of chimney sweeps, he used his own money to purchase a blacksmith shop and haul it to a site he bought at Sixth and Lombard Streets. Renovated as a humble house of worship, it opened its doors for a dedication service officiated by Bishop Francis Asbury on June 29, 1794. Reverend John Dickens, the white Methodist elder recently assigned to Philadelphia, prayed "that it might be a 'Bethel' to the gathering of thousands of souls."[86] This marked the birth of "Mother Bethel," the first congregation of what became in 1816 the independent African Methodist Episcopal Church.

While the sources have allowed us primarily to follow the efforts of black leaders to point the way forward by organizing separate churches, it is important to measure the response of the mass of ordinary former slaves to the establishment of St. Thomas's and Bethel because it can tell us, if only imperfectly, about an emerging black consciousness in Philadelphia. Three sources exist for this: fragmentary membership records for the black churches, baptism and burial records that appeared in annual bills of mortality, and records of white churches. All of these sources indicate an extraordinary response by Philadelphia's free blacks to the establishment of separate churches were they might worship, organize themselves, and develop their own leadership apart from white supervision.

In 1794, in the year they were founded, St. Thomas's and Bethel churches recorded 246 and 108 members respectively; one year later they had increased their members to 427 and 121. Besides no less than 548 registered members in the two churches, "a floating congregation of at least a hundred or more persons" attended St. Thomas's according to the church's first historian, and a number of others must have done so at Bethel.[87] The proportion of black adults who joined the church must have been about 40 percent of some 1,500 who lived in the city.[88] This level of church participation was probably higher than among whites in general and perhaps twice as high as among whites of the laboring classes.[89] These figures are all the more impressive in view of the fact that about half of the city's free blacks were living in the households of whites, many as indentured servants, and therefore were less than fully free to act autonomously, while hundreds of others were French-speaking blacks recently manumitted by their Caribbean refugee masters or were newly arrived migrants, often destitute and old, from the South.

It is also apparent from marriage and baptismal records that Philadelphia's free blacks warmly embraced the separate black churches. A few still married in white churches and brought their children there to be baptized.[90] But whereas fifteen black marriages are recorded in white church records in 1792 and twenty-one in 1793, only fourteen can be found in 1795 and seven each in 1796 and 1797. The strong attraction of the black churches is also apparent in baptisms, for between 1797 and 1802 an average of one hundred a year were performed at St. Thomas's and Bethel.[91]

The independent black church movement led by Absalom Jones and Richard Allen was the first major expression of racial strength and the most important instrument for furthering the social and psychological liberation of recently freed slaves. Bishop White had been correct, though in ways he knew not, when he reacted in anger in 1791 to word that free blacks were planning their own church, charging that their plan "originated in pride." The pride was really a growing feeling of strength and a conviction that black identify, self-sufficiency, self-determination, and the search for freedom and equality could best be nurtured in the early years of the Republic through independent black churches.

NOTES

1. Rush to Julia Rush, Aug. 22, 1793, *Letters of Benjamin Rush*, L. H. Butterfield, ed., 2 vols. (Princeton, N. J., 1951), 2:639.

2. Gary B. Nash, "Slaves and Slaveowners in Colonial Philadelphia," *William and Mary Quarterly*, 30 (1973): 232–39.

3. Debra L. Newman, "They Left With the British: Black Women in the Evacuation of Philadelphia, 1778," *Pennsylvania Heritage*, 4 (1977): 20–23; Benjamin Quarles, *The Negro in the American Revolution* (Chapel Hill, N.C., 1961), chaps. 7–9. For the 1767 population estimate see Nash, "Slaves and Slaveowners," 241; the tax list of 1783 in City Archives, City Hall Annex, Philadelphia, shows about 400 slaves, and I have estimated a population of about 800 free blacks at this time.

4. *Heads of Families at the First Census of the United States Taken in the Year 1790: Pennsylvania* (Washington, D.C., 1908); *Return of the Whole Num-*

ber of Persons within the Several Districts of the United States [Second Census of the United States, 1800] (Washington, D.C., 1801).

5. Rush to Granville Sharp, Nov. 28, 1783, *Journal of American Studies,* 1 (1967): 20.

6. Papers of the Pennsylvania Abolition Society, General Meeting, Loose Minutes, Historical Society of Pennsylvania (microfilm edition, reel 9).

7. Letter of Newport Union Society to Free African Society of Philadelphia, 1787, and Free African Society reply, in William Douglass, *Annals of the First African Church in the United States of America, now styled The African Episcopal Church of St. Thomas* (Philadelphia, 1862), 25–29.

8. Winthrop Jordan, *White Over Black: American Attitudes Toward the Negro, 1550–1812* (Chapel Hill, N.C., 1968), 357; George S. Brookes, *Friend Anthony Benezet* (Philadelphia, 1937), chap. 6; Nancy S. Hornick, "Anthony Benezet and the Africans' School: Toward a Theory of Full Equality," *Pennsylvania Magazine of History and Biography* (hereafter *PMHB*), 99 (1975): 399–421; Sydney V. James, *A People among People: Quaker Benevolence in Eighteenth-Century America* (Cambridge, Mass., 1963), 279–80, 316.

9. According to Jean Pierre Brissot, who was visiting the city at the time, Benezet's funeral was attended by 400 blacks. Brookes, *Benezet,* 458, 461. Also see Roberts Vaux, *Memoir of the Life of Anthony Benezet* (Philadelphia: 1817), 150.

10. Roger Bruns, "Anthony Benezet's Assertion of Negro Equality," *Journal of Negro History,* 56 (1971): 230–38; Hornick, "Anthony Benezet." The quotation is from Benezet's *A Caution and Warning to Great Britain . . .* (Philadelphia, 1767), 11–12. For his views in 1762 see *A Short Account of that Part of Africa Inhabited by the Negroes* (Philadelphia: 1762).

11. Minutes of the Women's Committee for Free Blacks, Historical Society of Pennsylvania. In 1788 the Philadelphia Yearly Meeting advised all Monthly Meetings to begin visiting free blacks so as to support and guide them in their new status. James, *People among People,* 294.

12. David Brion Davis, *The Problem of Slavery in the Age of Revolution, 1770–1823* (Ithaca, N.Y., 1975), 254.

13. James, *People among People,* 316–19. On Quaker exclusion of blacks from membership in the Society of Friends see ibid., 234, 279–80, and Henry J. Cadbury, "Negro Membership in the Society of Friends," *Journal of Negro History,* 21 (1936): 172.

14. *Autobiography of Richard Allen,* in R. R. Wright, Jr., *Bishops of the African Methodist Church* (Nashville, 1963), 46–49; "Sketch of Rev. Absalom Jones," in Douglass, *Annals,* 118–22. Absalom Jones has gone virtually unnoticed in black history while Richard Allen, because he was the founder of what would become in 1816 the first completely independent black church in America, has been widely noticed in the historical literature. When William J. Simmons wrote the first dictionary of Negro biography in 1887, he did not include Jones but wrote passionately of Allen: "He put his foot on the neck of hellborn prejudice and stamped it so hard that hell resounded with anger and a new song was given to the angels in heaven." *Men of Mark: Eminent, Progressive and Rising* (Cleveland, 1887; reprinted, New York: 1968), 493.

15. *Autobiography of Allen,* 48–53; Charles H. Wesley, *Richard Allen, Apostle of Freedom* (Washington, D.C., 1935), 19–35. Allen's master, thought by historians to be a Mr. Stokely since that is the name Allen gives in his autobiography, was actually Stokely Sturgis, as is given in Allen's manumission papers, which I have located in Manumission Book A, p. 2, Papers of the Pennsylvania Abolition Society, Historical Society of Pennsylvania. The manumission papers also show that Allen had no surname when he was manumitted on Jan. 25, 1780, but went only by the slave name Richard.

16. Benjamin Wynkoop was the second son of Abraham and Mary Wynkoop, a wealthy Sussex County planter-merchant who died in 1753. He left Benjamin a 1,000-acre plantation in Cedar Creek Hundred, £400 in cash, and probably the slave family to which Absalom had been born in 1746. Sussex County Probates, A.109: 125–26, Delaware Archives, Dover.

17. "Sketch of Jones," in Douglass, *Annals,* 119–20; Richard I. Snelling, "William Sturgeon, Catechist to the Negroes of Philadelphia and Assistant Rector of Christ Church, 1747–1766," *Historical Magazine of the Protestant Episcopal Church,* 8 (1939): 393–95.

18. "Sketch of Jones," 119–21. Jones's marriage is recorded in Records of Christ Church: Marriages, 1709–1800, 4352, Genealogical Society of Pennsylvania, Philadelphia. His master's name is given there as Benjamin Wynkoop. Although this record gives only the slave name Absalom, it is certain that this is Jones because the marriage is to Mary, the slave of S. King. In his autobiographical sketch, Jones recorded that he had been married to Sarah King's slave.

19. "Sketch of Jones," 121. The wartime purchase of the house and lot from Edward Shippen and John Brickell on Jan. 25, 1779, is noted in a later deed for the property in Deed Book D20, 565–66, City Archives, City Hall Annex, Philadelphia. It is likely that Absalom and Mary Jones decided to purchase her freedom first because the status of any children born to them would follow the mother.

20. *American Daily Advertiser,* Feb. 19, 1818. Douglass made similar remarks about Jones's temperament in *Annals,* 121–22.

21. *Autobiography of Allen,* 53–54. An early black historian, George F. Bragg, says that Jones and Allen met first in Delaware, but this seems unlikely in view of the fact that Allen was born in Philadelphia in 1760 and sold to Sturgis in Delaware later in that decade, while Jones was brought to Philadelphia in 1762. Bragg, *Richard Allen and Absalom Jones* (Baltimore, 1915), unpaginated.

22. *Autobiography of Allen,* 54. The quotation about "often communing together" is from the preamble to the constitution of the Free African Society, in Douglass, *Annals,* 15.

23. W. E. B. Du Bois, *The Philadelphia Negro: A Social Study* (Philadelphia, 1899; reprinted: New York, 1967), 19.

24. Douglass, *Annals,* 18–41, where extracts of the Free African Society's minutes, no longer extant, are recorded.

25. Ibid., 17–18, 40–44; for Dougherty see James, *People among People,* 236.

26. Ibid., 18–23.

27. Carol V. R. George, *Segregated Sabbaths: Richard Allen and the Rise of Independent Black Churches, 1760–1845* (New York, 1973), 57.

28. Douglass, *Annals*, 9.

29. Donald G. Mathews, *Slavery and Methodism: A Chapter in American Morality, 1780–1845* (Princeton, N.J., 1965), 3–21; George, *Segregated Sabbaths*, 43.

30. Douglass, *Annals*, 24.

31. Rush to Julia Rush, July 16, 1791, *Letters of Rush*, 1:600.

32. Vaux, *Memoir of Benezet*, 35. On Clarkson's influence on Rush see David Hawke, *Benjamin Rush: Revolutionary Gadfly* (Indianapolis and New York, 1971), 360–61, although Hawke does not specify, as Rush did, that it was his reading of Clarkson's pamphlet that turned him to the abolitionist cause.

33. Rush to Jeremy Belknap, Aug. 18, 1788, *Letters of Rush*, 1:482.

34. *Extract of a Letter from Dr. Benjamin Rush, of Philadelphia, to Granville Sharp* (London, 1792), 6–7. Rush's letter in its full, original form is in *Letters of Rush*, 1:608–9. The quoted phrases are from the "Address of the Representatives of the African Church," the printed appeal for subscriptions. No copy of this document, published in Philadelphia in 1791, is extant, but Sharp appended it to the *Extract of a Letter from . . . Rush*. Rush noted in his jounal the "many hundred [of free blacks] who now spend that day [Sunday] in idleness," and the Pennsylvania Abolition Society reported that "all these poor People profess some system of Religion" and noted that "many frequent some place of public worship." *The Autobiography of Rush*, George S. Corner, ed. (Princeton, N.J., 1948), 202; Minutes of the Committee of 24 (April 1791), Pennsylvania Abolition Society Papers (microfilm edition, reel 6).

35. *Extract of a Letter from Rush*, 4.

36. Gayraud S. Wilmore, *Black Religion and Black Radicalism: An Interpretation of the Religious History of the Afro-American People* (Garden City, N.Y., 1972), 114. For an illuminating analysis of the union church movement and other routes to independent black churches see Will B. Gravely, "The Rise of African Churches in America (1786–1822): Re-examining the Contexts," *Journal of Religious Thought*, 41 (1985).

37. *Extract of a Letter from Rush*, 4; Douglass, *Annals*, 45–46.

38. Frederick E. Maser and Howard T. Maag, eds., *The Journal of Joseph Pilmore, Methodist Itinerant* (Philadelphia, 1969), 235–47; Norris S. Barratt, *Outline of the History of St. Paul's Church, Philadelphia, 1760–1899* (Philadelphia, 1917), 113–24. Pilmore's register of marriages is in *Pennsylvania Archives*, 2d ser., 9:462–92. Very few black marriages were performed at St. Paul's before Pilmore's arrival, none before 1786 and only six between Jan. 1786 and May 1789.

39. *Extract of a Letter from Rush*, p. 4. Rush and Jones presented the plan to "a dozen free Blacks," undoubtedly the deacons and elders, on July 25, 1791. Three days later it was adopted, perhaps with some alterations. William Gray thanked Rush the following summer for "the great pains and trouble you

have taken in prescribing the rules and regulations which ought to be observed in the Africans Church." Two days later Gray requested Rush to draw up "a form of the credentials or whatever is necessary for the Elders and Deacons to have after their Ordination in Order to Authorize them to sit in their respective stations." Gray to Rush, Oct. 24, 26, 1792, Mss. Correspondence of Rush, 24:116–17, Library Company of Philadelphia.

40. "Address of the Representatives of the African Church," in *Extract of a Letter from Rush*, 6–7.

41. Ibid.

42. Wilmore, *Black Religion and Black Radicalism*, 106. Also see George Levesque, "Interpreting Early Black Ideology: A Reappraisal of Historical Consensus," *Journal of the Early Republic*, 1 (1981): 281.

43. Douglass, *Annals*, 3, 11. Benjamin Quarles writes that "racial pride was ... a central motif in antebellum black history. Like other Americans of their day, blacks were engaged in the quest for self-identity. Because blacks bore heavy burdens, however, black self-identity more readily flowed into group identity, with history a connecting link, in effect becoming history-as-identity." "Black History's Antebellum Origins," American Antiquarian Society *Proceedings*, 89 (Worcester, Mass., 1980), 94.

44. Rush to Julia Rush, July 16, 1791, *Letters of Rush*, 1:599–600.

45. Ibid.; *Autobiography of Rush*, 202.

46. *Autobiography of Rush*, 202; *Autobiography of Allen*, 55–56. For a more positive view of White's role see Ann C. Lammers, "The Rev. Absalom Jones and the Episcopal Church: Christian Theology and Black Consciousness in a New Alliance," *Historical Magazine of the Protestant Episcopal Church*, 51 (1982): 159–84.

47. Benjamin T. Tanner, *An Apology for African Methodism* (Baltimore, 1867), 16.

48. Rush to Granville Sharp, [Aug. 1791], *Letters of Rush*, 1:602, 608–9; Sharp to Rush, [Sept. 1792], Mss. Corr. of Rush, 28:106; receipt for £25 from Rush, Benjamin Rush Papers, Box 9, Hist. Soc. of Pa.

49. *Autobiography of Allen*, 56–57. The decision of the Free African Society to draw up subscription papers in Mar. 1792 is recorded in their minutes; Douglass, *Annals*, 44. The purchase of lots, which caused some controversy, was minuted on Feb. 17, 1792; ibid., 43.

50. Rush to Jeremy Belknap, June 21, 1792, *Letters of Rush*, 1:620.

51. *Autobiography of Allen*, 55.

52. The misdating of the incident at St. George's seems to have originated in Richard Allen and Joseph Tapsico's introduction to the *Doctrines and Discipline of the African Methodist Episcopal Church*, published in 1817 after Allen has finally split with the Methodists. The introduction—a "brief statement of our rise and progress"—dates the incident around November 1787. Many early Methodist historians and almost all historians writing since have accepted this date. Milton C. Sernett has provided convincing evidence, however, that Allen, writing a quarter of a century after the fact, telescoped events between 1787 and 1792. In his autobiography Allen related that the incident

occurred after the galleries and new flooring had been installed, but, as Sernett shows, the building records in the vault of St. George's Church show that the galleries were not finished until May 1792. Moreover, the initials of the elders and pastors that Allen recounted as connected with the incident cannot be associated with any St. George's officials in 1787 but correspond to those serving in 1791–92. *Black Religion and American Evangelicalism: White Protestants, Plantation Missions, and the Flowering of Negro Christianity, 1787–1865* (Metuchen, N.J., 1975), 117–18, 219–20.

53. Richard Allen and Jacob Tapsico, *Doctrines and Discipline of the African Methodist Episcopal Church* (Philadelphia, [1817]) in Wright, *Bishops of the AME Church,* 60; *Autobiography of Allen,* 55.

54. Rush to John Nicholson, Nov. 28, 1792, *Letters of Rush,* 1:624. On Nicholson see Robert D. Arbuckle, *Pennsylvania Speculator and Patriot: The Entrepreneurial John Nicholson, 1757–1800* (University Park, Pa., 1975).

55. Jones and Gray to John Nicholson, Dec. 3, 1792, Feb. 7, 9, 1793, John Nicholson Papers, General Correspondence, 1772–1819, Pennsylvania State Archives, Harrisburg (microfilm edition at Hist. Soc. of Penna., fr. 1300–01, 1303, 1305). Also see Jones and Gray to John Nicholson, May 11, 1793, ibid., fr. 1307, and Jones, Gray, and William Wilshire to John Nicholson, Nov. 28, 1792, Mss. Corr. of Rush, 24:118.

56. *Autobiography of Allen,* 57. Details on the building contracts and donations of building materials by white Philadelphians are recorded in the minutes of the African Society; Douglass, *Annals,* 50–57.

57. For the cost of building, ibid., 50; for seating capacity, William Catto, *A Semi-Centenary Discourse . . . in the First African Presbyterian Church . . .* (Philadelphia, 1857), 107.

58. For white Philadelphians reneging and Gray's trip to Baltimore see Jones to John Nicholson, Aug. 2, 1793, and Gray to John Nicholson, Aug. 13, 1793, Nicholson Corr., fr. 1308–9, 1311–12, and Joseph G. Bend to Rush, Aug. 12, 1793, Mss. Corr. of Rush, 22:82.

59. Nicholson to Absalom Jones and William Gray, Aug. 8, 1793, Mss. Corr. of Rush, 12:16; Gray to John Nicholson, Aug. 13, 1793, Nicholson Corr., fr. 1311–12; Rush to John Nicholson, Aug. 12, 1793, *Letters of Rush,* 2:636.

60. J. H. Powell, *Bring Out Your Dead: The Great Plague of Yellow Fever in Philadelphia in 1793* (Philadelphia, 1949), 8–63.

61. Ibid., 64–89. The quotations are from Carey's pamphlet *A Short Account of the Malignant Fever* (Philadelphia, 1793).

62. Powell, *Bring Out Your Dead,* 90–113.

63. Rush to Richard Allen, [Sept. , 1793], Mss. Corr. of Rush, 38:32.

64. Absalom Jones and Richard Allen, *A Narrative of the Proceedings of the Black People, During the Late Awful Calamity in Philadelphia, in the year 1793 . . .* (Philadelphia, 1794), 24–25.

65. Powell, *Bring Out Your Dead,* pp. 96–98; Rush to—, Sept. 7, 1793, *Letters of Rush,* 2:654.

66. Rush to Julia Rush, Sept. 13, 25, 1793, *Letters of Rush,* 2:663, 683–84.

67. Jones and Allen, *Narrative of the Black People,* 15–16; *Minutes of the Proceedings of the Committee . . . to Attend to and Alleviate the Sufferings of the Afflicted . . .* (Philadelphia, 1794), 204. According to the house census recorded in these minutes, only 209 blacks left the city.

68. Jones and Gray to John Nicholson, Dec. 20, 27, 1793, Nicholson Corr., fr. 1313–15.

69. Martin S. Pernick, "Politics, Parties, and Pestilence: Epidemic Yellow Fever in Philadelphia and the Rise of the First Party System," *William and Mary Quarterly,* 29 (1972): 559–86.

70. See Jones and Allen, *Narrative of the Black People.* The pamphlet was published on Jan. 24, 1794.

71. Ibid., 7–12.

72. Ibid., 15–16. Carey had distorted the evidence despite Benjamin Rush's description of the heroic work of many blacks. Rush to Mathew Carey, Oct. 29, 1793, *Letters of Rush,* 2:731–32. The Abolition Society investigated the matter at the request of Jones and Allen and concluded in June 1794, after examining the evidence, that the black leaders had actually suffered financially from their services. Committee for Improving the Condition of Free Blacks, Minute Book, 1790–1802, pp. 83–84, Penn. Abol. Soc. Papers, reel 6.

73. For the Irish see Edward Carter, II, "A 'Wild Irishman' Under Every Federalist's Bed: Naturalization in Philadelphia, 1789–1806," *PMHB,* 94 (1970): 331–46.

74. *Autobiography of Allen,* 57–58. The first election of deacons and elders in 1792 is recorded in Douglass, *Annals,* 49.

75. *Autobiography of Allen,* 57–58. For a history of the heterogeneous and generally "low-church" character of the Anglican churches in Philadelphia see Deborah Gough, "Pluralism, Politics, and Power Struggles: The Church of England in Colonial Philadelphia, 1685–1789," (Ph.D. diss., University of Pennsylvania, 1978).

76. *Autobiography of Allen,* 58–59.

77. Bragg, *Allen and Jones,* unpaginated.

78. The constitution is in Douglass, *Annals,* 96–99. White's statement is quoted in Edgar L. Pennington, "The Work of the Bray Associates in Pennsylvania," *PMHB,* 58 (1934): 22.

79. Douglass, *Annals,* 101. St. Thomas's leaders understood the quid pro quo to be temporary, but their successors found that when their black ministers were able to satisfy the Latin and Greek requirements the diocese still denied them representation in the Convention. Not until after the Civil War would the Convention concede to St. Thomas's claim. Ibid., 140–71. For further discussion see Lammers, "Jones and the Episcopal Church," 178–79, 183–84. Bishop William White ordained Jones as deacon on Aug. 23, 1795, and nine years later as priest. An invitation to the ordination ceremony to John Nicholson, Aug. 22, 1795, is in Nicholson Corr., reel 10, fr. 1318.

80. *A Discourse Delivered July 17th 1794, in the African Church of the City of Philadelphia, on the occasion of opening the said Church and holding public worship in it for the first time* ([Philadelphia, 1794]), reprinted in Douglass, *Annals*, 58–81.

81. Jones and Allen, *A Narrative of the Black People*, 23–24.

82. "Causes and Motives for Establishing St. Thomas's African Church of Philadelphia," in Douglass, *Annals*, 93–95. It may be significant that Jones left the word "Episcopal" out of the title. The quotation is on p. 94.

83. Douglass, *Annals*, 95.

84. Rush to Richard Price, Oct. 15, 1785, *Letters of Rush*, 371. The Pennsylvania Abolition Society reiterated this observation in 1787. General Meeting, Minutes, 1787–1800, p. 17, Penn. Abol. Soc. Papers, reel 1.

85. *Census of 1790: Pennsylvania*, 242, 244; Rush to Granville Sharp, Aug. 1791, *Letters of Rush*, 1:608; Committee for Improvement of the Condition of Free Blacks, Minute Book, 1790–1802, 112 (Nov. 30, 1795), Penn. Abol. Soc. Papers, reel 6.

86. *Autobiography of Allen*, 59. Allen had gathered ten black Methodists at his house on May 5, 1794, and it was there that the group decided to proceed with forming their own church. Wesley, *Richard Allen*, 77–78.

87. A list of St. Thomas's members in 1794 is given in Douglass, *Annals*, 107–10. Douglass's membership figure for 1795 and his comment on the floating congregation is on p.110. Bethel's membership is taken from *Minutes Taken at . . . Conferences of the Methodist-Episcopal church in America for the Year 1795* (Philadelphia, 1795). Benjamin T. Tanner reports a membership list for Bethel dated Nov. 3, 1794, with 108 names, but I have been unable to locate it. *An Outline of Our History and Government for African Methodist Churchmen . . .* (n.p., 1884), 19.

88. Based on an extrapolation from the 1790 and 1800 census data of free blacks in Philadelphia. Many other former slaves lived in Southwark and the Northern Liberties on the fringes of the city, and some of them probably gravitated to the city's churches. In a 1795 household census the Abolition Society counted 381 independent black families in the city. Committee for Improving the Condition of Free Blacks, Minute Book, 1790–1802, 112 (Nov. 30, 1795), Penn. Abol. Soc. Papers, reel 6.

89. Ira Berlin suggests similarly that a higher proportion of free blacks than whites belonged to churches in the South in the antebellum period. *Slaves Without Masters: The Free Negro in the Antebellum South* (New York, 1974), 287–303.

90. Francis A. La Rochefoucauld–Liancourt noted in 1798 that blacks in Philadelphia, in spite of having "The African church," went "to the other churches at their pleasure." *Travels through the United States . . . 1795–97*, 2 vols. (London, 1799), 2:387.

91. Calculated from the transcribed church records at the Genealogical Society of Pennsylvania and from the annual bills of mortality published in the city, which give the number of baptisms at Bethel and St. Thomas's Churches. By the late 1790s only an occasional black baptism occurred in the white

churches. Douglass used a "Baptismal Record" and interment book to give the total number of baptisms and burials at St. Thomas's from 1796 to 1818, but I can find no trace of these records. See Douglass, *Annals*, 123.

INDEX

economic changes, 197, 215, 251; economic conditions in America compared to Europe, 245–46; and economic crises, 249, 251, 254–57; economic power of, 195, 254, 255; group consciousness, 20, 243–62; and individualism, 249; intergenerational continuity of, 244; internal stratification of, 243, 246–48, 253, 261–62; merchant elite vs., 257–62; political activity and power, 144, 147, 154, 156, 212, 222, 223, 228, 235, 243–62; poverty of, 186, 255–56; and role in American Revolution, 243, 260–62; social status of, 243–44, 246–48, 251–62. *See also* Boston; Philadelphia; Unemployment
Asbury, Bishop Francis, 346
Atkin, Edmond, 55
Auchmuty, Robert, 225

Bacon's Rebellion, 16
Bailyn, Bernard, 211
Baptists, 109; black, 279. *See also* Blacks, free; Religion
Barbados, 23. *See also* West Indies
Barnard, John, 131
Barnard, Thomas, 127–28, 131
Batt, Jasper, 80, 84
Bayard, William, 196
Baynton, John, 104, 196
Bay of Fundy, 275, 277
Becker, Carl, 149
Belcher, Andrew, 196, 216–17
Belcher, Gov. Jonathan, 153, 196, 220
Belknap, Jeremy, 333
Bender, Thomas, 21–22
Benezet, Anthony, 95, 109, 326–27, 332–33, 344, 346
Berlin, Ira, 293
Bermuda, 274
Bernard, Gov. Francis, 200, 224, 225, 232
Beverley, Robert, 53, 55–57
Bidwell, Percy, 11
Birthrate. *See* Population
Black Guides and Pioneers, 273, 276
Blacks, 26-28; in the American Revolution, 269, 272–74, 280; culture of, 26–28; family, 28; influence on "white" culture, 28; religion, 28; social adaptation of, 27; white attitudes toward, 26–27, 105

Blacks, enslaved. *See* Slaves
Blacks, free
—Political activity and power: voting, 325
—religious life: Anglican Church, 294, 328, 330, 335, 342–47; Baptists, 279; churches, 307–10, 323–24, 328–47; Methodism, 328, 330–33, 336–37, 342, 346–47; role of church, 333–34, 343–47. *See also* African Church of Philadelphia; Allen, Richard; Jones, Absalom; Quakers; Philadelphia
—social and economic conditions: in Canada, 275–79; and community, 288, 293, 294, 307–12; family, 289, 298, 301–7; labor and laboring classes, 283–84, 287–89, 291–93, 301, 325; mortality rates, 93, 95, 98–100; naming patterns, 293–98; neighborhoods, 307–9, 311; in Nova Scotia, 275–79; occupational structure, 289, 291–92; population, 99–103, 283–91, 293, 310, 324, 341, 345, 346–47; schools, 307, 310, 311, 326, 327, 333; social adaptation, 293–94, 296–310, 324–28, 331; urban migration, 284, 287–89, 324, 346; women, 289–93, 299, 301–6. *See also* Boston; Canada; New York; Philadelphia; Slavery
Bollan, William, 228
Bond, Thomas 104
Boston
—government and political life: caucus, 148, 217, 220–21, 228, 230, 233; changes in political organization, 146–47, 148–49, 223, 224–33; Boston Port Act (1774), 259; economic conditions and, 153, 180, 217, 220–27; elections, 146, 148, 159, 228; factions and political parties, 146, 219, 220–21, 223–33; and political press, 149, 150, 151, 221, 225–30; and radicalization of politics, 141–42, 148, 223–24, 227–311; and social class, 142, 146, 220–33; town meeting, 122, 127, 146, 220, 221, 225–27, 229. *See also* Artisans; Crowd actions; Labor and laboring classes; Political press
—religious life: Pope's Day, 153. *See also* Great Awakening; Puritans; Quakers; Religion

88; in mid-Atlantic region, 9–10; native Americans, 17, 23; in New England, 8; ownership, 91–110, 298–99; in rural Pennsylvania, 101–4; in the South, 13–18, 23, 27; Swedes' attitudes toward, 82; trade, 269–70; in urban vs. rural areas, 271. *See also* Abolition; Blacks; Labor and laboring classes; Quakers
Slaves: and the American Revolution, 273; Cape Fear Uprising (1775), 272; and crowd actions, 216; culture, 26–28; and family, 99, 101, 271; loyalists, 272–74; population, 283, 284, 286–91, 324; and revolutionary rhetoric, 272–73; transition to freemanship, 283–84, 287–89, 291, 298–307; women, 105, 129–30. *See also* Blacks, free; Boston; Labor and laboring classes; New York; Philadelphia; Women
Smallpox. *See* Disease
Smith, John (Quaker), 173
Smith, John (Virginia leader), 45–48, 51, 53
Smith, Samuel, 155
Smith, William (Philadelphia), 151, 155, 157–58
Smith, William (New York), 149
Social class: antagonisms, 25, 216–35; in cities, 20–22; and crowd actions, 216; Great Awakening and, 221–22; history of, 3; Penn, William, views of, 72; and politics, 141–61, 199–201, 218–19, 223; and the press, 150; religious revivals and, 156; in the South, 15–16. *See also* Artisans; Economic conditions; Labor and laboring classes; Merchants and shopkeepers; Poverty and poor relief; Wealth, distribution of
Social development, 3–28; American, compared to English and French, 4, 35; in the Chesapeake, 14, 52; in cities, 18–21, 173–201; in mid-Atlantic region, 12; native Americans' influence, 25–26, 52; in New England, 12, 18; and occupational specialization, 19; and rise of professions, 19; in seaport towns, 22; in the South, 13–18; and wealth, 179, 195
Social structure: in cities, 22; and Great Awakening, 12, 221–22; and growth of

poverty, 174; and political activity and power, 141–61, 211–35; and Puritans, 7; in the South, 15–16, 52. *See also* Artisans; Boston; Economic conditions; Labor and laboring classes; Merchants and shopkeepers; Philadelphia; Social class; Wealth, distribution of
Society of Friends. *See* Quakers
Sons of Africa, 310
Sons of Liberty, 272
South, the, 12–18; agriculture, 13, 15; Bacon's Rebellion, 16; Culpepper's Rebellion, 16; economic conditions, 13, 14, 15, 16, 23; family, 15, 16; immigration, 14–15; labor, 13–15, 16, 18; land, 13, 15, 16; native Americans, relations with, 17–18, 22; population, 14, 15, 16; race, 16–18, 22–23; slaves and indentured servants, 13–18, 23, 27; social class, 15, 16; social development, 14–15, 18; social structure, 15–16, 18; trade, 14, 17; women, 14, 16. *See also* Carolinas, the; Chesapeake, the; Native Americans; North Carolina; Slavery; South Carolina; Tobacco; Virginia
South Carolina: native Americans, 52–55; slaves, 17, 23, 27. *See also* Carolinas, the; South, the
Spain, 25, 35, 38–39, 40, 41, 52, 120; and native Americans, 52; and New World, exploration of, 36, 37, 38; war vs., 120
Spanish Armada, 41
Spelman, Henry, 47
Stamp Act (1765), 142, 160, 200, 231–33
Steel, Murphy, 273, 275
Stith, William, 53
Strachey, William, 44, 47
Sturgeon, William, 329
Swedes. *See* Immigration; Philadelphia; Political activity and power; Slavery

Tanner, Benjamin, 335
Taxes: in Boston, 120, 123, 126, 127, 128, 176–78; effects of war and, 196, 214; in New York, 176–78; in Philadelphia, 100, 176–78; regulation of, 234. *See also* Economic conditions; Inflation; Poverty and poor relief; Recession/depression; Social class

A Note on the Author

GARY B. NASH is a professor of history at the University of California, Los Angeles. The author or editor of several books, including *Quakers and Politics, Red, White, and Black, The Private Side of American History,* and *The Urban Crucible,* he has been honored for his literary contributions to American history by such organizations as the American Historical Association (1970), the Daughters of Colonial Wars (1976), the Pulitzer Prize Committee (runner-up in history in 1979), and the Commonwealth Club of California (1980). He has published more than sixty articles, review articles, and reviews in such journals as *William and Mary Quarterly, Journal of American History, Journal of Interdisciplinary History, Reviews in American History,* and the *Journal of Ethnic Studies,* and is currently writing a book entitled *Forging Freedom: The Making of the Free Black Community in Philadelphia, 1740–1820.*